The Politics of Trade in Safavid Iran

Silk for Silver, 1600–1730

Rudolph P. Matthee's book offers a sophisticated, revisionist interpretation of the economy of Safavid Iran. Using a wide range of archival and written sources in languages ranging from Persian to Dutch and Russian, the author considers the economic, social and political networks established between Iran, its neighbors, and the world at large, through the prism of the late Safavid silk trade. In so doing, the author demonstrates how silk, the only commodity which spanned Iran's entire economic activity, was integral to various aspects of late Safavid society, including its approach to commerce, export routes, and, crucially, to the political and economic problems which confounded the Safavid state in the early 1700s. In a challenge to traditional scholarship, the author argues that, despite the introduction of the maritime, western-dominated channel, Iran's traditional land-based silk exports continued to expand and diversify right up to the end of the seventeenth century. The book makes a major theoretical contribution to the current debates on the social and economic history of the pre-modern world.

RUDOLPH P. MATTHEE is Associate Professor of History at the University of Delaware.

Cambridge Studies in Islamic Civilization

Editorial board
DAVID MORGAN (general editor)
VIRGINIA AKSAN   MICHAEL BRETT   MICHAEL COOK   PETER JACKSON
TARIF KHALIDI   ROY MOTTAHEDEH   BASIM MUSALLAM
CHASE ROBINSON

The Politics of Trade in Safavid Iran

Silk for Silver, 1600–1730

RUDOLPH P. MATTHEE

CAMBRIDGE
UNIVERSITY PRESS

CAMBRIDGE UNIVERSITY PRESS
Cambridge, New York, Melbourne, Madrid, Cape Town, Singapore, São Paulo

Cambridge University Press
The Edinburgh Building, Cambridge CB2 2RU, UK

Published in the United States of America by Cambridge University Press, New York

www.cambridge.org
Information on this title: www.cambridge.org/9780521641319

First published 1999
This digitally printed first paperback version 2006

A catalogue record for this publication is available from the British Library

Library of Congress Cataloguing in Publication data
Matthee, Rudolph P.
The politics of trade in Safavid Iran: silk for silver, 1600–1730
/Rudolph P. Matthee.
    p.   cm. – (Cambridge studies in Islamic civilization)
Includes bibliographical references.
ISBN 0 521 64131 4
1. Silk industry – Iran – Economic aspects.   I. Title.   II. Series.
HD9926.I852M38   1999
380.1´4567739´0955–dc21   99–12830   CIP

ISBN-13 978-0-521-64131-9 hardback
ISBN-10 0-521-64131-4 hardback

ISBN-13 978-0-521-02844-8 paperback
ISBN-10 0-521-02844-2 paperback

To my mother, Gerardina Matthee-Verspoor,
and my late father, Antonius Matthee

This book is published with the generous assistance of the College of Arts and Sciences at the University of Delaware.

Contents

Plates

Preface

In the last quarter-century the study of long-distance trade in south and southwest Asia in early modern times has developed into a serious field of inquiry. The Mughal state and, to a lesser extent, the Ottoman Empire in particular have seen a rich production of monographs on various aspects of domestic trade and traders, the activities of the newly founded European maritime companies in Asian waters, the commodities they exchanged and conveyed, the place of merchants in society, and their interaction with the state. With the notable but partial exception of Niels Steensgaard's and Stephen Dale's studies – neither of which deals with Iranian trade per se – Iran in the Safavid period has not shared in this surge in scholarly interest. This lacuna may have had its origins in the geopolitical position of Safavid Iran, a country squeezed, as it were, between two empires of admittedly greater wealth and resources, and more remote from the West than either; yet it remains curious and unjustifiable – curious in the light of the celebrated encouragement of long-distance trade by Shah 'Abbas I, the Safavid ruler whose reign is virtually synonymous with commercial efflorescence, which thus remains in isolation, suspended as a unique burst of energy and foresight without antecedents or follow-up, and unjustifiable because of the existence and availability of rich source material in the form of the archival records of the Dutch and English East India Companies and, to a lesser extent, of documentation in the Russian archives.

The present book seeks to contribute to a redressing of this situation. It examines aspects of long-distance trade in Safavid Iran, focusing on one commodity, silk. It does not claim to be a comprehensive study of silk in early modern Iran; it considers raw, unprocessed silk, pays some attention to its cultivation, but virtually none to the mechanics of silk manufacturing or the technicalities of silk textiles. Those interested in the latter two topics will therefore have to look elsewhere. This study does aspire to being more than an examination of silk and how it was exchanged and transported, however; by way of silk, it seeks to uncover the nexus of commerce and political power in late Safavid Iran. Silk is not an obvious key for this purpose: silk famously counts as a luxury commodity, and as such is often seen as being of limited value for the study of social and economic processes in non-modern societies. In the Safavid period, however, silk formed Iran's most valuable and lucrative export product. Central to the royal court as a source of revenue and a resource in state-controlled textile manufacturing, and crucial to the long-distance trade radiating out of Iran, silk affected much more than the elite. Its economic and political significance therefore greatly exceeded that of a preciosity, and it thus serves to illustrate one of this study's main arguments – that commerce can only be studied fruitfully in its political context.

Owing to its centrality to the state – and the nature of the available source material – silk in Safavid Iran forces the researcher's attention on the royal court, the locus of power and the arena where decisions were made that involved the entire realm, at least in theory. This focus places the book somewhat outside the mainstream of current scholarship on Asian trade and its practitioners, which tends to concentrate on the periphery, often confining itself to port cities, and to look for regional variation, resistance to central control, and the potential for regeneration in the face of a disintegrating center. These themes will be addressed as part of this study's concern with the economic and political crisis that befell Safavid Iran in the late seventeenth century. Yet the central state and the part it played in procuring, negotiating, and distributing silk remain the primary focus. Through this focus Safavid Iran emerges as a distinct political entity ruled by an elite with a clear sense of self, and as a territory that paired fluid cultural and social boundaries with rather well defined geographical and even economic borders marked by unambiguous crossing points.

Iranian silk in the Safavid era, finally, crossed regional and national boundaries and changed hands and was carried halfway around the globe in the context of one of the great processes of all time, Europe's maritime expansion and the global intercultural contact it spawned. Safavid silk was one of the commodities that helped integrate economic regions across imperial and cultural boundaries. It did so in more than one way, for even after the opening up of the maritime connection, linking Iran with Europe via the Indian Ocean and the Atlantic, Iranian silk continued to be exported to the Mediterranean basin along the terrestrial trade routes traversing the Ottoman territories of Anatolia and Mesopotamia. In documenting the continued vitality and, to some extent, increased activity of the latter routes, the study revisits and, by adducing a great deal of new evidence, modifies Steensgaard's well-known thesis about the decline of the overland trade following the entry of the European maritime companies. By the same token, it demonstrates the limited impact of the European companies on the economy and society of seventeenth-century Iran, revealing this to be a combined function of difficult, even inaccessible terrain and the limited attractiveness of Iran as a provider of commodities.

Acknowledgments

I have incurred a great many debts in the process of researching and completing this book. More than anyone, it has been Nikki Keddie who made me an historian. Her intellectual stimulation and generosity have made a lasting impression on me. I will always be grateful for her suggestion that, as a Dutchman, I explore the Safavid era from the angle of the Dutch maritime sources. By following that advice, I have been able to catch two birds with one stone: a rich and fascinating period in Iranian history has opened up to me, and while exploring it, I have come to learn a great deal about my own past. Michael Morony, always challenging in his questions and never satisfied with easy answers, has done his part in honing my critical faculties.

I am grateful to those colleagues and friends who read the book in its various incarnations. Willem Floor, Edmund Herzig, and Nikki Keddie read the entire work in typescript and made many incisive comments and valuable suggestions. I appreciate Ahmad Ashraf's comments on an individual chapter, and Robert McChesney for inviting me to present some of my ideas at New York University. All those who made suggestions will recognize where I followed their advice and where I did not. None is in any way responsible for any errors and poor judgment; all that's mediocre in these pages is mine alone. I thank Iraj Afshar and Asghar Mahdavi for assisting me with the *siyaq* part of the silk receipt, and Stefan Heidemann for helping me procure a photograph of the drawing of Ketelaar's 1717 mission to Iran. I am greatly indebted to Charles Melville for drawing my attention to a passage in the third volume of the "Afzal al-tavarikh," recently discovered by him, with the proclamation of the silk export monopoly, the only such reference in the Persian-language sources. Afshin Matin-Asgari has been a kindred spirit for years. I appreciate him for that as well as, more mundanely, for copying, among other things, more pages of Chardin than he will care to remember. I also would like to thank Stefan Troebst for sending me unpublished work, and John Emerson, Michelle Marrese, and David Shearer for their help in locating sources.

I received institutional support from the Social Science Research Council for dissertation research. Though the book has little in common with my dissertation, some of its archival research was done while preparing my thesis. Travel grants from the Mellon Foundation and the Gustave von Grunebaum Center at the University of California, Los Angeles, and a General University Research grant from the University of Delaware, made subsequent overseas research possible. I gratefully acknowledge the subvention toward publication offered to me by the Dean's Office at the University of Delaware, as well as the subvention toward the drawing of the maps awarded to me by the Persian Heritage Foundation in New York. I thank Barbara Broge for drawing the maps. The librarians and archivists of the India Offfice Library in London, the Archives des Affaires Etrangères, the Archives Nationales, and the Archives des Missions Etrangères, all in Paris, the Carmelite, Jesuit, and Propaganda Fide Archives in Rome, and the Algemeen Rijksarchief in The Hague all deserve credit for their efficiency and helpfulness. Marigold Acland and Philippa Youngman of the Cambridge University Press saw the manuscript through to publication in a most gracious and professional manner.

My family members are my real role models. Ruth O'Brien, constant source of inspiration and emblem of integrity and creative thinking, I thank for her intellectual companionship and love. Max, with his incomparable lust for life, has made every day a joyful one for the last two years. My final and most heartfelt thanks go to my mother and my late father. I cannot remember a time when they did less than put their full trust in me by letting me pursue my own intellectual interests. Though they must, at times, have been wondering where it all would lead, they never showed their apprehension. I hope I haven't disappointed them. This book is a token of my gratitude. I dedicate it to them.

Note on transliteration

The Arabic and Persian transliteration used in this book follows the Library of Congress system without the diacritical marks. Exceptions are non-Roman place names, such as Ganja, and terms such as *jizya*, which are spelled without the final *h*. Dates are given according to the Common Era calendar, except when the source is a Persian-language work, in which case the solar *hijri* reckoning is added. Russian spelling, too, conforms to the Library of Congress system.

Abbreviations

AE	Archives des Affaires Etrangères
AME	Archives des Missions Etrangères
ARA	Algemeen Rijksarchief
BN	Bibliothèque Nationale
BSOAS	*Bulletin of the School of Oriental and African Studies*
CMR(S)	*Cahiers du Monde Russe (et Soviétique)*
EHR	*Economic History Review*
EIC	East India Company
EIr	*Encyclopaedia Iranica*
FOG	*Forschungen zur Osteuropäischen Geschichte*
IOR	India Office Records
IS	*Iranian Studies*
IZ	*Istoricheskie Zapiski*
JA	*Journal Asiatique*
JEH	*Journal of Economic History*
JESHO	*Journal of the Economic and Social History of the Orient*
JGO	*Jahrbücher für Geschichte Osteuropas*
KSINA	*Kratkie Soobshcheniya Instituta Narodov Azii*
MOOI	*Le Moyen Orient et l'Océan Indien*
REA	*Revue des Etudes Arméniennes*
VOC	Verenigde Oostindische Compagnie

Map 1 Silk routes between Iran and Europe, seventeenth century.

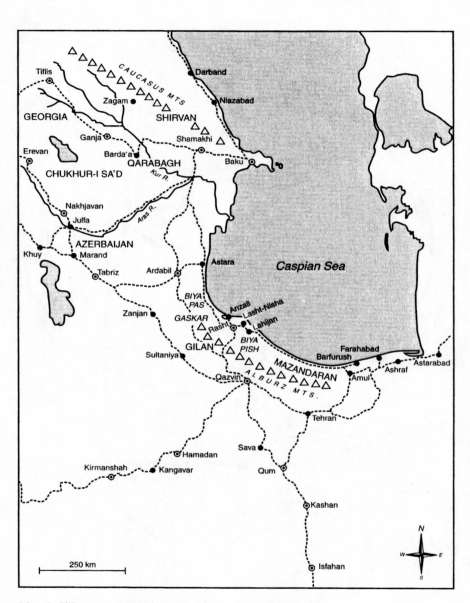

Map 2 Silk routes through northern Iran, seventeenth century.

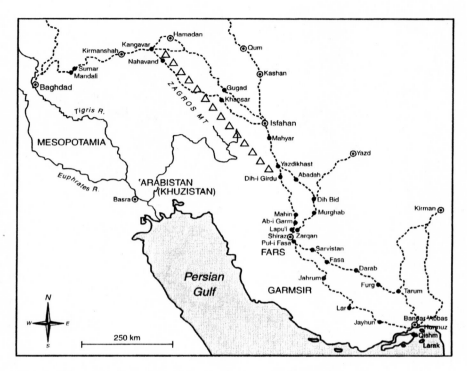

Map 3 Silk routes through southern Iran, seventeenth century.

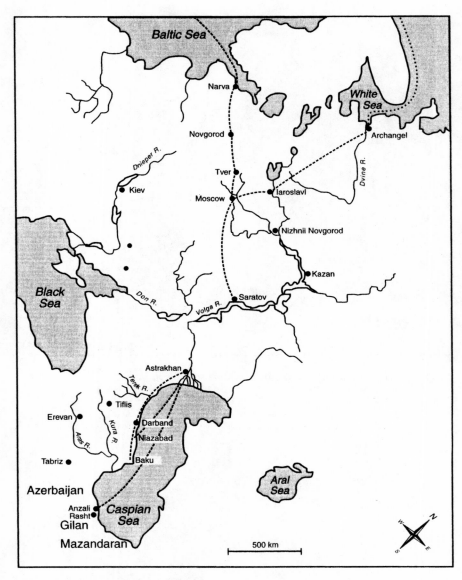

Map 4 The Volga route, seventeenth century.

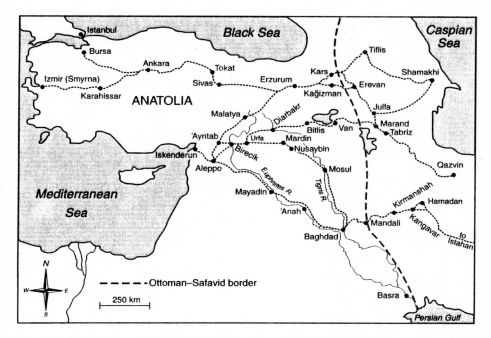

Map 5 Silk routes to the Levant, second half of the seventeenth century.

Introduction

Long-distance trade has forever been a quintessential part of life on the Iranian plateau. A crossroads between the Indian subcontinent, Central Asia, Russia, and the Mediterranean basin, Iran was the scene of east–west commerce even before the early days of the fabled Silk Road, an important branch of which traversed the country. Of the many commodities ferried across Asia, silk was invariably one of the most precious. In the West, however, silk has never readily been associated with Iran, not even in the form of the country's well-known carpets, the most priceless of which have always been made of silk rather than wool. The popular identification of silk with China has obscured the fact that silk did not just pass through Iran but that for many centuries the country was also an important producer of raw silk as well as of silk textiles. The latter were among the commodities carried to Byzantine textile workshops in late antiquity. Sasanian silk patterns remained popular in Asia long after the fall of the dynasty in the seventh century. In the Middle Ages raw silk from Gilan and Mazandaran was coveted by Italian merchants who imported it to feed an expanding textile manufacturing industry at home. In the fifteenth and sixteenth centuries, Iranian silk transported to the Levant provided the raw material for textile manufacturing in the Ottoman city of Bursa. And in the 1600s, Western travelers marveled at the high-quality brocades and taffetas produced by Iran's workshops, while Dutch and English merchants purchased large quantities of Iranian raw silk to satisfy a growing demand in Amsterdam and London.

Iranian silk long remained embedded in what Marshall Hodgson has called the Afro-Eurasian Oikoumene, the world between the Mediterranean and Central Asia that was knitted together by common cultural patterns and a comprehensive trading network.[1] This world was challenged in a process that, though known under different names, can be summed up as the "rise of the West." Historians differ about the precise timing of this process, but most have placed it in the context of the great maritime

[1] Hodgson, *Venture of Islam*, ii, 330–5.

1

discoveries and the "commercial revolution." Fernand Braudel sees a "turning point" in the late sixteenth century, when Spain retreated from the Mediterranean and the Atlantic became the world's center stage.[2] Immanuel Wallerstein's European world-economy "emerged" in the mid-fifteenth century and was "consolidated" after 1640.[3]

Situating the critical moment of European hegemony before 1800 easily leads to a conflation of ascendance and hegemony, rendering Asia subordinate and peripheral in a manner that is as inexorable as it is anachronistic. It makes early modern Europe prematurely cast a shadow over Asia, projecting power borrowed from a nineteenth-century reality that extends far beyond its actual influence on the world in the 1600s. Conversely, it turns Asia's history into mere reactive behavior to European commercial entrepreneurship and doomed resistance to Western political and military hegemony. In the master narrative thus scripted, anything beyond the purview of Western merchants recedes over the horizon. Trade with Russia becomes trade initiated by Europeans, and activity beyond Moscow, if addressed at all, is viewed as an extension of English ventures; merchant operations east of Izmir and Aleppo occur in the penumbra of the light cast by western Levant Companies; commerce in the Indian Ocean turns into an offshoot of a Western-dominated maritime trading world that touches little more than port cities and their immediate hinterland, leaving Asia's vast interior waiting to be opened up by nineteenth-century Western commercial and military initiative.[4]

In the last few decades scholars have been busy revising the picture of early modern Asia as a continent impervious to change, lacking in agency, and wanting in commercial sophistication. Ottomanists have begun to look into the ports of the Levant beyond the activities of Western merchants and consular representatives, while students of pre-colonial India have initiated the study of trade and merchants indigenous to the subcontinent and operating across Asia.[5] Much of this work represents a shift from European expansion in Asia to the maritime history of Asia and continues to explore the sea and the littoral rather than the hinterland.[6] More recent studies have shifted attention to the interior but in the process often lose sight of the maritime connection.[7]

---

[2] Braudel, *Mediterranean*, ii, 891, 1165, 1176.
[3] Wallerstein, *Modern World-System*, i, 10, 63, 68.
[4] Even J. C. van Leur, a lone dissenter who in the 1930s argued that the extent of commercial innovation and impact of the European East India Companies on Asia had been minimal, assumed an unchanging Asia. See van Leur, *Indonesian Trade*. This study, van Leur's dissertation, was originally published in Dutch in 1934.
[5] For the Ottomans, see Masters, *Origins*; and Brummett, *Ottoman Seapower*. Among the more numerous studies on India and the Indian Ocean, see Das Gupta, *Indian Merchants*; Chaudhuri, *Trade and Civilisation*; and Subrahmaniyam, *Political Economy*.
[6] For a discussion of this trend, see Wills, "European Consumption," 135.
[7] A good example of this development is Dale, *Indian Merchants*.

Safavid Iran has yet to become fully integrated in this revisionist discourse. Excellent work exists on some aspects of its economic history. We have a number of thorough studies of land ownership, mostly carried out by Russians,[8] and institutional–administrative history, pursued mainly by German scholars concerned with questions of chancery documentation, historiography and urban geography, is well represented, too.[9] Its commercial history, by contrast, remains underdeveloped compared with the state of the field in Mughal studies especially. Good general overviews are available and various aspects of trade have been highlighted in articles, but more probing studies have yet to be written. Serious impediments account for this situation, ranging from a dearth of surviving indigenous archives, a strong cultural and idealist bias in Iranian historiography, to the postwar failure of Iranian scholars to translate their quest for answers about material backwardness into solid research on the pre-nineteenth-century period. Inquiries into trade, moreover, either bear the imprint of what Martin Dickson has called the "Curzon–Sykes school," in reference to British scholars who have studied commerce as a derivative of Western-oriented political and diplomatic history,[10] or view Iran as a giant clearing house through which a considerable volume of trade passed on its way to somewhere else – following the seventeenth-century French cleric du Mans who compared Iran to a caravanserai with one gate open to Turkey and another to India.[11] Scholars continue to marvel at the commercial infrastructure set up by Shah ʿAbbas and the expansion of trade effected by him, but thus far have done little to examine critically the commercial approach and practice of this most famous of Safavid shahs, let alone that of other rulers.[12] Even Niels Steensgaard's study on Iran's role in the transformation of Eurasian trade patterns, to date the only monograph that deals with Safavid trade, falls short in this regard.[13] Steensgaard, keen to demonstrate how the English and Dutch maritime companies rendered their Portuguese predecessors uncompetitive, and land-based trade obsolescent, touches on Safavid commercial policy, but his focus and concern lie elsewhere, and his

---

[8] Examples are Petrushevskii, *Zemledelie i agrarniye otnosheniia*; Papazian, *Agrarnye otnosheniia*; and Lambton, *Landlord and Peasant*.

[9] This German tradition goes back to the scholarship of Walther Hinz and Hans Robert Roemer.

[10] Dickson, "Fall of the Safavi Dynasty." See also Emerson, "Some General Accounts." For a defense of the "traditional" school of Safavid historiography, see Savory, "Tahlili."

[11] Richard, *Raphaël du Mans*, i, 149–50.

[12] Excellent recent dissertations by René Barendse and Rüdiger Klein discuss Iran's important role in intra-Asian commerce but do not address the role of the (central) state in trade. See Barendse, *Arabian Seas*; and Klein, "Trade in the Safavid Port City." Stephen Dale's study on Indian merchants in Iran does include a discussion on commerce and the state. Edmund Herzig's first-rate dissertation on the merchants of New Julfa explores the wide-ranging trade practices of an important group among Iran's indigenous merchants. See Herzig, "Armenian Merchants."

[13] Steensgaard, *Asian Trade Revolution*.

work has been rightly faulted for its Eurocentric bias, overreliance on Western maritime sources, and scant attention to chronology, technology, and geography.[14]

The present study seeks to explore the dynamics of the interaction between political power and commercial activity in Safavid Iran. Its focus is the approach of the Safavid political elite to commerce and, more particularly, long-distance, transregional, and intercontinental trade, as seen in the role and place in society of Iran's domestic merchants and the encounter between the royal court and the agents of foreign trading companies. It does so by concentrating on one commodity, silk, from its productive source to its distribution and sale for export, between the reign of Shah 'Abbas I (1587–1629) and the demise of Safavid power in the 1720s, a period when relations between Europe and Asia reached a new level of intensity without yet bearing the weight of inequality that would subsequently mark them.

Within the field of Safavid economic and commercial history, the rather narrow topic of silk has received considerable scholarly attention. However, in keeping with the above-mentioned trend, historians interested in it have generally treated the subject as part of arguments external to Iran. Exemplifying this tendency, British scholars, the pioneers of the study of silk in Iran, have let an interest in political history and concern with Western commerce determine their approach to the Safavid silk trade, which thus became part of their study of the diplomatic forays of English envoys and adventurers and the activities of the English East India Company. In addition, their fascination with great rulers and the rise and fall of empires has led to a concentration on the reign of Shah 'Abbas, seen as a visionary in his state-building project and a European-style mercantilist in his approach to economic issues, at the expense of other periods in Safavid history.[15] Iranian scholars, hampered by limited access to the Western archival records, have done little to undermine the nationalist myth of Shah 'Abbas the Great, dispenser of justice and economic prosperity, one of the "good" kings in the Iranian tradition of statecraft.[16]

As Iran's most important export commodity and the mainstay of trade between the Safavid realm and the outside world, silk is ideally suited as a telescope bringing into focus a world far more complex and intricate than one perceived as a mere passive supplier of raw materials and an inert recipient of foreign envoys. To be sure, the study of Safavid silk points up fundamental changes in Eurasian commerce that seem to confirm Europe's

---

[14] See the critique of Steensgaard's book by Meilink-Roelofsz, "Structures of Trade."

[15] See Savory, "The Sherley Myth"; Ferrier, "British–Persian Relations"; "European Diplomacy"; Stevens, "Robert Sherley." For a critique of this view, see Steinmann, "Shah 'Abbas," 16. Edmund Herzig's recent studies, "Volume of Iranian Raw Silk Exports," and "Iranian Raw Silk Trade," have initiated a reexamination of Shah 'Abbas's involvement with silk and the role of Iran's Armenian merchants in its procurement and distribution.

[16] See, for example, Falsafi, *Zindigani*; and Bastani-Parizi, *Siyasat va iqtisad*. For the tradition of the good king, see Christensen, *Decline of Iranshar*, 27–31.

poise for hegemony. Increased demand led to intensified trade relations and greater competition. Its economy expanding, Europe imported a greater volume of (new) Asian commodities and explored various avenues in a competitive search for secure and cost-effective supply lines. Asia, in turn, and especially India, absorbed unprecedented amounts of gold and silver, most of it originating in the New World, in exchange for its products. Europe's quest for Asian goods and Asia's hunger for Western bullion added complexity to existing networks and arterial flows. The opening up of the oceanic route around the Cape of Good Hope gave Western merchants a direct presence in the Indian Ocean. In a pincer movement, they also began to explore the land-based access route to Asia through Russia. Their modus operandi in all this was new. Unlike their medieval predecessors, who hailed from individual city states and maritime republics such as Genoa or Venice and who tended to operate as private individuals or as envoys-cum-traders in the Asian ports where they engaged in business or took up residence, the new merchants served as commission agents or salaried employees of powerful chartered companies that at once operated as bureaucratic, state-like organizations far away from home and in various ways derived legitimacy from the power of the states that backed them and oversaw their activities. Whereas medieval trade had proceeded in stages, passing through many hands en route, the new commerce carried goods in single unbroken voyages linking producers and consumers.[17]

Yet the abundant documentation on (northwestern) European entrepreneurship easily obscures the Iranian dimension of these changes. First, the Europeans by no means held a monopoly on any commodity originating in or being supplied to Iran, including silk, bullion, or spices. Asian merchants joined their European colleagues in partaking of the intensified activity unleashed by the great changes of the sixteenth century. Armenian and Indian mercantile elites based in south and west Asia displayed a degree of energy and enterprise that owed little to Europe, operating as they did in family firms that often successfully competed with the maritime companies. Elusive because of the paucity of surviving documentation, these groups are just now emerging from obscurity.[18] The merchant diasporas they constituted shared in the greater complexity and the extension of existing networks as well. The Dutch and English established maritime (and military) superiority in some of the ports where they settled. In terms of the aggregate volume of trade and precious metals handled by them they were, however, no match for the Indian merchants who carried the bulk of the regional maritime trade, or the Iranian Armenians who, aside from being very active

---

[17] Chaudhuri, *Trade and Civilisation*, 95–6.
[18] For the Armenians, see Herzig, "Armenian Merchants"; idem, "Family Firm"; idem, "Rise of the Julfa Merchants"; Baghdiantz, "Armenian Merchants"; and Bayburdyan, *Naqsh-i Aramanah*. The Indian merchant diaspora in Iran, Central Asia and Russia has received its first scholarly treatment in English in Dale, *Indian Merchants*.

in regional commerce, created a near-monopoly for themselves on the Anatolian trade route and managed to secure a privileged position in the overland transit link through Russia, where they outdid the notoriously inefficient and undercapitalized Russian merchants. Nor did the Armenians simply engage in private trade. In the early seventeenth century, the Safavid state turned its domestic Armenian merchant community into what may be called a service gentry, employing them in ways that are reminiscent of the links between the contemporary Russian state and its *gosti* merchants.

A second development that tends to receive short shrift concerns the alternative to the maritime link, the land-based connections. To be sure, scholars concerned with continuity in the overland trade have begun to examine the "horizontal" axis linking Iran with the Ottoman Empire, the Mughal state, and Central Asia, long the main avenue for cross-cultural transmission.[19] The "vertical" axis connecting Iran and Russia via the Volga route, by contrast, has not received the same amount of interest.[20] Long the subject of research among Russians and Armenians,[21] the Volga route was until recently little studied by Western scholars, who mostly concentrated on the (limited) extent to which it was used by English merchants in the sixteenth century.[22] Whereas silk formed a small proportion of the oceanic trade, it represented a large share of the wares carried via the Levant route and made up the bulk of the goods exported from Iran via Russia, and as such may be called emblematic of continuity and change along those routes.[23]

All three routes form the subject of this book, as do all merchants who competed for a share of the trade carried along them. If the study pays disproportionate attention to English and Dutch attempts to capture a share of Iran's silk market, it does so only in deference to the fact that most of the extant documentation relevant to trade in Safavid Iran springs from the quills of the Western company agents and that most Persian-language sources yield virtually no data on trade, indigenous and international alike. Aside from being factually informative, the European sources are also the only ones that permit an exploration of the personal and dynamic encounter

---

[19] See Rossabi, " 'Decline' of the Central Asian Caravan Trade"; Klein, "Caravan Trade."

[20] The terms are borrowed from Allen, *Problems of Turkish Power*, 39.

[21] See, for example, Kukanova, "Russko-iranskie torgovye otnosheniia"; idem, "Iz istorii russko-iranskikh torgovykh sviaziei"; idem, "Rol' armanskogo kupechestva"; idem, *Ocherki*; Iukht, "Torgovye sviazi"; and idem, *Torgovlia*.

[22] Exceptions to the scant Western attention to the Russian trade link are Mattiesen, "Die Versuche"; and Emerson's pioneering dissertation "Ex Oriente Lux." The "opening up" of eastern Europe in the 1990s has dramatically altered this situation. Aside from Dale, *Indian Merchants*, see Sartor, "Die Wolga"; Troebst, "Isfahan–Moskau–Amsterdam"; idem, "Narva und der Aussenhandel Persiens"; idem, *Handelskontrolle*; Matthee, "Anti-Ottoman Politics"; Ahmedov, "Export of Iranian Silk"; and Heller, "Zur Entwicklung."

[23] In her critique of Steensgaard, Meilink-Roelofsz rightly called silk less an index than emblematic of such developments, but failed to differentiate between the various itineraries. See Meilink-Roelofsz. "Structures of Trade." 5.

between the world of the merchant and that of the political elite. Yet the importance of Armenian (and other Iranian) merchants will be fully acknowledged and, whenever possible and appropriate, their role and participation in the silk trade – which at all times exceeded that of the Europeans – will be integrated into the narrative.

Safavid silk permits a diachronic study of the interaction of political structures and economic processes in early modern Iran. Silk connects production to sale, sale to distribution and transportation, and all of these to manufacture. Silk involves the question of the extent of penetration of the production process by commercial capital, the expansion of the latter, and ultimately the potential for indigenous development. Silk connects the interior to the coast and is in fact the only commodity that crosses boundaries in Iran's fragmented economy. It thus tells us a great deal about geographical linkages, trade routes, and infrastructure. Above all, the trade in Safavid silk invariably involved the state. Its study therefore ought to encompass the intersection of state power and mercantile activity, and not just for the (brief) period in the early 1600s when Shah 'Abbas "monopolized" the country's silk export. From taxing production to engaging in embassy trade to levying export tolls, the state at all times had a role in the trajectory from production to export. Although Safavid silk cannot be understood simply through the lens of government involvement, a comprehensive picture of the silk business is impossible without recognizing that, until its demise, the Safavid state continued to have a crucial role in the collection, sale, domestic manufacturing and distribution of silk.

Unlike students of Mughal India and the Ottoman Empire, Safavid scholars have done little to reexamine the role of the state in commercial life in the light of new historiographical insight and perspectives. Most continue to emphasize the interventionist nature of the state's approach to economic life, focusing on the reign of Shah 'Abbas I as the period when intervention was beneficial rather than detrimental.[24] Recently, some have opted for a "non-etatist" approach to the study of economic process, which makes a more or less explicit case against the inhibiting effects of state organization and behavior on commercial activity.[25] Not surprisingly, its advocates primarily focus on maritime trade and port cities, the area where (central) governments are least visible, where commerce is most unregulated, and where "ecumenical trade zones" appear to prevail.

The present study rejects the notion of trade as spontaneous diffusion and directly confronts the role of the (central) state in it, analyzing the ways in which the profit-seeking merchant interacted with the revenue-seeking

---

[24] See, for example, Bastani-Parizi, *Siyasat va iqtisad*; Savory, *Iran under the Safavids*; and Tajbakhsh, *Tarikh-i Safaviyah*.

[25] This trend is currently prominent in the study of Mughal India. See Arasaratnam, *Merchants*; and Subrahmanyam, *Political Economy*. For Safavid Iran, see Klein, "Trade in the Safavid Port City"; and, for a more implied example, Dale, *Indian Merchants*.

state. One of its premises holds that, while the autonomous market – as a place of economic exchange – is an ideal-type rather than an historical reality, its logic is fundamentally different from that of the state. While the former operated on the basis of exchange between neutral partners, the latter made itself felt in the market on the basis of extra-economic mechanisms such as force, tribute, expropriation and monopolization. The Safavid state was a command polity (at least in its ambition) that operated on the principles of reciprocity and redistribution. It did not "monopolize" trade as such, nor did all commercial (or manufacturing) activity occur in its orbit. It rather coexisted and interacted with an active mercantile economy of indigenous and foreign merchants operating on calculations of loss and gain.[26] The apparent similarities with many contemporary European states, meanwhile, should not tempt us to treat Safavid Iran as the equivalent of the early modern European state or to divide its historical record into a short moment of capitalist potential inadvertently thwarted by internal distress or outside pressure. There is no a priori reason why the Safavid approach to trade should have resembled that of contemporary European states. A specific cultural, legal, and social context naturally lent Iran its own norms and practices, some of which were akin to the ones found elsewhere, some superficially similar, and some wholly different.[27] If we have to reexamine the state in Middle Eastern history, it ought to be a different kind of state, a more complex agent than one that either engages in rapacious policies or remains indifferent to economic activity, with equally deleterious consequences for order and profitability, but not necessarily a doppelgänger of the governing elite of the Dutch Republic or the administration of Restoration England. The Safavid state's approach to commerce is best analyzed on its own terms, both with regard to its objective – fiscal revenue – and its methods, which ranged from active encouragement to blatant exploitation. Silk permits insight into this approach, into the coexistence and interaction between the Safavid political–military elite and Iran's merchants, and into the ways in which the state dealt with the accumulators of wealth through a range of mechanisms between accommodation and coercion that included infrastructural services, licensing, taxation, protection mechanisms, price fixing, and outright confiscation.

In addition to being a command polity, the Safavid state was also a forum of negotiation rather than simply a place or a set of (fixed) institutions. The "state" centered on the shah and his entourage regardless of location, and institutions, though they existed, were fluid and flexible inasmuch as circumstance and royal disposition directly influenced their composition, function, and effectiveness. Rather than forming a fixed set of hierarchical relationships, the state acquired and dispensed power and profit

---

[26] The term "command economy" derives from Hicks, *Theory of Economic History*.
[27] For this, see Lieberman, "Abu Lughod's Egalitarian World Order," 547.

through a process of bargaining whose main characteristics were inclusion and manipulation.

Here, too, Iran's silk trade reveals the notion of trade as spontaneous diffusion to be misleading. In its trajectory between production and export, silk went through numerous transactions. Each and every one of these involved negotiation, a process in which economic realities interacted with political modalities, the dynamic of personal encounter and, in the case of the contact between Iranians and Europeans, different cultural premises and "mentalities." To follow the intricate negotiations surrounding silk is to follow the working of Safavid power in ways that neither court chronicles nor foreign travelogues allow us to reconstruct. The process reveals a network of power and authority at once far more fluid and personal than is portrayed in the formalized officiousness of the *Tadhkirat al-Muluk* and the *Dastur al-muluk*, and yet far more intricate and dynamic than what emerges from the accounts of foreign travelers, many of whom lacked insight into the workings of the Iranian state or failed to spend enough time in Iran to get acquainted with its bureaucratic norms and vagaries and the shifts in its power constellation.[28] It also reveals an indigenous merchant community of great resilience and resourcefulness ready and able to engage political forces in negotiation, manipulation, and resistance.

The Safavid trade in raw silk, aside from representing a fascinating case study of cross-cultural contact, also reveals that the encounter between the European maritime merchants and the Safavid court cannot be viewed in simple terms of unequal power or of Iran's incorporation into the world market. Steensgaard's contention that the European companies were successful because they managed to "internalize" protection costs and that those who "produced" violence also maximized their revenue only stands as long as one disregards the political dimension of trade. Far from enhancing the so-called transparency of the market, the Europeans in their quest for silk found themselves as dependent as any domestic merchant on forces they could not control, most of them having to do with the intricacies of the Safavid power structure.

Jacob van Leur's claim that the European political and cultural impact on early modern Asia was minimal is as true for Safavid Iran as it is for China and Japan.[29] The failure of the chartered companies to establish territorial control in Iran is related to the limited economic attractiveness of the country as much as to physical and political impediments. Aside from silk, Safavid Iran had few resources for which outsiders were willing to take great logistical and financial risks. Add to that Iran's particular physical and political circumstances. Unlike India, where nature made the interior relatively accessible from the coast, Iran could only be approached from the

---

[28] Minorsky, *Tadhkirat al-Muluk*; Rafi'ah, *Dastur al-muluk*.
[29] Van Leur. *Indonesian Trade*. 21. 238.

southern ports of entry, which were separated from the capital and the country's most productive regions by 1,000 km of semi-desert and formidable mountain ranges. Unlike Ceylon and most of southeast Asia, including the Indonesian archipelago, where fragmented political power enabled Europeans to establish local footholds, Iran was a centralized state or at least a state with a central power structure, and a polity based on a set of clear assumptions and values transmitted over countless generations.[30] Even if their actual power often did not reach far beyond the confines of Isfahan and the major provincial cities, the Safavids never faced a serious challenge to their legitimacy before the Afghan invasion of the early 1700s, and until then represented the only authority with which outsiders could hope to make workable and lasting arrangements. The Europeans were backed by powerful navies, whose might was at times invoked and applied but, in (later) Safavid Iran at least, never successfully deployed for the furtherance of commercial objectives, let alone for the extension of political domination. Safavid authorities, in sum, never found reason to give up their autonomous power or even to question the age-old universal claims of Iranian kingship. Inevitably this bred the (mistaken) conviction that the Europeans were willing to pay any price for their trading privileges.

The student of late Safavid Iran inevitably labors in the shadow of the fall of Isfahan in 1722. Decline is still the operative word in much of our thinking about the period, accentuated, it seems, by the lingering notion that the Safavid state was somehow the first "national" Iranian state, the one that might have taken Iran into the modern age. Were it not for Shah 'Abbas's reputation as state builder, the demise of the Safavids would have been unremarkable, the passing of one dynasty in a long sequence in Iranian history. Safavid historians, moreover, find themselves in a less comfortable position than their Ottoman and Mughal colleagues who can circumvent or even dismiss the notion of decline either because the regime survived, because the dissolution of the core matched the emergence of the periphery, or because fragmentation and failure are attributable to other than orthogenetic causes. Though weakened, the Ottomans in the eighteenth century held on to power, and even managed to "restore public trust in government."[31] In the case of the Mughals, retrenchment at the center was arguably accompanied by invigoration in the provinces.[32] The demise of Mughal rule, moreover, formed the prelude to the region's incorporation into the British Empire. The disintegration of the Safavid state, by contrast, did not spawn viable and lasting regional centers. Nor are the main causes of centrifugal tendencies and their outcome – instability and collapse – easily externalized.

---

[30] In this respect Iran was rather like China. See Murphey, *Outsiders.*
[31] Idem, "Continuity."
[32] As demonstrated by Bayly, *Rulers.*

The notion that unmitigated decline was Iran's fate following Shah 'Abbas's reign needs to be revised, and the study of silk can contribute to such revision. Though weakened, the state remained active as a mediator between production and the market. The shah's retreat from public life had grave consequences for administrative cohesion and direction. Yet a series of competent grand viziers concerned about economic problems continued to make efforts to regulate the flow of silk and the income deriving from it. Most importantly, "private" initiative picked up where the state left off. Armenian merchants operating under state auspices explored new outlets for silk and were largely responsible for opening up the Russia link. Many state measures and activities might seem misguided; a great many were either counterproductive by their very nature or negated by structural problems. Rather than reducing them to irreversible and teleological "decline," however, we should seek to identify motivations and consequences in an effort to establish a more accurate periodization and to construct a more plausible causal framework for the interplay between the political and the economic elements contributing to the problems that confronted late Safavid Iran.

Organization

This study alternates chronological with thematic chapters. Chapter 1 offers a largely narrative overview of silk in the Iranian world until the late sixteenth century, when Iranian silk became a "hot" commodity in European markets. It discusses the evolution of the trade in silk, and traces the origins of and shifts in the various silk routes radiating out of Iran as part of political and economic change and development. In its attention to the vicissitudes of the route between Iran and the ports of the Levant, it focuses on the enmity between Safavids and Ottomans, examining how strategic interests informed their economic policies and how intermittent warfare affected the silk trade. It also charts the origins of the north–south route that connected Iran with Russia, underscoring its emerging importance as an alternative to the Levantine trajectory.

Chapter 2 addresses the logistics of the Safavid silk trade. It discusses issues concerning cultivation, transportation, sale, and distribution and shipping, while touching on questions of capital formation, taxation, and the formal role of the government in the business of silk. This chapter further charts the three main silk routes radiating from Iran, the maritime outlet, the Anatolian itinerary, and the Volga route, in a comparative analysis that centers on physical characteristics, infrastructure, and cost-effectiveness.

Chapter 3 analyzes the late Safavid state as a patrimonial state that used its political power to mobilize the resources of its realm by maximizing the flow of tribute to the center. Borrowing some of Michael Mann's adaptations of Weberian theory, this chapter presents the organization of political, social, and economic power in Safavid Iran as a complex mixture of centrifugal and centripetal elements in which the mobilizing power of the state was huge in appearance but limited in practice and tenuous in its interaction with the forces of society.[33] It focuses on the reign of Shah 'Abbas I, the most advanced phase of Safavid "absolutism" and centralization, analyzing that ruler's economic approach and the nature of Safavid state interpolation in economic life. It explores the objectives of Shah 'Abbas's manipulation of wealth and power, and the extent to which he followed a *conscious* economic policy and can be considered a mercantilist, raising the question of the cross-cultural validity of such terminology. It will discuss four aspects of his reign that involve silk – the incorporation of the silk-producing Caspian provinces, the question of European attempts to divert the Safavid silk trade to the maritime route, Iran's relationship with Russia, and the recruitment of Armenians as a commercial elite – to show that in harnessing his commercial resources for the furtherance of strategic ends even a remarkable ruler like Shah 'Abbas operated within the strictures of his time and environment.

One salient feature of the mercantilist phase in European history is the establishment, around 1600, of a series of maritime chartered companies, the most important and successful of which were those of Holland and England. Their arrival on the shores of the Persian Gulf in the early 1600s marks the beginning of a long-standing encounter between Iran's political and economic elite and the agents of commercial institutions endowed with new forms of knowledge and power. The documentation the latter left for posterity allows the historian to go beyond the reconstruction of isolated moments and phenomena and to chart the process and sequence of negotiation involved in that encounter. This will be done in chapter 4, which examines the nature of the interaction, the stakes involved, and the bargaining process, through the lens of the most conspicuous government effort to maximize revenue and control through involvement in productive and commercial activity – the famous silk export monopoly of Shah 'Abbas I.

Although periodizing history on the basis of great rulers and their dynasties might seem out of date, it is arguable that some constitutive segments of Safavid history are coterminous with the tenure of individual monarchs, reflecting not just a coincidence between political process and economic dynamic, but also the crucial position of the shah, the apex of the system and the locus of legitimacy and direct power. The reign of 'Abbas I is a case in point, as is the succession of his grandson, Safi I, the ruler who abolished the silk export monopoly following his enthronement in 1629. Chapter 5 will consider the reverberations of this measure through an

---

[33] Mann, *Sources of Social Power*, vol. 1, *History of Power*.

assessment of how the state reconciled the relaxation of its control over silk with a continued need for revenue accruing from the same resource. This will be interwoven with another dramatic change in the Safavid power constellation, the growing influence of the bureaucracy, evidenced in a strong involvement of the grand vizier in political and economic state management.

As a commodity spanning Safavid politics and the international market place, silk mandates its own periodization, which by nature tallies only partly with dynastic succession. Chapter 6 reflects this by discussing the period between 1639, the date of the accord of Zuhab which ended a century and a half of intermittent Safavid–Ottoman hostility, and the 1660s, a time of important shifts in Iran's political and economic fortunes. The impact of Zuhab on silk was momentous: Safavid rulers ceased to conduct a foreign and commercial policy around the Ottoman threat and the need to find allies among the Christian powers of Europe. The peace agreement also unleashed the potential of the Anatolian route, which, no longer imperiled by warfare and threatened by commercial boycotts and diversion schemes, expanded rapidly. The position of the maritime companies changed as well. On one hand, the lifting of restrictions on travel and trade across the Ottoman borders made them lose leverage with the Safavid crown. On the other, the shah's failure to supply contractual quantities of silk, falling silk prices in Europe and the availability of alternative, cheaper sources elsewhere in Asia diminished their appetite for Iranian silk. No longer keen on purchasing silk, the Europeans now became engaged in a massive exportation of bullion from the country. The Iranian reaction to this was remarkably muted given the court's increasing penury. Growing corruption and the inability of the state to command silk at will from the Caspian region goes some way toward explaining the haphazard enforcement of Dutch silk quotas, for bribery made Safavid officials connive at the bullion hemorrhage, and a series of low silk yields caused them to put but little pressure on the Europeans to make purchases. Most important, however, is the fact that silk was now more profitably exported via different channels, most notably to the ports of the Levant.

The loss of state control continued in the period discussed in chapter 7, the mid-1660s to the early 1690s, which saw the rule of a relatively weak Shah, Sulayman, balanced by the tenure of a strong grand vizier, Shaykh 'Ali Khan, whose incumbency marks the culmination of the process of concentration of power in the hands of the chief minister begun under Shah Safi I. Shaykh 'Ali Khan's attempt at economic and fiscal reform grew out of the first overt manifestations of economic distress – commercial bankruptcies, a diminished inflow of silver, and monetary debasement. Bureaucratic inertia, corruption and half-hearted royal support doomed his policies, which thus remained an isolated effort incapable of halting the process of decentralization. Silk, meanwhile, continued to be exported in great quantities, through the Ottoman Empire as well as via Russia, where the state in the 1660s embarked on a policy that combined efforts to increase commercial revenue with a new attempt to isolate the Ottomans. The outcome, significant concessions granted to Iran's Armenian merchants, inaugurated regularized commercial traffic between Iran and western Europe through Russia.

The turn of the eighteenth century witnessed a significant shift in the external demand for Iranian silk. Following a brief period of silk shortages and high prices in the European market in the 1690s, the European maritime companies definitively gave up on raw silk from Iran. Having switched to new commodities, such as wool, and to more profitable destinations, above all India, they continued to make up the balance with bullion exports. As exports via the Persian Gulf trailed off and the Levant fell prey to insecurity, exports of Iranian raw silk to Russia underwent a significant increase. Among the factors contributing to this was Tsar Peter's policy to turn Russia into the hub of East–West trade, which culminated in an invasion of Iran and the seizure of its silk-producing provinces in 1722–23.

These developments coincided with the acceleration of the decentralizing process that would lead to the Afghan invasion, the fall of Isfahan in 1722, and the eclipse of central Safavid rule and foreign occupation in its aftermath. Chapter 8 will explore the coincidence between this mounting political disorder and changing trade routes, paying particular attention to the question, vigorously debated in Mughal and Ottoman history, of the linkages between the devolution of central authority and economic viability, and most notably to the extent to which local, peripheral, and private initiative survived in the face of a disintegrating center.

CHAPTER 1

The Iranian silk trade: from the Silk Road to the Safavids

Iran and silk have been linked since the inception of the Silk Road, the commercial trail that connected the Chinese city of Lo-yang on the Yellow River with the ports of the Black Sea and the Mediterranean from antiquity to Mongol times.[1] Besides being a conduit for silk originating elsewhere, Iran also produced its own. A reference in Herodotus suggests that in ancient times so-called wild silk was cultivated in the country's northeast.[2] A famous legend situates the origins of regular silk production in the fifth century C.E., claiming that Chinese silkworm eggs were smuggled into Khotan from the Tarim basin in western China by a Kushan princess. Regardless of the date of introduction, sericulture is likely to have spread to Iran from Yargand and Farghana in Central Asia, in a movement whose direction and timing are suggested by the similarity of the Pahlavi word for silk *apreshum, apareshum* (New-Persian *abrisham*), with *warshum*, and *warshüm*, in Pamir dialects, and *wresham* in Afghan.[3] Until Mongol times the evidence for silk growing continues to center on Khurasan in the northeast, where production was widespread in the vicinity of Khaf, Sabzavar and Nishapur.[4]

It is only in the thirteenth century, following the Mongol invasion, that the Caspian provinces Gilan and Mazandaran come into focus as the main source of Iranian silk.[5] It is also in this period that Iran first appears as a source of raw silk in the East–West trade link. Benefiting from the *Pax Mongolica* and eager to satisfy the demands of a newly established silk

---

[1] The Silk Road is a term coined by the nineteenth-century German geographer F. von Richthofen to designate the trade link between China and Central Asia from 114 B.C.E. to 127 C.E. See Herrmann, *Die alten Seidenstrassen*, 10.

[2] Haussig, *Die Geschichte Zentralasiens in vorislamischer Zeit*, 63–4. As its natural color was either too dull or too bright, it was only marketed in colored form.

[3] Laufer, *Sino-Iranica*, 537–8. See also Eilers, "Abrišam." Some claim that sericulture is original to Iran. China, according to this theory, was the origin of the worm that produces a white cocoon, while Iran originally produced the yellow cocoon. See Petrushevskii, *Zemledelie i agrarnye otnosheniia*, 165–6.

[4] The extent of silk production in Khurasan under the Sarbidaran dynasty (r. 1336–81) is underscored by the fact that civil servants in this period were paid in silk. See ibid., 169.

[5] For references, see Barthold, *Historical Geography*, 235–6.

manufacturing industry at home, many Italian merchants frequented
Tabriz, the Il-Khanid capital, which had evolved into a commercial nexus
where routes from Ayas on the Mediterranean and Trabzon on the Black
Sea intersected with those coming from the Persian Gulf and Khurasan.
Equidistant from Gilan and Trabzon, Tabriz proved a hospitable environment for Western, mostly Italian, merchants who exchanged European
cloth and linen for silk and other eastern wares.[6] Both Genoa and Venice
had consulates in Tabriz in the early fourteenth century. Venice also sent
numerous embassies to Iran and in 1320 even concluded a commercial and
administrative treaty with the Il-Khanid ruler Abu Sa'd.[7]

The thriving trade between Iran and the Mediterranean was eclipsed by
the political turmoil and the Black Death pandemic of the fourteenth
century. Shortly after Abu Sa'd's death in 1336, the Il-Khanid state
disintegrated into a series of warring successor states, causing both Venice
and Genoa to boycott the Tabriz market. Despite attempts by the Jala'irids,
one of these states, to bring stability to western Iran, official relations were
suspended, the foreign merchant community dwindled, and commercial
traffic slowed to a trickle. Chaos in the Black Sea and the rise of the
Mamluk dynasty in Egypt simultaneously caused the center of trading
activity to move toward the southern Mediterranean.[8] With the Mamluk
conquest of Armenia in 1375 and the destruction of the Mediterranean port
of Ayas, Iran became even further isolated from the Levant. The rise of the
Ottomans to dominance in west Asia completed this process.

Ottomans, Mamluks, and Safavids

At the turn of the sixteenth century, three Muslim powers loomed over the
area bounded by the eastern shores of the Mediterranean, the Red Sea basin,
the Zagros mountains, and the mouth of the Persian Gulf: the Ottomans in

---

[6] Heyd, *Geschichte des Levantehandels*, ii, 108–12. See also Petech, "Les marchands italiens";
and "Testamento di Pietro Vioni." For an overall discussion of the west Asian trade routes
prior to the maritime discoveries, see Gaube and Wirth, *Aleppo*, 230–1.

[7] Ashtor, *Levant Trade*, 58, 60. That much of the silk transported for manufacture in Italy at
this time indeed originated in Iran is seen in contemporary Italian records, and is further
suggested by the well-known list of silk grades that refer to Iranian geographical regions
given in the narrative of the Italian merchant Pegolotti. Thus *seta ghella* refers to Gilan, while
seta masandroni clearly indicates silk from Mazandaran. Pegolotti further lists *seta stravai* or
stravatina, silk from Astarabad, *seta amali*, silk from Amul, *seta talani*, silk from Talish, *seta
mamutava*, silk from Mahmud Abad, *seta gangia*, silk from Ganja, and *seta merdacascia*, silk
from Marv. Other varieties are more difficult to associate with known places. *Seta canare*, or
chaunaruia, probably refers to Kinara in Qarabagh, while *seta siechi*, or *sacchi*, is most
probably related to Shaki in northern Azerbaijan. See Pegolotti, *La pratica della mercatura*,
208, 297–300. The list is also reproduced in Heyd, *Geschichte des Levantehandels*, ii, 650–3;
and in Petrushevskii, *Zemledelie i agrarnye otnosheniia*, 167. *Canari, talani*, and *mamodevi* are
also mentioned in Giovanni Rota's report of 1504. See Jodogne, "La <<vita del Sofi>>,"
228.

[8] Bautier. "Relations." 273–86; and Ashtor, *Levant Trade*, 64–5.

Asia Minor, the Safavids in eastern Anatolia and Azerbaijan, and the Mamluks in Egypt and Syria. Of these, the Safavids were upstarts. The latest Turko-Mongol tribal formation to rise in the borderlands of eastern Anatolia, they were inspired by a strong ideology that combined millenarian zeal with a tribal warrior ethos. Their leader, the youthful and charismatic leader Isma'il, relied on the fighting power of his Turkman warriors, the Qizilbash, to established his ruling house as the dominant power in eastern Anatolia and Azerbaijan. In 1501 Isma'il seized Tabriz as a prelude to a more comprehensive bid for regional supremacy. Crowned shah, Isma'il in the next few years mounted successful campaigns against the remnants of the Aq-quyunlu in central Iran, subjugated Fars, reduced Khuzistan and Basra to vassalage, and captured Mazandaran and Gilan. Emboldened by these initial successes, the young Safavid ruler in 1507–08 engaged in a series of clashes with the Dhu'l Qadr tribe in Anatolia and risked open conflict with the Mamluks by demanding the cession of the Aleppo region.

Isma'il's more formidable opponents proved to be the Ottomans, whose own spectacular expansion brought them into conflict with the Safavids. The fall of Constantinople in 1453 had given the Ottomans control over the entrance to the Black Sea and the main overland route between Asia and Europe. They next turned to the Black Sea, subduing Trabzon into tributary status in 1456. The Crimean port cities of Kaffa and Tana, long home to a Genoese merchant diaspora, were the next to fall under their control. By 1480 the Ottomans had incorporated all the former lands of the Byzantine Empire and were in the process of turning the Black Sea into a domestic lake.[9] The battle of Chaldiran, the culmination in 1514 of the first major Ottoman–Safavid confrontation, failed to stop the Ottoman advance. Routed by their opponents' artillery, the Safavids had to give up their territorial claims in Anatolia, with the victorious Ottomans extending their hold as far east as Erzurum. Their victory also enabled the Ottomans to take on the Mamluks. They first seized Syria in 1516, gaining control over the Levant. Their conquest of Egypt itself the following year ended Mamluk rule altogether and gave the Sublime Porte power over the most important of Arab lands, including the holy cities of Islam, as well as naval hegemony over the Red Sea basin.

In the next few decades the Ottomans further closed in on the Safavids by extending their control over Mesopotamia. They first took Kurdistan and Arab Iraq, seizing Baghdad in 1534, and incorporating Basra in 1549, and thereby gained an outlet to the Persian Gulf. They even invaded Azerbaijan twice between 1534 and 1548, and on both occasions briefly took Tabriz, exposing the city's vulnerability to outside attack and prompting Shah

---

[9] As Inalcik, "Question of the Closing," 108–09, points out, strictly speaking this process was only completed in 1538, when southern Bessarabia was annexed to the Ottoman Empire. Inalcik further argues that the closing of the Black Sea to international trade was a gradual process that was only completed at the turn of the seventeenth century.

Tahmasp, Isma'il's successor (r. 1521–76), to move his capital to Qazvin in the interior. Yet, as their supply lines extended too far and as campaigning was a seasonal affair, the Ottomans were never able to hold on to western Iran. This fact was acknowledged in 1555, when the two exhausted parties signed the agreement of Amasiya, which recognized Ottoman suzerainty over Iraq and eastern Anatolia while leaving Iran in control of Azerbaijan and the southeastern Caucasus. Amasiya thus affirmed boundaries that, though frequently shifting over the next three-quarters of a century, would prove remarkably enduring.

Scholars disagree about the motives behind these expansionist wars. Some argue that the Ottoman advance toward the Red Sea and the Persian Gulf was inspired by a desire to dominate the Indian Ocean trade. Others maintain that the Ottomans were driven less by immediate commercial objectives than by a bid for supremacy over the Islamic world and a desire to halt the westward thrust of the Safavids. Iran's impulse for moving west, in turn, tends to be associated with the (religious) zeal of the fledgling Safavid state. Indigenous sources are rarely explicit in offering motives, though the court chronicles suggest that geopolitical interest and imperial grandeur took precedence over faith and revenue. This is not to say that religious conviction and commercial advantage played no role in the flux and reflux of war and conquest. Fighting always took place under the banner of the true faith, and the fertile river basins of the Middle East and the corridors between the Mediterranean and the Indian Ocean had long been the target of rulers attracted by the prospect of rich agricultural and commercial income.[10] The politics of silk in particular suggest that the rivalry between Ottomans, Mamluks, and Safavids did involve issues of commercial control and revenue.

The silk trade between Iran and the Levant

The westward trade in Iranian silk, though periodically interrupted by dynastic change and conquest, survived all political turmoil – even the

---

[10] The various motives modern Western scholarship has ascribed to the Ottoman eastward expansion are discussed in von Mende, *Muṣṭafa 'Ālī's Furṣat-nāme*, 1–5, 42–6. Soviet scholars tended to give priority to economic motives, focusing on a desire for control over commercial routes. See, for example, Pigulevskaia et al., *Istoriia Irana*, 258–9. Brummett, *Ottoman Seapower*, passim, similarly (over)emphasizes the conscious commercial designs of the Ottomans in moving into the orbit of the Indian Ocean. Robert Mantran more convincingly argues that, while control over the commercial channels to India was part of the Ottoman thrust, they were motivated more by the prospect of revenue from existing routes and enterprises than by a desire for its expansion by active engagement. See Mantran, "L'Empire ottoman," 170–3. W. W. Clifford has recently (re)drawn attention to Ottoman geopolitical interests and strategic considerations, fueled by memories of recurrent Turko–Mongol eastward expansionism. See Clifford, "Some Observations," 275, 278. Exceptions to the tendency to ascribe religious motives to Safavid expansionism are Kissling, "Šāh Ismâ'îl Ier"; and Niewöhner-Eberhard, "Machtspolitische Aspekte."

convulsion that marked the invasion of Timur Lang in the late 1300s. In fact, the Spanish envoy to the Timurid court, de Clavijo, described Sultaniya as the principal market where raw silk was brought, sold, and from which it was further distributed, a town frequented by Indian, European, Turkish, and Syrian merchants. According to de Clavijo, "all the silk which is made in Gheelan comes here ... ," and this silk of Gheelan, he insisted, "is sent to Damascus and Syria and Turkey, and many other countries ... and all the merchants who come from the land of the Christians, from Caffa, and Trebizond, and the merchants of Turkey and Syria come every year, at this time to the city of Sultanieh, to make their purchases."[11]

Following Timur Lang's death Sultaniya declined as a commercial hub, its position taken by cities such as Tabriz, Ardabil, and especially Kashan.[12] We lack good information about the distribution network of Iranian silk in the fifteenth century but do know that, after Bursa had become the Ottoman capital, a great deal of it began to be redirected from the Trabzon route toward western Anatolia. Caspian silk in this period continued to supply the Italian weaveries, but a growing volume also began to feed the emerging silk weaving industry of Bursa itself.[13] Snippets of information about this link turn into concrete evidence in the second half of the sixteenth century, with records from Bursa suggesting that much of the raw silk used in the city's manufacturing industry came from Iran. Between 1460 and 1494, Bursa's customs revenue from silk increased threefold. Silk not processed by local manufacturers was re-exported.[14]

Given the ravages of the scorched-earth warfare practiced by the Safavids, several outbreaks of pestilence in Azerbaijan, and the reported plundering of silk caravans by Shah Isma'il's troops, the years immediately following the establishment of Safavid power in Iran are unlikely to have been propitious for the caravan trade across Anatolia and Mesopotamia.[15] Nor did conditions improve when in the second decade of Safavid rule Qizilbash revolts in Anatolia spilled over into Azerbaijan, leaving a trail of plunder and destruction.[16] Under the Ottoman Sultan Selim I (r. 1512–20), moreover, the Ottomans added economic warfare to their armory. In 1512

---

[11] De Clavijo, *Narrative*, 93, 95.
[12] Morgan and Coote, *Early Voyages*, ii, 389, 428.
[13] Inalcik, "Question of the Closing," 89–90; and Çizakça, "Sixteenth Seventeenth Century Inflation," 14. For the Italian use of silk from Gilan in the fifteenth century, see de Roover, "Andrea Banchi," 238–40, 274.
[14] Dalsar, *Türk sanayi*, 142.
[15] Jodogne, "La <<vita del sofi>>," 218; Bacqué-Grammont, *Les Ottomans, les Safavides*, 56–7; and Aubin, "L'Avènement des safavides," 69ff. Traffic was not altogether absent. In 1504, for example, Iranian silk arrived in Damascus. See Scarcia-Amoretti, *Šāh Ismā'īl I*, 70.
[16] Rumlu, *Ahsan al-tavarikh*, 165–6. The Qizilbash revolts in Anatolia, the most important of which was the uprising of Shah-quli of 1511–12, are detailed in Sohrweide, "Der Sieg der Safaviden." 145ff.

they arrested a number of Iranian silk merchants in Bursa and forcibly sent them to Istanbul and Rumeli.[17] Relations reached a nadir following the battle of Chaldiran, when Istanbul intensified its efforts to deprive the Safavids of revenue. Upon leaving Tabriz, the Ottomans took with them a number of merchants and artisans as well as a great volume of silk.[18] This was followed by the institution of a commercial blockade of Iranian products, which proved most damaging for Iran's silk exports but also affected the Ottoman economy, since it led to a dramatic fall in customs dues in Bursa.[19] Iranian merchants at first attempted to evade the blockade by rerouting their trade through Mamluk territory, but as of early 1515 the Ottomans sought to prevent this by introducing strict controls on products coming from the east at all entry posts, on land as well as along the coasts.[20] They confiscated the goods of Iranian merchants, transported the latter to Rumeli and Istanbul, and saw to it that Iranians as well as their own subjects would not sell Iranian merchandise. The only ones to be partly exempted from the boycott were Armenian and Jewish merchants; perhaps seen as less susceptible to Safavid religious propaganda than Muslims, they were permitted to purchase Iranian silk in Erzurum under Ottoman supervision.[21]

Thus cut off from the Mediterranean outlet, Iranian merchants sought alternative outlets for their export wares. Attempts to transport silk via the as yet unpacified Russian steppes remained unsuccessful, however, as did efforts to loosen the Ottoman stranglehold by approaching the Portuguese with a request to be allowed to use Indian ports for their products.[22] Relief came with Selim's death in 1520, for his successor Sultan Suleyman relaxed the boycott, moved to act by a drop in revenue for his treasury and by manifold complaints of merchants who had their goods confiscated.[23]

Though resumed, the westward flow of Iranian silk continued to suffer from intermittent Ottoman–Safavid warring between 1538 and 1555. In 1539, merchants wishing to visit Iran from Ottoman territory needed a special permit from the sultan.[24] A scorched-earth policy conducted by both parties did great damage to the borderlands of Shirvan and Azerbaijan in 1548–49.[25] The Ottoman invasion of Azerbaijan in 1554 devastated Tabriz and caused great suffering in Nakhjavan and Qarabagh.[26] But it was

---

[17] Dalsar, *Türk sanayi*, 131.

[18] Bacqué-Grammont, *Les Ottomans, les Safavides*, 167–8.

[19] See the table giving the value of customs receipts in Inalcik, "Ottoman Economic Mind," 210.

[20] The blockade is discussed in Inalcik, "Osmanli Imperatorlugunun kurulus," 661–76; Bacqué- Grammont, "Notes sur le blocus"; 66–8; idem, "Notes sur une saisie"; idem, *Les Ottomans, les Safavides*, 53ff.

[21] Ibid., 68.

[22] Bacqué-Grammont, "Notes et documents," 244, 265, fn. 31; and idem, *Les Ottomans, les Safavides*, 128ff.

[23] Ibid., 57, 68–71.   [24] Berchet, *La Repubblica*, 179.

[25] Hinz, "Schah Esma'il II," 28–9.   [26] Geidarov, *Goroda i gorodskoe remeslo*, 101.

especially the outbreak of the Ottoman–Venetian war of 1570–73 and rebellions in Anatolia in the same decade which negatively affected the silk trade.[27] The Italian envoy d'Alessandri, describing Qazvin in 1574, noted that

This city is commercial, as in it the goods and caravans of all parts of the kingdom come together, but its business has suffered much from war. As for instance, in the past, two loads of silk, with which the country abounds, were worth more than four hundred sequins, and are now worth only two hundred.[28]

On the receiving end the drop in silk supplies was felt as well, for in the same year Aleppo experienced a fall in silk imports from Iran.[29]

Nor did matters improve in the next few years, with Celali rebellions raging all over Anatolia, and Iran in turmoil in the aftermath of Shah Tahmasp's death in 1576. Two years later a new round of Safavid–Ottoman warfare erupted – triggered, it is said, by an Iranian refusal to pay indemnification for an attack on an Ottoman silk caravan near Zanjan[30] – that would continue until 1590. Georgia was the initial target of Sultan Murad III's attempt to establish control over parts of Transcaucasia with a Sunni majority. Shirvan, where heavy taxation had sparked an anti-Safavid uprising, soon followed. Assisted by Crimean Tatars, the Ottomans advanced as far as Baku and Darband on the Caspian Sea in 1579. Travel along the western shore was made impossible, and the Ottomans blocked maritime traffic by establishing naval supremacy on the Caspian Sea. In the frequent clashes with the Safavids Shamakhi, the capital of Shirvan and the center of Iran's northern silk trade, was destroyed. In 1585 the Ottomans briefly seized Tabriz, massacring its population. As roving Tatar bands spoliated the countryside, the Iranians contributed to the area's destruction by engaging in their usual scorched-earth policy.[31]

The Safavid–Ottoman wars of 1578–90 have been held responsible for a long-term economic decline of Shirvan and northern Azerbaijan.[32] The silk trade was indeed badly affected, and a simultaneous ban on bullion exports to Iran further inhibited traffic to the point where Bursa experienced such silk shortages that prices went up by 300 percent, forcing many of the city's silk weavers out of business.[33] The long-term effect of such shortfalls was the establishment of an independent sericulture in the Bursa area. Still, a greater volume of available silk did not obviate imports, for at the same

[27] Faroqhi, "Bursa at the Crossroads," 122.
[28] Grey, Narrative of Italian Travels, 225.
[29] Berchet, Relazioni, 61, Relazione di Soria del console Andrea Navagero, eletto il 16 aprile 1574.
[30] For the Iranian refusal to pay damages for the attack, see Kütükoğlu, Osmanlı–Iran siyasi münasebetleri, 17–18.
[31] Kortepeter, Ottoman Imperialism, 51–75; and Kütükoğlu, "Les relations."
[32] Ashurbeili, Gosudarstvo Shirvanshakhov, 287, 291.
[33] Geidarov, Goroda i gorodskoe remeslo, 102–3; Dalsar, Türk sanayi, 173. For the price increase, see Çizakça, "Price History," 536–7.

time a growing European demand developed for Iranian silk, considered to be of superior quality.

The caravan trade, inherently insecure due to harsh climatic conditions, inhospitable terrain, and frequent epidemics, was often interrupted by the Ottoman–Safavid clashes, but commercial traffic never came to a halt for any extended period of time.[34] One reason for this was the important role which the Armenians began to play in the trade link between Iran and the Mediterranean port cities. They may have been active on this route as early as the thirteenth century, when Maku, one of the way stations in the Trabzon link, was home to a considerable Armenian population.[35] The exemption of Armenian traders from the 1514 boycott suggests how prolonged Safavid–Ottoman conflict stimulated Armenian participation in the west Asian transit trade. Their "neutral" status seems to have worked to their advantage in circumstances where Iranian Muslims were not allowed to traverse Ottoman territory.[36] Iran's rulers also seem to have accorded them preferential treatment of sorts. Already under the Qara-quyunlu, merchants from Armenian towns such as Julfa and Agulis enjoyed special status and were exempted from commercial taxes.[37] Shah Ismaʿil saw the Armenian community as a useful ally in his struggle with the Ottomans.[38] Shah Khudabandah in 1586 granted one Khajah Nazar individual protection and the freedom to trade in Iran.[39] Though there is no evidence that either ruler accorded them favored group status, the approach of both prefigures the privileges Armenian merchants would obtain under Shah ʿAbbas I.

To be sure, the Armenians were by no means the only ones to ply their trade between Iran and the Levant. In fact, in the fifteenth century most of the merchants frequenting the Anatolian route appear to have been Azerbaijani Iranians, who may have found it easier to travel in Ottoman territory because they were turkophone and insofar as they were Sunnis.[40] The Portuguese traveler, Tenreiro, in 1525 called Tabriz a silk emporium where merchants from Russia, Venice, and Turkey converged.[41] A generation later the English merchant, Edwards, claimed that "there is in those parts to be had three or fowre thousand horses lading, every horse loade being 50 to 60 batmans, beside silke of Grosine [Georgia]. Great aboun-

---

[34] Even during the Ottoman Iraqi campaign of 1533–35, traffic of persons and merchandise seems to have continued between Safavid and Ottoman territory. See Gökbilgin, "Rapports d'Ibrahim Paša," 194.

[35] Martirosian, *Armianskie poseleniia*, 176.

[36] Zekiyan, "Xoğa Safar," 361. Especially after 1593, when the shaykh al-Islam of Qazvin declared all non-Twelver Shiʿis unbelievers, travel in Ottoman territory must have become problematic for many Iranians. See Stewart, "Taqiyyah as Performance," 6.

[37] Bayburdyan, *Naqsh-i Aramanah*, 17–18.

[38] Zulalian, *Armeniia*, 63.

[39] Gregorian, "Minorities of Isfahan," 660.

[40] Inalcik, "Question of the Closing," 90.   [41] Tenreiro, *Itinerarios*, 30.

dance of silke at times is sent out of these parts, to wit, 4 or 5 hundred horse loades, by the Turkes . . . "[42] It is clear, however, that as of the mid-sixteenth century Armenians became the pre-eminent mediators in the silk trade between Iran and the ports of the Levant. "One village of Armenians," Edwards wrote in 1566, "yeerely carrieth 400 and 500 mules lading of silke to Aleppo, and bringeth thence 800 or a thousand Mules laden with karsies & Venice clothes."[43] Their activity centered on various towns in eastern Armenia, of which Julfa was the most prominent. Situated on the river Aras and at a crossroads of overland routes connecting Transcaucasia and Iran with Anatolia, Syria, and the Mediterranean, Julfa in the later 1500s grew rapidly, despite the frequent turmoil and destruction of the times.[44]

Europe's growing demand for Iranian silk

The growing participation of Armenian merchants in Eurasian trade in the 1500s was not simply a function of outsider status and royal favor. It owed as much to their resourcefulness and efficiency inherent in a tendency to operate as family firms. Most importantly, the Armenians benefited from rapidly expanding East–West trading opportunities that were triggered, for the most part, by the arrival in the Levant of European trading companies eager to buy Asian commodities. This process is epitomized by the tremendous growth of Armenian expatriate communities in many Mediterranean port cities in the late sixteenth century. By the 1550s a great number of Julfan Armenian merchants active in international trade resided in Aleppo. Before the end of the century they had virtually monopolized the supply of Iranian silk, establishing themselves as the main intermediaries between local markets and the European maritime companies.[45] Livorno (Leghorn) in 1593 had twelve Armenian trading houses, six of which were managed by Levantine Armenians.[46] Armenians had begun to migrate to Venice as early as the eleventh century, and their number had greatly increased after the eclipse of the Armenian Republic of Cilicia in the early 1400s. The earliest reference to Julfan Armenians in Venice dates from 1570.[47] A generation later, Armenians only ceded place to Ottoman Muslims among the number of eastern merchants residing in the city.[48]

This rapid increase in the number of Armenians, in Italy as elsewhere, matched the simultaneous growth of the Levantine port cities in response to Ottoman but, above all, European economic expansion and the attendant

---

[42] Morgan and Coote, *Early Voyages*, ii, 401, letter of Arthur Edwards, Aug. 8, 1566.
[43] Ibid., 397. The actual number of kersies is given by the same source as "four, five, and six thousand pieces."
[44] For details, see Herzig, "Rise of the Julfa Merchants."
[45] Sanjian, *Armenian Communities*, 48–9.
[46] Tékéian, "Marseille," 10
[47] Herzig, "Armenian Merchants," 131.   [48] Vercellin, "Mercanti turchi," 246.

growing demand for luxury wares from Asia. The rise of Aleppo as an entrepôt between the overland route to Iran and the maritime link with Europe exemplifies this development. Aleppo's rise to commercial prosperity, commonly associated with the period following the Ottoman conquest of the early 1500s, may in fact have begun in the last decades of Mamluk rule, when Turkish campaigns into Anatolia caused the main east–west commercial artery to shift southward.[49] Nevertheless, Ottoman control in 1516 accelerated the city's expansion. With the Ottoman annexation of Baghdad in 1534 and of Basra in 1549, Aleppo became the terminus of trade from Iran and India. In time, the city overtook Damascus as the third largest city of the Ottoman realm, after Istanbul and Cairo. Underscoring Aleppo's rise at the expense of Damascus, Venice moved its consular representation from the former to the latter city. By the mid-1500s the Venetians bought the bulk of their silk in Aleppo, which by then was said to receive 350,000 ducats worth of silk from Iran.[50] The European Levant Companies which entered the trade in the same period established their consular legations in Aleppo as well. The French took up residence as early as 1557, while the English Levant Company moved its agency from its initial location in Tripoli on the coast inland to Aleppo by 1586. Soon, Iskenderun, Aleppo's port city, received an Ottoman customs station and became the site of European warehouses, thus developing into the major outlet for trade with Europe.[51]

What initially attracted the Europeans to Aleppo was not only or even principally silk, but commodities such as cotton, indigo, and spices. While the Venetians imported considerable amounts of silk, which may have formed one-third of their trade in the Levant, the commodity at first was fairly insignificant for the newly founded Levant Companies. English raw silk imports were quite minimal until the closing years of the sixteenth century. Illustrative of the relative unimportance of silk is the fact that Ottoman port officials long levied a customs fee on silk that was much lower than that on spices and cotton.[52]

Interestingly, it was the direct import of east Asian spices by the Dutch and English East India Companies which made the Levant traders search for an alternative, which they found in silk.[53] As the English observed in 1598:

The truth is all men have such cold advice out of England, of the glut of indigo and

[49] Wirth, "Alep et les courants commerciaux," 54. Masters, *Origins*, 11–12, emphasizes Aleppo's rise as a commercial center with its incorporation into the Ottoman Empire in 1516.

[50] Berchet, *Relazioni*, 19; Chesneau, *Voyage de monsieur d'Aramon*, 254. Twenty-five years later it was claimed that close to two-thirds of the wares brought to Aleppo from Iran consisted of silk. See Tucci, "Un ciclo di affari," 104.

[51] Masters, *Origins*, 15.   [52] Heeringa, *Bronnen*, i, 450.

[53] Steensgaard, *Asian Trade Revolution*, 160.

spices here, that noe man dare as yet venture upon anything. But all men's orders are for raw silk which commodity at present not here to be had for any money ... [54]

The European run on silk was sudden and dramatic. The frenzy among Western merchants by the end of the sixteenth century is captured in the words of William Clark, an English Levant Company merchant in Aleppo, who in 1598 reported that merchants were ready to pull the silk off the camels' backs as soon as the caravans arrived, and that many bought without even opening the bales.[55]

This search for new products appears to be the key to the paradoxical circumstance that the opening of the Cape route, far from dealing a huge blow to the Levant trade, coincided with its revival. Scholars used to see the balance between the Levant and the Indian Ocean trade as a zero-sum game. More recently it has been argued that if the surge in oceanic commerce following the European exploration of the Cape route led to an immediate fall in the volume of the Mediterranean trade, this was a temporary outcome. Richard Rapp has gone even further by claiming a revival of commercial vitality in the Mediterranean basin. He suggests that changing trade routes alone did not cause shifts in European economic strength and that the rise of the northwestern European countries at the expense of the old hegemon, Venice, must be seen as the outcome of successful competition in established markets rather than of the exploration of new ones. In his view it was "the invasion of the Mediterranean, not the exploitation of the Atlantic, that produced the Golden Ages of Amsterdam and London."[56] The latter claim remains contested by those who argue that neither the Atlantic nor the Mediterranean trade, but rather the Baltic connection fueled the prosperity of the Dutch Republic.[57] In either case, there is little doubt that the Mediterranean trade underwent a revival after a period of retrenchment. In a classic study, Frederic Lane demonstrated that, after their initial retreat, the Venetians in the mid-sixteenth century were able to reemerge as major spice traders against the Portuguese.[58] The Venetian merchants, whose return cargo consisted mostly of woollen cloth, ultimately lost their pre-eminence because of high cost and their inability to respond to fashion changes, but they held their own in the Levantine market until the early 1600s.[59] We also know that the English "disappearance" from the Levant trade in the 1550s only prefigured their enhanced presence in the form of the Levant Company. This presence, soon reinforced by the arrival of the French and the Dutch, thrived in part on old commodities, like spices, in part on new wares, among which silk was

[54] Quoted in ibid., fn. 36.
[55] Harris, "An Aleppo Merchant's Letter-book," 67.
[56] Rapp, "Unmaking."
[57] See the discussion in Israel, *Dutch Primacy*, 12–37.
[58] Lane, "Venetian Shipping"; and idem, "Mediterranean Spice Trade."
[59] Wilson. "Cloth Production," 212.

important. Braudel, discussing the flourishing state of the Levantine trade in the last decades of the sixteenth century, notes that "every single letter from Venetian or Marseilles merchants from Aleppo, Tripoli, or Alexandretta, carries a reference to silk" in this period.[60] Venetian imports of Iranian raw silk for 1590 have been estimated at 1,425 bales, while for the following decade 845 bales are given as the annual average.[61] As the demand for silk increased, its price went up accordingly.[62] While earlier, silk was hardly an important commodity in the Levant trade for any nation but the Venetians, by 1600 all merchants operating in the Levant realized its promise.[63]

European demand for silk had been expanding ever since the creation of an Italian manufacturing industry and received a huge stimulus from the end of the Italian monopoly over the silk trade with France and the emergence of Provence in the fifteenth century as a silk-producing region and Lyon as a manufacturing center under French royal patronage. This northern shift of silk manufacturing even affected the lands across the Alps, where as early as the fourteenth century the German towns of Regensburg and Cologne had begun to process silk.[64] In the Flemish cities of Ghent and Bruges a silk industry was established in the fifteenth century. Antwerp, which had long been an entrepôt for silk wares from Italy, acquired its silk processing industry in the 1500s. The urban centers of the northern Netherlands, finally, owed the establishment of their silk manufacture to the migration of artisans and craftsmen from France and the Spanish Netherlands in the 1570s and 80s.[65]

These developments epitomized the growth of Europe's urban industry, and ultimately signaled an economic expansion that, by giving greater numbers of people more spending power, increased the demand for luxury goods, including silk. Traditionally used almost exclusively in ecclesiastical clothing and the attire of the very rich, silk as of the late fifteenth century became a symbol of social mobility to an urban elite of greater financial means and increasingly refined taste. As a result, silk manufacturing turned into a key industry in many European countries.[66] Merchants began to explore all possible avenues to beat their competitors in gaining access to Iranian silk, and one was the Russian connection.

[60] Braudel, *Mediterranean*, i, 563–5.
[61] Sella, *Commerci*, 111–13.
[62] Foster, *Travels of John Sanderson*, 131; and Baulant, *Lettres de négociants marseillais*, 157–61.
[63] Steensgaard, *Asian Trade Revolution*, 160–1.
[64] Heimpel, "Seide aus Regensburg"; and Haussig, *Die Geschichte Zentralasiens in islamischer Zeit*, 146–50, 221–2.
[65] Van Nierop, "De zijdenijverheid," 23–5, 32.
[66] Braudel, *Civilization*, ii, 178, 312–13.

The "longitudinal axis"

In the sixteenth century, the Anatolian and Mesopotamian route had a virtual monopoly as the western outlet for Iranian silk. It was not, however, to remain the only one. Over time a "longitudinal" axis emerged in competition with the Ottoman "latitudinal" link.[67] The southern component of this axis ran from the Caspian provinces to the ports of the Persian Gulf. The latter body of water had played a role in Iran's external trade links since time immemorial and, as the thriving trade of the port of Siraf in the tenth century suggests, had at times been a vital commercial outlet for the Iranian interior. In the fifteenth century, its shipping lanes progressively gained in importance, resulting in the emergence of Hurmuz as an entrepôt in the trade between south and southwest Asia. The north–south trade route expanded accordingly, with silk, raw as well as manufactured, being among the goods transported to Hurmuz.[68]

On the eve of the Safavid rise to power, the Persian Gulf littoral and the adjacent parts of the interior, the so-called Garmsir, were ruled as semi-independent principalities. The most important among these, the kingdoms of Hurmuz and Lar, had long paid fixed sums to the successive rulers of Iran proper, Timurids, Qara-quyunlu, and Aq-quyunlu, to assure safe passage of caravans through their territories.[69] Shah Isma'il I was thus merely the latest in a series of Iranian rulers when in 1503 he invaded Fars and in the process forced Hurmuz, by then severely weakened by internal strife, to pay tribute to him. Hurmuz was not to remain an exclusively Safavid outlet to the Indian Ocean, though: the island also became the target of the Portuguese who, prompted by the Ottoman hold over the eastern Mediterranean to explore the Atlantic route, entered the Persian Gulf in search of power and revenue. Occupying Hurmuz in 1507, they proceeded to build a fort but soon withdrew, leaving its ruler tributary to their king. In 1515 they returned and equipped the island with a garrison. In the same year Shah Isma'il, under pressure from the Ottoman boycott of Iranian goods and presumably searching for alternative outlets, approached the Portuguese Afonso de Albuquerque with a request for a treaty that would include the sharing of toll revenue, the right to utilize Portuguese ships, and trading rights for Iranian merchants in Hurmuz and Portuguese India.[70] In the following years an intensive diplomatic exchange developed between the two. The results were meager, however. The Safavid ruler must have been reluctant to engage in an open anti-Ottoman alliance with the

---

[67] Allen, *Problems of Turkish Power*, 39.

[68] Pires, *Suma Oriental*, i, 20; Barbosa, *Book of Duarte Barbosa*, i, 93; Texeira, *Travels*, 252.

[69] Aubin, "Le royaume d'Ormuz," 141. The rulers of Hurmuz, in turn, seem to have secured safe trade by paying tribute to those of Lar. See de Gouvea, *Relation*, 483.

[70] De Bulhão Pato, *Cartas de Affonso de Albuquerque*, ii, 233–50, Descripção da jornada que fizeram os embaixadores que foram ao Xeque Ismael.

Lusitanians, and the end of the boycott in 1520 obviated the quest for Indian Ocean exit lanes.[71] In 1543, the Portuguese took control of the toll house of Hurmuz, thus depriving the Safavid rulers of customs revenue and unhindered access to the Persian Gulf.

Hurmuz was one of the pre-eminent ports of trade in the Indian Ocean basin in the sixteenth century, and silk was among the articles that went through it, much of it arriving from Kashan, Iran's entrepôt for southward bound commerce. According to Michele Membré, who visited the city in 1540, a great deal of silk arrived in Kashan from Gilan, Varamin, Shirvan, and Mazandaran "for at the said city they load the caravans and go to Hormuz."[72] The Portuguese admiral Albuquerque confirmed the Indian destination by insisting that the Persian Gulf ports supplied "Ormuz with a great quantity of silk which is exported to India."[73] The fact that customs tariffs in Hurmuz favored silk products from the Iranian workshops suggests that silk textiles as well as raw silk were exported to India.[74]

The northern end of the longitudinal axis connected Iran with the lands to the north via the Caspian Sea and the Volga basin. This route also gradually came into its own in the sixteenth century. Traffic via the Caspian Sea and the Volga, which goes back to the pre-Islamic period, had always fluctuated according to political circumstances, but no sustained commercial exchange along this itinerary could develop until the emergence of a stable political center in the north. The rise of Muscovy (Moscow) in the fifteenth century created such a center and led to a (modest) revival of trade relations between Russia and the Islamic world, as is seen in visits of trade representatives from Shirvan to Moscow in 1465 and 1494.[75]

It was not so much the formation of the Safavid state as the tensions between the Iranians and the Ottomans which spurred initial Russo–Iranian contacts. Indeed, what may have prompted Shah Isma'il to seek contact with Tsar Vasili III (r. 1505–33) was the same Ottoman boycott of Safavid export wares that led him to approach the Portuguese. The blockage of the link with the Levant led Iranian merchants to seek alternative routes via the Persian Gulf as well as across the Caucasus, and was one of the reasons why in 1516 Isma'il sought a rapprochement with the Shirvanshah rulers, who controlled the western Caspian Sea littoral.[76] The same circumstances may have caused the shah in 1520 to send an envoy to Moscow in what represents the earliest diplomatic contact with Safavid Iran recorded in the Russian sources.[77]

[71] Bacqué-Grammont, *Les Ottomans, les Safavides*, 128–37.
[72] Membré, *Mission*, 46.
[73] Albuquerque, *Commentaries*, iv, 187.
[74] Aubin, "Le royaume d'Ormuz," 172.
[75] Ashurbeili, *Gosudarstvo Shirvanshakhov*, 289.
[76] Bacqué-Grammont, *Les Ottomans, les Safavides*, 69–70.
[77] Bushev, *Istoriia posol'stv v 1586–1612*, 36. Since the envoy was in Moscow in 1521, it may be presumed that he had been dispatched in 1520.

Though necessary, the formation of stable states was not a sufficient precondition for direct and durable Russo–Iranian trade relations. Until the 1550s few Russian merchants ventured south into a region that lacked the most basic facilities for commercial traffic.[78] Tatars acted as the main intermediaries in the north–south trade. The Italian Contarini in the later 1400s noted that a caravan left Astrakhan for Moscow every year "accompanied by a great many Tartar merchants who ... take with them silk manufactured in Gesdi [Yazd] and fustian stuffs to exchange for furs, saddles, swords, bridles and other things which they require."[79] On the part of Iran, the first to engage in commercial traffic with the north were probably the same Julfan Armenians who progressively increased their market share in the Anatolian trade. They seem to have traded with Moscow long before Russia controlled the Caspian Sea route and may also have been instrumental in attempts to transport Iranian silk to Europe via Russia when the Ottomans struck Iran with their commercial blockade.[80] In time the presence of Iranian Armenians along the northern route became as institutionalized as it did in the Mediterranean basin. In 1544 the beglerbeg of Shirvan asked Ivan IV to renew existing privileges for Armenian merchants in their trade with Russia.[81] Moscow housed an Armenian caravanserai in the late sixteenth century, and the records of the city of Lvov, in Galicia-Volynhia, after 1570 list a number of resident Armenian Iranians.[82]

The extension of Russian control over the Volga route must be seen as a land-based variant of the maritime expansion undertaken by European merchants and soldiers at the turn of the sixteenth century. While the consequences for the Ottoman Empire and Iran of Europe's maritime explorations are well known, however, Russia's simultaneous advance and the efforts by Western merchants to forge an overland link with Iran and India via its territory remain relatively obscure. The Portuguese exploration of the Atlantic route was a direct response to the Ottoman hegemony over the Levantine connection; the search for the riches of India via Russia, in turn, was undertaken in reaction to the Iberian monopolization of the sea route to Asia. In an attempt to break the latter monopoly by creating a new overland alternative, the Genoese Paolo Centurione in 1522 endeavored to open up a route from the Baltic Sea via the Volga and Astrakhan to central

---

[78] See Contarini's observation about the Volga route in the late 1400s, in Stanley of Alderley, *Travels to Tana*, 151–4; and Jenkinson's reference to the lack of victuals between Astrakhan and Kazan about a century later, in Morgan and Coote, *Early Voyages*, i, 99.

[79] Stanley of Alderley, *Travels to Tana*, 151.

[80] Zevakin, "Persidskii vopros," 157. Armenian merchants, though not necessarily from Iran, are mentioned in Moscow as early as the fourteenth century. See Voskanyan, "Les Arméniens à Moscou," 425.

[81] Bushev, *Istoriia posol'stv 1586–1612*, 40.

[82] The existence of the caravanserai is noted by Gregorian, "Minorities," 662. For the Armenian presence in Lvov, see Nadel-Golobič, "Armenians and Jews," 352.

Asia and India.[83] Such efforts met with little success as long as the lands lying astride this fluvial route remained unpacified. Pacification, in turn, had to wait until after the Russian annexation of the khanates of Kazan (1552) and Astrakhan (1556), as a result of which the Caucasus and the Caspian Sea were made accessible via the Volga route.

The Russian incorporation of Astrakhan proved to be of momentous importance for commercial relations between the Slavic and the Islamic worlds, for it made the town emerge as the principal crossroads where merchants from Russia, Iran, Central Asia and India met and exchanged their wares. From Astrakhan Russian merchants began to venture further south. They not only participated in the exchange of silk and other wares in Shamakhi (Shamakha in Russian), the terminus for most merchants arriving from the north, but their presence was noted in Iranian cities such as Tabriz, Ardabil, and Kashan as well.[84] Russia's annexation of Astrakhan also prefigured an active governmental role in trade with the Muslim world. Extending its ambit beyond Astrakhan, Muscovy established contacts involving trade with the central Asian khanates as well as with the region of Transcaucasia and Iran proper. Thus the beglerbeg of Shirvan, 'Abdallah Khan, in 1562–63 sent envoys to Moscow for trade talks.[85] Tsar Ivan IV in 1567 dispatched two agents with royal wares as far south as Hurmuz.[86] Russia exported leather, metal objects such as arms, fur, wax, and tallow. Merchants from Iran frequented Kazan and Nizhnii Novgorod with goods that ranged from carpets and morocco leather to saffron and precious stones.[87] Silk, most of it manufactured, was also included in their assortment. Jenkinson in 1558 observed that Astrakhan was a meeting place of Tatar merchants who brought "diuers kindes of wares made of cotton wooll, with diuers kinds of wrought silkes," and merchants from Shamakhi in Iran who carried "sowing silke, which is the courrest that they use in Russeland."[88] The velvets, satins and taffetas woven in Yazd, Kashan, and Isfahan that were taken to Russia often made up 70 percent or more of the total value of goods transported.[89] Relatively little raw silk seems to have been carried to Russia until the growing demand from western Europe in the later sixteenth century opened up the possibility of re-export.[90]

Armenian Iranians, Indians and Russians were not the only ones to explore the route between Moscow and Iran following Russia's annexation of Astrakhan. Tsar Ivan IV, negotiating peace with Sweden in 1557, offered King Gustav the right of Swedish merchants to travel through his realm to

[83] Kellenbenz, "Der russische Transithandel," 483.
[84] Fekhner, *Torgovlia*, 27; Purchas, *Hakluytus Posthumus*, viii, 507, Observations of Master John Cartwright in his voyage from Aleppo to Hispaan, and backe again.
[85] Bushev, *Istoriia posol'stv 1586–1612*, 42.   [86] Ibid., 45.
[87] See Fekhner, *Torgovlia*, 52ff., and 79–80 for the exchange of goods in both directions.
[88] Morgan and Coote, *Early Voyages*, i, 59.
[89] Fekhner, *Torgovlia*, 67.   [90] Ibid., 79–80.

Iran in return for free transit for Russian merchants to western Europe via Sweden.[91] The project never materialized. The Swedes declined the offer, and when Ivan captured the transit port of Narva the following year the proposal lost its attractiveness for the Russians as well. Other Western ventures were more successful. Among the first to take advantage of improved communications and greater safety were the English so-called Muscovy merchants who, faced with a Portuguese and Spanish monopoly of the Atlantic connection and a strong Armenian, Venetian, and Ottoman presence on the Levant route, decided to explore the northern itinerary in their quest for Indian wealth. To that end the Russia Company, which had been chartered in 1555, undertook a series of missions to Iran. The first of these set out in 1561 and was led by Anthony Jenkinson, the same person who earlier had undertaken a fact-finding mission to the Caspian Sea and Central Asia. Jenkinson failed to make an agreement with Shah Tahmasp, who was reluctant to endanger the peace of Amasiya, but did obtain trading privileges from the ruler of Shirvan, 'Abd Allah Khan, and brought back the Company's first raw silk. Upon Jenkinson's return to Moscow, Ivan IV, desirous to secure munition and technicians from England and thus to circumvent a Habsburg, Swedish, and Polish embargo imposed on Russia, granted the Russia Company toll-free trade throughout his realm and possibly the right to trade with Iran as well.[92] When the English also obtained toll-free trading rights from Shah Tahmasp, in 1566, the stage was set for a regular traffic.

In the next fifteen years the Russia Company engaged in various commercial expeditions to Iran. None of these were very profitable. The route alongside the Caspian littoral remained far from secure, devoid of facilities and infested with bandits as it was. Robberies were common, and even caravans protected by armed troops of up to 1,000 men might be attacked.[93] If anything, conditions worsened in the last third of the sixteenth century. Crimean Tatars marched on Moscow and in 1571 torched the city. A year later the Volga Tatars rose in revolt. In and around Astrakhan things were hardly better. In 1569 the Ottomans launched a campaign against the city to forge a link between Anatolia and Central Asia.[94] When they took Azerbaijan and the Caspian Sea littoral between Baku and Darband, the western side became impassible and travel temporarily shifted to the eastern shore. The last of the expeditions undertaken by the Russia Company epitomized the hazards of the journey. Dispatched in 1579, it found all of Shirvan occupied by the Ottomans and after much delay and hardship returned with a mere forty-eight bales of silk.

Poor infrastructure and the vagaries of war and rebellion were not the

[91] Troebst, *Handelskontrolle*, 169.
[92] Baron, "Ivan the Terrible," 566.
[93] Bushev, *Istoriia posol'stv 1586–1612*, 61–2.
[94] Bennigsen, "L'expédition turque"; and Bushev, *Istoriia posol'stv 1586–1612*, 57.

only reasons for the demise of the Russia Company in the 1580s. As T. S. Willan notes, by traveling to Iran via Russia the English may have tried to fill the vacuum created by their withdrawal from the Levant. Conversely, the resumption of English trade in the Mediterranean in the 1580s must have dimmed their enthusiasm to explore the hazardous Russian connection.[95] A final, less well recognized reason for the cession of the English missions is the fact that the Russian government, under pressure by its indigenous merchants, at this point began to restrict the movements of foreigners. Russian merchants, spearheaded by those who operated in the service of the state, the *gosti*, had long resisted the activities of foreign competitors on Russian soil. Initially ignored by Ivan IV, they gained a partial victory in their struggle to control the domestic market when in 1569 they managed to have foreigners banned from retail trade. Following Ivan's death in 1584, foreigners were restricted to the newly founded White Sea port of Archangel in a measure that shows the hand of the *gosti* as well. This not only affected the English but also merchants from the southern Netherlands who, keen to join their neighbors in the exploration of the Russian route, in 1578 had created a rival trading company.[96] Eastern merchants, who under Ivan IV may have had full freedom to trade in cities all over Russia, saw their movements curtailed as well under his successors. They were obliged to operate in so-called *gosti* hostels, and their imports were subjected to higher tax and toll rates. No longer permitted to buy Russian goods directly from producers and manufacturers, they were forced to use Russian merchants as intermediaries. Lastly, the state monopolized or restricted the export of a whole array of wares known as *zapovednye torgovy*, forbidden wares, and banned the export of gold and silver.[97]

The *gosti* in time grew into a formidable pressure group. Yet the Russian state, while often heeding their complaints and requests, was never interested in totally eliminating the activities of foreign merchants whose capital helped fill its treasury and whose participation was vital to Russia's other objective: to deal a blow to the Ottomans by way of a northern diversion of the Levant trade. The end of the Livonian war in 1582 and the conclusion of an anti-Ottoman alliance with the Habsburg Empire five years later allowed the Russians to pursue both goals, in a reorientation that coincided with the coming to power of Shah 'Abbas I in Iran.

---

[95] Willan, *Muscovy Merchants*, 30–3; and idem, *Early History*, 56–62, 152–4.
[96] Most of these hailed from the city of Antwerp, which at that time was dependent on the Venetian market for its raw silk. The negative effect of the Ottoman–Venetian war of 1570–73 on Antwerp's silk supply was one incentive for them to travel east. The other was the prospect of English dominance in the silk trade. See Wijnroks, "Jan van de Walle." Unlike the representatives of the English Russia Company, the Dutch merchants never seem to have gone directly to Astrakhan, let alone all the way to Iran. See Baron, "Ivan the Terrible," 574–5.
[97] Fekhner, *Torgovlia*, 61–2, 102–4, 110.

CHAPTER 2

Procedures, logistics, and finances

Cultivation

No seventeenth-century Persian or European sources include extensive descriptions, let alone eyewitness accounts, of the silk cultivation process in the Caspian region. The precise role of labor and capital in this process is therefore unclear and may only be inferred – at the risk of anachronism – from conditions in the early 1800s, when a sharecropping system involving owners, cultivators and merchants called *musalisa* (*muthallatha*) was common in Iran's sericulture. In this arrangement, merchants distributed silkworm eggs among the landowners and assisted them with loans or advances on the crops, free of interest. The landlords, in turn, assisted the actual cultivators, for the most part poor peasants, in similar fashion. Having invested either raw material, money, or labor in the cultivation process, the three parties involved, speculator, proprietor, and cultivator, also shared the profits accruing from the cultivation. Alternatively, the landowner would let his estate to the peasants who worked it for a fixed amount of the yield.[1]

We have no way of knowing if the same system was common in the seventeenth century and whether the role of provincial government agencies representing the Safavid crown went beyond revenue extraction. Conditions in the 1600s are, however, likely to have been similar to nineteenth-century practice whereby the "governor of the district exacts almost what he pleases or is able to get from him [the cultivator]" whenever the latter owned the soil.[2] Our general knowledge about the landed system in Safavid Iran, including the Caspian region, a crown (*khassah*) domain where silk was cultivated in small quantities by poor peasants, reinforces this likelihood.[3]

For a description of the various stages of the actual cultivation process we are rather better informed, although with the exception of the accounts of Herbert, Olearius, de la Maze, and de Bruyn, the earliest sources are

---

[1] Issawi, *Economic History of Iran*, 226–7. [2] Ibid.
[3] Della Valle, *Delle conditioni*, 41.

again not contemporaneous but derive from European travelers who, following the demise of the Safavid state, visited northern Iran as part of their journeys to or from Russia. Yet in this case, too, the fact that in many respects their descriptions match later, nineteenth-century observations, suggests a continuity that reaches back at least as far as the 1600s.[4]

Sericulture was a seasonal operation. The process began around the end of March, when the cultivators, *nuqandar*, would put those eggs, *kirm*, that they had secured from the previous year and that had survived the winter, in a warm spot or in a cotton cloth, the women often carrying the latter on the warmest parts of their bodies, so that the eggs might hatch. Within eight to ten days the eggs would thus produce the silkworms.[5] These were then spread out on sieve-like beds inside rectangular open barns, called *tilimbar*, which were erected around wooden stakes and covered with a straw roof. Thomas Herbert, describing Gilan and Mazandaran in the 1620s, said that "in every village and cottage one might behold sheds fild with industrious people and inriching silkworms."[6] The worms were fed once a day with the most tender leaves from the mulberry trees, which by then had begun to turn green. Again according to Herbert, "Hyrcania [Gilan and Mazandaran] is a continual forrest, and of all the trees I saw, none exceeded the mulberries, for numberlesse numbers, none more notable for use; ten, yea thirty miles spreading in them."[7] Most of the trees de Bruyn saw were young and very short, "that they may always have leaves upon young branches, the worms not caring for the leaves of old wood."[8] De la Maze confirmed this by noting that, following the defoliation in the spring, the mulberry trees in Gilan were pruned to a height of about five feet.[9]

This first stage would continue for the next ten days. In the following period the frequency of feeding gradually went up, first to twice every day, and then to three times, at which stage it was no longer necessary to select only the most tender leaves. At this point the worms also no longer lay on the sieve but were allowed to crawl freely on the floor. By the time the

---

[4] The later descriptions, by various British consuls such as K. E. Abbott, and F. Lafont and H.-L. Rabino, are reproduced and discussed in Issawi, *Economic History of Iran*, 226–7, 231–8.

[5] The Persian terms occur in nineteenth-century descriptions and are mentioned here on the assumption of unchanged terminology. Gilaki women in the nineteenth century still placed the eggs under their clothes. See Bazin and Bromberger, "'Abrišam," 232.

[6] Herbert, *Some Yeares Travel*, 181.   [7] Ibid.

[8] De Bruyn, *Reizen over Moskovie*, 115. The English quote is from the trans., *Travels into Muscovy, Persia, and Part of the East-Indies*, 2 vols. (London, 1737), i, 162. It is not altogether clear which mulberry tree was the most common in Iran. The so-called black mulberry, *morus nigra*, is also called "Persian," implying that it originated in Iran. The medieval Persian agricultural manual *Kitab al-falahah*, on the other hand, mentions two kinds, the black variety, and the white mulberry *morus alba*, and implies that both were common in Iran. The eighteenth-century German botanist Gmelin noted that in Gilan the white and the black, as well as the red mulberry tree were known. See Gmelin, *Reise nach Russland*, iii, 374–5; and Petrushevskii, *Zemledelie i agrarnye otnosheniia*, 165.

[9] De la Maze, "Journal," 48.

worms were fed five to six times a day they would finally spin themselves into their cocoons. The entire maturation process took about forty days.[10]

Once the cocoons reached their final shape they had to be suffocated so that they could yield their silk thread. According to Hanway, this could be done in three different ways; 1) "by covering it [the cocoon] in blankets or 2) by the heat of the sun, unless 3) they wind off the silk immediately for then warm water answers the same purpose."[11] The third method, which combined suffocation with soaking in boiling water, seems to have been the most common in Safavid times. The process is described by Herbert in the 1620s, in greater detail by de Bruyn, who in 1703 witnessed it in a village in Shirvan, and in the mid-eighteenth century by Hanway. De Bruyn's description is as follows:

... at this work they require no more than the assistance of one person at a time. There was, on the right hand going in, a stove which they heated from without, and in which there was a great caldron of almost boiling water, in which were the cods of the worms. The person that wound off the silk sat upon this stove on one side of the caldron and with the small stick frequently removed the cods; in the small cottage I also observed a large wheel of eight or nine palms diameter, and which was fixed between two posts, which he turned with his foot as he sat upon the stove, just as we turn a spinning wheel; and before the stove there were two sticks, upon which there was a reed, round which turned two small pullies which guide the silk from the cods to the wheel. They assured me that this manner and method of winding off silk is the common one all over Persia; and confessed it must be that this way they do it with surprising ease and dispatch.[12]

As eggs would be needed for the following year, a limited number of worms were allowed to complete their natural process by boring themselves out of their cocoon, emerging as moths, and mating, after which the females would lay new eggs before dying.

The reels used to wind the silk tended to be very large. While manufacturers, in Iran as well as in Europe, preferred smaller reels because large ones were much more difficult to unwind – and as late as the nineteenth century complained about what they saw as a stubborn Iranian refusal to accommodate the European preference – large reels were more convenient for the cultivators and, more specifically, diminished the chances of the silk sticking or "gumming" in the damp climate of Gilan. As Hanway explained:

In moist weather the silk wound on a large wheel is not so apt to stick or be gummed together in those parts where it lays on the bars, or divisions of the wheel, where it is often rendered black and so hard that it cannot without great difficulty be separated.[13]

[10] Hanway, *Historical Account*, ii, 17; Soimonov, "Auszug aus dem Tage-Buch," 515–8; Gmelin, *Reise nach Russland*, iii, 374–6.
[11] Hanway, *Historical Account*, i, 190.
[12] De Bruyn, *Reizen over Moskovie*, 115; trans., *Travels into Muscovy*, i, 162.
[13] Hanway, *Historical Account*, ii, 18.

Not all silk was of the same quality. According to Hanway, silk must be "equal, strong, and round as wire, and also clean."[14] It was more important for silk to be even in quality than to be of the finest sort. As Hanway noted, "the threads of silk being thus even, that is, as near as possible to one size, and not coarse and fine intermixed, can be most easily separated in the winding; but otherwise the coarse is apt to tear the fine, and make waste in manufacturing it."[15] The best silk, Hanway and Gmelin claimed, was pure white and lustrous in appearance. In the 1700s this silk invariably was sent to the manufacturing workshops in Rasht and Kashan. Most silk from Gilan, however, was yellow. Yellow silk passed for good silk, too, provided it had all the other requisite characteristics of cleanliness and quality.[16]

The quality of Iranian silk varied a great deal, but one consistent foreign complaint concerned the dirty state in which it tended to arrive in Europe. The Dutch as early as 1632 grumbled about the poor quality of some of the silk that arrived in Holland.[17] Their subsequent records are replete with similar complaints about damp silk, low-quality grade, and the various states of impurity in which the raw silk was received. Hanway sums up the problems and the difficulty of detecting some of the flaws:

the cleanness and clearness of raw silk constitute a good part of its goodness; inferior silk has many knits and course stuff sticking to the threads. The moss, or head of silk often appears fair to the eye, when much coarseness is concealed under it; for it is a trick of the peasants of Gilan to hide the defects as they wind it off from the pod.[18]

Varieties, grades, and prices.

In the first report on Iranian silk written by a representative of the English East India Company (EIC), Agent Barker listed three grades of Iranian raw silk: *ardas*, *ardasset* (*ardassin*), and *connorsee* (*canarsie*). Most other contemporaneous sources leave out the latter, which is probably identical to Pegolotti's *seta canare*, *kinar* silk from Qarabagh, but otherwise expand on the range. The very best and most expensive silk came from Gilan and was called *sha'rbafi* (weaving) silk. This lustrous grade came in two colors, white and yellow, with the white variety being the most beautiful.[19] *Sha'rbafi* silk was mostly processed inside Iran, in Yazd, Kashan and Isfahan, where it was used for the production of precious cloth.[20] Some was exported via the Levant, as was the slightly less desirable *ardassin* grade, which was similar

---

[14] Ibid.   [15] Ibid.   [16] Ibid.; Gmelin, *Reise nach Russland*, iii, 376–7.
[17] Dunlop, *Bronnen*, 379–80.
[18] Hanway, *Historical Account*, ii, 18.
[19] Savary, *Le parfait négociant*, v/2, 716.
[20] Dunlop, *Bronnen*, 665, report Overschie, Dec. 15, 1638; Kotov, *Khozhenie*, 71; Chardin, *Voyages*, iv, 162–5. For the etymology of the terms *sha'rbaf* and *sha'rbafi*, see Bastani-Parizi, "Sha'r-i gulnar," 172–5.

in color and fineness.[21] Khurasan, specially the area of Khaf, also produced silk of extraordinary fineness. Of this little or none was "transported into any parts of Christendom but all is wrought in the Persian own country into silk stuffs or is carried into India."[22]

A second high-quality silk was *kadkhuda pasand*, much of which was exported to the Levant by the Julfan Armenians and by Ottoman merchants. The same was true for *kharvari* or *laji* silk, called *legia* by the European traders, which originated in Lahijan – from which it probably took its name – and was called a second-grade silk by the Dutch, who ordinarily preferred to receive either this kind or the *kadkhuda pasand* variety.[23]

The least desirable export grade was *shirvani* silk, called *ardas* by the Europeans – possibly deriving its name from the river Aras – which was labeled "ugly and coarse" by Chardin, but, depending on the market, was not necessarily unpopular in Europe.[24] A better kind of *ardas* silk was cultivated in Mazandaran.[25] The lowest grade, finally, was so-called *las* silk. Coarse and irregular, *las* silk was mostly manufactured in Mazandaran. In Europe this variety was known as *salvatica*.[26] *Las* silk came from Mazandaran and possibly from Astarabad, which produced Iran's worst silk, according to Hanway, who added that the silk harvested there, mixed in with cotton, served only for the manufacture of clothing.[27] Silk from Gilan was generally considered the best, followed by that from Mazandaran. Silk from Georgia, Qarabagh, and Ganja was said to be of lesser quality and was mostly exported to the Ottoman Levant.[28] Kirman and Yazd, finally, produced small quantities of unclear quality, all of which was locally manufactured.[29]

Among contemporary foreigners a broad consensus existed with regard to ranking in quality and preference. Besides intrinsic quality, taste and market conditions influenced demand, in Iran as much as in Europe. Thus the Dutch initially preferred *ardas* silk, which was mostly used in the southern Netherlands, though it seems to have been popular elsewhere in Europe as well. In the early 1630s, complaints about the quality of silk caused this preference to change. *Legia*, the directors of the Dutch East

[21] Savary, *Le parfait négociant*, v/2, 717.
[22] IOR E/3/6/792, Barker to London, ca. April 28, 1618, fol. 8. Witsen, *Noord- en oost Tartarye*, 485, mentions Khaf as a production area.
[23] Dunlop, *Bronnen*, 665, report Overschie, Dec. 15, 1638; Chardin, *Voyages*, iv, 162–5.
[24] Chardin, *Voyages*, iv, 162–5.
[25] ARA, Coll. Hoge Regering Batavia 877, Radicale beschryving van 's-Companies handel in Perzië, ch. 10, unfol.
[26] Dunlop, *Bronnen*, 198, Visnich, Isfahan to Heren XVII, Aug. 17, 1626; van Dam, *Beschryvinge*, ii/3, 283.
[27] Hanway, *Historical Account*, ii, 16.
[28] Dunlop, *Bronnen*, 612, Overschie, Gamron to Batavia, March 25, 1637. For the exports to the Ottoman Empire of *kinar* silk, see Zarinebaf-Shahr, "Tabriz under Ottoman Rule," 173. Silk from the Caucasus was still considered inferior in the nineteenth century. This was blamed on the way in which it was reeled, which left it dirty and of uneven quality. See von Nasackin, "Die kaukasische Seidencultur," 30.
[29] IOR E/3/6/792, Barker to London, ca. April 28, 1618, fol. 8.

Table 2.1. *Prices in* mahmudis *for three grades of silk in Gilan, 1618–1698*

| | mann-i shah (5.6kg) | | |
	sha'rbafi	kadkhuda pasand	kharvari (legia)
1618[30]	118	100?	
1638[31]	150	125	110
1641[32]	120–150	100–110	88–95
1651[33]	100–140	76–100	
1690[34]	100–115	80	40–70
1691[35]	65–77	65–70	57–65
1696[36]	140–145		120
1698[37]	160	140	110–120

If we take a 125:100:80 proportion as average, and convert these prices to *tumans* per load, assuming that 36 *mann-i shah* of 5.6 kg made up one load, *sha'rbafi* sold for 45 *tumans*, *kadkhuda pasand* for 36 *tumans* and *kharvari* for 28.8 *tumans*. The difference between *kadkhuda pasand* and *kharvari* in this ranking conforms to van Dam's assessment that, depending on the quality of either, the difference would be 5 to 10 *tumans*.[38]

India Company (VOC) claimed, was now the most favored kind in Europe, selling at 3 Dutch *stuivers* per pound more than *ardas*. They therefore requested *legia*.[39] In 1640, by contrast, supplies of *ardas* being low, its price exceeded that for *legia* by 1 *stuiver* per pound.[40] In the later part of the century *kadkhuda pasand* appears to have become the most desired grade. In the early 1700s *ardas* was being replaced by Bengal silk in England, which continued to import mostly *legia*.[41]

Overall, prices in the Caspian region reflected the perceived quality of the various grades in a proportion that remained fairly constant over time, as is seen in Table 2.1.

[30] IOR E/3/6/792, Barker to London, ca. April 28, 1618, fol. 8.
[31] Dunlop, *Bronnen*, 665, report Overschie, Dec. 15, 1638.
[32] ARA, VOC 1134, van Oostende, Isfahan to Heren XVII, Feb. 13, 1641, fol. 200.
[33] ARA, VOC 1195, Sarcerius, Gamron to Batavia, Nov. 27, 1651, fol. 780.
[34] IOR, E/3/48/5734, Gladman, Gombroon to London, Oct. 27, 1690, unfol.; and G/36/110, Gladman, Gombroon to London, Jan. 13, 1691, fol. 64; prices for silk in Isfahan.
[35] IOR G/36/110, Gladman, Gombroon to Bombay, Jan. 12, 1691, fol. 63.
[36] IOR E/3/52/6289, Major, Tabriz to London, Oct. 14, 1696, unfol.
[37] ARA, VOC 1611, Hoogcamer, Gamron to Heren XVII, June 5, 1698, fols. 41–2. The large difference in price between 1690 and 1696–98 is explained by the fact, discussed in chapter 8, that in the former year the market in Europe was anemic, while in the latter years a shortage in Europe had caused steep price increases (in Isfahan in 1698 *sha'rbafi* fetched 190 and 195 *mahmudis* and *kadkhuda pasand*, 170–175).
[38] Van Dam, *Beschryvinge*, ii/3, 283.
[39] Dunlop, *Bronnen*, 379–80, Heren XVII to del Court, Isfahan, Feb. 29, 1632.
[40] ARA, VOC 864, Batavia to Persia, Aug. 28, 1640, fol. 492b.
[41] Davis, *Aleppo*, 140. Davis, by equating *legia* with *sha'rbafi* silk, confuses the two.

Figures on production and export levels

Estimates of the level of production of Iranian silk are all by Westerners
and vary widely. Robert Sherley at the turn of the seventeenth century
ventured a total yield of 34,000 bales, Olearius in the 1630s claimed that
Iran's annual harvest was 20,000 bales,[42] while VOC Agent Overschie in
1635 put the country's total production at a lowly 1,073 bales. He acknowledged that this was an exceedingly low yield, adding that in 1629 –
presumably a "normal" year – total production had been 4,000 bales. For
1636 he estimated a production of 2,800 bales.[43] In later years estimates
tend to be much higher. An anonymous Frenchman in the 1660s insisted
that Iran yielded a total of 40,000 bales, Chardin put the number at 22,000,
and Israel Ori at the turn of the eighteenth century made the excessive claim
that Shamakhi's annual production was 30,000 bales, while Gilan, according to him, produced the same amount.[44] Russian estimates generally
are high as well. The Russian archives cite 2,800,000 pounds, or some
14,000 bales, for Gilan alone.[45] The Russian scholar Geidarov does not
consider the production figure of 20,000 *puds* for Shirvan (ca. 3,300 bales)
and 15,000 for Qarabagh (ca. 2,500 bales), both based on Olearius,
exaggerated; instead, arguing that these figures do not represent Azerbaijan's entire silk production, he estimates a total output of no less than
100,000 to 125,000 *puds*, or between 15,000 and 20,000 bales.[46]

Edmund Herzig rightly argues that none of these estimates can be taken
at face value and that all sources have to be evaluated separately for biases
and motives.[47] As Overschie intended to "prove" to his superiors that he
had managed to export a significant share of Iran's total silk production, it
was in his interest to downplay the latter. Indeed, Overschie's data do not
seem to have convinced anyone; they were immediately gainsaid by his
superiors who argued that much more silk had arrived in the Levant than
his figures warranted. The anonymous Frenchman's figures can be dismissed as those of an uninformed observer who was wont to exaggerate in
other respects as well. It is unclear where Olearius got his data, which, in
turn, may have informed Chardin's later estimate.[48] As for Israel Ori, his
estimate should not be taken at face value, either, for he intended to whet
Russia's military appetites for Iran. The same may be true of other Russian
figures.

The main problem with outsiders giving figures of annual output is that

[42] Olearius, *Vermehrte newe Beschreibung*, 601.
[43] Dunlop, *Bronnen*, 599, Batavia to Heren XVII, Dec. 28, 1636.
[44] Ezov, *Snosheniia Petra Velikogo*, 38, Donesenie Izraelia Oriia Pfal'tskomu kurfirstu Ioannu
Vil'gel'mu.
[45] Kukanova, "Russko-iranskie torgovye otnosheniia," 251. The author calls this estimate
improbably high.
[46] Geidarov, *Remeslennoe proizvodstvo*, 48–50.
[47] Herzig, "Volume of Iranian Raw Silk Exports," 62–3.   [48] Ibid., 75.

none had a complete overview of Iran's silk producing areas. Of all the non-Iranian observers whose documentation has survived, the Dutch may be expected to have been most reliably informed about matters of volume; yet, even if we assume that *anyone* had any comprehensive information about Iran's silk output, their local (Armenian) informants may have been reluctant fully to disclose real figures for their own particular reasons. Extreme fluctuations in the harvest due to disease and devastation, moreover, make it difficult to determine whether *any* figure represents an *average* yield. Some VOC agents cite figures that are considerably higher than the low ones given by Overschie, though substantially lower than the extreme ones quoted above. Thus an estimate from 1643, based on "reliable sources" states that in most years Iran's production of raw silk was about 4,000 bales.[49] The fact that the year in question yielded a poor harvest, causing small quantities to arrive in Aleppo, may have accounted for this low volume. Yet VOC director Sarcerius in 1653 similarly reckoned that during the previous season Iran had produced 4,160 bales.[50] Four thousand bales, however, not only constitutes a rather low volume, but also contrasts with a much higher figure put forth in a VOC report from 1649. Iran's annual output, according to Verburgh, the author of the report, was about 8,000 bales.[51] Verburgh's estimate is close to a figure that appears in the VOC sources for 1686,[52] as well as similar to one that comes up time and again in negotiations for the opening up of the Russian transit trade to Armenians in the 1660s and 70s, which put Iran's annual production at approximately 8,000 bales.[53] This figure also approximates Barker's claim that the country's annual silk production was 168,000 *mann-i shah*, or 9,333 bales,[54] yet ill accords with the 15,000 bales quoted by van Dam, the VOC lawyer whose history of the VOC dates from 1700. The sources of the latter, while presumably derived from first-hand VOC reports, remain unclear.[55] A Dutch merchant dealing with the Russia trade, finally, in 1634 claimed an annual average production of approximately 6,000 bales.[56]

Unfortunately no firm conclusions can be drawn from all this information. Disregarding the hyperbole of some observers and the improbably low figures given by others, we might conclude that in "average" years in the seventeenth century Iran produced approximately 8,000 bales, a figure that

[49] ARA, VOC 1150, diary Constant and Bastinck, Dec. 1643, fol. 250.
[50] ARA, VOC 1201, Sarcerius, Gamron to Batavia, April 5, 1653, fols. 779–80. This, as well as a similar figure from 1651, has led Willem Floor to conclude that 4,000 bales is a "reasonable estimate of the annual production in a 'normal' year during the 17th century." See Floor, "The Dutch and the Persian Silk Trade," 339.
[51] VOC 1170, Verburgh, Gamron to Heren XVII, Feb. 12, 1649, fol. 871b.
[52] Coolhaas, *Generale missiven 1675–1685*, 63, which lists 7,000 loads.
[53] Parsamian et al., *Armiano-Russkie otnosheniia*, 39, 56, 55–6.
[54] IOR E/3/6/792, Barker, ca. April 28, 1618, fol. 9.
[55] Van Dam, *Beschryvinge*, ii/3, 284.
[56] Attman et al., *Ekonomiska förbindelser*, 49.

might well have dropped by half in years of natural disaster, disease, and warfare.

If it is impossible to reach satisfactory conclusions about Iran's total raw silk yield, the production of the various regions cannot be established with any greater degree of reliability. Olearius gives the following figures: Gilan in a good year yielded 8,000 bales, Shirvan 3,000, Khurasan 3,000, Mazandaran 2,000, Qarabagh 2,000. He offers no data on Georgia.[57] Overschie asserted that of the total of 2,800 bales harvested in 1636 Gilan had produced 2,100, Farahabad and Mazandaran 150, and Kirman 250, while Georgia, Qarabagh, and Ganja had yielded a total of about 300 bales.[58] Sarcerius claimed that Gilan in 1652 had yielded 2,580 bales, of which 800 were *sha'rbafi*, 400 *kadkhuda pasand*, and 1,180 *legia*. Mazandaran's production had been 200 bales, Khurasan's 80, all *sha'rbafi*, Shirvan had yielded 700 bales, of which 100 were *sha'rbafi* and 600 *ardas*, while Qarabagh had produced 600 bales, 80 of which were *sha'rbafi* and 520 *ardas*.[59] Chardin's figures are as follows: Gilan produced 10,000 bales, Mazandaran 2,000, Media (western Iran) and Bactria (eastern Iran) each 3,000, Qarabagh and Georgia each 2,000 bales.[60] His figure for the quantity manufactured in Tabriz alone, 6,000, is higher than some of the estimates for the country's total silk production.[61] The only firm conclusion to be drawn from all these data is that Gilan was by far the most productive region. We can also be fairly certain about an expansion of Iran's silk cultivation in the early seventeenth century. Not only did the northwestern silk-producing regions recover from the protracted Safavid–Ottoman wars at that time, but Shah 'Abbas I, having subdued Georgia, ordered that in future the province would have to yield a great quantity of silk.[62] In 1617 it was reported that "the king daily plants silk in all parts."[63] It remains unclear if that expansion was sustained in later times, though the stability of silk prices throughout the seventeenth century suggests that production was able to keep up with growing demand.

Given the twin difficulty of arriving at reliable figures for production and export, it is scarcely surprising that little is known about the volume of raw silk destined for the domestic market. We know that much of the finest silk was used in the royal workshops, and in particular in the *sha'rbaf-khanah*, the weaving factory. A large volume of silk was also worked into luxury weaves, such as *zarbaft*, for the private market. Kashan, traditionally a silk manufacturing center, continued to maintain its position throughout the

[57] Olearius, *Vermehrte newe Beschreibung*, 601.
[58] Dunlop, *Bronnen*, 599, Batavia to Heren XVII, Dec. 28, 1636.
[59] ARA, VOC 1201, Sarcerius, Gamron to Batavia, April 5, 1653, fols. 779–80.
[60] Chardin, *Voyages*, v, 163.
[61] Chardin, *Voyages*, ii, 327–8.
[62] IOR, E/3/6/792, Barker to London, ca. April 28, 1618, fol. 8.
[63] IOR, E/3/11/1282, quoted in Steinmann, "Royal Silk Trade," 69.

seventeenth century. Isfahan was another important manufacturing center for high-grade silk. The province where the largest number of carpets with floral, vegetal, and aviary motives was manufactured was Khurasan.[64] Lar, too, had its silk manufacturing, much of it done by Jews who could also be seen in all of Kirman province selling textiles.[65] Silk was also processed in the northern urban centers of Tabriz, Rasht, Shamakhi, and Baku.[66]

The available data permit us to form a broad idea about the proportion of silk destined for export versus that used for local manufacturing purposes. Barker claimed that of 9,333 bales two-thirds were exported.[67] Of a total yield of 2,800 bales, the amount manufactured in Iran itself, according to Overschie, was as follows: 150 in Gilan, 600 in Kashan and Rasht, and 250 bales in Isfahan and Lar.[68] According to Olearius, of the total of 19,000 bales no more than 1,000 were used inside the country for manufacturing purposes.[69] Neither figure carries much conviction. The 1643 VOC report which claimed that about half of the total yield of 4,000 bales was used domestically may have had Gilan and Mazandaran in mind.[70] A more comprehensive picture is gained from information given by Verburgh, who in 1649 insisted that of the 8,000 bales annually produced in Iran 6,000 were transported to the Levant and Russia, while the remaining 2,000 bales were used domestically in the manufacture of silk draperies and gold thread cloth and velvets.[71] These figures sit well beside the early eighteenth-century estimate made by the Russian, Soimonov, whose informant was an Armenian merchant. According to him, prior to the fall of Isfahan Gilan alone had exported an annual quantity of 5,000 bales to Turkey.[72] Savary's estimate of Iranian silk exports via Izmir as about 2,900 bales in the 1670s is not in contradiction with this.[73] The figure of 9,000 bales exported to the Levant, given to Tsar Peter by an Indian merchant in Astrakhan, is almost certainly too high.[74] Whether or not these later figures reflect a longitudinal expansion in production, they do suggest that, regardless of total output, between one-half to three-quarters of the total silk harvest was destined for export. Spilman's figures from the late 1730s, finally, suggest that one half of Iran's silk continued to be exported after the fall of Isfahan, following a dramatic drop in production. According to him, Gilan alone produced no

[64] Bedik, *Chehil Sutun*, 321–2.
[65] Schillinger, *Persianische und Ost-Indianische Reise*, 266.
[66] Lystsov, *Persidskii pokhod*, 36; and Geidarov, *Remeslennoe proizvodstvo*, 61.
[67] IOR E/3/6/792, in Ferrier, "English View," 198–9.
[68] Dunlop, *Bronnen*, 612, Overschie, Gamron to Batavia, March 25, 1637.
[69] Olearius, *Vermehrte newe Beschreibung*, 601.
[70] ARA, VOC 1150, diary Constant and Bastinck, Dec. 1643, fol. 250.
[71] ARA, VOC 1170, Verburgh, Gamron to Heren XVII, Feb. 12, 1649, fol. 871b.
[72] Soimonov, "Auszug aus dem Tage-Buch," 267.
[73] Savary, *Le parfait négociant*, v/2, 616–8.
[74] Lystsov, *Persidskii pokhod*, 51.

more than 12,000 to 15,000 *puds* (2,000 to 3,000 bales), half of which quantity was consumed in Iran and half taken to Europe.[75]

Sale and purchasing practices

We are relatively well informed about the process of collecting and distributing the silk and the role of government authorities and private merchants. The cultivation process would come to an end in August, the time when the silk was available in the north.[76] The gathering of silk seems to have been a small-scale operation, so much so according to Hanway that "cargo cannot always be collected."[77] A century earlier VOC Agent Overschie had similarly insisted that buying in Gilan was a matter of collecting it bundle by bundle, from door to door and from village to village. In order to purchase 100 bales of silk, he noted, one would need no fewer than twenty employees.[78]

The question of the role played by capital in the distribution process is an intriguing one. In rural parts of Iran much trade took place on the basis of barter, and Membré gives an example of a local market in Mingrelia where silk was exchanged for cloth rather than cash.[79] Yet it is clear that from production to distribution the regular silk trade was fully monetized. Already in the mid-sixteenth century the English called the silk business a "ready-money trade."[80] Time and again the agents of the chartered companies reminded their superiors that without cash no silk could be obtained. Soimonov is most explicit in his statement that "in order to buy raw silk, one has to dispose of pure silver," adding that, to facilitate this, anyone could go to the mint in Rasht and have silver bullion minted into *'abbasis* of pure silver.[81]

Silk was generally sold on the basis of outstanding credit. The capital for the silk growers was provided by the merchants in the forward contracting system that also operated in the case of goats' wool in the Kirman area and the weaving industry at Kazirun, and that lay at the basis of much of the intersection of production and commerce in Safavid Iran, as it did in Asia all the way from Yemen to Sumatra.[82] The procedure, called *pish-furush* (advance selling) in Persian, involved the payment of money in anticipation

[75] Spilman, *Journey*, 29.
[76] Dunlop, *Bronnen*, 428, Overschie, Qazvin to Batavia, June 30, 1633.
[77] Hanway, *Historical Account*, ii, 17.
[78] Dunlop, *Bronnen*, 670, report Overschie, Dec. 15, 1638.
[79] Membré, *Mission*, 12, 14.
[80] Morgan and Coote, *Early Voyages*, 11, 413, fourth voyage into Persia made by M. Arthur Edwards; and Foster, *Travels of John Sanderson*, 133.
[81] Soimonov, "Auszug aus dem Tage-Buch," 353–4.
[82] For the Kirman wool trade, see Matthee, "East India Company Trade." The Kazirun wool trade is mentioned by Lambton, "Internal Structure," 254. A good description of the system in the case of Bengal silk may be found in Chaudhuri, *Trading World*, 355–8.

of the following year's harvest, and thus was based on a revolving IOU system that bound the producers to their creditors.[83] Even Safavid political authorities ordinarily abided by this system of forward commodity dealing. Although the shah enjoyed artificially low prices, he, too, had to prepay for his silk to prevent the producers from selling their silk to third parties. The only way the latter could avoid this was by hiding a portion of their silk.[84]

Little is known about the identity of those who furnished the capital that lubricated the trade. Hanway claimed that the business was mostly done by brokers, but that "the buyer attends to pay the money."[85] Most of these brokers may have been Banian Indians, who all over Iran and elsewhere in west Asia were active as moneylenders and providers of capital. The most actively engaged in the trade itself were the Julfan merchants. Leaving for Gilan in April or May, they would reside there until June or July, when the silk was spun. This proximity to the source of cultivation allowed them to make choice purchases when the silk was offered for sale.[86] Jews played a role as well. Along with 40,000 Armenians, Shah 'Abbas I relocated 8,000 Jews from Georgia to Farahabad in Mazandaran when he built the town in 1621. Dutch sources refer to Jews involved in the Caspian silk trade and in 1632 claim that the "powerful Jew Khajah Davud" shared control over Iran's silk with the grand vizier Mirza Muhammad Taqi.[87] A Jewish role in the trade is corroborated by the *Afzal al-tavarikh*, which mentions Khajah Lalazar Yahud, one of those who were relocated to Farahabad, as a loyal servant of the shah to whom silk from Gilan was to be consigned following the institution of the royal silk export monopoly in 1619. The same source lists Jews among the merchants taking silk to the Ottoman Empire.[88] Indians, finally, participated in the trade as well, mostly, it seems, with Russia. Shamakhi in the late 1600s was home to some 200 Indian merchants.[89]

Since Gilan and Mazandaran provided much royal revenue, Safavid political authorities naturally had an important role in the purchase and sale of silk. The liaison for those who purchased silk from the court was the shah's factor, or commercial agent. The two most prominent individuals mentioned as such in the sources are Lalah Beg, who is also known as Muhibb 'Ali Beg, and Mulayim Beg. Significantly, both combined their

---

[83] The sources do not tell us whether prepayments were made for fixed amounts or for the entire harvest. It is also unclear whether this gave the creditors the absolute right or merely the first right of purchase.

[84] Dunlop, *Bronnen*, 199, Visnich, Isfahan to Heren XVII, Aug. 17, 1626; ARA, VOC 1178, Sarcerius, Gamron to Batavia, Oct. 16, 1649, fol. 630b.

[85] Hanway, *Historical Account*, ii, 17.

[86] ARA, VOC 1152, Constant, Gamron to Batavia, March 11, 1645, fols. 82b–3; also in VOC 1157, fol. 622.

[87] Dunlop, *Bronnen*, 357, del Court, Isfahan to Heren XVII, Dec. 20, 1630.

[88] Khuzani Isfahani, "Afzal al-tavarikh," fol. 406a.

[89] [De la Maze], "Mémoire," 27.

function as *malik al-tujjar* (chief of merchants) with that of controller of the assay and mintmaster, *mu'ayyir al-mamalik* and *zarrab-bashi*. The *malik al-tujjar* supervised the silk and gold and silver brocade weaving operations, controlling the selection of samples, the preparation of the raw materials and the storage of the finished products. He was also head of all the court workshops that involved the manufacture of clothing.[90] He typically used his clout and capital to gain market advantage. In 1635, for instance, the then *malik al-tujjar* Khajah Qasim proposed to purchase VOC merchandise at market prices, but only on condition that he be allowed to acquire the entire supply, in order to "be able to dominate the market."[91] As of the 1630s, the shah's factor lost much of his relevance with regard to silk, to be replaced by a series of bureaucratic and financial officials, most notably the grand vizier.

Khassah land since the early reign of Shah 'Abbas I, Gilan and Mazandaran were administered by viziers, who stood under constant supervision by the *mustawfi khassah*, the treasurer who monitored the flow of crown revenue. It was the task of the vizier to purchase and collect the silk for the royal treasury. The mechanism for this may have been the same as what the *Tadhkirat al-Muluk* outlines for the royal purchase of textiles, whereby the *nazir* (head of the royal workshops) summoned experts and with their help fixed the price to be paid by the shah.[92] Just as the court was not exempt from advance payments, so it had to offer presents (*pishkash*) to producers and suppliers.[93] Royal silk buying, in sum, seems to have involved negotiation procedures similar to the bargaining that ordinary buyers engaged in. Soimonov suggests the strength of local interests by stating that, the powers with which a vizier was invested notwithstanding, he was unable to accomplish anything without the cooperation of the local population.[94] Peasants used every possible subterfuge to underreport their yield. Since the shah paid below market rates, the officials responsible for collecting silk for the crown also had an incentive to minimize deliveries to the royal warehouses. To achieve this they were willing to pay the viziers handsomely.[95] The viziers, in turn, not only gave in to such practices, but were also in the habit of reselling high-grade silk they had bought for the shah to private merchants, using the money to purchase low-quality silk for delivery to the maritime companies.[96] Local officials also seem to have engaged in *tarh*, the practice of forced sales. Mirza Ibrahim, the governor of Azerbaijan, in 1670

[90] Kaempfer, *Am Hofe*, 155. Chardin, *Voyages*, vii, 329–30.
[91] Dunlop, *Bronnen*, 476, v/d Trille aboard *Bueren* to Batavia, June 1634.
[92] Minorsky, *Tadhkirat al-Muluk*, 66.
[93] ARA, VOC 1324, memorandum Sarcerius for Berkhout, May 1655, fols. 684–700; and van Dam, *Beschryvinge*, ii/3, 283.
[94] Soimonov, "Auszug aus dem Tage-Buch," vii, 352–3.
[95] ARA, VOC 1255, res. Isfahan to Roothals, Gamron, July 9, 1667, fol. 915; Chardin, *Voyages*, v, 387–90.
[96] ARA, VOC 1667, request Hoogcamer to Safavid court, Aug. 13, 1701, fols. 366–7.

forced the inhabitants of the town of Agulis to buy 40 *litry* of silk worth 8,000 *dinars* per *litra* for a price of 12,500 *dinars*, or more than 50 percent above the market rate.[97] In response to such practices the shah could do little more than replace the viziers frequently, as was indeed often done, but this brought no real change. Too many hopeful officials were waiting impatiently to take on the lucrative position of vizier.

Nothing definitive can be said about the nature of silk taxes and the share of silk in total state income. Provincial authorities are said to have creamed off one-fifth of the silk harvest.[98] The central state collected revenue on raw silk as well. In keeping with customary practice with regard to crown land, the tax on silk was ordinarily paid in raw silk – which the state would convert into cash by selling it to merchants – though at times of capital shortages Safavid authorities required payment in cash.[99] Two kinds of royal taxation must be distinguished – a production tax and a commercial tax. The fee levied on producers amounted to one-third of the harvest.[100] A VOC report from 1680, claiming that the shah made 14–15 *tumans* on a load (worth 48 *tumans*), probably refers to the same tax, as does van Dam's assertion that the shah took 12 *tumans* on every load of silk.[101] Olearius, on the other hand, probably refers to a commercial fee in claiming that the duty on silk was 20 *Reichstaler* (rix-dollars), or 1.4 *tumans* per load.[102]

The fragmentary nature of our information on both the volume of silk production and the various taxes levied on it makes it difficult to arrive at reliable conclusions with regard to the total income the Safavid treasury derived from silk. Two sources give figures on silk revenue for the crown. One figure is given by Sanson, who in the 1690s stated that silk from Gilan netted the shah 80,000 *tumans*.[103] The other figure, given by the Russian envoy Artemii Volynskii, who visited Iran in 1717, is higher but not contradictory since it includes the entire country. According to him, Iran's silk-producing provinces yielded some one million *rubles*, or 125,000 *tumans*, for the shah's treasury, or some 16 percent of the monarch's total revenue of approximately 6 million *rubles*, or 750,000 *tumans*.[104]

[97] Papazian, *Agrarnye otnosheniia*, 241.
[98] Sotavov, *Severniy Kavkaz*, 43.
[99] ARA, VOC 1170, Barenssen, Gamron to Heren XVII, Jan. 29, 1649, fol. 868.
[100] Chardin, *Voyages*, v, 398; Minorsky, *Tadhkirat al-Muluk*, 180.
[101] ARA, VOC 1343, resolution Gamron Council, Feb. 13, 1680, fol. 601; van Dam, *Beschryvinge*, ii/3, 283.
[102] Olearius, *Vermehrte newe Beschreibung*, 668–9.
[103] Sanson, *Voyage*, 98–9.
[104] Lystsov, *Persidskii pokhod*, 45; and Bushev, *Posol'stvo Artemiia Volynskogo*, 166. The latter source does not mention *rubles* but speaks of 100,000 *tumans*. Volynskii's figure for total Safavid state income is remarkably close to other estimates, such as Olearius's 8,000,000 rix-dollars, or 560,000 *tumans* (*Vermehrte newe Beschreibung*, 668), Chardin's 700,000 *tumans* (*Voyages*, v, 412–4), du Mans' 600,000 *tumans* (Richard, *Raphaël du Mans*, ii, 11), and Sanson's 800,000 *tumans* (*Voyage*, 102).

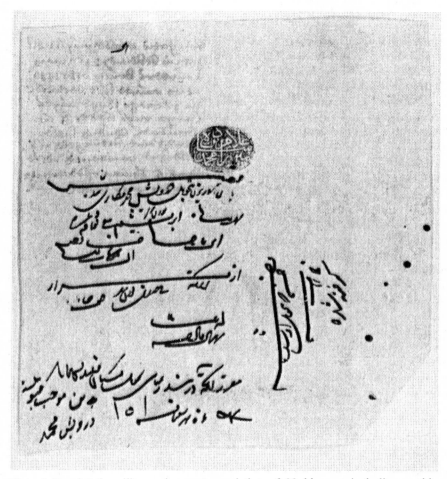

Plate 1 Receipt for silk consignment consisting of 38 *kharvar*, including packing material (3,800 *mann-i Tabriz*, equaling some 11,000 kg or about 125 bales) handed over to and accepted by Darvish Muhammad Makari, who is charged to deliver the silk to the Dutch agent (captain) in Bandar ʿAbbas, signed by Darvish Muhammad, sealed by Mirza Muhammad (the *tahvildar* of Isfahan?), dated Shaʿban 1051 (November 1641). In ARA, 1e afd., Coll. Gel. de Jongh 298. Courtesy of Algemeen Rijksarchief, The Hague.

Packing, handling, and transportation

Gilan to Bandar ʿAbbas: silk for the maritime companies

From Gilan, silk destined for Isfahan was first transported by mule caravan to Qazvin, the transmontane collection point where the royal storage facilities were located. This transport took place around *Nawruz*, the Iranian New Year, that is, toward the end of March.[105] The central position of Qazvin as a distribution center made the city an ideal location for the warehouses of private merchants as well.[106]

Royal silk remained in storage, under the supervision of an official called *tahvildar*, until early May, when it was transported to Isfahan, the gathering place for silk purchased by the Europeans.[107] The silk was then weighed. The weight as recorded by the Iranians frequently differed from the actual weight upon delivery and after drying. Silk is very hygroscopic and retains as much as a third of its weight in moisture without feeling damp, a problem that was exacerbated by the difference between the humid climate of the Caspian provinces and the semi-arid conditions in the interior. In normal circumstances a bale would lose 5 to 6 percent of its weight between Qazvin and Isfahan.[108] The Dutch, moreover, suspected the Iranians of deliberately increasing the weight of bales by packing extra wet silk and even sprinkling the bales with water, and complained about the alleged preference of the shah's factor to deliver silk in the winter, when dampness was at its maximum.[109] They solved the problem by leaving the bales to dry in the sun upon arrival in Isfahan, constantly turning them over and weighing them every day, until they no longer lost weight, all the while trying to ignore protests by the *tahvildar*, who invariably preferred the bales to be weighed immediately and would stop by every day to press the point.[110]

As weighing was a sensitive operation, it was done in the presence of a number of officials, including the vizier of Isfahan, the city's *kalantar* (city prefect), the *mustawfi khassah*, the *malik al-tujjar*, and a few lesser functionaries. The bales would first be weighed by the Iranians, after which the VOC agents reweighed them on company scales. Any difference was to be immediately reported, since a failure to protest on the spot might later give rise to disputes.[111] The weight standard used by the Iranians was the *mann-i Tabriz*, which equaled almost 3 kg.[112] From an ordinary bale, weighing some 16 *mann-i shah* or 90 kg. half a *mann*, or approximately 3 kg was

[105] The Russian ambassador Volynskii in 1718 lost forty-six camels and forty-seven horses between Qazvin and Rasht. See Bushev, *Posol'stvo Artemiia Volynskogo*, 186.
[106] Dunlop, *Bronnen*, 523–4, Overschie, Gamron to Batavia, March 15, 1635.
[107] ARA, VOC 1360, memorandum Casembroot to van Heuvel, March 4, 1679, fol. 1902a. The position of *tahvildar* preceded the Safavid period. Katib, *Tarikh-i jadid-i Yazd*, 224, mentions the existence of a *sahib-i tahvil-i abrisham* for the year 849/1445.
[108] Dunlop, *Bronnen*, 389, del Court, Isfahan to Surat or Batavia, Oct. 26, 1632.
[109] Ibid., 505, Overschie, Isfahan to Heren XVII, Oct. 27, 1634.
[110] ARA, VOC 1611, memorandum Hoogcamer for Casteleyn, May 31, 1698, fol. 51.
[111] Ibid.
[112] The Dutch pound was the so-called Amsterdam pound of 494.090 grams. In Shirvan a different weight, the *tiluni*, was used. This weight, one-fourth heavier than the *mann*, equaled 3.75 kg. See IOR, G/36/110, Gladman to Bombay, Jan. 12, 1691, fol. 63.

subtracted for tare. The weighers ordinarily received a "voluntary" gift of between 1 and 2 *tumans*.[113]

Much time and energy went into packing the bales, checking them, and repacking them if necessary, for the Iranians not only were in the habit of mixing different grades together but often stuffed bales with rocks and rags after the initial packaging, carefully resewing the wrapping.[114] The silk was packed in bales whose weight ranged from 70 to 90 kg each. The silk strands inside the bales were at first tied with rope, but this changed in 1642 when Dutch protests that the ropes were too heavy made the Iranians replace them with silk bindings.[115] Inside each bale a note was put with the sequential number, the exact weight, and the grade, to be signed by the head factor and the second in command, who were both present at the packing. The bales, made of cloth, were tied with rope and wrapped in a cotton cover, after which a cloth woven of animal hair would be sown over it. The resulting bundle was again tied with rope. The front was then marked with the company label and the number of the bale.[116]

Once agreement was reached over the net weight and the price of the silk, the contract was signed. The actual signing only took place after at least half of all the bales had been repacked, so that dirty silk and impurities detected during the packing could still be subtracted. The functionary in charge of the payments was the *tahvildar*, a position which was given to a new person each year who received an honorarium of 200 to 350 *tumans*, depending on the incumbent and the amount of silk changing hands.[117]

Once the silk was packed and the contract signed, a camel or mule caravan had to be arranged. Most merchants, especially the foreign ones, did not own their own pack animals and relied on the services of others. Camels were the usual beasts of burden, but in mountainous areas or in rainy conditions, both of which applied to the Caspian region, asses and mules were often used as well.[118] Caravans typically included horses and mules, which were used as riding animals by accompanying merchants.[119] A camel was loaded with two bales of silk, even though the animal was physically able to carry much more. An ass could carry no more than 100 kg or one bale, while a mule's carrying capacity was 150 to 180 kg, the equivalent of two small bales.[120] According to della Valle, in an opinion that was to be echoed by Tavernier, camel drivers were almost always

[113] Speelman, *Journaal*, 315, 317; and ARA, VOC 1349, report Bent to Batavia, Nov. 25, 1679, fol. 1708b.
[114] Dunlop, *Bronnen*, 668, report Overschie, Dec. 15, 1538.
[115] ARA, VOC 1141, Van Tuynen, Qazvin, to Gel. de Jongh, Isfahan, Sept. 11, 1642, fol. 560b.
[116] ARA, VOC 1349, report Bent to Batavia, Nov. 25, 1679, fol. 1709b.
[117] ARA, VOC 1360, memorandum Casembroot to van Heuvel, March 4, 1679, fol. 1906b.
[118] Dunlop, *Bronnen*, 251, Verhoeven, Gamron to v/d Broecke, Surat, Sept. 20, 1628.
[119] Tavernier, *Les six voyages*, i, 121.
[120] Ferrier, "English View," 195; de Thévenot, *Voyage*, 415.

Muslims.[121] The same was true for muleteers. The breeding and commercial application of mules seems to have been a tribal specialty. The sedentary "Turkish Lapu'i" tribe had a reputation as muleteers. They inhabited two villages, Lapu'i, and Zarqan, both situated northeast of Shiraz, near Persepolis. Mule drivers from these places were known all over Iran, and the ones from Zarqan had a virtual monopoly on the traffic between Isfahan and Bandar 'Abbas.[122]

The process of contracting a caravan combined elements of reputation and trustworthiness with the need for care and circumspection. For insurance purposes, the Dutch usually withheld full payment upon departure to those camel owners whose reputation was insufficiently known. The duration of the journey would also be stipulated by contract. The *qafilah-bashi* would carry two *rahdari* (toll) notes, signed by the head of the VOC in Isfahan, with requests for free passage at the *rahdari* stations at the pass in the Urchini mountains, at Mahyar, Ab-i Garm, and Lar on the basis of the agreement between the shah and the Company.[123]

Caravans were led by the so-called *qafilah-bashi*. Tavernier claimed that the composition of the majority of the merchants who constituted a caravan determined the identity of its leader. If a caravan was made up mostly by Turks, a Turk was chosen; if Armenians formed the majority, the caravan was led by an Armenian. This sounds plausible in the light of Tavernier's additional remark that the *qafilah-bashi* was always suspected of keeping money for himself.[124] In addition to the transportation fee, the *qafilah-bashi* expected a present, *khil'at*, which might consist of some precious cloth.[125]

The traveling time between Isfahan and Bandar 'Abbas would be stipulated in the contract made between the Company and the caravan leader. Usually a clause in the contract stipulated that the transport price would be reduced in case the agreed-upon traveling time was exceeded. The contract also involved a guarantee of quantity. Silk transports were not free from the risk of theft, and not just by marauding bandits. In keeping with Tavernier's claim that camel drivers themselves could not always be trusted, in 1638 VOC silk was stolen from closed bales by camel drivers from Lar, who apparently buried their booty and later sold the silk to Jewish merchants in Lar.[126] In reaction to this incident, VOC Director Geleynssen de Jongh in 1641 suggested enhancing the responsibility of the camel drivers by making them carry a list containing every single item transported by

---

[121] Della Valle, *Viaggi*, i, 541; Tavernier, *Les six voyages*, i, 120.
[122] Witsen, *Noord- en oost Tartarye*, 465. For Zarqan, also see Speelman, *Journaal*, 105; Fryer, *New Account*, ii, 218, and de Bruyn, *Reizen over Moskovie*, 206.
[123] ARA, VOC 1611, memorandum Hoogcamer to Casteleyn, May 31, 1698, fol. 54.
[124] Tavernier, *Les six voyages*, i, 120.
[125] Speelman, *Journaal*, 308.
[126] Dunlop, *Bronnen*, 669, report Overschie, Dec. 15, 1638.

DE KARWANSERA MAJAER.

Plate 2 Caravanserai of Mahyar, 42 km south of Isfahan on the road to Shiraz, 1704, as drawn by Cornelis de Bruyn, and published in *Reizen over Moskovie, door Persie en Indie*, 2nd edn, 1714. Courtesy of Koninklijke Bibliotheek, The Hague.

their caravan, with specifications for weight and volume, signed or sealed by him in the presence of witnesses of the same faith. Upon arrival, this list was to be handed to the receiving agent. Each bale also bore the stamp of the camel driver under whose supervision it was transported, making him responsible for errors.[127]

Isfahan was the point of departure for the silk that the European companies negotiated and that was subsequently transported to the Persian Gulf coast across high mountain ranges and vast stretches of semi-desert. The route led from Isfahan to Shiraz via Mahyar and Yazdikhast, where it split between a direct "summer" and a longer "winter" route. The former passed through Dih-i Girdu, Shahkuh, and Mahin. The main stops on the latter were Abadah, Dih Bid, Murghab, Naqsh-i Rustam (Persepolis), and Zarqan.[128] From Shiraz to Bandar 'Abbas caravans went via Pul-i Fasa,

---

[127] ARA, Coll. Gel. de Jongh 97a, Gel. de Jongh, Gamron to van Oostende, Isfahan, Jan. 6, 1641.

[128] Emerson, "Ex Oriente Lux." 205–7.

Jahrum, Lar, and Jayhun, or alternatively via Sarvistan, Darab, Furg, Tarum, and Issin. Severe weather conditions made travel during the summer only feasible at night and during the winter months all but impracticable. The journey would take some thirty-five days.

VOC caravans heading for the coast generally did not leave Isfahan until September and had to arrive in Bandar 'Abbas by January in order to be on time for the departing home fleet. The Indian monsoon determined the rhythm of shipping in the Persian Gulf and thus the timing of arrival and departure of ships. These would typically leave from Europe in the spring so as to take advantage of the southwest monsoon between April and early October. The moment to arrive in Surat, on the northwest coast of India, the usual port of call before sailing for Bandar 'Abbas, was in the first half of October, due to the chance of heavy storm before that time and adverse winds later in the season.[129] As of October, when the northeast monsoon facilitated east–west travel, ships would arrive in the Persian Gulf from Surat. They would leave again in December or January, but no later than February. The trading season at Bandar 'Abbas was therefore in the autumn, when many Banian and Jewish merchants arrived to buy merchandise, continuing into the winter, when government officials intent on purchasing wares for the royal household or the households of local magistrates would come down from Isfahan. In the summer virtually no activity took place. In July and August the torrid heat forced all who could afford it to seek refuge in Issin, a little town above Bandar 'Abbas, or further in the interior, around Lar. Not even beasts of burden could be hired during this period.[130]

The other routes

As was noted before, Qazvin was the central entrepôt for much of the silk collected in the north. It was here that the merchants stored their silk in anticipation of transportation to various destinations inside and outside Iran, according to road conditions and anticipated profit.[131]

The overland journey to the Levant ports naturally took longer than the trip to Bandar 'Abbas. Several alternative routes existed between Tabriz and Aleppo. The shortest one, via Cizre and Diarbakr, was not ordinarily

---

[129] EIC ships would leave England in March or April, and linger in Madagascar or the Comoros so as not to reach Surat before early October.

[130] VOC ships ordinarily called at Batavia before sailing for Surat and Bandar 'Abbas on the way from Europe *and* on the homeward journey. Between 1623 and 1637 the Heren XVII (XVII Gentlemen, the directors of the Dutch East India Company) experimented with a direct route between Iran/India and Holland. This meant, however, that export goods, including silk, had to arrive on the coast no later than late September, which created the problem of getting silk ready on time and of having to transport it during the summer months. See Dunlop, *Bronnen*, 434, 454; and van Dam, *Beschryvinge*, ii/3, 111, 292–3.

[131] Dunlop, *Bronnen*, 523, 524, Overschie, Gamron to Batavia, March 15, 1635.

Table 2.2 *Duration of caravan travel to the Persian Gulf, the Levant, and Russia*

	Days (approx.)
Isfahan–Bandar 'Abbas[132]	60
Qazvin–Istanbul/Izmir[133]	110
Qazvin–Aleppo (via Tabriz and Diarbakr)[134]	65
Isfahan–Aleppo (via Baghdad and Mosul)[135]	70
Qazvin–Archangel[136]	105–135

used by merchants because it was considered dangerous.[137] A longer and more common one passed through Marand – where victuals were bought[138] – Van, Bitlis, Diarbakr, Urfa, Birecik, and 'Ayntab (Gaziantep).[139] Various routes connected Isfahan with Aleppo. One reached Baghdad via Khansar, Nahavand, Kangavar, Kirmanshah, and Mandali, the border town with the Ottoman Empire, with an alternative itinerary to Kangavar via Gugad. In Kirmanshah all merchandise was registered and the lists were signed and sealed by the khan of that town. At Sumar, the last village on Iranian territory, the registers had to be handed over to the local khan, who performed a final inspection of each caravan.[140] From Baghdad it was possible to cross the so-called "little desert," reaching Aleppo via 'Anah and Mayadin. This was the shortest route but the last stretch especially exposed the traveler to bedouin raids. It was therefore more common to follow the Tigris to Mosul, and to proceed to Aleppo via Nusaybin, Mardin and Urfa.[141]

With the rise of Izmir in the seventeenth century the route from Iran to Izmir through Anatolia became the more popular one. Camel caravans took some three and a half months to cover the distance between Qazvin and Izmir, traveling via Tabriz, Erevan, Kars, Erzerum, Tokat, Ankara,

---

[132] Speelman, *Journaal*, 280.
[133] Heeringa, *Bronnen*, ii, 163, Warnerus, Istanbul, Feb. 22, 1663; Bedik, *Chehil Sutun*, 325. Twelve days have been subtracted for the trip between Isfahan and Qazvin.
[134] Tavernier, *Les six voyages*, i, 311–13, who gives thirty-two days for horse travel. Camels traveled at half the speed of horses.
[135] Ibid., 315–18. Traveling in the winter, William Hedges needed seventy-one days just to cover the distance from Isfahan to Baghdad in 1686. See Hedges, *Diary*, i, 218.
[136] AE, Perse 5, report on foreign trade in Persia, 1718, fol. 188; Bedik, *Chehil Sutun*, 325; Witsen, *Noord- en oost Tartarye*, 707; Fekhner, *Torgovlia*, 28–9; and Bushev, *Istoriia posol'stv 1586–1612*, 71, 143.
[137] Tavernier, *Les six voyages*, i, 313.
[138] Van Ghistele, *'T voyage*, 273.
[139] Berchet, *Relazioni*, 122, report Vicenzo Dandelo, consul in Syria, read in Senate Feb. 27, 1602; and Tavernier, *Les six voyages*, i, 300ff.
[140] Bembo, "Viaggio e giornale," fols. 257, 267, 272.
[141] Tavernier, *Les six voyages* i, 316–17, 177.

and Karahissar.[142] The first caravans, and the ones carrying the best silk, arrived in Izmir in January; others, carrying *ardas* silk, followed in February and March, and arrived as late as September.[143]

Silk produced in Gilan and transported via Russia was first carried to Rasht, the center of the Caspian provinces and a city with more than fifty caravanserais where merchants from east and west converged. From there it was taken to Anzali, the port of Gilan, to be ferried across the Caspian Sea to Astrakhan. Silk originating in Shirvan tended to converge on Shamakhi, from where it was transported to Niazabad (Nizovoi in Russian), one of the few viable ports on the western Caspian littoral and a lively entrepôt in its own right, situated south of Darband.[144] Because of the danger of banditry north of Darband, the next segment of the journey was ordinarily done by boat, at least until the later seventeenth century, when peace between the shamkhal, the ruler of the fiery Lezgis, and the Safavids (temporarily) diminished the risk of robbery and plunder.[145] In Niazabad the silk was loaded into flat vessels, so-called *strugi*, each with a capacity of up to 250 packs, which followed the western coastline as far as Astrakhan at the mouth of the Volga.[146] Frequent winter storms limited the duration of the shipping season on the Caspian Sea, which lasted from late April, the time that the ice on the upper Volga had melted, to early October.[147] Ships from Anzali therefore had to leave port by late August.[148] From Astrakhan, where freight was reloaded onto smaller vessels, the course of the Volga was followed as far as Saratov, where the merchandise was reloaded onto wagons. Climate conditions in Russia circumscribed the traveling season. The wagons between Saratov and Moscow operated from May to late August, after which ice formation on the Volga would interrupt traffic. Merchandise arriving too late in Astrakhan to be carried up in time had to wait until early January, when an annual caravan on sleds set out across the frozen Volga. From Moscow merchandise went to Archangel on the White Sea, in part following the river system, while in the winter the entire journey took place on sleds, or was (as of the early 1700s) taken to St. Petersburg, to be shipped across the Baltic.[149]

---

[142] Heeringa, *Bronnen*, ii, 163, Warnerus, Istanbul, Feb. 22, 1663. Masson, *Histoire du commerce français*, 419, gives an exaggerated duration of seven months between Isfahan and the Levant.

[143] Savary, *Le parfait négociant*, v/2, 715–16.

[144] Lystsov, *Persidskii pokhod*, 73–4. Niazabad was hardly an ideal harbor. Ships had difficulties mooring and the town had no lodging or storage facilities. See Bushev, *Posol'stvo Artemiia Volynskogo*, 38–9.

[145] [De la Maze], "Mémoire," 32. The shah paid the shamkhal protection money for safe passage. Whenever these payments stopped, the shamkhal allowed Lezgi tribesmen to plunder caravans and ships. Ibid., 28.

[146] De Bruijn, *Reizen over Moskovie*, 96. It is unclear if these were equivalent to bales.

[147] [De la Maze], "Mémoire," 31.

[148] Elton and Greame, *Journey through Russia*, 62ff.

[149] AE, Perse 5, report on foreign trade in Persia, 1718, fol. 188.

As elsewhere, the traveling time on the northern route depended on the season and circumstances. The journey from Qazvin to Ardabil on average took six days; from Ardabil to Shamakhi was another eight days, while the distance between Shamakhi and Niazabad was ordinarily covered in five.[150] The boat trip between Niazabad and Astrakhan lasted from five to nine days.[151] The trip from Astrakhan to Saratov took anywhere between twenty and forty days, while the stretch between Saratof and Moscow took another twenty-five to thirty days. The total traveling time between Qazvin and Astrakhan was thus about one month, and the journey between Astrakhan and Moscow lasted anywhere between forty-five and seventy days.[152] The last stage, between Moscow and Archangel, took between thirty and thirty-five days.[153]

As well as being transported via the maritime, the Anatolian, and the Russian routes, smaller amounts of raw silk were carried overland to India and central Asia. Other than that the silk originated in Khurasan, there is virtually no information about this traffic. An English report from 1618 notes that silk from Khurasan used to be transported to Lahore, there to be "wrought into stuffs." Currently, the report continues, these merchants found "so little profitt therein that they had rather carrye the proceede of theire sould goods in ready money then invest it in that comoditie," choosing to transport "a great parte of their retournes in sylke stuffs."[154] The absence of further information makes it impossible to draw conclusions from this presumed switch from the export of raw material to that of finished products. The Portuguese cleric Manrique, visiting Tabas in Khurasan in 1642, noted that its trade was "extensive owing to the collection in the town and the neighborhood of much excellent silk."[155] A report from the late 1600s avers that "Herat has a great deal of silk; so that one can obtain there in one day three to four thousand camel loads."[156]

Transportation costs

The expense of moving silk from the area of production to the place of sale depended on transportation costs and toll and customs fees. Transportation costs depended on the terrain and the season – which determined the state of the roads, the anticipated duration of the voyage, and the availability of animals and fodder – and fluctuated considerably according to conjunctural

---

[150] Ibid.; and Witsen, *Noord- en oost Tartarye*, 707.
[151] [De la Maze], "Mémoire," 31.
[152] Fekhner, *Torgovlia*, 28–9, estimates a rather short forty days. Bushev, *Istoriia posol'stv 1586–1612*, 71, on the other hand, noting the unpredictability of the route, gives a figure of 45 to 131 days. Elsewhere, p. 143, he mentions three months.
[153] AE, Perse 5, report on foreign trade in Persia, 1718, fol. 188.
[154] IOR, E/3/6/792, Barker to London, ca. April 28, 1618, fols. 9–10.
[155] Manrique, *Travels*, ii, 352–3.
[156] Witsen, *Noord- en oost Tartarye*, 484.

circumstances as well. Caravan leaders did not like to travel in the summer, and would charge more if they were called upon to do so. As Cunaeus had the silk he contracted in 1653 transported in July, he was charged considerably more than the average freight price (see table 2.3). The grazing season and the resulting scarcity of pack animals or a period of drought leading to food shortages affected prices as well. A scarcity of fodder, for instance, accounts for the high price paid by the VOC in 1678 (see table 2.3). Such "anomalies" underscore the need for caution in extrapolating long-term trends from isolated figures.

Regardless of the expenses involved, it should be borne in mind that transport costs for a high-price commodity like silk had a marginal effect on its overall sale price.[157] As table 2.3 shows, even after prices between Isfahan and Bandar 'Abbas shot up sharply after 1618 – no doubt because of increased competition caused by the arrival of the maritime companies – they rarely exceeded 1 *tuman* per load in the seventeenth century. Half that, or 52 *mahmudis*, was said in 1651 to be the "normal" freight price for a load.[158] Willem Floor has calculated that, on average, the cost of handling and transporting VOC silk carried from Isfahan to the coast amounted to no more than about 3 percent of the invoice price.[159]

Of much greater consequence was the level of road tolls, *rahdari*, and especially customs fees, which must be integrated in a comparative discussion for it to be meaningful. Comparing freight prices between the various routes is difficult. A combination of incomplete figures for most single years and seasonal and conjunctural variations makes it hazardous to generalize from data scattered over a longer period. Moreover, it is not always possible to separate freight costs, *rahdari*, and customs fees. Some tentative conclusions can nevertheless be drawn from the available data.

A VOC report from the 1660s maintained that a load of silk privately purchased in Gilan for 29 to 30 *tumans* was first charged with a royal fee of 1.25 *tumans* and a 0.20-*tuman* fee for the vizier. Weighing increased the price by 0.36 *tuman*, while *rahdari* and freight charges from Gilan to Isfahan added 5 *tumans*, so that the total price came to 35.5–36.5 *tumans*.[160] An EIC report from 1690 claimed that moving silk between Gilan and the Safavid capital cost 6 to 7 *mahmudis* per *mann-i Tabriz*, equaling 3.6 to 4.2 *tumans* per load.[161] This may not, however, have included the initial fees in Gilan.

We have an abundance of data on freight prices for the stretch between Isfahan and Bandar 'Abbas but, since the Dutch paid no road tolls, aggregate transport costs for ordinary merchants are not easy to distill from

[157] Steensgaard, *Asian Trade Revolution*, 39.
[158] ARA, VOC 1323, Bent, Gamron to Batavia, May 21, 1678, fol. 656b.
[159] Floor, "The Dutch and the Persian Silk Trade," 366–7, appendix 2.
[160] ARA, VOC 1259, memorandum van Wyck to Lairesse, March 22, 1666, fol. 3392.
[161] IOR. E/3/48/5734. Gladman. Gombroon to London. Oct. 27. 1690. unfol.

Table 2.3 *Freight prices, Isfahan to Bandar 'Abbas, per 100* mann-i Tabriz
(600 pounds) and per load (72 mann*)*

	tumans	
	100 *mann-i Tabriz*	1 load
1618[162]	0.25–0.275	0.180–0.198
1634[163]	1.0	0.72
1635[164]	1.1	0.79
1637[165]	1.50	1.08
1644[166]	n.a.	0.48
1651[167]	0.72	0.52
1653[168]	1.10	0.79
1656[169]	0.74	0.53
1661[170]	0.72	0.52
1678[171]	1.30–1.40	0.94–1.01

their records. One missive, written in 1645, states that private merchants
paid 6 *tumans* per load for transport between Isfahan and Bandar
'Abbas.[172] Assuming expenses of 5 *tumans* between Gilan and Isfahan, this
brings the total price for the journey between Gilan and Bandar 'Abbas to
11 *tumans*.

Table 4 shows the various reported customs and road fees levied on silk
between Iran and Izmir in the late 1600s, totaling more than 6 *tumans*. This
sum falls some 2 *tumans* short of figures given by Savary, who claimed that
silk carried between Gilan and Izmir at the turn of the eighteenth century
cost 40 *piasters* (2 *tumans*) to transport and incurred 122 *piasters* (6.1
tumans) in tolls and customs fees before reaching Izmir. Upon entering
Izmir, he noted, another 46 *piasters* (2.3 *tumans*) per load had to be paid.[173]
We either lack information about some toll stations and the fees they
charged, or fees went up after the 1660s, the period for most of the earlier
information, as some sources seem to suggest. While Tavernier claimed a

162 Ferrier, "English View," 194.
163 Dunlop, *Bronnen*, 496, invoice for 420 packs of silk, Isfahan, Aug. 10, 1634.
164 Ibid., 545, invoice for 621 packs, Nov. 10, 1635.
165 Ibid., 629, invoice for 500 bales, Feb. 5, 1637.
166 ARA, VOC 1150, invoice for silk, March 10, 1644, fol. 144a.
167 ARA, VOC 1185, Sarcerius, Gamron to Batavia, May 18, 1651, fols. 563–4.
168 Speelman, *Journaal*, 280.
169 ARA, VOC 1217, silk invoice, Sept. 5, 1556, fols. 422–3.
170 Floor, "The Dutch and the Persian Silk Trade," 367.
171 ARA, VOC 1323, Bent, Gamron to Batavia, May 21, 1678, fol. 656b.
172 ARA, VOC 1152, Constant, Gamron to Batavia, March 11, 1645, fol. 84b; ibid., Bastincq, Isfahan to Heren XVII, Dec. 14, 1645, fol. 214.
173 Savary, *Le parfait négociant*, v/3, 716. Ülker, "The Rise of Izmir," 80–1, claims that customs upon arrival in Izmir were 200 *piasters* per bale. Silk in transit paid an extra fee, as did silk sold in situ.

Table 2.4 *Toll charges between Tabriz and Izmir, per load in the 1660s, in* tumans, *converted from* écus, piasters *and* 'abbasis, *at 15, 20, and 50 per* tuman, *respectively.* [1]

Tabriz	0.64	Erzurum	1.5
Marand	0.26	Tokat	0.025
Nakhjavan	0.2	Ezbider	0.025
Erevan	1.0	Hasan Kala	0.012
Kağizman	0.2	Izmir	2.3
		Total:	6.16 *tumans*

[1] All information is from Tavernier, *Les six voyages*, i, 181–92, with the exception of that for Tabriz, in Petis, *Extrait du journal*, 143 (information from the 1670s); Erevan, in IOR E/3/60/7515, Owen, Isfahan to London, March 24, 1701; and Izmir, in Savary, *Le parfait négociant*, v/3. 716 (information from the late 1600s).

customs fee of 24 *piasters* (1.2 *tumans*) at Erzurum, Pitton de Tournefort, who passed through Erzurum in 1701, insisted that Iranian silk paid 80 *écus* ($5\frac{1}{3}$ *tumans*) per load at the same customs station.[174] Yet rather than reflecting a systemic price increase between 1660 and 1700, the difference may merely illustrate how the toll system in Erzurum – and no doubt everywhere else – was based on the notion that the level of protection money depended more on the availability of alternative routes than on the value of merchandise passing through.[175] Indeed, when Pitton de Tournefort was in Erzurum, marauding bedouins made the desert routes to Aleppo via Baghdad impassible.[176]

In any case, the expense of the Anatolian route cannot have been much different from the cost of taking silk to Aleppo. In the late 1620s transport costs from Isfahan to Aleppo totaled 13–14 *tumans* per load,[177] a price that remained fairly stable over time. In 1645 freight, road tolls, and miscellaneous expenses between Isfahan and the Levant totaled 10 to 12 *tumans*, as a result of which the price went up from about 31 *tumans*, the purchase price in Gilan, to between 42 and 43 *tumans*. Selling silk in the Mediterranean ports for anywhere between 900 to 920 *reals of eight* (58 to 60 *tumans*), the Armenians in 1645 made profits of up to 20 *tumans*, or nearly 50 percent.[178] Even at times when silk was expensive in Iran, those who transported it across Ottoman territory managed to make good money. In

[174] De Tournefort, *Relation*, ii, 263.
[175] Tavernier's claim that silk from Shirvan paid higher fees in Erzurum than silk from Gilan is related to this. Unlike caravans from Gilan, those coming from Shirvan had no cost-effective alternative route at their disposal.
[176] De Tournefort, *Relation*, ii, 266. The issue of protection is discussed by Steensgaard, *Asian Trade Revolution*, 65–6.
[177] Dunlop, *Bronnen*, 547, Overschie, Isfahan to Heren XVII, Dec. 15, 1635.
[178] ARA, VOC 1152, Constant, Gamron to Batavia, March 11, 1645, fol. 83.

Table 2.5 *Prices of raw silk in Moscow 1650–1739, in* tumans *per load*

	Grade	
	legia	*ardas*
1650–1656	67	36–78
1667	45–60	39–52.5
1672–1676	67.5–90	30–39
1680–1696	52.5–180	42–48
1707–1718	76.5–108	30–81
1724–1728	112.5	66–90
1733–1739	96–180	66–90

Source: Sartor, "Die Wolga," 241.

1635, for instance, silk, purchased in Iran at 50 *tumans* and burdened with 13–14 *tumans* en route, was sold in Aleppo at 85 *tumans*.[179]

Data for the northern route are spotty. De Rodes claimed that moving a load of silk from Gilan to Astrakhan cost between 2 and 4 rix-dollars (0.14–0.28 *tumans*), without indicating whether this price was just for freight or included tolls.[180] It cannot have included the substantial fees local khans levied on passing silk. An English report from 1701 claims that 0.8 *tumans* was taken in Ardabil, 1 *tumans* in Erevan, 4.16 *tumans* in Shamakhi and 0.6 *tumans* in Niazabad (diminishing central control at that time may account for the high level of these fees).[181] For the route beyond Astrakhan figures are virtually non-existent until 1667, when the Russian government introduced a uniform toll structure and imposed a 5 percent *ad-valorem* customs fee in Astrakhan on silk transported by the Armenians. The same charge had to be paid in Moscow and again in Archangel.[182] Such low customs may have offset freight costs, which must have been higher than those on the Levant routes. The lack of figures for freight costs makes it impossible to arrive at the total expenses of the Russian route. What we do have, however, are some data on the sale price of raw silk in Moscow between 1650 and 1739. These show overall stability except for times when silk was scarce in Europe, such as happened in the early 1690s, or when chaos prevailed in Iran, as was the case in the 1720s and occasionally in the 1730s.

The available information suggests that the Persian Gulf route was, by a fairly narrow margin, the cheapest of the three, and that the expenses of taking silk to Moscow or to any of the ports of the Levant were roughly

[179] Dunlop, *Bronnen*, 547. Overschie, Isfahan to Heren XVII, Dec. 15, 1635.
[180] De Rodes, "Beskrivning," 110; and Johann Philipp Kilburger, "Kurzer Unterricht," 310, who claims a maximum of 4 rix-dollars.
[181] IOR E/3/60/7515, Owen, Isfahan to London, March 24, 1701.
[182] AE, Perse 5, report on foreign trade in Persia, 1718, fol. 188.

comparable. If true, this was a function of the shorter distance of the first itinerary, coupled with the fact that the other two involved border crossings, where merchants had to pay substantial entry tolls and where forced gift-giving shading into extortion was often rife.[183]

Though significant, these figures by themselves do not account for the level of attractiveness and popularity of routes. For one, we have no information about expenses beyond Bandar 'Abbas, the ports of the Levant, and Moscow. More importantly, what made merchants prefer one route over another was not just the price level but a combination of factors that included overall profitability, security and predictability, or what Steensgaard calls transparency.[184] Logistical constraints and the inertia of existing infrastructure were other factors that made switching from one route to another little more than a theoretical option. Least capable of doing so would have been the maritime companies. The nature of their operation, a lack of infrastructural and logistical facilities, the fact that they would not have had toll freedom beyond Iran's borders and might, as Europeans, have paid more in tolls in Ottoman territory than indigenous merchants,[185] disqualified the Levant route as an option for the EIC and VOC. Similarly, the route to Bandar 'Abbas was not a viable alternative for the Armenians, even if its price level was advantageous. In the absence of a direct shipping link to Europe via the Cape, they would have been totally dependent on the European companies. They would also have been forced to pay 10 percent in customs in addition to a 4 percent export fee, a combined sum that would have canceled any advantageous freight expenses and road tolls. Their choice was therefore between the Russian and the Levant routes. It was seen how the first of these was the less attractive one due to the absence of facilities and the hazards of banditry. The Ottoman link was naturally not free from either political unrest and brigandage, or extortion by customs officials, but a multiplicity of routes gave merchants alternatives and its overall level of security and predictability seems, at least until the early eighteenth century, to have been greater than that of the Russian route.

---

[183] For an example of this, see Boullaye-le-Gouz, *Voyages*, 72.

[184] Steensgaard, *Asian Trade Revolution*, 40–1, argues that, while conveyance by ship was more expensive than caravan transport, overland trade still lost to maritime trade. Though he only adds the cost of maritime transportation from Bandar 'Abbas to western Europe and remains silent about shipping charges from the Levant to London and Amsterdam, Steensgaard is probably still right about the cost advantage of the Levant route.

[185] For examples of non-Muslims paying higher dues in Ottoman territory, see Emerson, "Ex Oriente Lux." 140–1.

CHAPTER 3

Shah ʿAbbas I and the Safavid political economy: territorial expansion, anti-Ottoman diplomacy, and the politics of silk

Though endowed with some of the characteristics of the early modern Western state – most notably the employment of firearms and gunpowder technology and a concept of "absolutist" kingship buttressed by institutionalized religion – the Safavid state remained a premodern socioeconomic formation in its physical setting, its cultural traditions, and its specific legal context. The Safavid polity exhibits many aspects of Weberian patrimonial rule, in which the state is an extension of the royal household. Over time, the Safavid state developed institutionalized bureaucratic features; yet it continued to show little functional division and its private and official spheres remained blurred; its offices continued to originate in the ruler's own household, and in its lawmaking tradition and arbitrariness were juxtaposed; power, in sum, continued to be the personal property of the ruler.[1]

A common criticism of Weber's social theory is the overbearing role it accords to the state. Weber was explicit about the fragility of patrimonial rule, yet he formulated state and society as a unitary system and, in his nineteenth-century (German) tendency to overrate the ability of the state to manage, arbitrate, and control, he paid insufficient attention to actual societal challenges to state power. Michael Mann's reformulation of Weber's ideas takes this into account by rejecting a simple antithesis between the state and civil society. Mann sees a dialectic relationship between the two, a relationship in which a "range of infrastructural techniques are pioneered by despotic states, then appropriated by civil societies (or vice versa); then further opportunities for centralized coordination present themselves, and the process begins anew."[2] Mann also views society less as a system and a structure than as a series of "multiple overlapping and intersecting sociopolitical networks of power."[3] This study follows these propositions, and specifically Mann's distinction between "despotic" (immediate) and "infrastructural" (logistical) power.

---

[1] For the features of the patrimonial state, see Weber, *Economy and Society*, i, 1006–10.
[2] Mann, "Autonomous Power of the State."
[3] Mann, *Sources of Social Power*, i, 1.

Weber's conception of patrimonialism will be further broadened by analyzing the Safavid polity as a tributary order, one that garnered its surplus through extra-economic means.[4] The Safavid state conforms to Tilly's model of a coercion-intensive apparatus that, operating in a cash-starved environment, sought tribute more than it sought stable control over the population and the resources within the territories it oversaw.[5] Coercion was, however, only one mechanism used by the Safavid regime to reproduce itself. The state was the only arbiter and no other body conferred power, yet all forms of surplus extraction in Safavid Iran, ranging from tax and rent to confiscation, from monopolization to forced partnership and royal visits to the provinces, were the outcome of bargaining processes in which central power and domination confronted local clout and peripheral recalcitrance. Real power was negotiated power and the state was, more than anything, a forum for negotiation. It was largely by balancing deterrence with inclusion and accommodation, by manipulating social forces and by playing them off against each other, that the Safavid state managed to maintain control.

The advantage of these emendations of Weber (and Marx) is that the resulting model subsumes a range in the distribution of power, accommodating a continuum between extreme political, social, and economic centralization and extreme fragmentation. It concurs with Weber's model in allowing a coexistence of a command state with (private) mercantile activity, but is more realistic in showing how such coexistence engenders alternatively mutualism and conflict, how challenges to the power and authority of the tribute-taker might make the latter dependent on the merchant (for capital) or the nomad (for military support). Finally, it avoids any inbuilt bias with regard to a linear progression toward capitalism by envisioning a potential for change *within* a precapitalist formation. As Mann argues, "it is the dialectic *between* the centralizing and decentralizing that provides a considerable part of social development."[6]

A perpetual tension between centralizing tendencies and the forces of fission and fragmentation characterizes Safavid history from beginning to end. Maximizing bureaucratic and economic control was a primary and perpetual objective for the Safavids, who went as far as any pre-industrial Islamic dynasty in evolving from a nomadic to a sedentary order. Landmark measures in this process are the introduction of a new military and bureaucratic apparatus and the choice of a centrally located city as the capital and its subsequent evolution as the realm's administrative center and locus of a

---

[4] The tributary mode as suggested by Wolf, *Europe*, 80, is meant to erase the traditional Marxian distinction between the Asiatic and the feudal mode of production, and subsume all precapitalist systems under one model. The tributary mode seems flexible enough and sufficiently attuned to the (re)production of political and social power in Safavid Iran to fit into a Weberian model.

[5] Tilly, *Coercion*, 15.

[6] Mann, *Sources of Social Power*, i, 172–3.

stationary court. Despite all efforts and changes, however, the Safavid polity never fully evolved from a tribal steppe formation to an urban-centered bureaucratic and agrarian empire. Safavid ideology pointed to unquestioned royal legitimacy, and as time went on its bureaucracy became ever more complex and elaborate, yet unlimited court power and administrative sophistication continued to exist side by side with tenuous military control and haphazard management. In so far as political authority depends on control over the appropriation and distribution of surplus, it was severely limited by Iran's circumscribed productive capacity and the state's precarious hold over economic resources – the result of a forbidding physical geography and a deficient revenue-collection system. Governmental control thus never exceeded a negotiated balance between the center and the periphery, between bureaucrats and tribal khans, political authorities in Isfahan and provincial appointees, court officials, and foreign merchants.

The reforms of Shah 'Abbas I

The reign of Shah 'Abbas I (1587–1629) is commonly seen as the period in Safavid history in which the state was most successful in wresting itself free from societal restraints by gaining the upper hand in negotiations over power and surplus. The many measures Shah 'Abbas I took with the aim of concentrating power at the center are sufficiently well known not to need much elaboration. His centralizing policy intensified a process that had begun with Shah Isma'il, when imported Georgian and Circassian slaves had been made part of the Safavid military apparatus, and that had continued under Shah Tahmasp, who allowed these so-called *ghulams* to infiltrate the bureaucracy as well. Shah Tahmasp had only been partly successful in employing these new forces to neutralize the Qizilbash, the mainstay of the Safavid military and administrative order, who had nearly overwhelmed him in the first decade of his reign. Mounting the throne at a time when the Qizilbash had regained virtual control of the Safavid state, Shah 'Abbas was determined to break their influence and power. He did so by further depriving the leaders of the Qizilbash of their fiefs, much of which became crown – *khassah* – land administered by *ghulam* viziers, or governors. Most importantly, he eliminated Qizilbash control over the army, granting key positions in the military establishment to *ghulams* and effectively creating a standing army loyal only to the ruler.[7]

Shah 'Abbas's reforms were costly, necessitating a substantial increase in royal revenue. This was in part achieved by the conversion of state land to crown land that also weakened the power of the Qizilbash. Other measures that were taken with an eye toward greater political control and revenue

---

[7] Röhrborn. *Provinzen*. 32: and Haneda. "L'Evolution." 5.

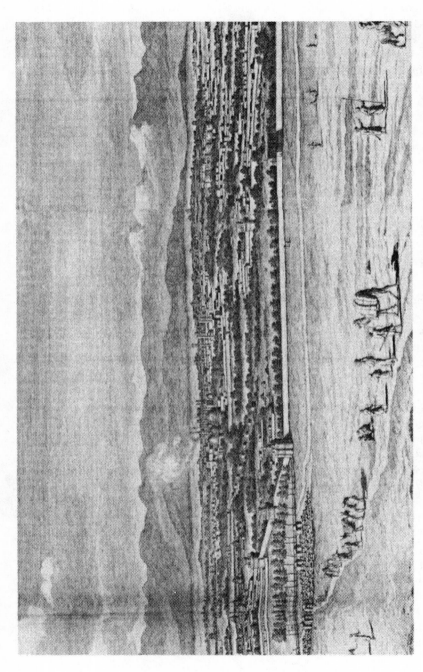

Plate 3 View of Isfahan, 1703–04, as drawn by Cornelis de Bruyn, and published in *Reizen over Moskovie, door Persie en Indie.* 2nd edn, 1714. Courtesy of Koninklijke Bibliotheek, The Hague.

DE MEY DORN.

Plate 4 View of the *Mayan-i naqsh-i jahan*, the Royal Square of Isfahan, 1703, as drawn by Cornelis de Bruyn, and published in *Reizen over Moskovie, door Persie en Indie*, 2nd edn, 1714. Courtesy of Koninklijke Bibliotheek, The Hague.

enhancement include the shah's choice of Isfahan, initially as the site of the royal *qishlaq* or winter quarters, and eventually as the court's administrative center and main residence, and the integration of commercial and political space in Isfahan's center, which the shah achieved by constructing an entirely new quarter centering on the royal square and combining a vast market area and a new royal palace. The move from Qazvin to Isfahan did not immediately end the court's peripatetic habits, but it did enhance the infrastructural control of the regime by creating a capital near Iran's geographical center (and away from the Ottoman sphere of influence and theater of war). Strategically located on the crossroads between the Iranian plateau and the Persian Gulf area, the city also became the country's largest market, generating new income for the royal treasury.[8]

A strong link between court and commerce and the intertwining of political legitimacy and revenue under Shah ʿAbbas – seen, for instance, in the integration of commercial and political space in Isfahan's new center – is often cited as proof of his innovative genius. Yet Shah ʿAbbas's reign can scarcely be considered the *beginning* of a close relationship between the state and the world of trade and manufacturing, and his policies, rather than bringing about dramatic change, either revived traditions or enhanced the scope and scale of existing arrangements. Many Iranian rulers, including the early Safavid ones, had shown concern for commercial security in their severe punishment of highway brigands and their efforts to facilitate trade. Like Shah ʿAbbas, Shah Ismaʿil was kindly disposed toward his Armenian subjects, who might not have been able to gain their important share in Iranian trade without the toleration and encouragement of early Safavid political authorities.[9] Shah Tahmasp had wells dug in caravanserais and standardized weights and measures.[10] Another example is the *karkhanah* (royal workshop) system, which was part of the royal establishments (*buyutat-i saltanati*). These workshops, manufactories producing necessities and luxury goods for the royal household, bear resemblance to the *bayt al-tiraz* of ʿAbbasid times. In Iran the institution goes back to the Ghaznavid era, existed in the Mongol period, and continued into Safavid times. We know that Shah Ismaʿil I established a number of silk and cotton cloth manufactories.[11] Shah ʿAbbas expanded their number throughout his realm and under him all major cities of Iran had royal workshops, many of which appear to have been engaged in the manufacture of silk textiles.[12] Administrative offices that regulated merchants and artisans, finally, such as the *malik al-tujjar* (head of the merchants), the *darughah* (police prefect),

[8] Sainsbury, *Calendar of State Papers*, 199–200, Pettus, Isfahan to London, Sept. 27, 1618.
[9] Zulalian, *Armeniia*, 63.
[10] Bacqué-Grammont, *Les Ottomans, les Safavides*, 55; and Bayburdyan, *Naqsh-i Aramanah*, 23.
[11] Astarabadi, *Tarikh-i sultani*, 41; and Anon., *ʿAlam-ara-yi Shah Tahmasp*, 82, 118.
[12] Della Valle, *Viaggi*, i, 584; Dorn, "Beiträge zur Geschichte," 379.

the *kalantar* (supervisor of city wards and the guilds), and the *muhtasib* (market inspector), are all known to have existed before Shah ʿAbbas.

Shah ʿAbbas's intervention in the economic activity of his realm combined stimulating and prohibitionist measures. He encouraged cotton cultivation and the wearing of cotton cloth in Iran so as to reduce the importation of Indian cloth and to increase domestic silk exports.[13] The same intent underlay the introduction of *zarbaft*, gold brocade, as clothing.[14] He had an interest in promoting the indigenous cultivation of indigo, used as a textile dye and mostly imported from India, as well as the growing of Bengal rice, requesting the Mughal court to send him a horticulturalist with expertise in handling these products.[15] An example of labor manipulation in the service of what might be termed a "proto-industrial policy" is ʿAbbas's quest for specialized artisans. He decided to build an indigenous ceramics industry by settling 300 Chinese potters in Iran,[16] and had his agents search as far as Venice for people who worked satin.[17] A similar design can be recognized in the shah's settlement of artisans from Tabriz after the completion of Isfahan's new bazaar area. More brutal but conducted in the same vein was the forcible resettling of the Armenians from Old Julfa to his new capital, to be discussed below.[18] Active economic engagement is also shown in the project that Shah ʿAbbas launched to increase the flow of the Zayandah Rud by directing the Kurang (Karun) river toward the capital in order to expand the region's irrigation potential.[19] The best-known of such infrastructural projects is the expansion of Iran's caravan network, which included the construction of a great number of caravanserais on existing and new routes. Their number tends to be wildly exaggerated – a total of 999 is traditionally cited – and many caravanserais built before or after his reign are habitually attributed to Shah ʿAbbas, but his building activity is impressive nonetheless. Shah ʿAbbas is finally credited with having re-established road security, which had lapsed in the chaotic period preceding his rule, by making provincial governors responsible for the safety of travelers and their goods.[20]

Prohibitionist in nature and epitomizing the spirit of the early modern era were the measures that Shah ʿAbbas took to forestall the drain of bullion from Iran, a perennial problem caused by the structural imbalance of Iran's

---

[13] [Chick], *Chronicle*, i, 156; Berchet, *Relazioni*, 31, 158, Relazione di Soria del console Girolamo Morosini, July 4, 1611 and Feb. 9, 1614; and Della Valle, *Viaggi*, ii, 157.

[14] Ibid., i, 567.

[15] Islam, *Calendar*, i, 164.

[16] Pope, *Introduction to Persian Art*, 95.

[17] Della Valle, *Viaggi*, i, 562.

[18] The shah in 1611 also resettled Tabrizi artisans. See Munajjim, *Tarikh-i ʿAbbasi*, 413.

[19] Iskandar Munshi, *Tarikh-i ʿalam-ara*, ii, 1170, 71, 1180. Unfinished at the time of the ruler's death in 1629, the project was abandoned under Shah Safi I, to be considered again in the 1680s. The project was only executed in the twentieth century.

[20] Röhrborn, *Provinzen*, 62.

economy vis-à-vis the Indian subcontinent. In 1618 he issued a ban on the export of gold and silver.[21] A similar preoccupation with currency flight is reflected in his decision to discourage the hajj, which drained enormous quantities of gold ducats out of the country. In an attempt to substitute an indigenous alternative, he stimulated the veneration of Imam Riza and the visitation of his tomb in Mashhad.[22]

Infrastructural projects, measures to stimulate import substitution, and bans on bullion export were not the only manifestations of the Safavid penchant for intervention in economic life. Trade, considered an important source of taxable wealth, yielded a significant part of state revenue in the form of custom dues and road tolls. Commerce was subject to the *tamgha* (or *baj*), an impost on trade commodities of varying size that was levied at the country's borders. In the interior, so-called *rahdari* or road tolls had to be paid.[23] Even caravanserais built by the shah and his courtiers were designed to do more than just facilitate trade. Many were leased or administered to cover the shah's "table expenses." All were subject to taxation.[24]

Beyond taxation lay more drastic intervention. The shah and provincial rulers routinely claimed as tribute the best agricultural and manufactured products from a region or a group of producers. In addition, Safavid authorities often resorted to commodity monopolization, *tarh*, the practice of forcing producers or merchants to sell to or to purchase from the court. Its obverse, temporary bans on the sale of merchandise desired by the court, was standard as well.[25]

Such procedures were subsumed under the general practice of purveyance (*suyursat*), which included the provisioning and billeting of troops during military campaigns and providing for passing foreign envoys, all of which go back at least to Mongol times.[26] Purveyance could and often did reach extortionate proportions. The provisioning and quartering of troops, for instance, tended to be a heavy imposition on the people affected by it. Another government prerogative that easily degenerated into arbitrariness was the right of *chappars* (express messengers) serving the royal and the provincial courts to requisition horses from whomever they encountered en route.[27]

The most conspicuous form of state participation in trade was commerce

---

[21] Sainsbury, *Calendar of State Papers*, 199, Pettus, Isfahan to London, Sept. 27, 1618.
[22] Tavernier, *Les six voyages*, i, 588–9; and Matthee, "Between Venice and Surat."
[23] Emerson and Floor, "Rahdars," 318–27.
[24] Tavernier, *Les six voyages*, i, 446, 448; Chardin, *Voyages*, vii, 399–400; and Kaempfer, *Am Hofe*, 123.
[25] De Thévenot, *Relation d'un voyage*, ii, 188.
[26] Lambton, *Continuity and Change*, 217.
[27] Ange de St. Joseph, *Souvenirs de la Perse*, 86–7; and Tavernier, *Les six voyages*, i, 686. Purveyance was, of course, by no means restricted to Safavid Iran. It existed in Russia from as far back as the sixteenth century. In various western European countries, too, it was customary for the palace to appropriate choice wares.

conducted on behalf of the court. Supervision lay with the shah's personal chief merchant or factor, who was charged with the negotiation of commercial deals for the royal household. Merchants commissioned by the shah also routinely accompanied diplomatic missions abroad. Aside from the status and legitimacy the accompaniment of a diplomatic mission conferred upon merchants, they also benefited from protection and the opportunity of evading customs duties.[28] Diplomatic missions often had important commercial mandates or were little more than trade missions in disguise. Such embassy trade was common in relations with India and even more so with Russia, where it involved the exchange of a number of so-called restricted goods such as arms, and sable fur, leather skins, and wax.[29]

As is true of purveyance, the blurring of diplomatic and commercial missions and the importance attached to royal trade were hardly peculiar to the reign of Shah 'Abbas I or, indeed, to Safavid Iran. Nor did the convergence of politics and commerce reach extreme proportions under the Safavids. Iranian shahs never institutionalized the practice of the court merchant as Russian tsars did with the so-called *gosti* merchants, whose direct ties to the court gave them first right to make purchases and a monopoly in the trade in sensitive export products.[30] In the West, too, royally commissioned trade was common, as is evidenced in the employment of Jewish "court factors" by early modern European rulers.[31]

Import and intent

Shah 'Abbas's policies raise many questions with regard to the interface between politics and economics in Safavid Iran. His approach to commerce does not seem to conform to dominant Western views of the relationship between state and trade in the Muslim world, which either see benign neglect on the part of governments or perceive Middle Eastern states as predatory institutions whose proclivity to intervene in economic life had nothing but deleterious effects on the latter. According to the first, the state approached the economy with a laissez-faire attitude and, as long as government interests were not detrimentally affected, would keep its hands off commerce and industry.[32] In the second, the state, bent on revenue maximization regardless of consequences, engaged in policies of coercion and expropriation that discouraged entrepreneurial initiative. Shah 'Abbas's numerous economic measures, on the other hand, and in particular

[28] Bushev, *Istoriia posol'stv 1613–1621*, gives many instances of merchants evading tolls by traveling in the suite of envoys.
[29] For the Indian case, see Monahan, "Trade and Diplomacy," 76ff.; for Russia, see Fekhner, *Torgovlia*, 61–2.
[30] Fekhner, *Torgovlia*, 111.
[31] For the "Court Jew" in early modern Europe, see Israel, *European Jewry*, 123–44.
[32] See, for example, Goitein, "Minority Self-Rule"; and Udovitch, "Merchants and Amirs." For the Mughal empire, this has been argued by Pearson, *Merchants and Rulers*.

his active involvement with commerce, seem to reflect not just what Palmira Brummett calls "economic intentionality" but to bespeak a foresight and vision that justifies the term "conscious economic policy."[33]

To discern the contours of a conscious economic policy in the aggregate of economic measures adopted by Shah 'Abbas is to ask the question of intent and priority. On the face of it, he might appear as an Asian mercantilist, a ruler implementing a version of doctrines preached and practiced by (some) contemporary European states. Simply defined as an "effort to increase royal revenues indirectly, through economic improvements,"[34] mercantilism indeed seems an appropriate label for Shah 'Abbas's policies. His infrastructural projects appear consciously designed to facilitate the expansion and profitability of commerce. His "import-substituting" policies hint at a willingness to sacrifice current revenue for long-term dividend, and the accumulation of specie, and reflect an unusual measure of creativity at a time when fiscalist policy was typically designed to preserve existing tax revenue among rulers who, on the whole, did not stimulate exports for fear of shortfalls in domestic consumption. His multilateral approach to commercial relations bears resemblance to contemporary European practice as well.

Yet equating Shah 'Abbas's economic management with European models raises several problems. For one, a focus on action and practice to the exclusion of theory easily leads to Procrustian interpretations as it fails to do justice to the mutuality between principle and practice in European mercantilism as much as to the embeddedness of Safavid economic practice in normative tradition. The term "mercantilism" has undergone much revision since its (retrodictive) introduction in the eighteenth century, when it was interpreted as a system that subordinates economic to political concerns and an ideology that sees wealth as a means to increase national power.[35] Having lost much of its formerly unproblematic character, mercantilism is currently regarded less as a uniform pattern of economic policy than a set of specific responses to immediate and varying problems. Irrespective of how much coherence we attribute to it, however, mercantilist thinking was novel, even in early modern Europe, because it represented a new level of understanding of economics articulated in new terminology. By according an autonomous space to economic process and behavior and by channeling self-interest toward a useful purpose, mercantilists separated thinking about the economy and the market from the sphere of moral reasoning.[36] Whereas traditional ideas about economic behavior remained

---

[33] Brummett, *Ottoman Seapower*, 3. For a critical analysis of the use of the term "conscious economic policy" (as used in the context of the Ottoman state), see Peter Sluglett's review of Masters, *Origins*, in *British Journal of Middle Eastern Studies*, 19 (1992), 203.

[34] Wolfe, "French Views on Wealth," 202.

[35] Viner, "Power versus Plenty."

[36] Grampp, "Appreciation of Mercantilism," 62–3.

embedded in a system of thought that condemned selfishness and stressed social justice and that saw a balance between consumption and redistribution as the best way to achieve such justice, the advocates of mercantilism, while not wholly unconcerned with the imperatives of a divinely ordered universe, grappled with issues of public finance and the division of labor, and sought to integrate the forces of production and consumption; thus they proposed changes in the tax structure and criticized the practice of royal hoarding for hindering the circulation of cash. Rather than just addressing the balance of trade as a zero-sum equation of bullion and commodity flows, mercantilists focused on the value-added content of export products.

It may be – and it has been – argued that European practice rarely followed mercantilist theory and that European rulers merely pursued traditional dynastic concerns with new means. Yet, new principles did inform practice through process. Colbert's elaborate and comprehensive scheme to establish an East India Company reflects an effort that went far beyond royal concerns. The project's ultimate goal was greater riches for the sake of greater power, but inasmuch as its architects sought popular support for investment to underwrite it and included issues of increased property and reduced unemployment in their discussions, French political economy under Louis XIV cannot be reduced to a royal quest for profit and power.[37] In Restoration England, too, the debate concerning the need for an aggressive commercial policy helped the state formulate such a policy. Though mercantilism *explains* government policy in neither case, its assumptions and terminology affected and gave meaning to the policies pursued by these states.[38] Mercantilist ideas about the creation of wealth and the working of the market were carried and reinforced by a public debate conducted by way of pamphlets, treatises, and lectures which reminded rulers not just of their errors and abuse but also suggested concrete ways of mending them. Mercantilism was at the very least a restraining influence on rulers, and at best convinced state policy makers that profit was an essential component in the pursuit of power.

Iranian statecraft had its own tradition of limitation and restraint. The classical Iranian notion of the cycle of justice, articulated in the typical *Nasihat namah*, or counsel for rulers, obliged the monarch to promote the integrity and well-being of the community by extending protection to his subjects, including road security, the supervision of market practices, and fixing prices for basic necessities in times of need. Iranian rulers had to pay more than lip service to such theoretical precepts, but since economic management remained integral to an overarching moral code rather than evolving into a separate practical realm subject to its own logic, scrutiny and criticism often remained hypothetical, and fiscal practice was allowed

---

[37] Ames, *Colbert*, 23.   [38] Brewer, *Sinews of Power*, 169.

to operate on the premise that royal revenue and societal wealth were antithetical, that the king's taxes were the people's loss. Economic gain remained wedded to notions of tribute and gift-giving, in practice as much as in theory.

As importantly, mercantilist thinking *and* practice evolved in the framework of the emerging nation-state and viewed its constituency as a community of people endowed with shared interests and living and working in a competitive relationship with other such communities. The (exclusionary) national state in which mercantilism was formulated was characterized by the loss of a certain social and economic fluidity and a hardening of boundaries, territorial as much as social. Manifestations of this were the erection of tariff barriers and a changing attitude toward domestic and foreign merchants. In keeping with a long-standing Muslim tradition, the degree of toleration shown by Safavid rulers toward merchants adhering to other faiths than (Shiʻi) Islam far exceeded that exhibited by their Spanish or French colleagues toward non-Catholic merchants such as Huguenots, Jews, and Armenians. Conversely, Safavid rulers did little to "protect" their indigenous merchants in the same manner that European states began to enact exclusionary policies expressly designed to favor their subjects or in the way that Russian rulers shielded their *gosti* merchants from foreign competition by protecting their market share.[39] The Safavids accorded certain privileges to their Armenian merchants, but did not "protect" them, either diplomatically or militarily, much less did they consider them "national" merchants. They employed non-Muslim merchants in part for the same reasons that some medieval European rulers invited Jewish merchants to settle in their realm: because they were outsiders who lacked the means to acquire political power yet possessed financial resources, skills, and contacts that were useful, even indispensable, for long-distance trade, investment, and the accumulation of capital. Iran's Armenian merchants show many of the features of an incipient commercial bourgeoisie. They were, however, unable to make their interests converge with those of the political elite, and remained subordinate to the latter in a way that English and Dutch merchants were not.

Finally, mercantilist thought and practice grew out of a societal order that imbued commercial activity, investment and above all property rights and principles such as escheat with a legal title. It is arguable that the Safavid preoccupation with official decrees, the granting and guaranteeing of trading permits, entrepreneurial privileges and tax exemptions was not qualitatively different from the legal ambience that framed European economic activity. Yet the latter knew an institutional quality that included

---

[39] Though the Russian state ignored the concerns of its *gosti* whenever these clashed with "reasons of state," the *gosti* merchants managed to keep foreign competition at bay by getting the state to make merchants from abroad pay higher toll fees and use Russian merchants as intermediaries. See Fekhner, *Torgovlia*, 102–4.

the parallel rise of a market geared toward new forms of capital accumulation and thus made it go beyond the person of the ruler and his immediate interests in ways not found in Iran. The very emergence of the chartered maritime companies, commercial institutions that went beyond the traditional family firm in their reliance on the mechanism of joint stock, is a function of the adoption and working of such principles and practices. Here, too, practice and theory can only be divorced at the risk of imprecison and apparent similarity.

The foregoing is not meant to contrast Iran negatively with Europe, but rather to lay the groundwork from which to approach and understand the specific means, goals, and constraints of the economic measures taken by Shah 'Abbas and his successors. Regardless of the moral impulse and notwithstanding the innovative quality of Shah 'Abbas's methods, the principal impetus behind his policies was the maximization of royal power and revenue. As Amin Banani has noted: "Most of 'Abbas I's reforms may be regarded as structural manipulations calculated to enhance his immediate power and wealth."[40] Like most of his contemporaries, Shah 'Abbas was a fiscalist, though one who implemented policies that cannot be dismissed as rapaciousness and that were not incompatible with judicious policy making. Filling the treasury meant maximizing personal wealth and control, yet did not come at the expense of equitable governance and a strong army capable of resisting internal and external enemies.

Profit, control, and traditional notions of morality join with the very foundations of the Safavid polity in explaining the nature of the government's approach to commerce. The tribal background of its elite and their prevailing ethos made Safavid Iran above all a state built on military might and centered on the imperatives of war-making. Military exigency thus had priority over the integral order of the land-based economy.[41] As the court chronicles, with their emphasis on diplomatic and military relations with Iran's neighbors, abundantly suggest, the government's main concern was not the "national" economy – the orderly procedure and expansion of agriculture and commerce – but the protection of the realm against outside invaders and internal rebellion. Despite numerous examples of official encouragement of trade, during as well as after Shah 'Abbas I, the structure of society militated against a sustained complementary relationship between the political and the mercantile worlds. Politics and trade overlapped. Political officials engaged in trade; indeed the shah himself was the largest merchant of the realm. As the interaction between the state and Iran's Julfan Armenian merchants suggests, mutual interests and reciprocal benefits existed – the court depended on its merchants for certain commodities, for revenue in the form of bullion, and for information, and in return gave them favored status, to the point where one might even speak of a symbiotic

---

[40] Banani. "Reflections."   [41] Ibid.. 90.

relationship – but these were contingent, not fundamental aspects of policy making. The state and the marketplace did not interact as equal partners; the state by definition operated in the market on the basis of extra-economic mechanisms such as tribute, expropriation, and monopolization. Commercial wealth did not generate power in the same way that (political) power generated wealth. The traditional state concern for merchants and peasants notwithstanding, the world of commerce and agriculture and the realm of politics operated in a climate of distrust of one another. Badly and irregularly paid political officials saw merchants as a source of income; merchants, like peasants, tried to minimize political involvement.

In Shah 'Abbas's involvement with silk we observe a similar pattern of intervention designed to increase royal power and revenue and grafted upon a societal structure in which commercial and political imperatives intersected without necessarily operating in a mutually reinforcing relationship.

The role of silk

Shah 'Abbas's domestic involvement with silk can be divided into a number of phases. In the first decade of his reign he established effective control over the main regions of cultivation, Gilan and Mazandaran. In the 1590s, the shah appropriated the surplus from these provinces for his treasury by turning them into crown land. In 1604–05 he brought the Armenian involvement in silk under closer state control by forcibly resettling the population of the Armenian town of Julfa on the Aras river in a newly built suburb of Isfahan, called (New) Julfa. At the same time he launched a series of diplomatic initiatives designed to find new outlets for Iran's silk surplus. In 1619, finally, the shah monopolized the export of Iranian silk.

Though the multifaceted and protracted nature of these measures makes it tempting to label the shah's involvement with silk part of a concerted economic policy, it might be rather more appropriate to view it as consonant with his overall approach to economic issues and to analyze it as a series of interventions that reflect an acute awareness of ways in which revenue might be enhanced and whose timing was in part determined by geopolitical considerations, in part by contingency and fortuitousness. Revenue enhancement in the form of a maximum inflow of the bullion that Iran was unable to procure from indigenous mines was the primary goal of 'Abbas's silk policy, but his involvement with the commodity also formed part of his centralizing policies, while at all times the backdrop was Iran's problematic relations with the Ottomans.

The conquest of Gilan and Mazandaran

According to a famous dictum, Shah 'Abbas faced the task of "reconquering" his own country when he came to power in 1587. The two areas of contestation were Khurasan in the northeast, which was threatened by the emerging Uzbegs, and the northwestern regions of Georgia, Shirvan, and Azerbaijan, all of which were under Ottoman control. Rather than confronting the Ottomans head-on in his attempt to regain lost territory, Shah 'Abbas first made peace with Istanbul, ceding Shirvan and Qarabagh to his archenemies so as to have a free hand against the Uzbegs. He did not, however, postpone action in Gilan, a safe haven for dissident Qizilbash forces and a region that was about to fall under Ottoman influence as its ruler, Ahmad Khan, requested Istanbul's protection against the Safavids.[42] It took half a decade and several expeditions by Shah 'Abbas's general, Farhad Khan, before the rebellious province was subdued. By 1593 Farhad Khan, having occupied Lahijan, was appointed governor and *tuyuldar*, landholder, of the area's eastern half, Biya Pish.[43] Shortly thereafter Biya Pas, the western half, fell to the Safavids as well, but full control had to wait until 1595–96.[44] In 1597, Shah 'Abbas, sensing that Farhad Khan had become too powerful, had him executed. A year later Gilan was turned into crown domain.[45] Henceforth *ghulams* were appointed as viziers and as much as one-third of the region's revenue was now directed toward the shah's treasury.[46]

To the east of Gilan lay Mazandaran, another region of high rainfall and rich agricultural yield. Long ruled by the Qavvami (Mar'ashi) sayyids, Mazandaran resembled Gilan in being tributary to the Safavid crown but, not least due to poor accessibility, the region was in practice autonomous prior to Shah 'Abbas's reign. Its four districts, Kujur, Larijan, Savad Kuh, and Hizar Jarib, were all ruled by local rulers who were habitually at war with each other. Using this turmoil as well as benefiting from a lull in his external wars, Shah 'Abbas in 1596 ordered Farhad Khan to subjugate the province, a task that was completed in little over one year.[47] In 1599 Mazandaran became crown land, and Aqa Muhammad Abhari, a *ghulam*, was appointed as its vizier.[48] The area continued to hold a special importance to the shah – whose mother hailed from Mazandaran – as a venue for summer stays and hunting parties. In 1612 'Abbas built the town of Farahabad as a pleasure resort filled with mosques, bathhouses and caravanserais, and nearby had the town of Ashraf constructed. Access to the region was facilitated with the construction of a paved all-weather

[42] Falsafi, *Zindigani*, iii, 1032; and Nawzad, *Namahha-yi Khan Ahmad Khan*, 303. Ahmad Khan belonged to the Malati or Kar-Kiya'i dynasty, which had ruled Gilan since 762/1361. See Rabino de Borgomale, "Les dynasties locales."
[43] Afushtah'i Natanzi, *Naqavat al-asar*, 540–6; Iskandar Munshi, *Tarikh-i 'alam-ara*, 634–7.
[44] Ibid., 634–7, 689–90; and Fumani, *Tarikh-i Gilan*, 170–1.
[45] Fumani, *Tarikh-i Gilan*, 173, erroneously gives 1006 as the year of Farhad Khan's execution.
[46] Chardin, *Voyages*, v, 398.
[47] Iskandar Munshi, *Tarikh-i 'alam-ara*, 693–8; Munajjim, *Tarikh-i 'Abbasi*, 143–9; Mar'ashi, *Tarikh-i khandan*, 341–8.
[48] Gilani, *Tarikh-i Mazandaran*, 100.

causeway of some 250 km, running from Kvar, south of Tehran, to Farahabad,[49] and a road of about 500 km in length that followed the entire Caspian shore from Khurasan to Azerbaijan.[50] The entire Muslim, Armenian, and Jewish population of the Georgian capital of Zagam, numbering almost 15,000, was resettled to Mazandaran to help develop the area.[51] Della Valle noted that

The Georgians, both Christians and Jews, accustomed to tend the labours of the worm, are occupied in the gathering and manufacture of silk; to facilitate the means for which an incredible number of mulberry trees has been planted in the neighborhood of Ferhabad, the soil being better adapted to their growth than that of any other in the world.[52]

Having annexed Gilan and Mazandaran, Shah ʿAbbas turned his attention to the northwestern regions of Georgia, Qarabagh, and Shirvan, all of which had intermittently been tributary to the Safavid state since the days of Shah Ismaʿil I. The latter two regions had been under Ottoman control since 1590. Reconquering them proved to be a long process, since his continuing problems with the Uzbegs forced the Safavid ruler to devote considerable time and resources to the stabilization of the northeast. Only in 1606 did Shah ʿAbbas manage to capture Ganja, Qarabagh's capital, and Erevan, which would serve as the springboard for the seizure of Shirvan. In 1607 Shamakhi fell into Safavid hands after a long siege. With the incorporation of Shirvan, Safavid control finally extended over all the silk producing areas south and west of the Caspian Sea.[53] Shirvan was never converted to crown land, but, as in the case of Gilan and Mazandaran, almost all of its governors were to be *ghulams*.

Silk and the search for alliances

The Russian connection

Shah ʿAbbas's silk policy is inextricably bound up with his diplomatic activities. This is as true for his efforts to find alternative routes for Iran's raw silk as it is for his treatment of the Julfan Armenians after their resettlement to Isfahan. Intertwined with these policies was the shah's main preoccupation, to stand up to his principal enemies, the Ottomans, and to isolate them through foreign alliances.

---

[49] Iskandar Munshi, *Tarikh-i ʿalam-ara*, 850, 990; and Marʿashi, *Tarikh-i khandan*, 362.
[50] Rabino di Borgomale, *Mazandaran*, 7.
[51] Iskandar Munshi, *Tarikh-i ʿalam-ara*, 881; and Arakʿel Davrizhetsʿi, *Girkʿ patmutʿeantsʿ*, trans. in Brosset, *Collection*, i, 488.
[52] Della Valle, *Viaggi*, i, 598. The translation is from della Valle, "Travels in Persia," in John Pinkerton, ed., *Voyages and Travels* (London, 1811), ix, 50.
[53] For the history of Shirvan under Safavid rule, see Dorn, "Beiträge zur Geschichte," 317–434; and Ashurbeili. *Gosudarstvo Shirvanshakhov*, 235ff.

Modern scholarship has mainly concentrated on the contacts between Shah 'Abbas and the western European powers, most notably Portugal, Spain, England, and the papacy, considering these his earliest and most significant contacts with the outside world. The well-publicized travelogue of the English Sherley brothers and the preponderance of British scholarship in modern research of the episode have, however, led to a skewed perspective in this regard. While the excessive attention paid to the Sherley brothers has not gone unnoticed,[54] little attempt has been made to put their role in Iran's diplomacy in proper perspective. As seen from Iran rather than from England, the Sherleys were rather minor agents who were manipulated by the shah in the service of a much larger diplomatic offensive.

In truth, the earliest contacts between Shah 'Abbas and the (non-Muslim) outside world were not with western Europe but with Russia, a country whose anti-Ottoman sentiments had long paralleled those of Iran. Moscow, prompted to seek Muslim allies by the fall of Constantinople in 1453 and Turkish expansion into the Balkans and the area north of the Black Sea, sent its first mission to Shamakhi in 1464–65.[55] Sporadic Russo–Iranian contacts marked the first half century of Safavid rule, until the Ottoman expedition against Astrakhan in 1569 and their occupation of Georgia and Shirvan a decade later led Shah Khudabandah to dispatch the first serious Safavid mission to Moscow, that of Hadi Beg, in an effort to create an anti-Ottoman alliance. As Russia at that point was embroiled in an exhausting war against Poland, nothing came of this, and it was not until the termination of the Livonian War in 1582 that Moscow was again in a position to turn its attention southward.[56]

This reorientation in Russia's foreign policy virtually coincided with the coming to power of Shah 'Abbas I in 1587, and led to a regular exchange of envoys, beginning with the 1588 embassy of Gregori Boris Vasil'chikov to Qazvin. Although 'Abbas's decision to make peace with the Ottomans made these contacts rather desultory, they were not entirely fruitless. In 1589 the Russians sent Hadi Beg once again to Iran, expressing a desire for economic relations and a commitment to free trade for Iranian merchants.[57] Shah 'Abbas's northern diplomacy now began to involve trade relations as well. All four Safavid missions to Moscow between 1591 and 1594 had a commercial aspect, involving complicated discussions about the right of official merchants accompanying Safavid diplomats to engage in toll-free trade.[58] Silk soon formed part of the embassy trade that developed. The

---

[54] See, for example, Steensgaard, *Asian Trade Revolution*, 212ff; and Meilink-Roelofsz, "Structures of Trade."

[55] Bushev, *Istoriia posol'stv 1586–1612*, 35.

[56] Bennigsen, "La poussée," 31.

[57] Bushev, *Istoriia posol'stv 1586 1612*, 136ff., 149ff.

[58] These are the so-called Kay mission of 1591; the Hajji Khusraw mission of 1592; the Hajji Iskandar mission of 1593; and the Hadi Beg mission of 1594. See Bushev, *Istoriia posol'stv 1586–1612*, 177, 202, 205 8; and idem, "Iranskii kuptsina," 167.

royal merchants who accompanied the third Hadi Beg mission in 1594 carried some 450 lb of silk and bought "protected" goods such as arms and sable fur for the shah. Merchants carrying fine textiles were part of the Pir-quli Beg mission of 1599.[59] Moscow reciprocated by dispatching a series of missions designed to normalize trade relations.[60] The ill-fated Tiufiakin mission of 1597 – all three of its successive leaders perished before they had reached Iran – was to sign a commercial treaty with Iran. The same task seems to have been assigned to the full-fledged Zhirov-Zasiekin embassy dispatched by Tsar Boris Godunov in 1600.[61]

Not too much should be made of the Russo–Iranian commercial contacts at this point. The embassy trade was of rather limited frequency and import and was bound to remain relatively insignificant so long as Iranian and Russian geopolitical priorities and interests did not converge. Having signed an agreement with Istanbul in 1590, Shah 'Abbas was in no position to adopt an active anti-Ottoman stance. Besides, war against the Uzbegs and internal reforms for the time being absorbed all his energy, while Russia's aggressive policy in the Caucasus raised suspicions in Iran. It is telling in this context that neither then nor at any later time did 'Abbas attempt to open up the Russian route as an official outlet for his country's silk. Official Russo–Iranian relations were suspended altogether with the onset in Russia of the so-called Time of Troubles (1598–1613), a period of turmoil that severely diminished Russia's status as a credible military partner, aside from disrupting commercial relations. Ottoman and Crimean Tatar threats and peasant rebellions temporarily led to the closure of the route between Moscow and Astrakhan.[62] Safavid–Ottoman warfare in Azerbaijan and Shirvan in 1603–04, meanwhile, did a great deal of damage to Iran's northwestern regions.[63]

Relations with the western European powers

Contacts between Shah 'Abbas and western European rulers around a joint anti-Ottoman policy have antecedents that reach as far back as the European dream of enlisting the Mongols in an effort to reclaim Mamluk-held Palestine for Christianity. The Mamluks were succeeded by the Otto-

[59] Courbé, "Relation d'un voyage," 151–2. The Pir-quli Beg mission was different from the delegation which, led by Antony Sherley and Husayn 'Ali Beg Bayat, left Iran for Europe via Russia in 1599. The two did travel together between Astrakhan and Moscow.

[60] Russian missions to Iran include those of Zvenigorodski (1595), Tiufiakin (1597), and Zhirov-Zasiekin (1600).

[61] Bushev, *Istoriia posol'stv 1586–1612*, 362ff. Information is lacking about the embassy's dealings in Iran or the results achieved. Bushev speculates that the embassy may not have traveled beyond Astrakhan and that it may have been recalled as it became clear that Shah 'Abbas would not sign a treaty after all. Yet Maria Szuppe has shown that the Zhirov-Zasiekin embassy did stay in Iran in 1601. See Szuppe, "Un marchand," 90–1.

[62] Bushev, *Istoriia posol'stv 1586–1612*, 432–3; Bushev, "Iranskie kuptsina," 168.

[63] [Chick], *Chronicle*, i, 114.

mans, and by the time that Venice and Rome sent envoys to Uzun Hasan in the late 1400s, joint action against the Ottoman Empire had become the objective of Western diplomacy. The Christian powers approached Shah Isma'il and his successors for the same purpose, but their initiatives remained sporadic, and regular interaction had to wait until Shah 'Abbas, whose receptiveness to such initiatives may have been caused in part by the outbreak of the Time of Troubles in Russia. The first to visit Iran from the West during his reign was the English gentleman Antony Sherley who arrived in Qazvin in December 1598, representing the Earl of Essex but speaking in the name of all of Christian Europe in his call for an anti-Ottoman league. Shah 'Abbas launched his own diplomatic offensive the following year with the dispatch to Europe of Sherley and an Iranian envoy named Husayn 'Ali Beg. In the next two years some seven Safavid missions visited European capitals ranging from Rome to Paris and Vienna, to explore opportunities for joint anti-Ottoman alliance-building.

None of these efforts bore fruit, not just because the Europeans showed little inclination to lend effective support to Iran, but also because Safavid strategy was ultimately determined, more than by European concerns, by regional military considerations and domestic pressures.[64] Thus Shah 'Abbas decided to resume hostilities with the Ottomans before Husayn 'Ali Beg had returned to Iran with a (negative) response from Western rulers.[65] The Ottoman–Habsburg treaty of Sitva Torok of 1606 and the warning by his itinerant ambassador Zaynal Beg that the European powers secretly wished to see the mutual destruction of the Ottoman and Safavid states, must have convinced the Safavid ruler once and for all that he could expect little more than empty rhetoric from the West.[66]

In modern Safavid historiography much has been made of the question of diverting the flow of silk from the Anatolian to the Persian Gulf route in the context of these diplomatic contacts. Shah 'Abbas's European initiatives certainly coincided with a move to bring the southern regions of Iran under greater central control. In 1601 the shah ordered the ruler of Shiraz, Allah Virdi Khan, to occupy Lar province, and a year later he expanded his control over the Persian Gulf basin by seizing Bahrayn from the Portuguese.[67] The shah's search for a secure southern commercial outlet, made urgent by the renewed outbreak of war with the Ottomans in 1603, continued until the expulsion of the Portuguese from Hurmuz and the founding of the port of Bandar 'Abbas in 1622. The issue of silk in this endeavor remains problematic, however.

Presumably first proposed by Antony Sherley in a memorandum to the

---

[64] De Gouvea claims that the decision to resume war with the Ottomans was influenced by a religious faction at the Safavid court. See Steensgard, *Asian Trade Revolution*, 235.
[65] Ibid., 230.   [66] [Chick], *Chronicle*, i, 169.
[67] The campaigns are narrated in Iskandar Munshi, *Tarikh-i 'alam-ara*, ii, 614–6; and Munajjim, *Tarikh-i 'Abbasi*, 212–6.

Spanish King Philip III (Philip II of Portugal) in 1607, the idea of diverting Iran's raw silk initially met with a cool reception in Spain. Sherley thereupon managed to get the Spanish-Neapolitan viceroy Count de Benevento interested in the proposal, which seems to have been retransmitted to the Spanish court through Benevento. Having reconsidered its position toward the idea, the Spanish crown is said to have conveyed letters to Iran via the Portuguese viceroy in Goa.[68] Whatever the precise channels of transmission, it seems that the Portuguese Augustinian Antonio de Gouvea was the first to broach the issue personally with Shah 'Abbas when he visited Iran as head of a permanent Augustinian mission to Isfahan in 1608. De Gouvea maintains that the Safavid ruler reacted favorably to the suggestion and even put the proposal to the test with his decision to send a contingent of raw silk to Philip III with Khajah Rajabo, one of Shah 'Abbas's merchants, who accompanied de Gouvea, and an Iranian envoy named Jangiz Beg, on the return embassy to Rome and Spain. They seem to have carried a letter in which the shah spoke of a diversion of Iranian silk and a Spanish blockade of the Red Sea as ways to thwart the Ottomans. It is, however, not altogether clear which of the proposals presented to European rulers originated with Shah 'Abbas and which sprang from the minds of de Gouvea and the Sherley brothers. As for the silk accompanying the envoys, the shah wrote to his Spanish colleague that he was determined to deprive the Ottomans of future silk profits, suggesting that the king send representatives to Hurmuz to purchase the raw silk that Iran customarily exported via the Levant. In return he requested that Iranian and Armenian merchants be allowed the freedom to visit Goa. When no more than 1,600 *mann* of silk was found in the royal warehouse, Shah 'Abbas was so embarrassed that he decided to present the silk to King Philip as a gift and a sample of what Iran might provide in future.[69]

Steensgaard raises doubts about this version, pointing out that no one but de Gouvea calls the silk a gift, and that the volume, 19,200 lbs, and the estimated value, 60,000 ducats, suggest a business deal rather than a present.[70] Yet this suggestion appears to be gainsaid by a customs statement from Hurmuz which mentions the passing of the consignment, consisting of eighty-six bales of silk from Khurasan and Gilan, and clearly refers to it as a present, *sughati*.[71] The ambiguity of the meaning of gift-giving in the Iranian tradition, where a "gift" did not necessarily preclude monetary compensation, goes some way toward explaining the confusion. Della Valle further clarifies both the shah's intentions and de Gouvea's role. Shah

[68] Gulbenkian, *L'Ambassade*, 59–61; Steensgaard, *Asian Trade Revolution*, 264ff.
[69] De Gouvea, *Relation*, 456–9, 468.
[70] Steensgaard, *Asian Trade Revolution*, 269.
[71] Gulbenkian, *L'Ambassade*, 61, fn. 127, citing *O Archeologo Portugues*, 1904, vol. 9, Procès verbal de la douane d'Ormuz à propos de la soie que Chah 'Abbas roi de Perse, a envoyé au roi de Portugal.

ʿAbbas, della Valle states, sent his ambassador, Jangiz Beg, to Spain to explore the idea of sending his silk to Europe via India rather than via Ottoman territory. Desirous to learn if traffic in silk via this route would be feasible, he dispatched his ambassador with 100 bales of silk and "ordered him to sell these so as to find out how much they would yield."[72] According to the same source, it was de Gouvea who persuaded Jangiz Beg to present the silk to the Spanish king as a gift, with the argument that, if transported as a commercial commodity, the silk would accumulate so much overhead in transportation and customs fees that little profit would result. If the silk was presented as a gift, on the other hand, the king would surely return a present twice its value.[73]

Arriving in Spain in 1610, de Gouvea – here again speaking for himself – presented the silk diversion project as simple and favorable. Ships would be sent to Hurmuz twice a year to fetch silk, which Iranian merchants would then be allowed to transport to Europe on Portuguese vessels. As Steensgaard notes, the combined advantage would be Iberian–Iranian friendship, a solution to the question of Hurmuz, an economic blow to the Ottomans, and increased income for the Spanish-Portuguese king. The Spanish Council of State, though skeptical about the project, reacted favorably to de Gouvea's proposal by agreeing to the idea of sending ships from Goa to Hurmuz twice a year to fetch the silk. It also followed de Gouvea's advice to charge no customs on the goods exported.[74]

Nothing ever came of this project. The reasons for its failure are varied. For one, the proposal never seems to have evolved beyond the personal vision of Antony Sherley to the level of official Spanish policy. The Spanish court and its subsidiaries, the viceroys of Naples and Goa, at no time threw their full weight behind the idea. Secondly, a project of this kind would have been problematic enough if it had been restricted to matters of commerce and revenue. Since it was intimately linked to Shah ʿAbbas's strategies and, by extension, to the complex and fluctuating dynamic of war-making, it is difficult to conceive of the perfect long-term alignment of forces that would have made the rerouting of silk a feasible option. Thirdly and most importantly, the diversion of all of Iran's silk was ultimately not in the interest of either the Safavid court or Iran's indigenous merchants. Privileging the Armenians in the silk traffic ran counter to a diversion of trade, an operation in which foreign merchants inevitably would play the leading role in spite of a clause that gave Iranian merchants the right to carry the silk to

---

[72] Della Valle, *Delle condizioni*, 70–1; and idem, *Viaggi*, ii, 168–9. Other sources claim that ʿAbbas initially sent 120 loads, but that Jangiz Beg sold more than half before he reached Madrid, pocketing the money. See Florencio del Niño Jesus, *Biblioteca Carmelitano-Teresiana*, iii, *En Persia, 1608–1624*, 91.

[73] Della Valle, *Delle condizioni*, 70–1; idem, *Viaggi*, ii, 169.

[74] Steensgaard, *Asian Trade Revolution*, 284. The text of de Gouvea's memoranda with the details of the project is reproduced in Alonso, "La embajada persa," 55–66.

Europe. As for the Armenians, they are unlikely to have consented to an arrangement in which they would have lost their autonomy. In fact, *pace* Steensgaard's assertion, there is precious little evidence that 'Abbas ever seriously intended to divert his country's silk trade, his many declarations to the contrary notwithstanding. The shah's strategy was designed to intimidate the Ottomans as much as to manipulate the Europeans. Shrewd strategist that he was, the Safavid ruler must have realized that silk was his only bargaining chip with the European powers, and that his best chances lay in playing the various parties off against each other. His promise to divert the silk trade sounds less absurd than his pledge to hand over Jerusalem to the Christians in the event that he conquered the city, or his commitment to the Russians to yield Darband and Baku to them if he himself were to seize these cities from the Ottomans; like those promises, however, the idea of rerouting Iran's silk was mostly a diplomatic gambit, rhetorical in nature rather than reflective of realistic options.[75]

The subsequent stages in Iran's diplomatic activity bear this out. In 1610 Shah 'Abbas extended a peace offer to the Ottomans. In the autumn of the next year an Ottoman ambassador visited Isfahan for negotiations. When the latter departed for Istanbul he was accompanied by an Iranian envoy whose task it was to offer peace with the pledge of an annual tribute of 1,000 bales of silk.[76] The Ottoman–Safavid treaty which resulted in 1612 indeed included an Iranian obligation to send 400 bales of silk to the Ottomans in exchange for Tabriz remaining in Safavid hands.[77] In the interim Jangiz Beg returned to Isfahan. Instead of considering the proposals Jangiz Beg brought with him, 'Abbas, outraged that his envoy had presented the silk consignment to the Spanish as a gift rather than as part of a business transaction after selling more than half on his own account, had him executed. De Gouvea, who had been largely responsible for the mishap, had to answer to the shah with regard to the same issue when he arrived in Iran shortly after Jangiz Beg. The Spanish king, he replied to 'Abbas's query about the events, was not a merchant and, besides, he had sent goods that could be considered either a gift or payment for the silk. However, the merchandise in question, assessed for its value, was found to be worth 8,000 to 10,000 *scudi*, far less than the estimated 50,000 *scudi* the silk had been worth. When the shah demanded to be reimbursed for the difference by de Gouvea, the latter quickly left Iran.[78]

---

[75] For the promise of Jerusalem in 1609, see Steensgaard, *Asian Trade Revolution*, 288; for that of 1619, see de Silva y Figueora, *Comentarios*, ii, 409. 'Abbas's pledge to hand Darband and Baku to the Russians recalls a similar gesture that his father, Shah Khudabandah, had made in 1586. See Bushev, *Istoriia posol'stv 1586–1612*, 64, 119.

[76] Alonso, "Cartas del P. Melchior," 256–7, 261.

[77] Olson, *Siege of Mosul*, 19–20. In the event, no silk was never sent. Della Valle, *Viaggi*, i, 651, claims that the Iranian refusal to remit silk to Istanbul was the cause of the next Safavid–Ottoman war.

[78] Della Valle, *Viaggi*, ii, 169; and Steensgaard, *Asian Trade Revolution*, 293.

Following this disastrous mission, 'Abbas dispatched a letter to Spain in which he appeared to offer the Europeans one last chance to side with Iran in their struggle with the Ottomans. Yet the peace treaty that he simultaneously signed with the Porte suggests that the Safavid ruler now operated from the assumption that no European assistance would be forthcoming. A change in treatment of Iran's Armenians (other than the Julfans), who were put under pressure to convert to Islam, reflects the strained relations between the shah and the Catholic powers at this point. Nor is it a coincidence that 'Abbas directed his attention to the Persian Gulf coast, and in particular to the Portuguese stronghold of Gombroon. Acting as Shah 'Abbas's proxy, Imam-quli Khan, the ruler of the Garmsirat, in 1614 laid siege to Gombroon, forcing the town to capitulate before the end of the year.[79]

The aftermath of these events goes on to illustrate the difference between chimeral schemes and realistic scenarios. In 1615 the execution of Nasuf Pasha, the Ottoman grand vizier who had been a protagonist of peace with Iran, once again portended war. This may have led Shah 'Abbas to try and restore the damaged Iberian connection by sending Robert Sherley – who had returned to Iran in the same year – back to Europe. Though it is unclear what instructions Sherley received, his subsequent dealings at the Spanish court, which included further elaborations on the silk diversion project, appear increasingly removed from Iranian realities. This holds as much for the Spanish suggestion to strike at the Ottoman economy by blockading the Red Sea as for their demand of Iran for the restitution of Gombroon and the expulsion of the English who had meanwhile arrived on the Persian Gulf coast.[80]

Just as inconsequential was the mission of Don Garcia de Silva y Figueroa, who took over from Antony Sherley as representative of the Spanish crown. Although the origins of his journey go back to a Spanish decision to send an official embassy to Isfahan that had been taken in 1611, de Silva y Figueroa only left for Iran in 1614, did not set foot on Iranian soil until three years later, and arrived in Isfahan in the early summer of 1618. By that time, a new Safavid–Ottoman peace agreement had obviated any need for Iberian assistance and with it the rationale for continued negotiations about the silk diversion project, and it is therefore not surprising that the ensuing talks were marked by misunderstandings and an obvious lack of interest in the Spanish proposals on the part of the shah.[81] Just as importantly, new and more promising candidates, closer at hand and eager to please the Safavid ruler, had arrived in Iran by this time. In December 1616, the first ship of the English East India Company had

---

[79] Ibid., 294–6.   [80] Ibid., 310–11.
[81] De Silva y Figueroa, *Comentarios*, ii, 366–83; 408ff.

entered the Persian Gulf, offering the shah a fresh opportunity to diversify his diplomatic and commercial projects.

Promoting a new commercial elite: the resettlement of the Julfan Armenians

Every aspect of Shah 'Abbas's silk policy served his centralizing reforms and was designed to strengthen the royal domain. Gilan and Mazandaran became *khassah* land as soon as they fell under Safavid control; the two most prominent royal factors, Mulayim Beg and Lalah Beg (Muhibb 'Ali Beg Lalah), were *ghulams*; and the main impetus behind the shah's silk export monopoly, to be discussed in the next chapter, was the enhancement of royal control and revenue. The shah's treatment of his country's Armenian population fits into this pattern as well. It was seen earlier how the Armenian rise to commercial prominence centered on Julfa, the town on the river Aras that separated Azerbaijan from Qarabagh. In one of his most noteworthy measures, Shah 'Abbas in 1604–05 resettled the community from (Old) Julfa and its surroundings to his newly created capital Isfahan, where a town named New Julfa was built for them on the south bank of the Zayandah Rud. As such, there was nothing unusual about this. Resettling tribes and communities was a long-standing practice in Iran, and Safavid rulers, practicing a scorched-earth policy in times of war, frequently depopulated regions and shifted populations to dilute local power in peripheral areas or to strengthen defenses in border lands and newly conquered territories.[82] The Armenian deportation to Isfahan, however, is generally considered a unique case, the result of systematic planning rather than random events, and a great deal of economic significance has been attributed to it. In keeping with the image of Shah 'Abbas as a visionary ruler, modern historiography has portrayed the Armenian relocation as part of a deliberate policy designed to "enlist the industrious and thrifty nature and the commercial experience of the Armenian merchants in the service of the Safavid state."[83] The reality appears more complex, however.

Undertaken during Shah 'Abbas's campaign in Azerbaijan in 1603–04, the evacuation of thousands of Armenian families – a number of whom were resettled in various parts of the country other than Isfahan – occurred amidst the horrors of war and starvation afflicting the Safavid–Ottoman borderlands between 1591 and 1609.[84] The indigenous Persian and Armenian sources fully acknowledge this and do not portray the events as the orderly relocation project that later gained currency. The Persian chroni-

---

[82] Perry, "Deportations," 309–10; and Tumanovich, *Gerat*, 142, for examples in Khurasan.

[83] Savory, *Iran under the Safavids*, 174. A recent example of this interpretation is Ghougassian, *Emergence*, 17–32.

[84] For the chaotic and brutal conditions in the border region, see Schütz, "An Armeno-Kipchak Document," 256–60.

clers tend to focus on issues of strategy in their coverage of the events. One claims that the evacuation of the Armenians was related to the shah's decision to destroy Nakhjavan in retaliation for the collaboration of its Sunni population with the Ottomans.[85] Another puts the decision to resettle the population of the province of Chukhur-i Saʿd and the subsequent Armenian evacuation in the context of Iran's scorched-earth policy, and presents it as a move designed to prevent the Ottoman army from inflicting any harm on the local population as well as to discourage the Ottomans, confronted with a region in ruins, from building fortresses. The scene these works invoke – though never explicitly mention – is that of a Safavid army retreating before advancing Ottoman troops in chaotic circumstances, resulting in numerous casualties among those who were driven across the river Aras and who drowned in the process.[86] Armenian sources in particular provide details about the suffering of the Julfans, who were given three days' notice before they were rounded up and their town was razed to the ground.[87]

The picture that emerges from such accounts has led Edmund Herzig to cast doubt on the planned character of the entire project and to argue for a hasty and ad hoc operation rather than an orderly evacuation. According to him, whatever deportations initially took place did not involve the civilian population and were anything but systematic in being border raids for booty and captives. Nor was the decision to move the Armenians to Isfahan apparently taken until the winter of 1605, after it had become clear that those who had been driven from their villages would not be able to return because of the threat posed by Kurdish and Ottoman Celali marauders.[88]

While Herzig's revisionist scenario poses a serious challenge to those who want to see a "blueprint" in Shah ʿAbbas's economic "policy," a chaotic evacuation fails to explain the outcome, the eventual settlement of the Julfans in Isfahan. The fact remains that the entrepreneurial reputation of the (Julfan) Armenians predated their deportation and had been recognized by Shah ʿAbbas's predecessors. Junabadi calls the Armenians famous for their commerce and wealth, claiming that they were responsible for the prosperity of Nakhjavan.[89] They had enjoyed favors under Shah ʿAbbas himself, who had also employed them as royal merchants-cum-envoys before their evacuation to New Julfa.[90] In sum, their reputation as

[85] Junabadi, "Rawzat al-Safaviyah," fol. 320b.

[86] Munajjim, Tarikh-i ʿAbbasi, 270–2.

[87] Arakʾel Davrishetsʾi, Girkʾ patmutʾeantsʾ, trans. in Brosset, Collection, i, 286–96; Brosset, "Itinéraire," 223–5; Gulbenkian, L'Ambassade, 100–01, 104.

[88] Herzig, "Deportation of the Armenians." The sequence of events as narrated by Junabadi, "Rawzat al-Safaviyah," fol. 322b, confirms this.

[89] Ibid., fol. 320b.

[90] Arakʾel Davrishetsʾi, Girkʾ patmutʾeantsʾ, trans. in Brosset, Collection, i, 300; de Gouvea, Relation, 223–4; Berchet, La Repubblica, 192–5. There is no clear record of Shah ʿAbbas sending Armenians to Venice prior to 1600. Fekete, Einführung, 453–67 (docs. 80–3), is

resourceful merchants was clearly not lost on the Safavid ruler, who may have made up his mind in the period between the initial evacuation and the eventual settlement in Isfahan. In other words, an ad hoc deportation does not necessarily invalidate the intent, even if the intent did not perhaps precede the deportation.

Regardless of his original motives, Shah ʿAbbas secured a skilled work force by deporting the Julfans, and in addition brought the trade in the important commodity of silk under closer state supervision. Following their settlement, a complex and multifaceted relationship developed between the Julfan Armenians and the Safavid court. Allowed to live as a rather self-contained community, the Julfans enjoyed privileges beyond those customary for *dhimmis* in a Muslim environment, including permission to ride richly caparisoned horses and the right to sell land and property without restrictions. New Julfa, like the old Julfa before it, had the status of *khassah* land. Its taxes therefore accrued directly to the royal treasury. The community enjoyed the patronage and protection of the queen mother. The head of the community, the *kalantar*, was an official appointed by or at least with the approval of the shah who served as the intermediary between the court and the Armenians and who also represented the community in commercial matters.[91] In 1614 Shah ʿAbbas issued a decree that made the construction of the Vank cathedral in New Julfa possible, while in 1619 he bestowed the land on which the town was situated on the Armenian population.[92]

Shah ʿAbbas also arranged a mutually beneficial partnership with the most important of the town's merchant families, enlisting them as a commercial service class. A good understanding of the working of this partnership awaits a fuller examination of unpublished Armenian documents, but the available material permits insight into at least some of its aspects. The members of these families performed a number of commercial and diplomatic tasks on behalf of the court. Leaders of the Armenian business community formed a trade council that was often consulted by Safavid court officials regarding matters of (foreign) commerce. At times this council even acted as an officially appointed body representing the state in negotiations with foreign envoys. Their cosmopolitanism and knowledge of foreign languages made Armenians useful in dealing with visitors from abroad. As Armenian representatives were used as *mihmandars* (officially appointed hosts of foreign diplomats and merchants), emissaries from abroad often had their first encounter with Armenian agents upon entering

mistaken in giving 1585 as the year of ʿAbbas's first mission to Venice, since ʿAbbas only came to power in 1587. The other early dates for subsequent missions given by Fekete, 1587–88 and 1590–91, are in error as well. The documents in question apparently refer to missions in 1610 and 1621. See Steinmann, "Shah ʿAbbas," 109.

91 Herzig, "Armenian Merchants," 89, 99, 187.
92 See the decrees in Falsafi, *Zindigani*, iii, 1126–30; and docs. 2 and 3 in Ghougassian, *Emergence*, 204–09.

the Safavid capital.[93] The Armenians also acted as court financiers, extending loans to the shah. Khajah Nazar, the Armenian *kalantar*, at one point is said to have lent Shah 'Abbas the sum of 5,000 *tumans*.[94]

This partnership extended beyond Iran, for Shah 'Abbas's reign saw an intensification of the long-standing practice of sending Armenians abroad as envoys and merchants. In 1607, when war with the Ottomans made it difficult for Shi'i Iranian subjects to traverse Ottoman territory in an official capacity, one Khajah Shiush visited Venice as his special agent. A year later another Julfan Armenian, Hovhannes, went to Istanbul on a commercial mission.[95] Khajah Safar, a third Julfan (and not to be confused with his homonym, who was *kalantar* of New Julfa until his death in 1618) was sent to Venice to recover merchandise lost by the Khajah Shiush mission as well as to explore anti-Ottoman sentiments in Europe.[96] In 1613, two Armenians, Khajah Alredin and Khajah Shahsavar, arrived in Venice as royal agents, assuring the city magistrates that Venetian merchants would receive every possible favor in Iran.[97] The Julfans, finally, served the Safavid court in a purely commercial capacity as well, traveling abroad on royal missions with quantities of silk varying from 50 to 300 bales, charged to sell those at a certain price. Any profit exceeding that price they could call their own. Upon return and disbursement of the proceeds, the shah would regale them with presents.[98] The Armenians, in sum, played a crucial role in the raw silk for bullion trade that enriched Safavid coffers as much as their own, so much so that della Valle could claim a symbiotic relationship between the shah and the Julfans, noting that neither could live without the other.[99]

Not the least important aspect of the patron–client relationship forged under Shah 'Abbas is that it allowed the Armenian family firm, operating on the basis of the extended patriarchal household, to develop its full potential. The phenomenal rise of Old Julfa in the last decades before its demise testifies to the tremendous expansion that Armenian trading activity had undergone already before the relocation of the Julfan community to Isfahan. Armenians in the late 1500s built a trading network that stretched

---

[93] Szuppe, "Un marchand," 91. Dutch envoys later experienced this as well. Pacifique de Provins, a French cleric, in 1628 stayed at the house of an Armenian merchant Khajah Muchaq, whom he had met in Paris. His host and his relatives, whom Pacifique de Provins called "very influential with the King," acted as intermediaries in the interview the Frenchman had with the shah. See Pacifique de Provins, *Relation*, 250–3.

[94] Dunlop, *Bronnen*, diary Jan Smit, 741.

[95] Zekiyan, "Xoğa Safar," 361.

[96] Baiburtian, "Posrednichkaia rol'," 26–8; and idem, *Armianskaia koloniia*, 33ff.

[97] Berchet, *La Repubblica*, 49, 65. Venice in this period tried to maintain its position in the Levant trade in the face of growing competition from western European nations. Part of its strategy was to try and attract Iranian silk. In 1614 and 1626 the Venetian Senate exempted Iranian silk from import and export duties. See ibid., 67. The documentation in Fekete, *Einführung*, docs. 90–1, 499–507, shows that Muslim merchants were entrusted with such missions as well.

[98] ARA, VOC 1133, van Oostende, Gamron to Surat, Jan. 9, 1640, fol. 413b.

[99] Della Valle, *Viaggi*, ii, 215–16.

from England to the Philippines. They had representatives in European ports, operated an Asian trading network, and were active in conducting trade for the tsar in Moscow, where they had their own caravanserai.[100] Their social and commercial organization, centering as it did on the family firm, made them a very effective merchant community in the early modern world,[101] and some see in the association between the most prominent Julfa families an institutionalized commercial company.[102] Regardless of the label we attach to the organizational structure, the partnership dimension of their family firms, their extensive use of the *commenda* (a risk-sharing contract) and other partnership constructions in business transactions, their knowledge of local conditions, and their low overhead costs, moreover, lent Armenian merchants a flexibility and adaptability in the Iran trade with which no European commercial enterprise could compete.[103]

All in all, it is evident that the relationship between the Safavid state and the Julfan mercantile community did not correspond to a partnership between the overlord and the small-scale peddler.[104] To be sure, they manifested themselves in Iran's home market as small-scale merchants, for there they typically acted through peddlers, who, in groups of two or three, went around the country selling manufactured goods supplied on credit by their masters.[105] As an aggregate economic force operating at a distance, however, the Armenians were rather than peddlers, highly sophisticated merchants who in their skills, techniques and range of operation were every bit comparable to their European counterparts, great family firms such as the Fuggers, the Cranfields, and the Tripps.[106] Their formidable economic power is illustrated in the outcome of a governmental attempt to convert Iran's Armenians to Islam in 1621, following a deterioration of relations between the shah and the European powers. One caravan on the way from the Levant to Iran apparently turned back upon hearing the news and the shah, fearing the economic consequences, is said to have decided to call off the conversion campaign.[107]

While their commercial skill and financial wherewithal gave the Julfans a

---

[100] Gregorian, "Minorities," 662.
[101] Herzig, "Armenian Merchants," 169, 185.
[102] Sartor, "Die Wolga"; and Baghdiantz, "Armenian Merchants," 116–25. In reality no overarching Armenian Company ever seems to have been in existence. The Julfan merchant houses occasionally joined forces, as they did in 1666 during negotiations with the Russian tsar, when they may have presented themselves as a single trading company. Ordinarily, the individual family firms were engaged in fierce competition with each other. See Herzig, "Armenian Merchants," 191–2. Ferrier, "The Armenians and the East India Company," 58–9, shows how fierce intra-Armenian competition could be.
[103] For the strength of the family partnership, see Herzig, "Family Firm."
[104] The interpretation of the Asian merchant as a "peddler" originated with Van Leur and is a central part of Steensgaard's argument.
[105] Khachikyam "Typology of the Trading Companies."
[106] Herzig, "Armenian Merchants," 180.
[107] Della Valle, *Viaggi*, ii, 214–7.

measure of clout beyond their numbers and religious status, it did not make them fully fledged partners in the political arena. Merchants in Safavid Iran by definition operated outside the inner core of a polity that centered on military imperatives. The autonomy the Julfans enjoyed, moreover, remained that of a *dhimmi* community subordinated to the state and ever vulnerable to religious pressure.[108] Rather than to the European maritime companies with their quasi-governmental structure, the Julfan merchant community should therefore be compared to the early modern European court merchants.[109] Like the latter, they served the political elite rather than being part of that elite.

Conclusion

Sanjay Subrahmanyam has recently argued for a breakdown of the dichotomy between early modern trading states and agrarian states, the first characterized by "mercantilist" policies, the second by inward-looking, antimercantile policies.[110]

Iran under Shah ʿAbbas I arguably corresponds to neither model. Safavid Iran derived most of its revenue from agriculture, and landownership carried the most prestige after military service, yet its rulers did not neglect or spurn trade. Indeed, Shah ʿAbbas's approach to commerce was complex and multifaceted, as is evidenced in the multiple positions held by Mulayim Beg and Lalah Beg, the shah's personal factors. The former was also Master of the Mint (*zarrab-bashi*) and served as *malik al-tujjar*, while the latter had been building supervisor when the shah had his new commercial center in Isfahan constructed. Shah ʿAbbas's policies removed impediments and provided infrastructure support for commerce and industry. Rather than merely extracting revenue from existing routes and enterprises, he was actively and creatively engaged in the exploration of new ventures, harnessing the resources of his realm for greater revenue. These included the incorporation of the Caspian provinces into his realm and his extensive diplomatic activity, as well as his enlisting of the Armenians from Julfa as his "court merchants." His policies exhibit a concern for the precarious balance between commerce as a revenue producing venture and commerce as a mobile enterprise that, given excessive protection costs, might relocate. His drive to raise revenue was primarily motivated by a quest for personal

---

[108] Such religious "minority" status distinguishes (many) merchants in the Middle East from their counterparts in India. The current debate in Mughal scholarship on the status of merchants and, in particular, their political influence on and membership of the ruling classes, is therefore not wholly transferable to Iran. In India, too, a lack of ethnic or kinship connections might place a merchant community outside the ranks of the political elite. See Arasaratnam, *Merchants*, 225.

[109] Baghdiantz, "Armenian Merchants," 119, argues by contrast that the Julfan Armenians had more power than the European company directors.

[110] Subrahmanyam, *Portuguese Empire*, 19.

wealth and power, but this goal was not pursued at the expense of a strong central state and defensible borders, and the pursuit itself generally stopped short of abuse and neglect of those who produced the wealth. Given the inherent environmental, economic, political, and social constraints of the time, his achievements were considerable. Yet, while reminiscent of mercantilist practice, Shah 'Abbas's methods were deeply imbued with traditional notions of the tributary state which made no clear distinction between diplomacy and trade, between gift giving and investment. The Gouvea affair amply demonstrates what European merchants interested in silk would soon experience: that the tributary character of the Safavid state extended to trade as much as to politics.

CHAPTER 4

Government control and growing competition: the silk export monopoly and the advent of the European maritime companies

Though little is known about the volume, it is clear that most of Iran's raw silk destined for export in the early 1600s was carried via the Anatolian land route. Della Valle in 1620 claimed that the greatest part of commerce in Aleppo was in silk, which arrived from Iran and other areas, in spite of the war.[1] Then, as later, reliable figures are hard to come by. In 1621 it was said that Iran annually exported 6,000 bales to Europe via Aleppo, 500 of which went to Holland, 600 to England, 1,500 to Venice, 3,000 to Marseille, and the remaining 400 to Genoa, Lucca, Florence, and Messina.[2] These figures differ in varying degrees from other, mostly isolated estimates in the same period – such as a total Levant export via Aleppo of 4,000 bales claimed for 1620, or the approximately 1,500 bales France is said to have imported in 1621 – but are close enough to warrant serious consideration.[3]

Whatever the aggregate volume of Iranian silk converging on Aleppo in this period, there is no doubt that most of it was carried by the Julfan Armenians.[4] Taking advantage of the opportunities offered to them by the Safavid ruling house, Armenian merchants at the turn of the seventeenth century became the uncontested primary movers of raw silk between Iran and the ports of the Levant. Their continued expansion is reflected in the number of Armenians trading and residing in the Mediterranean basin and later in northwestern Europe. In Izmir and Aleppo, Armenian houses in about 1610 are said to have numbered 100 and 300, respectively.[5] In Venice the number of resident Armenians at that time was still small, though growing. The names of 2,500 Julfan merchants have been found in the Venetian archives, and there was even a Julfa street in Venice.[6] Holland, where Armenians from Iran were first recorded in 1560–65, became home

---

[1] Della Valle, *Viaggi*, i, 331.
[2] Dunlop, *Bronnen*, 11, Heren XVII to Batavia, March 4, 1621.
[3] Figures in Steensgaard, *Asian Trade Revolution*, 159, 161.
[4] Masters, *Origins*, 63, draws attention to the fact that non-Iranian Armenians were involved in the Levant trade as well.
[5] Herzig, "Armenian Merchants," 132–3.
[6] Baiburtian, *Armianskaia koloniia*, 55; and Herzig, "Armenian Merchants," 135.

to resident Armenian merchants as well in this period, especially after the Ottomans concluded a commercial treaty with the Netherlands.[7] The other Italian cities that began to compete with Venice, Livorno, and Genoa, saw the establishment of Armenian trading communities in the same period. Livorno had an Armenian population of about 120 in the early seventeenth century.[8] So many Armenians frequented the port of Marseille that the French state in 1622 issued a mercantilist decree that prohibited their trading activity.[9]

The reestablishment Russian link lagged far behind this. In fact, it is only with the end of the Time of Troubles, coinciding with the enthronement in 1613 of Tsar Mikhail Romanov, that private trade and official relations between Iran and Russia resumed. In 1616 the Dutch Russia merchant Isaac Massa noted that "the route to Astrakhan via the river Volga is completely open and free from robbers so that many merchants have arrived in Moscow with a lot of silk merchandise undamaged."[10] Shah 'Abbas's pacification of the north and the cessation of direct Ottoman–Safavid conflict in Armenia and Shirvan further contributed to a more propitious commercial climate. In 1623, seventy-five Russian merchants are said to have visited Iran, and a total of 4,440 ansyrs (lbs) of silk was shipped from Astrakhan to various Russian cities.[11] A report from 1626 notes that Russian merchants would come down the Caspian Sea to exchange their goods for silk in Gilan.[12]

Yet the northern flow of silk continued to face numerous obstacles. In the absence of formalized trade relations, merchants suffered many indignities. Russian merchants visiting Iran were routinely harassed and obstructed in their movements by the governors of Shirvan and Gilan, who subjected their wares to strict inspections, refused to grant them legal protection and even imprisoned them.[13] Nor were Iranians visiting Russia guaranteed safe passage, as is suggested by the steps the Russians took to increase the protection of Iranian merchants on Russian soil following the Safavid Muhammad Kazim mission of 1616.[14] Russia's official reception of foreign merchants, meanwhile, was mixed. Though they were made welcome in the first years of Tsar Mikhail's reign, they gradually faced new taxes, and restrictions were imposed on their visiting Moscow.[15] Finally, prospects for

[7] Van Rooy, "Armenian Merchant Habits," 347.
[8] Zekiyan, "Le colonie armene," 914.
[9] Tékéian, "Marseille," 12–13; Bayburdyan, Naqsh-i Aramanah, 100.
[10] Quoted in Wijnroks, "Jan van de Walle," 54.
[11] Buskovitch, Merchants of Moscow, 96.
[12] ARA, VOC 852, Batavia to Persia, Aug. 14, 1625, fol. 124.
[13] Bushev, "Iranskii kuptsina," 169; idem, Istoriia posol'stv 1613–1621, 203–4; idem, "Posol'stvo Korob'ina," 146–50; Kotov, Khozhenie, introd., 11.
[14] Bushev, Istoriia posol'stv 1613–1621, 139.
[15] Burton, The Bukharans, 470–1.

expanded private transit trade to Europe were dashed with Russia's rejection of Sweden's request for transit privileges to Iran in 1617.

The embassy trade, about which we are slightly better informed, resumed as well. In 1614 the Russians sent the Tikhanov mission to Iran in an attempt to renew commercial and diplomatic ties with the Safavid state. The Muhammad Kazim mission included a silk consignment. Ivan Afana'evich, a high-ranking merchant traveling with the Korob'in mission of 1621–23, carried merchandise with the aim of buying silk in Iran.[16] Yet, aside from the inherent irregularity of the embassy trade, divergent interests did little to boost trade relations conducted at the official level. Russia emerged from the Time of Troubles a weak and impoverished country, and the tsar's repeated requests for monetary assistance between 1615 and 1620 no doubt contributed to the poor reception enjoyed by northern emissaries in Isfahan.[17] Most importantly, Shah 'Abbas had, by that time, initiated a reorientation of his foreign policy. His victory against the Ottomans in 1618 temporarily obviated direct pleas for Russian assistance. The arrival of the Western companies on his southern shore, meanwhile, had prompted him to try and establish control over access to the Gulf and to explore a third export option, that of the maritime route. The Russian ambassador who in 1624 came to Iran to encourage the silk trade via the Caspian route experienced first-hand how irrelevant the Russians were to this project. Shah 'Abbas rejected his proposals and refused continued commercial traffic as suggested by the Russians.[18]

The English and Dutch maritime companies: origins and objectives

The English and Dutch decision to engage in trade beyond the Cape of Good Hope was motivated by the prospect of gaining a share in the lucrative Asian spice trade, much of which was in the hands of the Portuguese. Dutch maritime expansionism was also triggered by the Spanish trade embargo imposed on Holland in the late 1500s. What enabled both nations to widen their maritime horizons, finally, was an emerging naval superiority vis-à-vis the Iberian powers.

The English were the first to claim a stake in the Indian Ocean basin, but their early expeditions beyond the Cape of Good Hope were irregular and lacked a sound financial basis. In 1595 Dutch merchants launched their first venture. Its success resulted in the establishment of so-called *Voorcompagnieën*, ad hoc trading ventures created and equipped with joint-stock capital by various cities in the Dutch Republic. In response to this, the English in

---

[16] Bushev, "Posol'stvo Korob'ina," 126–8.
[17] Bushev, *Istoriia posol'stv 1613–1621*, 44–5, 53.
[18] ARA, VOC 852, Batavia to Persia, Aug. 14, 1626. Accompanying merchants bought ca. 150 bales of silk before returning to Moscow. Dunlop, *Bronnen*, 60, Visnich, Isfahan to Batavia, July 24, 1624.

1601 incorporated the East India Company with a charter that gave the king a monopoly over shipping between India and the mother country. A Court of twenty-four directors, annually elected by the company shareholders, was given authority over the organization. In reaction to this threat to Dutch mercantile interests, some of the *Voorcompagnieën* merged, until in 1602 all were united in the *Verenigde Oostindische Compagnie* (United East India Company, hereafter VOC), which for a period of twenty-one years received a monopoly on trade with the eastern hemisphere beyond the Cape of Good Hope.

The outward similarities between the two companies mask some significant differences which influenced their Asian operations and their relations with overseas rulers. The VOC was at once more representative of the country beyond Amsterdam and less of a private enterprise than its English counterpart. Authority in the new organization was vested in six headquarters located in Amsterdam, Delft, Enkhuizen, Hoorn, and Rotterdam, with Amsterdam providing one half of the investment, Middelburg one quarter, and the other towns each one-sixteenth. The Company was represented by the *Heren XVII* (Seventeen Gentlemen), a board with eight members from Amsterdam, four from the province of Zeeland, and one each from the other towns. The relationship with the Dutch Republic was equally as complex. Its mandate, accorded by the States General, gave the Company quasi-sovereign powers, which included the building of fortresses, the appointment of governors, the stationing of soldiers, and the conclusion of treaties. However, as this autonomy did not cover all aspects of political power, over time many conflicts over jurisdiction arose between the Company and the Dutch Republic.[19] Finally, while fighting and commerce were closely linked and naval service and company service were blurred, the VOC saw itself first and foremost as a trading enterprise and only reluctantly took on a military role in Asian waters.

This combination of mercantile, political, and military power was not matched by the EIC. Begun as a series of individual annual expeditions, the EIC in 1613 organized its first joint-stock capital, but in 1628 went back to a system whereby participating merchants remained in charge of their own capital. The Company's ad hoc character extended to the position of its employees who, unlike the VOC personnel, were paid on a commission basis rather than as salaried servants and who soon acquired the (circumscribed) right of private trade, something that remained strictly prohibited for VOC employees.[20] The organization overseas and the relationship between the Company and the state show similar differences. The VOC set up an Asian network under the supervision of a headquarters in Batavia

---

[19] Leue, "Legal Expansion," 129–58.
[20] Chaudhuri, *English East India Company*, 75–7, 83–4; and Meilink-Roelofsz, "Een vergelijkend onderzoek." 206–7.

(modern Jakarta), to which each individual factory reported. Over time, a complex division of authority developed between the governor-general in Batavia, who was responsible for the Asian operation, and the Heren XVII, who maintained ultimate jurisdiction over the entire commercial enterprise. Following the founding of Batavia in 1609, the VOC set out to build a complex trading network that thrived on intra-Asian trade and made use of permanent capital and a standing merchant fleet to carry goods between Asian ports and from Asia to Europe. The EIC, by contrast, lacked a unified command system in Asia and, instead, relied on a series of regional headquarters, of which the one in Surat in India was to be crucial for the Iranian operation. Nor did it benefit from a similar interactive Asian network. The EIC was more independent of the English crown, yet enjoyed less autonomy. Unable to count on the naval power and the financial means of the state, the EIC had to compete with interlopers who were sanctioned by the authorities at home. It similarly lacked the official war- and peace-making functions accorded to the VOC. Paradoxically, however, the English merchants in some ways found themselves bound to a much stricter governmental policy than the Dutch. The best example of this is the official English ban on bullion exports, a policy that greatly impeded the activities of the EIC once it became clear that the value of the exported English commodities failed to cover Asian imports (even if the state allowed the Company to violate the ban).[21] Its poor capitalization made it especially difficult for the EIC to compete with its Dutch rival. In sum, whereas the VOC exhibited a corporatist structure in a country where shared interests made the state cooperate with merchants, the EIC received a trade monopoly from a state which otherwise did little to stimulate and protect an essentially private enterprise.

The Dutch preceded the English in entering the Persian Gulf: their ships appeared before Hurmuz as early as 1607.[22] They were also the first to show an interest in shipping Iranian raw silk via the Persian Gulf. In 1611 a Dutch merchant named Gilles de la Faille approached the States General to gauge their interest in participating in Iran's silk trade. De la Faille's liaison was Robert Sherley, who a year earlier had visited Spain to encourage the formation of a European anti-Ottoman alliance. However, Dutch skepticism about Sherley's credentials as well as a reluctance to infringe on the monopoly granted to the VOC made this early venture fail.[23]

The entry of the VOC into the Persian Gulf formed part of a broader exploration of the western Indian Ocean and was directed from the port city of Surat in Gujarat, as of 1616 the VOC headquarters for the western Indian Ocean. India then served as a stepping-stone for the exploration of

[21] Chaudhuri, "East India Company and the Export of Treasure," 31, 34, 36.
[22] [Chick], Chronicle, i, 130.
[23] Meilinck-Roelofsz. "Earliest Relations." 5: and Davis. Elizabethans Errant, 234–6.

west Asia including Iran and Arabia. In the context of Dutch intra-Asian trade, Gujarat was to exchange textiles for east Asian spices, while Iran and Arabia were to provide the precious metal needed to purchase those spices.[24] Iranian silk, long known because of the Levant trade, was not initially the main objective of the VOC. The Dutch were rather more keen on silk from China, Asia's largest silk producer, their appetite whetted by the seizure in 1603 of a Portuguese ship loaded with Chinese silk and the profitable sale of the 1,200 bales on board. Known to be of better quality than Iranian silk, Chinese silk sold for at least 50 percent more in Holland and it was therefore expected that China and not Iran would become the focus of scarce company resources.[25] China supplied the Netherlands with silk as of 1621, and in 1624 and 1625, well after the VOC had exported its first Iranian silk, Amsterdam and Batavia still urged their agents to concentrate on Iran only as long as political unrest left the Chinese silk market uncertain.[26] However, as much of its silk was siphoned off by Japan, China never realized the anticipated annual volume of 72,000 pounds.[27] In the end, therefore, the Dutch market was to be supplied with Iranian silk.[28]

The EICs entry into Iran

The English may have trailed the Dutch in their initial appearance in the Persian Gulf, but they beat them in pursuing trade in Iran's interior. Disappointing Indian sales of English broadcloth made the EIC look for alternative markets, and this brought Iran into its purview. In 1615 Surat sent two agents, Richard Steel and John Crowther, to Iran with the task of exploring commercial opportunities. In Isfahan they managed, with the assistance of Robert Sherley, to lay the basis for future English operations by obtaining a *farman* (decree) from Shah 'Abbas which instructed Iranian officials "to kindly receive and entertain the English Frankes or Nation, at what time any of their ships or shipping shall arrive at Jasques, or any other of the Ports in our Kingdome: to conduct them and their merchandise to what place or places they themselves desire: and that you shall see them safely defended about our Coasts, from any other Frank or Franks whatsoever."[29]

Not everyone in the upper echelons of the EIC agreed to this foray into Safavid territory. Court members who also served on the board of the Levant Company were reluctant to sanction a trade link in competition with the overland connection through Anatolia. Some suggested focusing

[24] Coolhaas, *Pieter van den Broecke*, i, 4–5.
[25] Terpstra, *De opkomst*, 137; and Glamann, *Dutch–Asiatic Trade*, 112–13.
[26] Dunlop, *Bronnen*, 121, 134, 136, 172.
[27] Glamann, *Dutch–Asiatic Trade*, 114.
[28] Meilink-Roelofsz, "Earliest Relations," 3.
[29] Purchas, *Hakluytus Posthumus*, iii, 279.

on Bantam or Japan instead. Thomas Roe, who was sent on a mission to
the Mughal court, wished to concentrate on the Red Sea trade. Skeptical
about Iran's stability and viewing commerce in the context of Safavid–
Ottoman enmity, he providentially suspected that once the shah had made
peace with the Porte, he would never allow a diversion of the overland
trade. He was also correct in surmising that trade in Iran would require a
great deal of cash, which, as he foresaw, would not easily come from
England. Moreover, having inferred from talks with a Safavid ambassador
at the court in Agra that Iran's trade was small in volume and conducted
mainly by petty merchants, Roe expressed his doubts about its profitability.
The English, he insisted, "ayme not at gnatts and small flyes, but at a
commerce honorable and equall to two so mighty nations."[30] His suggestion
was that Shah 'Abbas be told that "it will be impossible for us to bear the
charge of transport up of ours and down of his commodities, but that if he
desire to entertain us, that he will be pleased to send his merchants to our
ports, at least to some fit place adjoining, where we may constantly reside
for trade, and not seek it like pedlars."[31]

Surat, disheartened by slow cloth sales in Gujarat and eyeing Iranian silk
made cheap by the Safavid–Ottoman wars, decided to ignore Roe's advice
and in 1616 authorized a first commercial venture, led by Edward Connock.
While the dilapidated appearance of Jask, where Connock and his men
landed later that year, seemed to confirm all of Roe's apprehensions, the
Englishmen, heartened by the courteous reception they enjoyed from the
local governor and anticipating richer rewards in the interior, proceeded to
transport their wares to Isfahan.[32] So sure was Connock in his anticipation
of a lucrative trade that, before he was even received by the shah, he wrote
to London and various Asian factories requesting to have a large supply of
spices and even the entire cargo of the next fleet from England sent to Iran.
Upon arrival in Isfahan, he also began to speak in grandiose terms of
diverting Iran's entire silk trade to the maritime route. The cause of
Connock's excitement, aside from a letter from Sherley he received in
Isfahan,[33] must have been Iranian promises, expressed most notably by
Lalah Beg, the shah's main factor in Isfahan, who spoke of Iran's wish to
weaken the Ottomans and mentioned 3,000 bales as the initial quantity that
might be shipped.[34] Convinced that the shah himself would be willing to
underwrite the deal, Connock set out toward the royal camp on the
Ottoman border. There the English cut a poor figure. To a court that used

[30] Foster, *Embassy of Sir Thomas Roe*, ii, 374, Roe to Robbins, Isfahan, Jan. 17, 1616.
[31] Ferrier, "English View," 185.
[32] Ferrier, "English View," 189–90.
[33] Steensgaard, *Asian Trade Revolution*, 327–8.
[34] Foster, *England's Quest of Eastern Trade*, 301; Chaudhuri, *English East India Company*, 53–4.

panoply to display its power and that measured the importance of visiting embassies by the same criterion, the English must indeed have appeared as "masters of neyther meanes nor money to by us bread ..."[35] Shah 'Abbas nevertheless does not seem to have disabused the English agents of their expectations, for the optimistic reports continued after their first audience. Connock claimed that the Safavid ruler had promised him "1,000, 2,000 or 3,000 bales of silk at reasonable prices," and on credit. In his exuberance he anticipated that "the whole quantity of silk made in these kingdoms, amounting to full one million sterling at 6s. the 16ozs (by my computation) may be henceforth by sea carried and dispersed throughout Christendom and not more through Turcky be transported."[36] Connock promised the shah payments of one-third in money and two thirds in English cloth and Indian commodities.[37]

Connock's hope that European cloth and tin, supplemented with Asian products, would pay for Iranian silk was quickly dashed. London remained cautious, wary as it was of high prices and unsure if the quantities mentioned would find enough demand in England. The agreement Connock made with the shah in mid-1617 was disappointing as well, for it included neither a silk monopoly nor the anticipated silk for credit. What is more, the shah may have promised the English toll exemption during the verbal phase of the negotiations, but the written contract did not exempt them from regular dues. Whereas the English (and Dutch) versions of the agreements are somewhat unclear on this point, the Persian original of the *farman* obtained by Connock indicates that the EIC was expected to pay the *baj* and the 10 percent duty known as the *dah-yik*.[38] This is further confirmed by two of Connock's companions, Barker and Monnox.[39]

Instead of the anticipated "whole quantity of silk made in these kingdoms," the Iranian payment for the goods the English had brought with them consisted of seventy-one bales of silk which were purchased at nearly 50 *tumans* per load.[40] Equally as ominously, the *Bee*, the ship that arrived in Jask in late 1617, failed to carry new capital and merchandise for future

---

[35] Ferrier, "European Diplomacy," 81, fn. 48.

[36] Foster, *Letters Received*, v, 35, 37, Connock, Persian Court to London, Aug. 4, 1617.

[37] Sainsbury, *Calendar of State Papers*, 152, Monox, Isfahan to London, April 18, 1618.

[38] Steensgaard, *Asian Trade Revolution*, 330, claims, on the basis of the Dutch translation of the *farman*, which appears in Dunlop, *Bronnen*, 675, that the English were exempted from paying any customs. Linda Steinmann, "Shah 'Abbas," 138–9, has argued that the Persian original shows beyond a doubt that the English were supposed to pay. She also notes the reference in Foster, *Letters Received*, v, 293, to the payment of the same duty. The fact that the Dutch version had been translated from the Italian makes mistranslation a real possibility. At bottom, it is unlikely that Shah 'Abbas intended to exempt the English from paying customs dues that all merchants were required to pay.

[39] Foster, *Letters Received*, v, 293.

[40] The EIC paid 280 *shahis* per *mann-i shah*. IOR E/3/7/815, Pettus, Isfahan to London, Oct. 28. 1619. fol. 46b.

purchases. Instead, it brought instructions from London to reopen negotiations with the shah.[41]

These negotiations were to be led by Edward Monnox and Thomas Barker, Connock's successors following the latter's death in December 1617. Having reconsidered their reluctance to invest in Iran, the EIC directors were now willing to buy an annual volume of 8,000 bales as part of a strategy designed to redirect Iran's silk trade. Yet Monnox and Barker were hampered by the conditions their superiors attached to continued trade, ranging from the granting of fixed customs rates and set prices for import and export goods, to the establishment of a protected port in the Persian Gulf.[42] Moreover, the negotiators appeared empty-handed in Qazvin in the summer of 1618. It is therefore hardly surprising that they achieved nothing new. The shah refused to buy English wares at anything but market rates. Nor was he prepared to grant the EIC a fortified port at Jask.[43] Ensuing negotiations, finally, confronted the English with the fact that the Safavid ruler had meanwhile instituted a silk export monopoly.

The royal silk export monopoly

Throughout history, government efforts to maximize revenue and control through involvement in production and commerce have often taken the form of trade monopolies of profitable and sensitive commodities.[44] The Byzantines made the purchase of silk a royal monopoly, and Emperor Justinian instituted a virtual state monopoly on silk manufacturing.[45] Shah Jahan, the Mughal contemporary of the Safavid Shah Safi, attempted to monopolize his country's trade in indigo.[46] The Muscovite tsars in the late 1500s controlled the sale of vodka, caviar, and wax, and reserved the right to buy and sell commodities on their own terms.[47] The Song rulers of China sought to administer the production of tea as well as its commerce.[48] Nor were these practices restricted to non-Western states. In contemporary Europe, too, royal or state monopolies were commonplace. In fact, a tendency toward monopolization was the hallmark of the bureaucratic and fiscal state that emerged in the fifteenth and sixteenth century, at which time the very word monopoly became the most frequently used of all economic

---

[41] IOR E/3/6/699, Pettus, Isfahan to London, Sept. 27, 1618; and Steensgaard, *Asian Trade Revolution*, 331.

[42] Foster, *Embassy*, ii, 462, 554–6, Roe's instructions to Barker and Connox in Persia, Feb. 4, 1618, and company instructions for negotiations in Persia.

[43] Steensgaard, *Asian Trade Revolution*, 333.

[44] For the proclivity of the patrimonial state to resort to commodity monopolization, see Weber, *Economy and Society*, ii, 1097–9.

[45] Lopez, "Silk Industry," 9–11; and Pigulewskaja, *Byzanz*, 85.

[46] Van Santen, "Verenigde Oost-Indische Compagnie," 162–7.

[47] Fletcher, "Of the Russe Commonwealth," 167–8.

[48] Gardella, "Qing Administration," 99.

terms.[49] The Portuguese king long held the monopoly of the Asian pepper trade. In 1621 there were allegedly 700 royal monopolies in England.[50]

The prime example of this phenomenon in Safavid Iran is Shah 'Abbas I's export monopoly in raw silk. The commonly accepted date for its establishment is 1619. Aside from the EIC records and Pietro della Valle's travelogue, no foreign source actually identifies this as the commencement of the restriction on the purchase of raw silk. This has led several scholars to argue that the creation of the monopoly antedated the arrival of the EIC. Bushev, following a tendency of Soviet scholars to attribute economic, largely silk-related, motives to Shah 'Abbas's policies, maintains that the shah's interference in the country's silk export goes back to the 1590s, when Gilan and Mazandaran were turned into crown domain.[51] Steinmann, suggesting that the export monopoly may have been in place long before 1619, submits that 'Abbas's initiative harked back to the pacification of the Caspian provinces twenty-five years earlier. She thinks it possible that "'Abbas's silk trading mechanism was firmly in place and working by 1617 but that he was relying mainly on indigenous traders." To her, the "coming of the East India Company's traders in 1617 merely provided an additional outlet for his silk, not a substitute one."[52]

There is no question that Iranian rulers had long interfered in the country's silk production and trade. In Mongol times tax payments from the Caspian provinces had been in silk. After his conquest of Gilan, the Il-Khanid ruler, Öljeitu Khudabandah, gave security of life to its governors on condition that they pay the *kharaj* tax in silk.[53] The same is true for Mazandaran under Timur Lang, who upon subduing the province in 1388 demanded only half of the 10,000 *mann* of silk due to him.[54] The local Kiya'i rulers, too, were in the habit of collecting silk as tax payments.[55] The Aq-quyunlu made considerable efforts to strengthen their hold over the Caspian region and the trade link through Anatolia. They married into the ruling house of Shirvan and on many occasions sent expeditions to get their Caspian vassal dominions to pay outstanding tribute, much of it in silk.[56] 'Uthman Pasha, the Ottoman governor of Shirvan in 1579, took 4 percent on local silk and forced all merchants to purchase it from him.[57] The importance of silk revenue for Shah Tahmasp's treasury, finally, emerges from the words of Arthur Edwards, who noted the shah's likely refusal to buy cloth from the English:

[49] Höffner, *Wirtschaftsethik*, 7–9.
[50] Hill, *Century of Revolution*, 33.
[51] Bushev, *Istoriia posol'stv 1586–1612*, 202.
[52] Steinmann, "Shah 'Abbas," 86.
[53] Natanzi, *Muntakhab al-tavarikh-i mu'ini*, 141.
[54] Shami, *Tarikh-i futuhat*, 295.
[55] Mar'ashi, *Tarikh-i Gilan*, 98, 117, 366, 376.
[56] Woods, *Aqquyunlu*, 147.
[57] Ashurbeiliv. *Gosudarstvo Shirvanshakhov*. 291.

... by report the *Shaugh* neuver tooke cloth into his treasurie all the dayes of his life, and will not now beginne; his whole trade is in raw silke, which he selleth alwayes for money to the Armenians and the Turkes, and such other as vse to buy it ... [58]

While silk designed for domestic manufacture and consumption had thus long been subject to some form of government regulation and supervision, no Iranian ruler prior to Shah 'Abbas ever seems to have instituted an actual export monopoly. The specificity, as well as the date, of its proclamation, emerge unambiguously from the only contemporary Persian-language source that mentions the measure, the recently discovered third volume of the *Afzal al-tavarikh*.[59]

The prevailing geopolitical and commercial circumstances seem crucial for a proper understanding of the timing and the motivation behind the monopoly's proclamation. Among these are increased competition for Iranian silk, the entrenched position of the Julfan merchants on the routes to the Levant, and the state of Safavid–Ottoman relations. The arrival of the English in Iran clearly had a catalytic effect on the shah's initiative. Their willingness to pay good money for Iran's silk in early 1619 prompted the Julfan Armenians to try and preempt changes in their privileged position as Iran's chief silk exporters by approaching the shah, at that moment residing in Farahabad, with rich gifts.[60] 'Abbas, benefiting from a lull in his latest war with the Ottomans, reacted to this move by turning access to the Levant route into a bargaining chip.[61] He is said to have granted the Armenians an audience only on condition that they would not discuss silk exports via Anatolia, pretending that the traditional routes could not be opened because peace with the Ottomans was only feigned and war would surely resume. This, della Valle claims, had made the Armenians willing to pay for the continuation of their privileges. One merchant had told the shah that the Julfans would be happy to pay him 5 *tumans* per load if the roads to the Levant would be opened for their silk exports. Corroborating English sources report that the Armenians had offered to pay either the 5 *tumans* per load, a lump sum of £150,000, or a customs fee equal to 12 d. on every pound of silk "to tollerate theire former free commerce by land."[62] The shah, it was said, was very interested in this proposal and, desirous to gain the 5 *tumans*, was inclined to allow silk to go via Ottoman territory.[63]

It is at this point that the silk export monopoly was instituted. The *Afzal*

---

[58] Morgan and Coote, *Early Voyages*, ii, 411, Fourth voyage made into Persia by M. Arthur Edwards.

[59] Khuzani Isfahani, "Afzal al-tavarikh," fol. 405b.

[60] Della Valle, *Viaggi*, i, 847–8. Della Valle claimed to have received this information from an Armenian arriving from Farahabad.

[61] Silk exports via the Ottoman empire were prohibited as long as the wars lasted. See Foster, *Embassy of Sir Thomas Roe*, 356, Roe, Camp of the Mughal Emperor to London, Nov. 30, 1616.

[62] IOR, E/3/7/815, Pettus, Isfahan to London, Oct. 28, 1619, fol. 46b.

[63] Della Valle, *Viaggi*, i, 847–8.

al-tavarikh gives the text of the decree as follows under the year 1028 (1619):

It is ordered that the viziers and kalantars of every silk-producing province, whatever silk [marginal note: there was in every district should be sold (or bought) for the royal workshops (*sarkar-i khassah-i sharifah*), and anyone who bought or sold one *mann* of silk without their permission should be punished and the merchants should be restrained from buying silk]. On this matter, inviolable orders were written to (the following):

Taqi Mirza Isfahani and Aslan Beg, the viziers of Gilan; Husayn Beg, vizier of Shirvan; Malik Sharif, *kalantar* and Sharif Beg, vizier of Ganja and Qarabagh; Malik Safar Kalantar and the *hakims* of Tabriz and Ardabil, and the places which were thought to trade in silk [?], and it was commanded that not a *mann* of silk should be transacted in those provinces [*mamalik*] without their knowledge; and a *kharvar* of twenty-five *mann-i sang-i Gilan* (each *mann* being 1600 *misqal*), should be brought from the cultivators by fixed arrangement for 30 Tabrizi *tumans*. If the merchants came from Anatolia to buy and (. . . qari?) is sold to them for 46 *tumans* they should have permission; otherwise they should carry it to Anatolia or Europe. Silk from the Gilanat should be consigned to Khajah Lalazar Yahud, whom the shah brought to Farahabad with 1,000 Jewish households from Kakht in Georgia, which was their original home, and who had gained complete distinction in his service, and who himself had 50,000 *tumans* in capital goods (*mayah*). Having given it to the inhabitants of Farahabad who came from Nakhjavan, Ganja, and Zagam [?] and the Jews (Yahud), he should send them to Turkey. While the silk of Shirvan and Qarabagh should be consigned to Khajah Safar and Khajah Nazar Julfa'i the Armenians, who were in Isfahan. It was decreed that, having taken it to Turkey, they should traffic in it. It was decreed with . . . [?] that, having gone to the Dar al-Saltanah of Istanbul he should be the treasurer of the cash raised [from sales]. Having bought the equivalent value of the silk in scarlet and gold [cloth?] and Turkish textiles, he should send it to Muhibb 'Ali Beg Lalah in Isfahan and get a voucher.[64]

European accounts add a few details to this. Barker wrote, "observing this eagerness among buyers, thereby to improve the price thereof and that he might bring the intyre and totall benefitt of the said improvement to his owne coffers hath caused it to be published that all Sylkes made throughout his domynions shall be brought into his Treasuyrie and thence to receive monye from the same by which meanes have made a monopolye thereof and engrossed all into his own possession."[65] Della Valle added that no one was allowed to sell silk to the merchants and that, by decree, silk producers would have to sell to the shah, who, paying in advance, would purchase the silk cheaply, perhaps at half the price for which he sold it to the Julfans. All those who wished to export silk would have to get theirs from the shah at the fixed price. Those merchants who had already bought silk from third

[64] Khuzani Isfahani, "Afzal al-tavarikh," fols. 405b–6a.
[65] Ferrier, "Armenians and the East India Company," 44–5.

parties would be able to export it provided they paid the shah the 5 *tumans* which the Armenians had earlier offered.[66]

Shah 'Abbas next staged a price war between all parties interested in silk. On September 17, 1619, an auction was held to fix the price of silk and to offer it to the highest bidder. Both the Julfan Armenians and the English were summoned to this gathering, as was the representative of the bare-footed Carmelites in Isfahan, because of letters regarding silk that had recently arrived from Spain. All were asked how much they would be willing to pay for the royal silk. The Carmelite Father spoke first, stating that the Spanish agents had no orders to offer a price but only to engage in trade under certain conditions. At first neither the Armenians nor the English were eager to tender their bid. In the end the former outbid the competition by quoting the extremely high price of 50 *tumans* per load, "in order to keep the traffic to themselves," as della Valle noted. The English, whose highest bid had not exceeded 43.2 *tumans*, argued that the Armenians were given an unfair advantage because of the credit extended to them; whereas others would have to come up with cash in advance, the Julfans would only have to pay upon returning from the Levant. When the shah denied that this was true, the English, claiming that in that case the Armenians must be trading at a loss, argued that at the price their competitors were willing to pay it was not worth their while to purchase silk. Assuming that the price offered by the Armenians was merely a ploy to entice them to bid higher, they decided not to take any royal silk that year.[67] Unable to buy on the private market, where no one dared to contravene the shah, the English indeed were left without silk.[68]

Shah 'Abbas in 1619 skillfully exploited an optimal constellation of circumstances to derive maximum benefit from Iran's export trade in raw silk, an objective that is not necessarily at variance with the purpose of the shah's action as reported by several sources: to keep vital revenue from accruing to the Ottomans.[69] Politically, the shah was in an advantageous position. As he had just made peace with the Ottomans, he was free from any pressure to make commercial concessions to the Spanish, whose continued efforts to redirect the silk trade had yielded nothing but empty promises. The recent arrival of new merchants with an interest in silk, combined with the Armenians' eagerness to maintain the status quo, enabled the shah to maximize his profits by manipulating competing parties, access to routes, and silk prices. The decree, finally, had the additional benefit of ensuring that lean years would not interrupt contrac-tual deliveries and thereby the flow of revenue. As an English report noted:

---

[66] Della Valle, *Viaggi*, ii, 58–9.
[67] Ibid.; IOR/E/3/7/815, Isfahan to London, Oct. 28, 1619, fols. 46b–7.
[68] Steensgaard, *Asian Trade Revolution*, 334.
[69] Isfahani, *Khulasat al-siyar*, 39; della Valle, *Viaggi*, i, 696–7.

Shaw 'Abbas by his commands prohibited all men of what nacion soever to buy any silke unles from his hands, and to the ende all should bee collected, and brought into his magazenes, he sent his servants with ready money to all places where silke grewe to buy from the countrey people, the inhabitance of those partts that made itt, at such rates as the owners could afford itt. With this silke thus gained he complied yearlie with the English and Dutch nacions, sould part unto the Jullfaleyne Armenians att 10 tumands the load proffitt which was transported by the way of Aleppo, some hee adventured with them on his proper account and the rest he hoorded upp in his magazenes, providentcie doubtinge silk in some years might faile and then such thus reserved would both satisfie his contracts and sell to his greater profitt.[70]

As this excerpt suggests, the monopoly did not exempt the Safavid court from having to deal with the silk producers according to the rules of the market. According to a Dutch report, producers were wont to sell their silk to merchants at lower prices, but the authorities sought to prevent this by providing them with fixed advance payments for the next harvest.[71] The reference to cash payments is particularly interesting, for the Safavid court would ordinarily do its utmost to avoid having to pay for goods and services in cash, preferring payment in kind or in drafts, *barat*.[72]

Contrary to the above report, it seems that (Iranian) merchants did not have to buy their silk directly from the court but could purchase it privately in the area of production provided they paid a 4-*tuman* fee per load for silk to be processed in Iran itself and 12 *tumans* for silk designed for export.[73] The monopoly was thus little more than a form of additional taxation. While noting that great care was taken that silk was only purchased via the court, VOC director Visnich stated that the Armenian merchants were allowed to buy silk on the spot in Gilan and Mazandaran provided they paid the 12 *tumans* per load in royal dues.[74] Otherwise they had to purchase their silk directly from the shah at 50 *tumans* per load, with the right to pay a few months after delivery. A discount price of 45 to 46 *tumans* was accepted for payment in cash.[75]

Unfortunately, further details about the subsequent working of the monopoly are rather scarce. The very term "monopoly" is misleading in that it implies a system capable of matching intent with implementation. That much silk eluded the control of the court is implied by Visnich's remark that producers were wont to hide silk and to sell it secretly, at the

[70] IOR, E/3/13/1379, Heynes, Isfahan to London, Sept. 26, 1631, fol. 70.
[71] Dunlop, *Bronnen*, 197–9, Visnich, Isfahan to Heren XVII, Aug. 17, 1626; and 234, report on the trade with Gujarat, India and Persia.
[72] Chardin, *Voyages*, v, 414; and Kaempfer, *Am Hofe*, 125.
[73] Steensgaard, *Asian Trade Revolution*, 381.
[74] Ibid. According to the English, the shah's profit was 10 *tumans*. See IOR, E/3/13/1379, Heynes, Isfahan to London, Sept. 26, 1631, fol. 70.
[75] Dunlop, *Bronnen*, 197–9, 234.

risk of confiscation, for export purposes.[76] Equally suggestive are the problems the Dutch had in 1628, when they received only *legia* silk. The *ardas* variety, which was cultivated in Shirvan, had not been delivered in Isfahan due to the "remoteness of the place, the scarcity of pack animals, and the deficient forwarding by officials."[77] Most explicit about the limits of the shah's reach is the testimony of the Dutchman Pelsaert, who in the 1620s visited Iran and India. He claimed that Iranians brought silk to Tatta on the coast of Makran, adding that this had to be done surreptitiously because it was prohibited by the Iranian monarch.[78]

The VOC's entry into Iran

The English may have intended to continue their buyer's strike in 1619, but they soon realized that their position was weak and their power to bring silk prices down minimal. The goods they offered in return were not much in demand in Iran, and the Iranians seemed quite indifferent as to whether they actually bought any silk, even with cash. The EIC thus turned to the Dutch, proposing to cooperate in the Iranian silk trade by dividing the exports to western Europe.[79] Uncertain about the volume and profitability of the trade – by 1620 the English had only been able to export the seventy-two bales they had received in 1617 – and anticipating that even the companies' combined capital would fail to pay for the silk unless supplemented by spices, sugar, and textiles, the Heren XVII decided to wait until more information could be gained.[80]

In 1620, the arrival of an Iberian fleet in the Persian Gulf, presumably sent to safeguard Hurmuz against Iranian and English attack, offered the English an opportunity to improve their standing in Iran. In December of the same year, an English squadron arrived before Jask and managed to defeat the Portuguese forces of Ruy Freire. If the Iranians were impressed by this show of force, they made no public display of it, for nothing changed in the shah's formal attitude toward the EIC. Yet the English

[76] Ibid.
[77] Ibid., 247, Visnich, Isfahan to Heren XVII, Aug. 6, 1628.
[78] Pelsaert, *De geschriften*, 279.
[79] Glamann, *Dutch–Asiatic Trade*, 114–15. This was part of an overall cartel agreement in Asian commerce. Realizing that they would not be able to compete with Dutch financial wherewithal, manpower, and ships, the English in 1611 had approached the Dutch with a proposal to pool resources and cooperate on pricing and purchasing policy. The Dutch agreed to friendly trade but, anxious to maintain their superiority, insisted on a trading monopoly in those regions where they had concluded treaties with local rulers. The agreement, concluded in 1619, upheld the principle of free trade, but bound the two companies to common price fixing and a shared defense strategy against the Portuguese. It lasted until the 1623 incident known as the Amboyna massacre. For the negotiations and the agreement, see Clark and Eysinga, *Les Conférences*.
[80] Dunlop, *Bronnen*, 6–11, Heren XVII to Batavia, March 24 and Oct. 26, 1620; Heren XVII to Surat, May 13, 1620.

performance is likely to have given Shah ʿAbbas the idea that their naval power might help him drive the Portuguese out of Hurmuz. When the latter proceeded to fortify the island of Qishm, strategically located across from Hurmuz, the Safavid ruler had Imam-quli Khan of Shiraz put pressure on the English to help him launch an attack on Hurmuz, threatening the loss of trading facilities if they refused and promising the town of Gombroon and a share in the port's future customs receipts if they complied.[81] The English agreed, turned against Qishm, and bombarded its fortress with their superior forces. On February 11, 1622, the Portuguese garrison of Qishm surrendered, and a few weeks later the Iranians entered the town. On May 1 the Portuguese finally gave up the fortress where they had been holed up.[82]

Pace Steensgaard, who sees the Portuguese defeat as a metaphor for a radical restructuring of trade in all of Asia, the main outcome of the fall of Hurmuz was the transfer of Iran's principal outlet to the Persian Gulf to the port of Gombroon (Gamron in the Dutch sources), henceforth named Bandar ʿAbbas.[83] The victory of the English, moreover, was a Pyrrhic one inasmuch as they failed fully to exploit the favor they had just rendered to the shah. In the 1622–23 season the EIC exported 820 bales of silk.[84] Yet already before the attack on Hurmuz, an economic slump in England which caused new restrictions on bullion exports deprived the EIC of a vital asset in Iran and made shareholders demand immediate dividend, caused London to revise its policy of two years and to decide that trade with Iran should be put on hold until the conclusion of a better contract.[85] Just as this new policy halted the sending of merchandise to Iran, it also led to an abrupt drop in EIC silk purchases. According to the Dutch, the English were only able to export sixty-three bales in 1624–25, and seventy the following season.[86]

It is at this point that the Dutch decided to join the EIC in Iran's silk trade, urged to act by rumors of the English naval assistance to the Iranians and regretful that they had arrived too late with a fleet to join in the Hurmuz venture.[87] By late 1622 Surat Director van den Broecke had decided that it would be desirable to send an agent to Iran, to see if cooperation with the EIC might not be obviated by concluding a separate agreement with the shah.[88] The choice fell on Hubert Visnich, a scion of a textile-dyeing family hailing from the town of Dordrecht, whose expert knowledge of the overland trade from Iran to Aleppo and smattering of

[81] Boxer, "Anglo-Portuguese Rivalry," 73–4.
[82] Steensgaard, *Asian Trade Revolution*, 341–3.
[83] Meilink-Roelofsz, "Structures of Trade," 26; Subrahmanyam, *Portuguese Empire*, 157.
[84] Ferrier, "British–Persian Relations," 347–8.
[85] Ferrier, "European Diplomacy," 85; Chaudhuri, *English East India Company*, 217–18.
[86] Dunlop, *Bronnen*, 139, Visnich, Gamron to Batavia, Feb. 9, 1625.
[87] Terpstra, *De opkomst*, 146.
[88] Dunlop, *Bronnen* 15–16, van den Broecke, Surat to Heren XVII, Jan. 1, 1623.

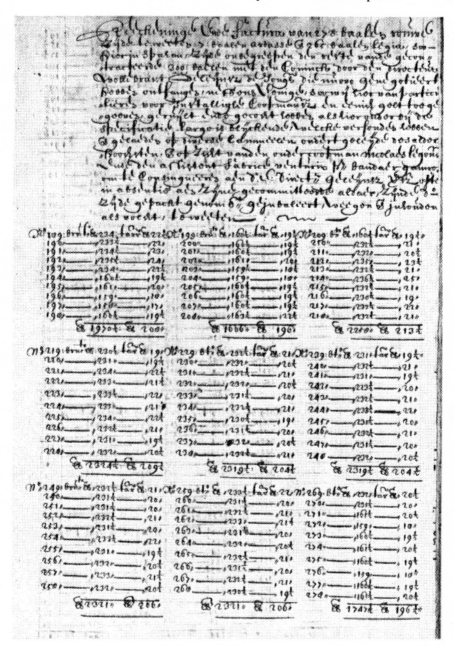

Plate 5 First page of a Dutch silk invoice, concerning a total of 272 bales, 7 *ardas* and 265 *legia*, 1641. In ARA, 1e afd., Coll. Gel. de Jongh 92. Courtesy of Algemeen Rijksarchief, The Hague.

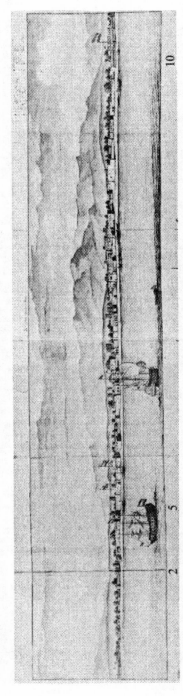

Plate 6 View of Bandar 'Abbas, ca. 1704, drawn by Cornelis de Bruyn. In ARA, 1e afd. 4. Aanw., Aanwinsten 1891, nr. 29. Courtesy of Algemeen Rijksarchief, The Hague. No. 2 is the governor's house, no. 5 the English factory, and no. 10 the Dutch factory.

useful languages such as Italian, Arabic, and Turkish, made him an excellent candidate.[89]

Visnich and his companion Lemmens arrived in Bandar 'Abbas in June 1623, received permission from the governor of Hurmuz to unload the cargo they had brought with them and, with some delay, set out for Isfahan. Upon his arrival in the capital, Visnich was well received by Shah 'Abbas, who asked him why he did not carry any official letters from the state of Holland but did not press the matter when the Dutchman explained that he represented the VOC. Visnich was able to sell his commodities to Mulayim Beg, the royal factor and mint master, and was promised silk in exchange, to be delivered in Isfahan.[90] On November 21, Visnich received his contract. Its provisions were similar to the terms concluded with the EIC six years earlier, in that it gave the VOC the right to conduct trade anywhere in Iran. Other concessions and facilities accorded to the VOC included the right to use Dutch weights and measures, an inviolable factory, cooperation on the part of Iranian officials, jurisdiction with regard to crimes committed within the Dutch community, and the stipulation that goods stolen from the VOC in Iran would have to be returned or paid for by the authorities of the district in which the theft had occurred.[91] The clause on tolls and dues shows the same ambiguity as the EIC contract. Article 3 of the Dutch text exempted the VOC "from paying any duties or tolls on goods and cash imported and exported." All merchandise would be free from any burden, except for the usual duties of the *rahdars* (collectors of road tax)."[92] It is quite possible that the Persian text of this agreement, which has not survived, was analogous to the counterpart of the Persian *farman* granted to the English. While it may have mentioned the payment of dues, these were left unmentioned in the translation, thus leaving room for a retraction of verbal promises. At any rate, the very same clause was to give rise to differences of interpretation for as the long as the VOC remained active in Iranian commerce.

Their late arrival in Iran had done little to place the Dutch at a disadvantage vis-à-vis the English. Shah 'Abbas clearly saw them as leverage with the English, just as the latter had served as a countervailing force against the Portuguese. The pending closure of the Levant route following the outbreak of a new war with the Ottomans must have convinced him of the usefulness of having two trading partners willing to outbid one another for silk that of necessity would be exported via the maritime route.[93] The Dutch also had a helpful mediator in the person of

---

[89] Meilink-Roelofsz, "Earliest Relations," 11–13.
[90] Dunlop, *Bronnen*, 30, Visnich, Isfahan to Heren XVII, Nov. 15, 1623.
[91] For the full text, see Heeres and Stapel, *Corpus diplomaticum*, 183–91.
[92] The full text appears in ibid., 186.
[93] The Levant route was indeed soon interrupted by the Safavid campaign against Baghdad. See Dunlop, *Bronnen*, 149, 153.

Jan Luykassen van Hasselt, a painter who resided at the court and who was on intimate terms with the monarch.[94] Besides, as they themselves surmised, their friendly reception in Isfahan was directly linked to the diminished standing of the EIC.[95]

A cordial welcome did not mean the absence of problems, however. For one, the contract obtained by Visnich remained ambiguous on the status of Imam-quli Khan, the ruler of Fars and the Garmsir, with regard to tolls and taxes in the area under his jurisdiction. Article 22 stipulated that the shah would consent to any rights and privileges granted to the VOC by Imam-quli Khan.[96] Implicitly recognizing the khan's autonomy in the south, including the port of Bandar 'Abbas, the article in effect gave him the right to impose his own duties on the Dutch.

Article 22 immediately gave rise to problems concerning regional jurisdiction. Prior to the agreement with Shah 'Abbas, Imam-quli Khan had issued to the authorities of Lar and Bandar 'Abbas decrees enjoining them to assist the Dutch and not to take any dues, including *rahdari*, from them.[97] In apparent violation of this decree, the governor of Bandar 'Abbas, presumably with a letter from Imam-quli Khan in hand, had demanded the payment of an 11 percent duty on the merchandise that the Dutch were about to transport from Bandar 'Abbas to Isfahan in early 1624. He demanded the same sum retroactively for the wares that had been carried to the capital the previous year. Violating another article, the ban on opening any VOC bales, he had forcibly taken a total of 5,220 *reals of eight*. Following Dutch complaints and monetary inducements, Imam-quli Khan reimbursed them for the entire amount save 400 *reals*, and honored their request for a confirmation of toll freedom as well.[98]

Nor did proceedings in Isfahan go smoothly. Mulayim Beg showed an interest in VOC merchandise and agreed to take spices and cash in exchange for 350 to 360 bales of *ardas* silk at 45 *tumans* per load – a reasonable price, Visnich noted, given that the English paid 50 *tumans*.[99] By the time the goods had been unloaded, however, the royal factor, referring to a fall in the price of spices since the arrival of a number of indigenous ships, refused to commit himself to taking these at anything above market rates. The shah

[94] Vermeulen, "La mission de Jan L. van Hasselt," 133.
[95] Dunlop, *Bronnen*, 45, van den Broecke, Surat to Batavia, March 24, 1624. The English had refused to participate in the attack that the khan of Shiraz decided to carry out against Masqat in the winter of 1622–23, claiming that the Iranians had reneged on their pledge to partition Hurmuz.
[96] For the text, see Heeres and Stapel, *Corpus diplomaticum*, 191.
[97] For the text, see ibid., 184–5.
[98] Dunlop, *Bronnen*, 48–9, resolution Gamron Council, March 31, 1624; 51–2, Visnich, Isfahan to Heren XVII, May 6, 1624; 54, instructions for Granyer, June 1, 1624; 65, Visnich, Isfahan to Heren XVII, Sept. 9, 1624. Visnich was probably right in suspecting the hand of the EIC in the latter incident, for the English were the losing party in an arrangement that exempted the VOC from paying tolls in Bandar 'Abbas.
[99] Ibid., 39–41. Visnich, Isfahan to Batavia, Jan. 18, 1624.

himself invalidated the preliminary written accord between the Dutch and his factor by declaring that no silk should be sold for less than 50 *tumans*. Invoking the ruler's authority, Mulayim Beg made it clear that this point was not negotiable, so that Visnich had no choice but to resign himself to this decision.[100] At the end of that summer the Dutch received their first 400 bales of silk. The price was indeed 50 *tumans* per load but, in an apparent gesture of goodwill, the shah had agreed on a 2 percent discount, reducing the actual price to 49 *tumans*, more than what was anticipated, as Visnich noted, but still 6 *tumans* cheaper than what the EIC was paying for silk that had to be acquired in Gilan itself.[101]

Visnich's version of this episode was soon to be refuted by his colleagues, who claimed that the price increase from 45 to 49 *tumans* had been due to his irregular procedures. Visnich was said to have prepaid the silk with wares and cash at the agreed-on rate of 45 *tumans* in exchange for the promise that the silk would be delivered in Isfahan as soon as possible. The consignment had, however, suffered a significant delay because the authorities of the silk-producing provinces had insisted on valid royal *farmans*, the procurement of which took a considerable time since the shah was in the process of besieging Baghdad. Visnich had thereupon requested the restitution of his money, claiming that, instead of buying more silk, he wished to procure different wares. After receipt of the money, he had furnished the cash to Julfan merchants as an interest-bearing loan. When the silk finally arrived a dispute had arisen between Visnich and Mulayim Beg over the price to be paid. Visnich had been brought before an Iranian court, which had ruled in Mulayim Beg's favor by concluding that Visnich had broken the old contract. He thus had been forced to purchase silk at 50 *tumans*, discounted to 49 *tumans* in return for gifts.[102]

Safavid embassies to Holland and England

Neither the English nor the Dutch ever imagined a reciprocal relationship when they began their commercial activities in Iran. Shah 'Abbas, however, in keeping with his habit of exchanging embassies-cum-trade missions with nations of his choice, following the arrival of the EIC and the VOC in his realm launched an initiative designed to establish precisely such reciprocity. In the winter of 1624–25 the Safavid ruler made preparations to send an ambassador to Holland with the task of concluding an agreement with the

---

[100] Ibid., 59, Visnich, Isfahan to Batavia, July 24, 1624; 140, Visnich, Gamron to Batavia, Feb. 9, 1625.

[101] Ibid., 64, Visnich, Isfahan to Heren XVII, Sept. 9, 1624.

[102] Ibid., 161, Wonderer, Surat to Heren XVII, May 10, 1625; 295 6, report van Hasselt to Coen. Visnich was also accused of trading for his own personal gain and of maintaining a private trade link with Aleppo. To avoid being arrested and brought to justice by the VOC, Visnich in 1630 fled to the Ottoman Empire, where he was executed on suspicion of being a spy.

Dutch States General. In February 1625, Musa Beg, accompanied by two merchants and van Hasselt, set sail on a ship that carried 511 bales of raw silk for Holland, 100 of which on account of the shah, to arrive in Holland one year later.[103]

The retrospective report written by van Hasselt suggests that Shah 'Abbas took his decision even before the arrival of the VOC in Iranian waters. Van Hasselt notes how he had been received by the shah, who had inquired about Holland. Told that the Dutch had been fighting the Spaniards for sixty years and were unrivaled in their trade in spices, the Safavid ruler had extended to them an invitation to participate in his country's trade, promising them fair and honest treatment. Afterwards 'Abbas had decided to send van Hasselt to Holland with letters of credence, and while he was waiting to leave the first Dutch trading mission had arrived.[104]

Van Hasselt's story sounds plausible enough, yet needs to be approached with caution. It was written seven years *post dato* – he claimed that he had written letters to Holland via Aleppo which had never arrived because of English and Portuguese machinations – and smacks of retroactive justification. Visnich is of little help in clarifying the circumstances and the timing of the mission. Defending himself against accusations that he had failed to consult his superiors about it, he later claimed that he had been faced with a fait accompli himself. The shah, he insisted, had one day accosted him and told him that he intended to send an envoy to Holland.[105]

The broader political context explains the motives as well as the timing of Shah 'Abbas's initiative. Having resumed his war with the Ottomans in 1623, the shah had conquered Baghdad and was planning a campaign against Basra as well, and thus had good reason once again to explore Europe's readiness to assist him in his efforts. His preference for dealing with political equals, moreover, explains 'Abbas's insistence on sending an embassy to Holland rather than to Batavia.

All this is clear from the demands and requests Musa Beg submitted while he was in Holland. Not only did he demand that the Dutch help Iran strike a blow at the land-based trade through Ottoman territory by recalling their consuls in the Levant. He also gauged Dutch interest in a common strategy against the Portuguese in Masqat. He further requested that the shah be allowed to transport his wares, including silk, on Dutch ships to Holland, where they were to be sold on his account. The 100 bales of royal silk he brought with him served as a sample of future deliveries.[106]

[103] Coolhaas, *Pieter van den Broecke*, ii, 305–6.
[104] ARA, VOC, 315, van Hasselt to Staten Generaal, June 26, 1630, unfol.
[105] Dunlop, *Bronnen*, 257, Visnich, Isfahan to Heren XVII, Nov. 1, 1628; 268, Heren XVII to Persia, Nov. 27, 1628. See also Vermeulen, "L'ambassade persane de Musa Beg," 145; and Floor, *Avvalin sufara*, 42.
[106] Vermeulen, "L'ambassade persane de Musa Beg," 150–1; Floor, *Avvalin sufara*, 46.

Musa Beg was well received by the authorities in Holland but, not surprisingly, the Heren XVII had little enthusiasm for Shah 'Abbas's commercial initiative. Nor were the Dutch States General pleased to hear a Safavid representative suggest that Holland disrupt its relations with the Ottomans. The Dutch authorities did not look kindly upon any of Shah 'Abbas's requests, and either rejected them outright, pleading a lack of jurisdiction, or reacted with deliberate vagueness. As it happened, Musa Beg soon became a liability and the mission turned into an embarrassing spectacle. Letters sent from Holland complained about his presumptuous behavior, listed his unreasonable complaints about poor treatment followed by threats to leave for England or even for Spain – Holland's enemy – and mentioned his womanizing and excessive drinking. The Heren XVII also grumbled about the cost of the embassy, a reported Dfl. 100,000. In addition, they were unhappy about the silk, which undermined the VOC monopoly on Dutch silk imports, and over the sale of which a dispute arose between the Company and the ambassador. In sum, the Musa Beg mission aroused so many negative feelings that the verdict was that no one in Holland "would be pleased to see Persian ambassadors again."[107]

Musa Beg was thus sent back to Iran, where he arrived – accompanied by Jan Smidt, the new VOC agent in Iran – in early 1629, shortly after the death of Shah 'Abbas. The latter had, before the mission's return, dispatched van Hasselt, who had come back from Holland earlier because of his quarrels with Musa Beg, as his ambassador to Holland. Upon arrival in Surat, his first stop, van Hasselt claimed to be heading for the Netherlands as 'Abbas's permanent representative with the task of facilitating the sending of Iranian wares to Holland under a capitulation-like agreement. Visnich, whose fraudulent practices van Hasselt had exposed to the VOC authorities, tried to make his compatriot suspect in the eyes of their superiors by claiming that van Hasselt also carried credentials for the French King, in order to seek profit for the shah in case the Dutch venture would fail.[108] Whether or not van Hasselt was charged with the latter task, his assignment provides even stronger proof that Shah 'Abbas was serious about reciprocity in the establishment of trade links between Iran and the outside world. In 1631 van Hasselt in fact managed to conclude a treaty with the States General on behalf of the shah, according to which Iranian merchants in Holland received the same rights as Dutch merchants in Iran. The VOC opposed the treaty and was not one of the signing parties. This remarkable document, the only treaty ever concluded between the Dutch Republic and an Asian power to include bilateral rights, was thus never

---

[107] Dunlop, *Bronnen*, 170, Batavia to v/d Broecke, Surat, Aug. 14, 1625; 242, instructions from Heren XVII for ambassador, July 18, 1628.
[108] Vermeulen. "Mission de Jan van Hasselt."

observed by the VOC and, for all intents and purposes, remained a dead letter.[109]

Shah 'Abbas in 1625 dispatched a similar mission to England. It was headed by Naqdi Beg and also included a merchant, Khajah Shahsavar, who carried fifty bales of silk with him. According to Visnich the English, jealous of the "favored treatment" accorded to the Dutch, had asked the shah to send a mission to their country as well. Visnich's claim that the small volume of silk carried by the envoy illustrated the decline of English prestige at the Safavid court was doubtless meant to reassure the authorities in Holland.[110] Ferrier concurs by calling Visnich's reasoning extremely unlikely. Arguing that English policy was "directed towards minimizing their charges, not augmenting them," he points to a more complex set of factors. These include the fact that the shah's campaign against Baghdad had blocked the Levant route and highlighted the maritime route as an alternative, 'Abbas's continued interest in the EIC following the arrival of the Dutch and given the presence of the Portuguese in the Gulf, and his wish to be updated about the situation in England where Robert Sherley had arrived as his envoy two years earlier.[111] In addition, Shah 'Abbas probably intended to gauge the chances of direct silk sales in England.

The problems created by the Naqdi Beg mission matched the imbroglio of the Musa Beg visit to Holland, both with regard to the envoy's behavior in England and the exasperation it provoked among English authorities. English opprobrium concerned not so much Musa Beg's pretensions as the conflict that developed between him and Sherley – both of whom claimed to speak on behalf of the shah – over jurisdiction, and squabbles with Khajah Shahsavar, who denied second rank to the ambassador and claimed to have the sole mandate over the sale of the silk. Problems over the sale of silk led Naqd 'Ali Beg to write scurrilous letters in which he accused the EIC of seizing his silk.[112]

The symmetry between the two embassies even extended to the aftermath: the Naqd 'Ali Beg mission prompted the English crown to send Dodmore Cotton as King James's personal emissary to Iran in the company of the returning Iranian (who committed suicide before reaching Iran for fear of the shah's reaction). Sherley, whose status as official envoy of the shah had remained unexplained, returned to Iran as well. The simultaneous dispatch of three envoys to Iran clearly failed to make a favorable impression on the Iranians. Shah 'Abbas received the two Englishmen in audience in Ashraf

[109] Barendse, "Zijde, zambouqs, zilver," 44. For the text of the treaty, see Heeres, *Corpus diplomaticum*, 246–50. The nature of the treaty is discussed in Alexandrowicz, *Introduction*, 119–24.

[110] Dunlop, *Bronnen*, 142, Visnich, Gamron to Batavia, Feb. 9, 1625; 145, Visnich, Gamron to Heren XVII, Feb. 9, 1625.

[111] Ferrier, "European Diplomacy," 84

[112] Ibid.. 85–9.

and verbally consented to the supply of an annual volume of 10,000 bales in return for cloth, yet they met with little courtesy at the court and failed to achieve anything before they both died in Mazandaran in the summer of 1628.[113]

From commodities to cash

Both the English and the Dutch entered Iran in the hope of exchanging merchandise for silk. The EIC from the outset was forced to pay for part of its silk with cash, however. Though the Iranians had initially allowed the Dutch – purveyors of valuable spices – to pay for their entire silk supply with goods, there was nothing inherent in this privilege, and it was to erode shortly after the VOC's arrival in Iran. Mostly responsible for this was the resumption of Safavid–Ottoman hostilities in 1623. The war may have made Shah ʿAbbas "more tractable,"[114] as the English claimed, enabling them to conclude a new contract which set fixed prices for cloth and tin and resulted in the procurement of 782 bales of silk in 1626.[115] Yet it also exposed the growing impecuniousness of the Safavid treasury, forcing Shah ʿAbbas to pay his troops with money printed on leather during his Baghdad campaign.[116] This naturally motivated the shah to demand cash for his silk. The growing impoverishment of the country at large, meanwhile, made it more difficult for the court to dispose of the import goods it received from the companies. Owing to lack of demand, Dutch and English merchandise often remained in the royal warehouses for years.[117]

Given these problems, it is hardly surprising that the contract the Safavid court offered the VOC in 1626 stipulated new terms of payment. It stated that the shah's factor would take all goods arriving on Dutch ships, provided that one-third of the value would be in gold and silver. In return the court would deliver silk, half *legia*, half *ardas*, at 48 *tumans* for the portion paid for by merchandise and 45 *tumans* for the portion covered by cash. In addition, the contract freed the VOC from the payment of customs and *rahdari* tolls for a period of three years.[118]

This new contract immediately caused controversy. Mulayim Beg complained that the VOC did not remit cash and grumbled about the bad

---

[113] Stodart, *Journal of Robert Stodart*, 23–32; Herbert, *Some Yeares Travel*, 156, 204–8.

[114] Sainsbury, *Calendar of Papers*, 213.

[115] Ferrier, "British–Persian Relations," 69. The Dutch were close in their estimate of between 750 and 850 bales. See Dunlop, *Bronnen*, 139, 180, 233, 269, 277. Visnich, however, was wide of the mark with his claim that the EIC bought 1,500 to 1,600 bales in 1627. See ibid., 218, Visnich, Isfahan to Heren XVII, Nov. 18, 1627.

[116] Arakʿel Davrizhetsʿi, *Girkʾ patmutʾeantsʾ*, trans. in Brosset, *Collection*, ii, 26–7.

[117] Dunlop, *Bronnen*, 234, report on the trade of Gujarat, India, and Persia.

[118] Ibid., 184–5, contract between Visnich and Mulayim Beg, April 23, 1626. This implies that the Dutch themselves were uncertain that their toll freedom was automatically included in their contract of 1623. Steensgaard, *Asian Trade Revolution*, 382, doubts that the VOC was held to supply cash.

quality of the sugar and the diminished market value of Dutch spices.[119] He also claimed that the Dutch failed to live up to the contract by not supplying sufficient quantities of sugar, spices, and tin.[120] Visnich, in turn, denied that the VOC was obliged to deliver the amounts indicated by Mulayim Beg, reminding the factor that the contract allowed the VOC to sell whatever was supplied by its ships at prices that had been established beforehand, and that in exchange the Company was to receive silk at 48 *tumans*. According to him, it was the Iranians who had failed to abide by the contract by not delivering half in Shirvani silk, adding that the price the VOC paid was higher than what it was currently sold for to the Armenian merchants. For two consecutive years Visnich was forced to seek recourse with the shah, traveling to Sultaniya in 1627 and to Mazandaran the next year, in order to commission silk and to secure contractual terms. On both occasions the shah, apparently in return for a monetary gift, ordered the authorities in Gilan to earmark silk for the Dutch, while issuing a *raqam* that exhorted Mulayim Beg to purchase VOC commodities at prices as arranged the year before and to supply them with silk upon its arrival in Isfahan.[121] In spite of these royal favors, it was clear that the VOC would have to comply with the one-third payment in cash, or be left with merchandise – a very costly option. The Heren XVII had long cautioned their agents in Iran not to fall into the English trap of paying for silk with cash. Batavia, too, calculating the relative profitability in Europe of goods bought in Surat and silk purchased in Iran, was loath to see any cash go to Iran. Yet, faced with the above dilemma and urged by Visnich to make sure that one-third of the remitted wares were *in specie*,[122] the VOC directors grudgingly agreed to send cash to Bandar 'Abbas, so that the fleet that in 1628 set out to provide Surat and Iran with merchandise also carried Dfl. 100,000 for Iran. The amount, far less than one-third of the cargo's total value of Dfl. 816,000, reflected the optimism with which the VOC dispatched Jan Smidt on the same ship. Ordered to negotiate the extension of the 1623 agreement by three to six years, Smidt was to make the Iranians accept far less than the one-third in cash.[123] Smidt, however, never had a chance to discuss these issues with the shah, for upon arriving in Bandar 'Abbas in February 1629, he was informed of the ruler's death.

---

[119] Dunlop, *Bronnen*, 228–9, 232, 251, 258–9. The VOC in 1628 supplied a mere 3,000 *tumans* against goods totaling 17,153 *tumans*.

[120] Ibid., 260–1, trans. request Mulayim Beg to Visnich, Nov. 1628.

[121] Ibid., 215, 218, 221–2.

[122] Ibid., 222, 229, 266.

[123] Smidt also was to convey Dutch readiness to lend assistance against the Portuguese and the Spanish, though not against the Ottomans. In addition, he was to prevent the Safavid court from sending another embassy to Holland. See Vermeulen, "L'ambassade néerlandaise de Jan Smit," 157–8; and Dunlop, *Bronnen*, 240–3.

Conclusion

The optimism with which the EIC entered the Iranian market in 1616 was short-lived. In 1618 the English called Iran "miserably poor of money with little trade in itself," adding that "this country [would] not vend as much as expected."[124] Though they briefly entertained hopes of appropriating and diverting Iran's entire silk export, their long-term experience confirmed their first impressions. As for the Dutch, they entered the Iranian silk market for fear that neglecting the Persian Gulf would give their main competitors the upper hand rather than because of an inherent preference for Iranian silk, which was known to be neither the cheapest nor the best available.

Though their operations from the outset were fraught with problems, the European merchants received a cordial welcome from Shah 'Abbas, who appreciated them as commercial and strategic assets. By extending the range of possible outlets for silk, he acquired a powerful weapon in the struggle against his archenemies, the Ottomans, and by stimulating the Persian Gulf trade, he secured an enhanced inflow of a scarce commodity, cash, into his coffers. To lure the English and the Dutch Shah 'Abbas may initially have shown himself more willing to grant concessions in the form of toll and customs reductions than he was fundamentally prepared to concede. He then used the intensified outside interest in Iranian silk to maximize the revenue derived from its trade by decreeing a royal export monopoly. The culmination of a long process of state intervention in matters of silk, Shah 'Abbas's initiative was brilliant in its strategy and timing. It forced the Julfan Armenians to pay an additional tax on silk they bought in the Caspian provinces, and made the newly arrived Westerners, who were unable to penetrate the area of production, accept above market prices for Iranian silk.

As long as the Dutch and English were able to exchange silk for merchandise, dealing with the shah had distinct advantages for them. The price they paid was high, but its stability cushioned the foreign merchants against market fluctuations. Equally as importantly, they sold their goods at relatively high prices as well and were not responsible for the cost and risks involved in distributing them across towns and regions according to projected absorption capacity. As one VOC agent acknowledged, the Dutch sold their wares in exchange for silk at a higher price than the "petty merchants" would be able to command for their merchandise, which made for a "very good and profitable trade for the Company." In his estimation the shah was able to sell their goods three times as fast as they would be able to.[125]

---

[124] Sainsbury, *Calendar of State Papers*, 199.
[125] Dunlop, *Bronnen*, 234, report on the trade of Gujarat, India and Persia.

The Dutch and English soon realized that the chances of establishing a political power base in Iran were limited. Elsewhere in Asia fragmented influence enabled both companies to gain authority, even dominion, in addition to commercial profit. In the shah's realm such aspirations would prove illusory. More than anywhere in Asia other than Japan and China, Westerners were forced to abide by local customs and to accept terms of trade dictated by the local authorities. The first decade of their presence in Iran taught the VOC and EIC agents that success in creating trading monopolies in places such as the East Indies and Ceylon was not to be replicated in Iran. Iran's rulers were too strongly aware of the competitive nature of the outside search for silk; in addition Safavid Iran had a centralized government whose effective power may not have been equally strong throughout the realm but whose jurisdiction was nowhere seriously contested. The Safavid authorities also proved to be astute negotiators, a fact with which the company agents would be confronted for as long as they operated on Iranian soil.

CHAPTER 5

The complications of privatization: from the abolition of the silk export monopoly to the peace of Zuhab, 1629–1639

The accession of Shah 'Abbas's grandson Shah Safi in early 1629 fore-shadowed significant changes in the political structure as well as the economic management of the Safavid state. The enthronement of the new monarch, who at the time was only seventeen years of age, took place in haste, no doubt in order to pre-empt various rival claims to the throne.[1] Beyond the customary panoply, the ceremony was accompanied by a series of magnanimous gestures to societal groups in the form of the payment of salaries in arrears, tax remissions, and grants. One contemporary chronicle insists that, within days after the accession, a sum of 200,000 *tumans* was distributed among the various courtiers, *qurchis* (tribal guards), *ghulams*, and other servants. The same source also claims that Imam-quli Khan, the powerful ruler of Fars, received the entire annual tax obligation of that province, in the amount of some 60,000 *tumans*, as a gift. In sum, the chronicler notes, the new ruler did not reject anyone's request in his liberality, and "no refusal passed his lips."[2]

Included in this outpouring of royal largesse was the cancellation of the silk export monopoly. Safavid chroniclers mention the abolition in passing; one refers to it in conjunction with other economic measures taken immediately after the inauguration. Among those was Shah Safi's decision to cancel his grandfather's project of conducting the waters of the Kurang (Karun) river to Isfahan as part of the city's planning project.[3] Another offers a causal framework by noting the harmful practices that had crept into the practice of taking the silk from the producers and supplying it to the merchants.[4] Later Safavid histories, linking the measure to royal

---

[1] Isfahani, *Khulasat al-siyar*, 33; Iskandar Munshi and Valah Isfahani, *Zayl-i tarikh*, 7.

[2] Isfahani, *Khulasat al-siyar*, 41–2. In Qazvini, *Fava'id al-Safaviyah*, 48, and Shirazi, "Tarikh-i Tahmaspiyah," fol. 117, which are not contemporary accounts, the sum disbursed in the first year of Shah Safi's reign has swollen to a fantastic 500,000 *tumans*.

[3] Isfahani, *Khulasat al-siyar*, 39.

[4] Iskandar Munshi and Valah Isfahani, *Zayl-i tarikh*, 13. See also Qazvini, *Fava'id al-Safaviyah*, 48.

benevolence, insist that the freedom to sell silk was designed to improve the condition of merchants, peasants, and other subjects of the shah.[5]

The coincidence of Shah Safi's enthronement and these changes is hardly fortuitous, though it would be naive to take Safavid annals at face value and ascribe them just to the shah's goodwill. As the Russian scholar Pavlova has argued, the events must be seen as a partial reversal of Shah 'Abbas's measures and as a sign that powerful societal groups took advantage of the shah's death to bring about changes in the state's political management and economic organization.[6] The *ghulams*, and especially the Armenians, who by that time held many high functions in the administration, including the top positions in the silk-producing regions, must be counted among these. The role of Yusuf Aqa, a courtier of great influence since the days of Shah 'Abbas who served as head of the secret royal council and master of the *ghulams* of the royal harem, may have been pivotal here. Various lines connected Yusuf Aqa to silk, the regions where it was cultivated, and the merchants who dealt in it. A relative of his, Qazaq Khan Charkas, was *beglerbeg*, governor, of Shirvan at the time. One of his intimates, Manuchihr Khan, administered Gaskar.[7] His own appointment in 1629 as *mirshikar-bashi* (master of the hunt) tied him directly to the Julfans.[8] In his capacity as supervisor of Isfahan's Armenian community, the *mirshikar-bashi* acted as their liaison with the court and carried their requests and grievances to the shah.[9] And it was the Armenian merchants who stood to gain the most from a diminished role for the state in trade, no doubt preferring unfettered commerce to a relationship with the court that offered as many restrictions as privileges. The abolition of the silk export monopoly indeed appears related to the influence the Armenians managed to exert on the new administration. The EIC factors, posing the rhetorical question of why, in the face of lost revenue, the new shah would not prolong his grandfather's monopoly, suggest as much in their answer:

The facion of Jullfalleynes Armenians and other merchants of Guyland and Sherwan, whoe have there trade to Alleppo by their extreame bribes to his Ducks, Nobles and Ministers preventeth him, who have alsoe there factors in those partts, to buy and sell yearly to there most advantage, regardinge more there one particular proffitt then there King's honor or benefitt of their Common weale.[10]

---

[5] Astarabadi, *Tarikh-i sultani*, 236; Shirazi, "Tarikh-i Tahmaspiyah," fol. 117.

[6] Pavlova, "Maloivestniy istochnik," 100.

[7] Vali Qazvini, "Khuld-i barin," fol. 53.

[8] Isfahani, *Khulasat al-siyar*, 47.

[9] ARA, VOC 1379, report Casembroot to Heren XVII, Nov. 25, 1682, fol. 2735. In 1632 Yusuf Aqa fell out of favor to become a victim of Safi's bloody purges. Qazaq Khan and Manuchihr Khan were deposed and imprisoned. Their death did not, however, end the Armenian hold over the positions they had held. Khusraw Sultan Armani succeeded Qujjah Beg, who in 1631 had taken over from Yusuf Aqa as *mirshikar-bashi*, Amir Beg Armani became *hakim* of Gaskar, and Farrukh Khan succeeded as governor of Shirvan.

[10] IOR E/3/13/1379, Heynes and Gibson, Isfahan to London, Sept. 26, 1631, fol. 70.

We know that the Julfans were willing to lavish funds on causes they deemed important – as they did when they paid Shah Safi 1,000 *tumans* to have rescinded an annual 100-*tuman* tax that Shah 'Abbas had imposed on the prelate of Echmenadzin.[11] The *kalantar* of Julfa, Khajah Nazar, was the second person to greet Shah Safi during the accession ceremony, depositing 150 *tumans* in gold coins at his feet.[12] It may be assumed that the Armenian businessmen offered the new monarch and his entourage a substantial amount of money beyond this ceremonial sum to have the commercial restriction abolished, as they had (unsuccessfully) attempted to do under Shah 'Abbas I. Yusuf Aqa would have been among those who benefited from any monetary gain made during and immediately following the episode, for when he was executed in 1632 the exorbitant sum of 450,000 *tumans* is said to have been found in his possession.[13]

The Gilan uprising

If the haste with which the governing elite proceeded to enthrone Shah Safi reflected fears of instability, an initially weak performance by the new incumbent did little to allay anxieties. Within a few months of his accession, the young shah was already said to be given to drinking. Courtiers, released from the grip of the strong-willed Shah 'Abbas, openly engaged in disputes in the presence of the new monarch, and rumor had it that chaos reigned in governmental circles.[14] Nor were the emerging divisions limited to the capital. The power vacuum caused by the transition of power and the monarch's feeble appearance inevitably unleashed the country's centrifugal forces. Many refused to recognize the decrees that Shah 'Abbas had issued and autonomous tendencies were visible everywhere. VOC officials experienced this when *rahdars* south of Isfahan forcibly took two bales of silk from a caravan transporting their goods to the coast, declaring that they did not acknowledge decrees issued by the former shah and that the territory now belonged to their leader, Zaman Beg.[15]

In a further manifestation of these inauspicious beginnings, within a year of Safi's accession insurrections broke out in various border areas. While Uzbeks raided the northeast, the severed heads of rebels were brought to Isfahan from Qandahar, the border city with the Mughal state. In the Persian Gulf the Portuguese attacked and plundered the town of Qishm, the main city on the eponymous island.[16] In Qazvin the regime was faced with a

---

[11] Arak'el Davrizhets'i, *Girk patmut'eants'*, trans. in Brosset, *Collection*, i, 419–20.
[12] Dunlop, *Bronnen*, 284, Stick, Isfahan to Visnich, Gamron, Feb. 3, 1630.
[13] Ibid., 422, Overschie, Isfahan to Heren XVII, May 8, 1633.
[14] Ibid., 747, diary Jan Smidt, July 26, 1628–June 16, 1630; and IOR E/3/13/1379, Heynes, Isfahan to London, Sept. 26, 1631, fol. 73b.
[15] Dunlop, *Bronnen*, 329, Mibaise, Gamron to Batavia, March 5, 1630.
[16] Ibid., 742, 750, 757, diary Smidt.

religious revolt led by Darvish Riza, a self-styled claimant to mahdihood.[17] The gravest threat, meanwhile, loomed on the western frontier, where the Ottomans invaded Safavid territory, moving to recapture Baghdad, which had been in Safavid hands since 1623. The prevailing discord in Safavid court circles manifested itself most clearly in the equivocal official response to this last threat: while some advocated a swift military operation, most members of the inner court, including the shah himself, showed themselves reluctant to take action.[18]

Part of the same response to the void caused by the death of Shah 'Abbas, and most significant for the availability of silk, was the rebellion that broke out in Gilan in the same year. In part a messianic movement, in part an attempt to regain autonomy, the uprising was above all a revolt against the heavy tax burden imposed since Gilan had been converted to crown land – one chronicler speaks of the hardship suffered by the population during seventeen years of rule by various viziers[19] – and it attracted thousands from among the population of the Caspian provinces.[20] The movement's leader was one Kalanjar Sultan, a descendant of the formerly ruling Kiya'i dynasty who took the name of 'Adil Shah and was called Gharib Shah by his opponents. Having been proclaimed ruler of Gilan, he set out from the town of Lashtah-Nisha and managed to capture the region's two central cities of Rasht and Lahijan and the territory in between, plundering and killing the population and doing great damage to the silk cultivation. From Gilan the revolt spread to Mazandaran.[21] The rebels are said to have broken open all the shah's warehouses and sold off the silk stored in them. Of the estimated 300 *kharvari* of royal silk in storage in Gilan, 200 were reportedly destroyed or carried off.[22] Nor were locals the only victims. Ten Russian merchants who happened to be in Gilan at the time of the revolt are said to have lost all their belongings, valued at some 15,000 *tumans*, to robbers.[23] The *Tarikh-i Gilan* mentions 300,000 *tumans* as the total damage done to the inhabitants of Gilan.[24] The shah, realizing the gravity of the situation, did react to this challenge which, after all, occurred in one of Iran's most profitable regions, and charged several provincial governors with the task of putting an end to the uprising. This was done in

[17] For a discussion of this revolt, see Babayan, "Waning of the Qizilbash," 148ff.

[18] Dunlop, *Bronnen*, 748–9, diary Smidt.

[19] Fumani, *Tarikh-i Gilan*, 261.

[20] Their number is variously given as 14,000 and 30,000. See Iskandar Munshi and Valah Isfahani, *Zayl-i tarikh*, 15; and Petrushevskii, "Narodnoe vosstanie," 230.

[21] Mar'ashi, *Tarikh-i khandan*, 312–13.

[22] Dunlop, *Bronnen*, 299, Visnich, Isfahan to Heren XVII, July 17, 1629; and 329, Mibaise, Gamron to Batavia, March 5, 1630; Fumani, *Tarikh-i Gilan*, 265; IOR E/3/12/1317, Burt, four days from Baghdad, to London, Oct. 6, 1630, fol. 151.

[23] When they appeared in Isfahan, they were reimbursed by the shah. IOR, E/3/12, Burt, four days from Baghdad, to London., Oct. 6, 1630, fol. 151; Dunlop, *Bronnen*, 306, Visnich, Isfahan to Heren XVII, Sept. 26, 1629; and Isfahani, *Khulasat al-siyar*, 51.

[24] Fumani. *Tarikh-i Gilan*. 265.

May of 1629; Gharib Shah was brought to Isfahan and executed in the city's main square on June 10, 1629. Of his followers 2,000 similarly paid with their lives.[25]

The destruction caused by the Gilan revolt naturally made itself felt in the availability of silk, especially since it came on the heels of the reported loss of all silk stored in the royal warehouses in the last year of Shah 'Abbas's reign, when Georgian rebels had seized 3,000 bales and burned an even greater amount deposited in Shirvan.[26] The loss had a devastating impact on the royal treasury and also affected the operations of the VOC and EIC. In the fall of 1629 it initially looked as if no silk whatsoever could be procured, despite the fact that the Dutch were willing to sell commodities to the value of 900 bales. Only with great effort did Mulayim Beg manage to have silk delivered from the north later in the year, so that the Dutch still managed to garner 279 bales, 233 of which came from the government.[27] The English fared worse, for they were told that the shah could not possibly comply with the existing contract and that only one-third of the quantity desired by them would be available.[28] Contrary to expectations, however, silk prices were low, either because of the amount of silk looted and sold off by the rebels or because the Ottoman threat to the western border lands and road insecurity made the Julfans wary of purchasing silk.[29] Once hostilities broke out and the Ottomans advanced toward Hamadan, the main outlet to the Levantine ports temporarily became blocked altogether.[30]

Circumventing the shah: the perils of private purchasing

The loosening of state control over silk benefited Iran's Armenian merchants far more than the foreign merchants. After all, nothing in the new situation absolved the Dutch and English companies from their obligation to abide by arrangements made with the shah. In fact, as the information on silk prices in 1629 illustrates, the relaxation of government strictures increased rather than alleviated their dependence on the court. Low sale prices would prompt private merchants to purchase most of the available silk, leaving the government with little to pass on to the foreign merchants. At times when prices were high, on the other hand, it would be tempting for the shah to keep supplies to the maritime merchants low as well, in the hope of selling large quantities on the private market. It was only if the price settled on a medium level that the Dutch and English could expect to get a

[25] Dunlop, *Bronnen*, 329, Mibaise, Gamron to Batavia, March 5, 1629; [Chick], *Chronicle*, i, 307; Olearius, *Vermehrte newe Beschreibung*, 545–6.
[26] IOR, E/3/13/1379, Heynes, Isfahan to London, Sept. 26, 1631, fol. 71.
[27] Dunlop, *Bronnen*, 329, Mibaise, Gamron to Batavia, March 5, 1630.
[28] IOR, E/3/12, Burt, four days from Baghdad, to London, Oct. 6, 1630, fols. 151–2.
[29] Dunlop, *Bronnen*, 306, Visnich, Isfahan, to Heren XVII Sept. 26, 1629.
[30] Ibid., 345, del Court, Isfahan to Heren XVII, Aug. 6, 1630; and 351, idem, Dec. 20, 1630; and ARA, VOC 1109, de Leeuw aboard *Utrecht*, Aug. 10, 1632, fol. 72.

full delivery from a court able to make purchases in the north and to sell its silk at a sufficiently large profit to the Europeans.

The political changes under Shah Safi further contributed to the companies' growing dependence on Isfahan. Safi's weakness and the attendant disarray in palace circles proved to be temporary: within a few years the new monarch managed to consolidate his power base by eliminating all of his existing and potential rivals and opponents, dismissing them, blinding them or, more often, having them executed.[31] Zaynab Bigum, Shah 'Abbas's aunt and a good example of the formidable power females wielded at the Safavid court, was expelled from the royal harem. 'Ali Beg, who had been the most influential courtier in the later reign of Shah 'Abbas, fell out of favor and was sent on a diplomatic mission to India. Court merchant Mulayim Beg became embroiled in financial scandal and saw his status dwindle until he ceased to play a role in the management of silk.[32] The army's commander-in-chief (sipahsalar) Zaynal Khan Shamlu, the qurchiba-shis 'Isa Khan and Chirag Khan Zahidi, the governor of Khurasan Muhammad Khan, and the grand vizier, Mirza Abu Talib Khan Urdubadi, were all murdered between 1630 and 1634. Most importantly for the European merchants, Imam-quli Khan, the powerful ruler of Fars, found himself in disagreement with Shah Safi's new favorites and became marginalized, until he too was executed at the ruler's orders.[33]

However much these purges concentrated power in the hands of the shah, they did not coalesce in the creation of a clearly defined power center. The firm hand of Shah 'Abbas gone, the governing elite under his successors was to be riven by fierce factionalism and Shah Safi, the first Safavid ruler to be brought up in the harem, was never able to rise above the fray. Even allowing for an idealized image of Shah 'Abbas I, the Safavid state under Shah Safi does seem to have lost some of its resolve and integrity. The effects of this on the management of silk are visible in various ways. Contrary to Shah 'Abbas's habit, the new ruler failed to have silk in storage but made contracts only on the basis of future harvests. Royal orders concerning silk deliveries were routinely ignored by those responsible for carrying them out. The Dutch claimed, moreover, that the demand for gifts had been much less under the old ruler, when it had "not been necessary to

---

[31] Iskandar Munshi and Valah Isfahani, Zayl-i tarikh, 90; Isfahani, Khulasat al-siyar, 110; Dunlop, Bronnen, 422–3, Overschie, Isfahan to Heren XVII, May 8, 1633. See also Olearius, Vermehrte newe Beschreibung, 654–62; and, for a modern study, Falsafi, "Dastha-yi khun-alud."

[32] IOR/E/3/13/1317, Burt, four days from Baghdad, to London, Oct. 6, 1630, fol. 151b; and ARA, VOC 1106, del Court, Isfahan, to Heren XVII, Nov. 3, 1632, unfol. Mulayim Beg became implicated in an embezzlement scheme that is said to have netted him the (implausibly high) sum of 300,000 tumans. See Vali Qazvini, "Khuld-i barin," fol. 76a.

[33] For a vivid description of these murders, see ARA, VOC 1106, Overschie, Isfahan to Heren XVII, May 8, 1633, unfol.

offer considerable presents to high officials."[34] Shah Safi himself, perhaps influenced by what has been called the "xenophobic" party at the court, also seemed less interested in foreign relations, including trade relations, than his grandfather had been.[35] In any case more preoccupied with an impending war with the Ottomans than with the need to renew commercial contracts with foreigners, the new ruler following his enthronement moved toward Hamadan to meet the advancing Ottoman army.

Among the first to experience the attendant changes was the new VOC factor Antonio del Court, whose task it was to improve relations with the Safavid court following the Visnich debacle. The backdrop to this initiative was a 60 percent profit on Iranian silk in Holland in 1629, a margin deemed sufficiently lucrative by the Heren XVII to encourage Batavia to order 1,200 bales a year.[36] Del Court arrived in Iran in early 1630, eager to renew the 1623 contract and all privileges, including the freedom from customs and road tolls, that had lapsed with the death of Shah 'Abbas, and to solve the problems that had arisen over Visnich's misconduct. Informed that EIC director Burt was also preparing to visit the royal camp, and worried at the rumor that the English had already been promised a share in the toll on Dutch goods, del Court decided to follow the court toward Hamadan.[37]

Though del Court achieved no formal renewal of the 1623 contract – mostly because Mulayim Beg claimed 3,000 *tumans* in indemnification for the damage done by Visnich – he did receive a royal *farman* that confirmed the Dutch freedom to trade as well as their exemption from road tolls. Yet contrary to del Court's reading of it, this *farman* did *not* explicitly reiterate the exemption from tolls and fees, much less offer the VOC more advantages than the old contract.[38] As for silk purchases, unsafe roads and the threat of war had left the royal warehouses overstocked with goods and the shah woefully short on cash, and his silk supply therefore fell far short of the 1,200 projected bales. Fluctuating market prices, moreover, limited the feasibility of private deals. Shipping problems and possibly a silkworm disease meant that no Iranian silk was included in the cargo of the fleet that reached Holland in 1632.[39] Del Court also had to pay dearly with gifts and bribes, mostly, as he put it, because courtiers had a free hand with a shah

[34] Dunlop, *Bronnen*, 475, v/d Trille, aboard *Bueren*, to Batavia, June 1634.
[35] The existence of a xenophobic faction at the Safavid court, noted by Ferrier, "European Diplomacy"; and Stevens, "Robert Sherley," 122, is confirmed in the VOC records. See Dunlop, *Bronnen*, 746–7, diary Smidt.
[36] Ibid., 303, Heren XVII to Batavia, Aug. 28, 1629.
[37] Ibid., 345, del Court, Isfahan, to Heren XVII, Aug. 3, 1630.
[38] Ibid., 359; and 367, del Court, Gamron, to Heren XVII, March 27, 1631. The 1623 contract may or may not have contained such freedom. The *farman* is reproduced in Heeres, *Corpus diplomaticum*, 254–6, where its date is erroneously given as 1629.
[39] Dunlop, *Bronnen*, 384, Heren XVII to Batavia, April 18, 1632. For the silkworm disease, see IOR, E/3/13/1379, Heynes, Isfahan to London, Sept. 26, 1631, fol. 71.

who had turned hunting into his favorite pastime.[40] Even more disturbing to the Heren XVII was the 7:3 cash-to-merchandise ratio of the contract that del Court signed in 1632. In his defense, del Court pointed to his limited leverage. If the VOC refused to buy silk, he noted, the shah would sell it to the English, who were eager to buy anything offered to them.[41] Dissatisfied with his performance, his superiors next relieved del Court of his function and appointed Nicolaes Overschie in his place.

Overschie, who arrived in Iran in early 1633, was supposed to restore the exchange of silk for commodities, to negotiate a substantial quantity of silk and drastically to reduce the cost of Dutch operations in Iran. Upon his arrival in Isfahan, Overschie found few bales in the VOC warehouse. Yet, with the EIC officials temporarily absent, he anticipated being able to buy silk at $41\frac{1}{2}$ *tumans* per load. Trade prospects looked bright, he noted, since the silk harvest was reportedly fine and the new shah, having completed his purges, was in good spirits.[42]

These rosy prognostications failed to materialize as expected. It is true that Overschie was promised better treatment for the Dutch. The Armenian Khajah Qasim, the former factor of Imam-quli Khan, was appointed to supervise the VOC's silk purchases and to look into Dutch grievances. Overschie also managed to get Shah Safi to confirm Dutch freedom from customs and *rahdari*, and under his supervision the VOC in 1634 managed to collect a total of 870 bales of silk. He failed, however, to secure a more regular long-term supply and proved unable to get the court to procure the total amount desired by the Dutch. Nor did he manage to get the surcharge abolished that had meanwhile been imposed on privately purchased silk.[43]

How to pay for silk became Overschie's most intractable problem, the more so because it was intertwined with the question of how to secure a timely supply. Isfahan's repeated failure to deliver the silk it was contractually obliged to hand over to the Dutch stemmed from the very same problem – a shortage of cash needed to make purchases – that also made the Safavids demand current coin from foreigners interested in silk. This demand had long rendered the Dutch ideal of simply exchanging silk for spices unattainable. The VOC agents in Iran therefore received strict orders to purchase their silk with the proceeds of import goods, but this ran into practical obstacles. The merchandise either did not arrive according to schedule, did not fetch the anticipated price, or remained unsold because of oversupply. By 1635 a shortage of money due to the closure of the

---

[40] Dunlop, *Bronnen*, 396, del Court, Isfahan to Batavia, Nov. 3, 1632; and 411, instructions Lucassen for Overschie, March 17, 1633. Del Court in two years spent Dfl. 31,077 on gifts and bribes. See ibid., 435.

[41] Ibid., 329, Mibaise, Gamron to Batavia, March 5, 1630.

[42] Ibid., 420, 424, Overschie, Isfahan to Heren XVII, May 8, 1633.

[43] Ibid., 426–7, Overschie, Qazvin to Batavia, June 30, 1633; 469, Overschie, Gamron to Batavia, March 28, 1634; 527, Overschie, Gamron to Batavia, March 15, 1635.

Anatolian route even depressed the price of some spices, which normally had no problem finding a market.[44] The Dutch thus had no choice but to take out interest-bearing loans, something to which the Heren XVII gave their grudging approval in 1633.[45]

Faced with these problems and officially freed from the fetters of the export monopoly, the VOC in the early 1630s began to explore the possibility of increasing its control over sales and distribution by circumventing the court altogether. Already in 1628 the suggestion had been made to safeguard investments by asking the shah to send silk in advance to Bandar ʿAbbas in anticipation of commodities, and then to ship as much as their value justified.[46] Needless to say, nothing had come of this idea. More drastic was the proposal, put forth by the Heren XVII, to relocate the entire trade by canceling the official contract, establishing a factory at Lar and encouraging the Julfans to sell their silk directly to the Dutch. To this their agents in Iran objected, arguing that it would unduly raise prices since the Armenians were sure to transfer the transportation costs to them. Second, they noted in a prescient observation, the shah would no doubt react by imposing the regular 11 percent customs fee on all Dutch goods, quite aside from domestic tolls levied *en route* which the VOC would have to pay.[47]

To purchase at least part of the silk from private merchants seemed a more realistic scenario. The first Dutch foray into the private market, prompted by frustration with the slow pace of court deliveries, occurred in 1630, when del Court managed to lay his hands on some 200 bales.[48] After that, the Dutch regularly bought from private merchants. Of the 870 bales Overschie purchased in 1634, 520 were thus acquired.[49] The following year he obtained 743 bales, of which 235 came from the shah and 508 were bought privately.[50] The Heren XVII, seeing a great opportunity for enhanced sales following their infiltration of the silk market of Antwerp, at first encouraged private buying. Intent on diverting a maximum amount from the Levant and the Volga routes, they requested a large volume and in 1635 ordered their agents in Iran to buy as much silk as they could.[51]

Dutch private buying did not go unchallenged. It met with resistance

[44] Ibid., 549, Overschie, Isfahan to Heren XVII, Dec. 15, 1635; 551, Smidt, Gamron to Surat, Dec. 26, 1635; and 555, idem, Jan. 10, 1636.

[45] Ibid., 454, Heren XVII to Isfahan, Nov. 25, 1633.

[46] Ibid., 234–5, v/d Lee, Report on the trade of Gujarat, India, and Persia, 1628.

[47] Ibid., 465, resolution Gamron Council regarding the continued employment of Overschie, March 15, 1634; and Colenbrander, *Daghregister Casteel Batavia 1635*, 333–4.

[48] Dunlop, *Bronnen*, 357, del Court, Isfahan to Heren XVII, Dec. 20, 1630.

[49] Ibid., 527, Overschie, Gamron to Batavia, March 15, 1635.

[50] Ibid., 547–8, Overschie, Isfahan to Heren XVII, Dec. 15, 1635; and 564, Overschie, Gamron to Batavia, March 25, 1636; and Colenbrander, *Daghregister Casteel Batavia 1636*, 116–17, 119. The number of bales listed for 1635 in Dunlop, *Bronnen*, 548, is 979, but 358 of these had been shipped in March 1635 and thus had been part of the 1634 harvest. To the remaining 621 bales should be added the 122 which arrived later in 1635.

[51] Barendse, "Zijde, Zambouqs, Zilver," 47.

from court officials, some of whom questioned whether the VOC should be allowed to purchase its silk privately and export it free of duty. In 1634 Overschie claimed that he would have bought more from Armenians, who, he said, preferred selling their silk to the VOC to taking it at great hazard to the Levant, but for Khajah Qasim, who, despite having received 6,500 *tumans* from the Dutch, had refused them permission to buy from private merchants. The Julfans, he insisted, would have been willing to sell him their silk in Lar at 45 *tumans*, but had ultimately declined, fearing the wrath of court officials.[52]

The question was not simply one of individual suspicion and obstruction, but also involved the interpretation of contractual terms. While the Dutch thought themselves entitled to absolute freedom, the Iranians made it unambiguously clear that, according to the contract, the rights enjoyed by the VOC only pertained to officially purchased silk and that Dutch sales were toll-free insofar as the proceeds were used to buy royal silk; on any amount beyond that an 11 percent fee would have to be paid.[53] The shah, in sum, was unwilling to allow the private market to operate at his financial expense, hence the decision to institute the afore-mentioned surcharge, in the amount of 14 *qazbegis* on each *mann-i shah* bought from private suppliers.[54]

If buying from the Safavid court had its drawbacks, the Dutch quickly learned that the free market held its own hazards. Delivery of official silk might be irregular and its price high, but at least it was fixed. The private market offered neither predictable prices nor guaranteed supplies, dependent as it was on the state of the Anatolian route. As it transpired in 1630 that the Ottoman invaders were not heading for Gilan but had turned their attention to Baghdad, prices shot up to 39 *tumans* per load.[55] In 1634 Overschie notified merchants in Gilan that he would be willing to receive silk in Isfahan at 40 *tumans* per load. Originally intent on selling 250 bales to the Dutch, the Julfans changed their mind upon hearing that the road to Aleppo had just reopened and that in Baghdad silk fetched 42 *tumans*.[56] Equally as important was the need for cash. While the cash ratio for silk bought from the court was open to negotiation, no such bargaining was possible with private merchants. The latter, moreover, insisted on being paid in advance. Interest-bearing loans typically ran from July or August, the time of the silk harvest, to the winter, when the next shipment of goods in Bandar 'Abbas could be made liquid.[57] The common annual interest on a

[52] ARA, VOC 1115, Overschie, Isfahan to Heren XVII, Aug. 9, 1634.
[53] Barendse, "Zijde, Zambouqs, Zilver," 47.
[54] Dunlop, *Bronnen*, 427, Overschie, Qazvin to Batavia, June 30, 1633.
[55] Ibid., 347; Heren XVII to Batavia, Aug. 27, 1630.
[56] Colenbrander, *Daghregister Casteel Batavia 1635*, 334.
[57] ARA, Coll. Geleynssen de Jongh 157, Gel. de Jongh, Isfahan to Heren XVII, Oct. 5, 1641, unfol.

loan was 20 percent, but rates could rise as high as 4 percent per month. Finally, the fragmented state of Iran's domestic market, which was dominated by peddlers unable to absorb the relatively large volume handled by the Europeans, left the latter no alternative but to deal with the shah. As the English put it, "For dealinge in those parties with any other merchant than the King, are soe poore and meane . . . never knew any man . . . to deal with us for 500 tomans."[58]

Dealing with the grand vizier

The demotion of Mulayim Beg in 1632 marked the end of the time when the European companies dealt primarily with the shah's personal factor.[59] The royal factor thereafter faded into the background and the grand vizier became more prominent in silk negotiations. VOC reports in the mid-1630s still refer to Mulayim Beg's successors, Husayn 'Ali Khan and Khajah Qasim, albeit with decreasing frequency. In the late 1630s the royal factor, by then Lachin Beg, is only mentioned sporadically by the Dutch, who by now dealt with Mirza Muhammad Taqi, the grand vizier, on a regular basis.

The rise of Mirza Muhammad Saru (blond) Taqi to prominence is at once a reflection of the diminished presence of the shah and a symptom of growing *ghulam* domination at the court. Castrated as an adult following accusations of pederasty, Mirza Taqi was given access to harem circles and over time built up a close relationship with the inner palace and in particular with the queen mother. In the course of his career he also gained ample experience with the cultivation, trade, and export of silk. His northern background, his experience as financial supervisor in Ardabil, and stints as head of the financial administration in Ganja, the capital of Qarabagh, and as vizier to the *beglerbeg* (governor) of the same province, must have made him thoroughly familiar with the production of silk, the methods of its procurement, and ways of taxing it. Mirza Taqi's appointment as governor of Mazandaran in 1616 further extended this familiarity. As vizier of Mazandaran he became active in the infrastructural projects surrounding the development of Farahabad, and in the same capacity may have played a role in the institution of the silk-export monopoly of 1619.[60] In 1629, following the quelling of the Gharib Shah revolt, Mirza Taqi was also appointed governor of the entire province of Gilan and charged with the task of

---

[58] Quoted in Ferrier, "British–Persian Relations," 79.

[59] It is unclear whether Mulayim Beg was dead or had merely been demoted in 1632. Del Court refers to him as "deceased" in a letter dated Oct. 26, 1632, in Dunlop, *Bronnen*, 389. Yet in 1642 he was said to be still alive. See ARA, VOC 1144, Gel. de Jongh, Gamron to Batavia, June 30, 1642, fol. 584.

[60] For Mirza Taqi's background, see Iskandar Munshi and Valah Isfahani, *Zayl-i tarikh*, 261–3; Vali Qazvini, "Khuld-i barin," fol. 73ff; and della Valle, *Viaggi*, i, 630. His further career is also discussed in Falsafi, "Sarguzasht-i 'Saru Taqi'"; Braun, "Ein iranischer Grosswesir"; and Floor, "Rise and Fall."

investigating the financial losses suffered by the crown during the revolt.[61] His hold on silk only increased in 1633, when he acceded to the highest bureaucratic post of grand vizier, while his brother-in-law, Muhammad Mu'min Beg, succeeded him as *vazir-i kull* of Gilan.[62] When Mirza Taqi received the grand vizierate, his brother Muhammad Salih Beg took over as ruler of Mazandaran.[63] Shortly thereafter the position devolved on another brother, Muhammad Khan Beg.[64] The family continued to have a hand in silk as long as Mirza Taqi stayed in office, for at the end of Shah Safi's reign Mazandaran was ruled by Muhammad Salih Beg's son, Mirza Qasim.[65] Muhammad Salih Beg himself served as *malik al-tujjar* at that point.[66]

In his various capacities Mirza Taqi managed at once to line the shah's coffers by significantly reducing government spending, and to enrich himself. The investigation of the financial record of his predecessor in Gilan, Mirza Isma'il, was only one of several anti-corruption campaigns undertaken during his tenure.[67] Western observers claimed that it was Mirza Taqi who enticed Shah Safi to increase royal revenue by converting the important province of Fars into crown domain following Imam-quli Khan's execution.[68] He is also said to have imposed heavy taxes, among others on the Armenian community of New Julfa.[69] His combined policy of revenue enhancement and cost cutting must in large part be held responsible for the neglect of the military that would soon diminish the fighting power of the Safavid army. Budgetary considerations, for one, may have impelled him to lobby for peace with the Ottomans. Yet none of this prevented him from behaving like most Safavid officials. One chronicle accuses him of having bribed his way into the vizierate of Gilan.[70] Mirza Taqi's venality was such, Olearius claimed, that all who wished to have the grand vizier's ear had to approach him with a "heavy hand."[71] The Dutch insisted that during his tenure as vizier of Gilan he had enriched himself by short-changing the English on silk while regaling the shah with gifts.[72]

[61] Isfahani, *Khulasat al-siyar*, 70.
[62] Muhammad Mu'min Beg had been vizier of Isfahan since 1630 and was succeeded in that function by his brother, Muhammad Khan. See Isfahani, *Khulasat al-tarikh*, 54; and Iskandar Munshi and Valah Isfahani, *Zayl-i tarikh*, 119, 296.
[63] Qazvini, "Khuld-i barin," fol. 89b; Astarabadi, *Tarikh-i sultani*, 250.
[64] Isfahani, *Khulasat al-siyar*, 189; Iskandar Munshi and Valah Isfahani, *Zayl-i tarikh*, 148.
[65] Vali Qazvini, "Khuld-i barin," fols. 157b–8. This source presents Mirza Qasim as the son of Muhammad Salih Beg and claims that he succeeded his father as governor of Mazandaran.
[66] Isfahani, *Khulasat al-siyar*, 163; Iskandar Munshi and Valah Isfahani, *Zayl-i tarikh*, 281.
[67] Iskandar Munshi and Valah Isfahani, *Zayl-i tarikh*, 233–4, 281.
[68] Tavernier, *Les six voyages*, i, 596; and Chardin, *Voyages*, v, 250–1.
[69] Iskandar Munshi and Valah Isfahani, *Zayl-i tarikh*, 210; Chardin, *Voyages*, vii, 315.
[70] Mar'ashi, *Tarikh-i khandan*, 396.
[71] Olearius, *Vermehrte newe Beschreibung*, 670. This issue is controversial. According to Chardin, who was in Iran long after Saru Taqi's death, the grand vizier was incorruptible. See Chardin, *Voyages*, vii, 306.
[72] ARA, VOC 1115, Overschie, Isfahan to Heren XVII, fol. 100b. In reaction, the English tried to have him convicted. Steensgaard, *Asian Trade Revolution*, 388, fn. 83.

Mirza Taqi became involved in negotiations concerning silk immediately after his appointment as grand vizier, offering the Dutch his services and informing them that one Khan Vali Beg had been sent to Gilan to buy all available silk so that the foreign merchants might receive all of their overdue silk.[73] In 1635, during talks with Overschie in Ardabil – where the court had moved – the shah's desperate need for cash to pay his troops translated into a request by Mirza Taqi for an 8,000-*tuman* loan from the VOC in exchange for silk at reduced prices. Following negotiations, the Iranians lowered their demand to 4,200 *tumans* and promised to supply 200 bales at 42 *tumans* per load. With 442 bales still in arrears, the Iranians now owed the VOC 642 bales.[74] In the end, however, the Company only received 235 bales, owing, it seems, to a meager harvest and high prices following abundant rains in 1634. Mirza Taqi, if he was responsible for the decision, may also have held off on selling (expensive) silk in anticipation of the reopening of roads and high prices in Aleppo and Baghdad.[75] Even more compelling must have been the same impecuniousness that had led the grand vizier to ask the Dutch for a loan and that stemmed from the fact that state funds ordinarily employed for silk purchases in the north had all been used to finance the continuing war effort.[76] Overschie that year purchased a mere 160 bales in Gilan, and in Qazvin contracted another 508 bales of *legia* from Julfan merchants who were hoping to transport this silk to Aleppo. The high price he paid, 50 *tumans*, must have dissuaded the merchants from carrying their silk to the Levant.[77]

Dealing with Isfahan did not become any easier in the next few years. As the Safavid court continued to owe the VOC more than 400 bales, Overschie in 1635 pursued the free market by making arrangements with an Armenian merchant named Khajah Safar Amirants, whereby the latter would deliver *legia* silk to the value of 5,000 *tumans*.[78] An outbreak of the plague made silk expensive that year. Possibly an extension of the epidemic that first became apparent in Georgia in the summer of 1634, that also afflicted parts of the Ottoman Empire, and that forced Shah Safi to set up camp outside Qazvin in 1635, the epidemic reportedly claimed the lives of one-third of the

---

[73] ARA, VOC 1115, Overschie, Isfahan to Heren XVII, Oct. 27, 1634, fol. 100.

[74] Dunlop, *Bronnen*, 547, Overschie, Isfahan to Heren XVII, Dec. 15, 1635; and 564, Overschie, Gamron to Batavia, March 25, 1636.

[75] Ibid., 503, Overschie, Isfahan to Batavia, Oct. 27, 1634. A load of silk was said to cost 42–43 *tumans* owing to the poor harvest.

[76] Ibid., 522, Smidt, Gamron to Surat, Dec. 26, 1635.

[77] Ibid., 547–8, Overschie, Isfahan to Heren XVII, Dec. 15, 1635; and 564, Overschie, Gamron to Batavia, March 25, 1636; and 599, Batavia to Heren XVII, Dec. 28, 1636. See also Colenbrander, *Daghregister Casteel Batavia 1636*, 116–17, 119. The total number of bales listed for 1635 in Dunlop, *Bronnen*, 548, is 979, but 358 of these had been shipped in March 1635 and thus had been part of the 1634 harvest and supply. To the remaining 621 bales should be added the 122 which were received later in 1635.

[78] Ibid., 582, Overschie, Gamron to Heren XVII, May 15, 1636.

population of the Caspian provinces.[79] Nevertheless, the VOC in 1636–37 managed to procure 1,000 bales, 500 of which were supplied by Khajah Safar.[80] The Dutch repeated their deal with him the following year.

The plague having subsided, the 1637 season looked better than that of previous years and by the summer many merchants from Iran and the Ottoman empire had gone to Gilan in anticipation of the silk harvest. The fierce competition this influx unleashed kept prices from falling; royal buyers acquired silk at 38 *tumans* in Gilan, and a privately bought load was said to cost 48 *tumans* in Isfahan.[81] The presence in Iran that same year of an embassy from the German principality of Holstein and designed to stake a claim in Iran's silk trade no doubt put upward pressure on prices as well. Voicing his unhappiness with VOC attempts to evade the court, Mirza Taqi refused to accept Overschie's excuse that the shah had been on campaign for years and was constantly in arrears on payment for delivered merchandise.[82] Arguing that the VOC's toll freedom was only good for transactions concluded with the shah, he forced the VOC to pay a $13\frac{1}{2}$-percent export toll amounting to 4,600 *tumans* on 593 privately purchased loads. Overschie thereupon decided to buy strictly from the court, and the Dutch laid their hands on a consignment of 1,120 bales, their largest ever.[83]

The end of the silk export monopoly, this episode shows, may have given private merchants greater latitude but did not signal the end of government involvement in the silk trade. Examples abound that the opposite was true. Shah Safi continued his grandfather's habit of sending Armenian merchants to Europe with silk consignments.[84] In 1638 the shah prohibited private merchants from buying *kharvari* silk so as to fill his own warehouses with a low-grade silk that could be foisted on the Europeans. At the same time, Lachin Beg ordered that all bales earmarked for the Dutch be inspected during packing in Gilan. This move, it was said, so intimidated the Gilanis that they kept substantial quantities hidden, for fear that annual fluctuations in the volume of available silk might expose them to accusations of having surreptitiously sold some to the Julfans. Many of those plying the Anatolian route had therefore come back to Isfahan without being able to

[79] Ibid., 612, Overschie, Gamron to Batavia, March 25, 1637; Vali Qazvini, "Khuld-i barin," fol. 104; Isfahani, *Khulasat al-siyar*, 179, 219–20; and Olearius, *Vermehrte newe Beschreibung*, 450, who reports that on his way from Shamakhi to Ardabil he entered a village that was totally deserted after the plague had carried off the entire population. The plague in Georgia in 1634 is noted in Alonso, *Missioneros agustinos*, 115.

[80] Dunlop, *Bronnen*, 611–12, Overschie, Gamron to Batavia, March 25, 1637. Of these, only 500 were shipped in early 1637. The other 500 bales arrived too late in Isfahan for transport that year and were included in the 1638 shipment.

[81] Ibid., 630, Overschie, Isfahan to Heren XVII, July 25, 1637.

[82] Ibid., 613, Overschie, Gamron to Batavia, March 25, 1637; and 622, idem to Heren XVII, June 15, 1637.

[83] Ibid., 612, Overschie, Gamron to Batavia, March 25, 1637; 640, Overschie, Gamron to Surat, Jan. 19, 1638; and 654, van Oostende, Isfahan to Heren XVII, Aug. 10, 1638.

[84] ARA. VOC 1133. van Oostende. Gamron to Surat. Jan. 9. 1640. fol. 413b.

make deals.[85] Mirza Taqi year after year declared his unwillingness to sell silk to the Dutch for less than 50 *tumans*. While each year they received permission to purchase some silk toll-free from private merchants, they were still forced to take the bulk from the shah.[86] Batavia, afraid that resistance might jeopardize trading privileges, by that time discouraged its agents in Iran from buying privately.[87] The authorities at home meanwhile issued ever sterner warnings that no more loans were to be expended on silk, arguing that the interest consumed half of the profits won in Holland, and urged their agents to explore the cloth trade from Surat and Coromandel.[88] Falling prices in Holland also prompted the Heren XVII to limit silk orders from Iran. Instead, they turned to Bengal and China, both cheaper sources. The most dramatic suggestion came from the Surat factory, which in 1639 inquired about the possibility of Iran sending specie to Surat instead of silk so that wares more profitable in Holland than silk could be purchased in India.[89] For the time being the suggestion remained unanswered, but it was reflective of changing perceptions that would have momentous repercussions for future Dutch dealings in the Safavid realm.

The EIC: broadcloth versus cash

The English, meanwhile, found themselves in a worse predicament than the Dutch. Having received the unusually high volume of 782 bales of silk in 1626–27,[90] the EIC in the next few years saw its trading activity diminish dramatically as a result of a low supply of new goods. Given the dismal ninety-three bales they procured in 1628, it is not surprising that the English were no longer perceived as serious rivals by the Dutch. So low did the fortunes of the EIC fall around the time of Shah 'Abbas's death that Surat came close to discontinuing the entire Iranian operation.[91]

Existing commitments, the expected cost and duration of closure, and fears that the spoils would fall to the Dutch, made the EIC decide to persevere. Bolstered by a supply of cargo, William Burt, the new EIC agent, in 1628 negotiated a contract that lowered silk prices while raising the price of English imports to the level which the Iranians paid for Dutch wares – with the exception of cloth, for which the EIC continued to receive less than

[85] Ibid., 666, report Overschie to Heren XVII, 15 Dec. 1638.
[86] ARA, VOC 1133, van Oostende, Gamron to Surat, Jan. 9, 1640, fol. 414; VOC 1135, van Oostende, Isfahan to Gel. de Jongh, Gamron, Nov. 22, 1640, fol. 704b.
[87] ARA, VOC 864, Batavia to Heren XVII, Aug. 28, 1640, fol. 493.
[88] ARA, VOC 862, Batavia to Heren XVII, Sept. 28, 1638, fol. 458; VOC 1132, Surat to Batavia, April 20, 1639, fol. 688b.
[89] ARA, VOC 1132, Surat to Batavia, April 20, 1639, fol. 688b.
[90] Ferrier, "British–Persian Relations," 69. The Dutch were close in their estimate of 750 to 850 bales. See Dunlop, *Bronnen*, 139, 180, 233, 269, 277.
[91] Ibid., 301, Visnich, Isfahan to Heren XVII, July 17, 1629.

the VOC. The contract also held the EIC to payment of one-fourth in cash as opposed to the previous two-thirds.[92]

Shah Safi initially confirmed the contract concluded with his predecessor.[93] When the Safavid authorities failed to comply with its clauses, Burt managed to conclude a revised contract, assisted in this by Imam-quli Khan and considerable bribery. In return for 23,000 *tumans* in broadcloth, kersies and tin and one-fourth that amount in cash, the Iranians committed themselves to a delivery of 400 bales of Gilan silk at 37 *tumans* and 600 bales of Shirvan silk at 43 *tumans*. Burt similarly negotiated a deal which would give the EIC 400 bales of silk annually for two years at 40 *tumans* per load, against a similar admixture of goods and current coin.[94]

The results lagged far behind these terms. By the time Burt's successor, Edward Heynes, had an audience with Shah Safi in the summer of 1631, only 520 bales had materialized from the contract. The shah told Heynes that, due to a silkworm disease, silk was scarce and expensive, adding that the English broadcloth was "soe course and bad condicioned that his people refused to receive itt for their pay," and that their tin, having accumulated in storage, commanded market prices lower than what the court had paid for it. The EIC would therefore have to lower the prices of its goods and accept an increase in the price of silk to 45 *tumans* for Gilan silk and 50 *tumans* for Shirvan silk. Otherwise, the shah would no longer be able to do business with the EIC. Alternatively, the English could choose to use the money and goods available in Isfahan and go up to the Caspian region to purchase silk there, in which case they would enjoy the shah's protection, and "more liberty and freedom than his own subjects."[95]

Heynes, fully aware that the second option would leave the EIC with a great volume of unvendible merchandise, saw little reason for optimism. Many dukes and nobles in the shah's presence, he noted, "sided with him and showed many reasons to induce the kinge thus to leave us." He also drew attention to the opposition the English met from the Julfan Armenians and other merchants who "had the greatest partt of the nobles in faccion with them to oppose stronglie our proceedings."[96] To improve his position, Heynes dispensed large bribes while soliciting the assistance of Imam-quli Khan, the EIC's "best friend and last hope to reconcile this difference." With his help, the English were able to negotiate slightly better terms with the *qurchibashi* and the grand vizier, who were put in charge of the next round of negotiations. Yet the basic conditions remained the same: the EIC could either choose to deal with the shah or use its freedom to visit the

[92] IOR/G/29/16 and 17, *farmans* to EIC, Shawwal 1037/May 1628.
[93] IOR/G/29/1, *farman* to EIC, Jan. 1629, fol. 325.
[94] IOR, G/29/1/22 and 23, Muharram 1039/Aug. 1629, *farmans* to EIC, fol. 326; and E/3/13/ 1317, Burt, four days from Baghdad, to London, Oct. 6, 1630, fols. 151–2.
[95] IOR/E/3/13/1379, Heynes, Isfahan to London, Sept. 26, 1631, fol. 71.
[96] Ibid.

Caspian region. Effectively forced to buy his silk in Isfahan, Heynes committed himself to a three-year supply of broadcloth kersies, and tin worth 32,000 *tumans*, and an additional one-third of that sum in cash, in return for which the Iranians were to provide the EIC with 800 bales of silk, at 40 *tumans* for silk from Gilan and 43 *tumans* for the Shirvani grade. To this Heynes consented "as of two evills the least." Pointing to the sealed contract he had received, he even showed himself buoyant about the prospect of doing business without further "disputes, delays, and bribes," and declared his faith in the shah's promise to prohibit "all transportt of silke by way of Turkie and not any man to buy a baile butt from his hand, the better to perform with us, makinge Spahan his martt and Gombroon his portt."[97]

Such naivete was bound to result in even greater disappointment than that experienced by the more realistic VOC agents. Needless to say, no efforts were made to halt commercial traffic to the Levant, much less to reinstate the export monopoly. As for silk, the EIC managed to ship no more than 224 bales in the 1632–33 season, a mere 110 bales in 1634, and a respectable 371 bales the following year.[98]

That the English fared so poorly in their silk buying was less a function of the shah's unwillingness or inability to comply with agreements than of their structurally weak position in the Iranian market. The prestige that had come with the seizure of Hurmuz had long worn off by 1630, though in Bandar 'Abbas, their mainstay, the English were still entitled to half of the toll income. In enforcing this, they had found a long-time supporter in the powerful Imam-quli Khan, whose desire to attract trade and revenue toward the south was reflected in his construction of numerous caravanserais in Shiraz and elsewhere in the Garmsir region.[99] Ever since the death of Shah 'Abbas, however, Imam-quli Khan's standing in Isfahan had begun to slip. When Shah Safi had him murdered in 1633, all the European merchants, but especially the English, lost a powerful mediator at the court.

An additional problem was that the English were more dependent than the Dutch on import products that were difficult to sell. Their broadcloth and kersies were ill-suited to the Iranian market. A great deal of cloth, moreover, arrived via the Qandahar route. Armenian merchants also imported large amounts of the same cloth from the Levant, accepting it in exchange for their silk at times when no cash was available. As silk in Iran could only be purchased with cash and as current coin was anyhow a most valuable commodity, they often had no choice but to sell the broadcloth at whatever price was offered.[100] In 1643, for example, the Armenians are said

---

[97] Ibid., fols. 71b–2.
[98] Dunlop, *Bronnen*, 421, Overschie, Isfahan to Heren XVII, May 8, 1633; and 528, Overschie, Gamron to Batavia, March 15, 1635.
[99] Tavernier, *Les six voyages*, i, 591.
[100] ARA. VOC 1152. Constant. Gamron to Batavia. March 11. 1645. fols. 82b–3.

to have dumped their broadcloth at cost price and to have used the cash proceeds for arbitrage purposes in India.[101] The English, in sum, were frequently undersold with prices they could not match. Worse, much of their own cloth was of inferior quality, "stained and rotten," as Heynes reminded his superiors, and so bad that the English received "many bitter curses from the poor souldiers as wee pass the streets, whoe are inforced to take on bad cloth for payment of their longe service."[102] This was a reference to the habit of the insolvent Safavid court to pay its soldiers in cloth that had deteriorated from long-term storage. Hard put, the soldiers were forced to sell such cloth at reduced prices, thereby further saturating the market and causing prices to drop.[103] The shah, fearing that he would lose money on English cloth, naturally was loath to buy these imports.

Most importantly, the English never overcame their perennial problem, their lack of ready money. As the Dutch noted: "their warehouses are filled with tin, lead, and cloth, yet cash they don't have."[104] A shortage of liquid funds made it especially difficult for the English to capitalize on the private silk trade, hence their rejection of the offer to buy silk on the private market during the 1631 negotiations. Whereas the VOC found ways to engage in private buying despite the obstacles involved, the EIC never had the wherewithal to do so, lacking the credibility that would have allowed it to take out interest-bearing loans.

Developments as of 1635 fully exposed the EIC's weakness. Having lost all their friends in Isfahan, the English incurred the shah's irritation when they concluded a truce with the Portuguese in India that admitted English ships into Portuguese-held ports.[105] The opening of the Anatolian road in 1636 did not help either, for this only increased the inflow of cloth of the type imported by the EIC, causing prices to tumble.[106] Rather than delivering silk, the Iranians that year returned 135 pieces of damaged cloth to the Company. By early 1636 the shah owed the EIC 600 bales of silk. So desperate were the English, Overschie noted in the spring of that year, that they were contemplating giving up their entire operation in Iran.[107]

An important force behind all this was Mirza Taqi, who proved to be an even more difficult negotiation partner for the EIC than for the VOC. Their dispute with the grand vizier dated from his tenure as vizier of Gilan, when the English had accused him of malversations with the silk supply, and over time little changed in their mutual antipathy. According to the Dutch, in 1636 Saru Taqi connived at the diversion to the Dutch warehouse of 100

---

[101] ARA, VOC 1141, Constant, Isfahan to Heren XVII, Oct. 16, 1643, fol. 516.
[102] IOR E/3/13/1379, Heynes, Isfahan to London, Sept. 26, 1631, fol. 73.
[103] Ibid.; and Dunlop, *Bronnen*, 391–2, del Court, Isfahan to Batavia, Nov. 3, 1632.
[104] Ibid., 480, report v/d Trille, June 1634.
[105] Ibid., 553, Batavia to Heren XVII, Jan. 4, 1636.
[106] Ibid., 587, Overschie, Isfahan to Heren XVII, Sept. 5, 1636.
[107] Ibid., 549, Overschie, Isfahan to Heren XVII, Dec. 15 1635; and 566, Overschie, Gamron to Batavia, March 25, 1636.

bales of silk originally destined for the English. The latter, in turn, failed to impress Mirza Taqi when, during an audience, they threatened to give up on Iran if they had to sell their tin and cloth at the low prices suggested by him. Mirza Taqi responded that they would be free to do so, but that in the event he would have his silk sent to England accompanied by officials who would also divulge the disorderly and opulent life style of the EIC employees in Iran.[108]

Contrary to Dutch claims, William Gibson, Heynes's successor, did manage in 1636 to sign a new contract with the shah following another round of acrimonious negotiations. The Iranians committed themselves to the delivery of 2,000 bales of silk at 42 *tumans* per load over a period of three years, to be paid for by English goods at a value of 28,000 *tumans* and one-third in cash.[109] Despite high hopes and a general upsurge of Indian Ocean trade in the following years, none of this had much positive effect on the Company's standing in Iran. The fundamental problems remained unsolved and the fate of the 1636 contract resembled that of earlier arrangements: the Shah never delivered the stipulated volume and the EIC was left with a great deal of unvendible merchandise.

The last contract between the EIC and the shah, concluded by Thomas Merry in 1638, failed to change this situation in any significant way. After the death of Gibson in 1637 Merry was appointed as head of a commission of investigation charged to look into the disorderly state of the Iranian agency. It was suspected that Gibson's bad relationship with Mirza Taqi had been the cause of the problems with the contract. But the new director found it just as difficult to come to terms with the grand vizier, who expressed a willingness to conclude a silk contract but now insisted on a price of 50 *tumans* and a two-thirds cash payment.[110] A contract for 600 bales was drawn up, with a concession on the proportion of ready money, which dropped to one-third, but not on the price, which remained at 50 *tumans*.[111] The English, in other words, fared even worse than the Dutch in their effort to buy silk for less than 50 *tumans* per load and with minimal cash outlays. Table 5.1 illustrates the combination of climbing silk prices and falling revenues for English merchandise in the period between 1628 and 1638.

The 527 bales which the English managed to procure in 1639–40 would be their last substantial consignment.[112] Around this time, prices for Iranian silk had begun to fall in Europe. The downward movement dated back to the late 1620s but became visible as a long-term trend only in the following

---

[108] Ibid., 612, Overschie, Gamron to Batavia, March 25, 1637.
[109] Ferrier, "British–Persian Relations," 83, 334.
[110] Dunlop, *Bronnen*, 656, van Oostende, Isfahan to Heren XVII, Aug. 10, 1638.
[111] Ferrier, "British–Persian Relations," 334–5; and ARA, VOC 1130, Westerwolt, Gamron to Surat, April 6, 1639, fol. 1295, which speaks of a contract for 700 bales.
[112] Colenbrander, *Daghregister Casteel Batavia, 1640–41*, 316.

Table 5.1 *Prices the EIC was made to pay for raw silk as compared with cloth*

Year	Silk price (*tumans* per load)		Cash ratio	Cloth (*shahis* per *covid*)	Tin (*shahis* per *mann-i shah*)
1628	48 (for wares)	45 (for cash)	1/4	38	70
1630	37 (Gilan)	43 (Shirvan)	1/4	33	56
1631	40 (Gilan)	43 (Shirvan)	1/3	33	56
1632	42		1/3	?	?
1638	50		1/3	?	43

Source: Ferrier, "British–Persian Relations," 331–5.

Table 5.2 *Prices per pound of Persian legia silk in England 1628–1643*

Year	Price	Year	Price
1628	25s. 10d.	1637	21s. 3d.
1629	24s.	1639	20s.
1633	22s.	1641	17s. to 17s. 2d.
1635	22s. 6d.	1642	17s.

Source: Ferrier, "British–Persian Relations," 350–2.

decade, as is evident from Table 5.2, which shows the sale prices of silk in England for the fifteen-year period between 1628 and 1643.

The reasons for this varied, involving the uneven quality of Iranian silk as much as a growing supply from elsewhere. Already in 1632, when no Iranian silk had been shipped to Holland, the European market was adequately supplied from other sources.[113] Raw silk from Iran, it was reported from Holland in 1639, was cheap, owing in part to the large flow of Italian silk.[114] The Heren XVII in 1641 noted that Europe was well supplied with silk, a fact which prompted them to enjoin their agents in Iran to temper their purchases and not to spend more than the proceeds of imports.[115] The following year a large volume arrived from Aleppo, with prices lower than those of silk carried around the Cape, so that Amsterdam suggested the purchase of Chinese silk as an alternative.[116] Slowly the awareness was setting in that Iranian silk transported via the maritime route might not be the most profitable of enterprises.

---

[113] Dunlop, *Bronnen*, 384, Heren XVII to Batavia, April 18, 1632.
[114] ARA, VOC 316, Heren XVII to Batavia, March 14, 1639, fol. 237.
[115] ARA, VOC 315, Heren XVII to Batavia, Oct. 22, 1641, fol. 340.
[116] ARA, VOC 316, Heren XVII to Batavia, April 11, 1642, fol. 368.

The Russian connection

The overall restructuring in Safavid political and economic orientation following the death of Shah ʿAbbas I was matched by considerable change in the relationship between Iran and Russia. Shah Safi's diminished interest in the outside world had its effect on relations with Moscow as well. The continuous interaction that had marked the reign of Shah ʿAbbas I began to level off to the point where the number of known Russian emissaries sent to Iran during Shah Safi's reign is confined to just a few. One was the envoy who in 1635 visited Iran to congratulate Shah Safi on his accession (and who may have been the same as the Russian envoy-cum-merchant who in 1634 appeared in Qazvin with about 10,000 *tumans* in cash, furs, and English cloth, for which he intended to purchase pearls, jewelry, and raw silk).[117] Olearius mentions the presence in Isfahan of Alexei Savinovich as Russian envoy, without giving any information about the purpose of his mission.[118] A delegation led by an obscure Iranian envoy may have been the extent of Shah Safi's interest in sending representatives to Russia.[119]

While the embassy trade slowed down, private trade appears to have undergone a continuing (modest) revival. Olearius' description of Shamakhi as a center of commerce with a great bazaar where all kinds of goods changed hands and with several caravanserais for foreign merchants, hints of a bustling trade.[120] So does the account of the Turkish traveler Evliya Celebi who a decade later praised Shamakhi and mentioned the existence of 7,000 well-built houses, seventy mosques, forty caravanserais "in each of which many thousand *tumans* of wares are deposited," and 1,200 shops.[121] Yet actual conditions varied a great deal for private merchants interested in conveying commodities via the Volga route. In 1629, at the time of the Gharib Shah rebellion, ten Muscovite merchants arrived in Isfahan after being robbed by Gilaki rebels. Claiming that their total cargo had been 500 bales of silk, they were reimbursed after the rebellion was quelled.[122] Cossacks repeatedly raided Gilan in the early 1630s and made shipping on the Caspian Sea a hazardous enterprise as well.[123] In addition there were the nomadic Kalmyks who had settled in the Caspian steppes in the 1620s and whose plunder of caravans in the next few decades did great damage to the

---

[117] ARA, VOC 1115, Overschie, Isfahan to Heren XVII, Oct. 27, 1634, fol. 102. The Julfans rejected his offer to buy silk for 42 *tumans*, half in cash and half in cloth.

[118] Olearius, *Vermehrte newe Beschreibung*, 506, 510, 513, 534.

[119] Floor, "New Facts," 306. Given the name "Ottoman," presumably "Uthman" in the original, it is more likely that an Ottoman envoy was involved.

[120] Olearius, *Vermehrte newe Beschreibung*, 444.

[121] Efendi, *Narrative of Travels*, ii, 160.

[122] Dunlop, *Bronnen*, 306, Visnich, Isfahan to Heren XVII, Sept. 26, 1629.

[123] Ibid., 424, Overschie, Isfahan to Heren XVII, May 8, 1633; 430, Overschie, Qazvin to Batavia, June 30, 1633; and Vali Qazvini, "Khuld-i barin," fol. 50.

trade between Moscow and the Islamic lands.[124] Between 1633 and 1637, the plague decimated the ranks of silk cultivators and merchants, including Russian ones, visiting the Caspian region. In 1635–36 a Russian doing business in Iran reportedly took back only 4,000 *tumans* of goods in return for the 6,500 *tumans* worth of copper, furs, and cash he had brought with him. His companions had almost all perished from the plague.[125]

Just how much silk was transported via Russia in this period is unclear. The estimates of 400 bales of silk transported to Holland via Archangel in 1630 and of 700 bales as the total annual volume carried via Russia in the early 1630s,[126] are no doubt uncharacteristically high, caused perhaps by the aforementioned seizure of 3,000 bales of royal silk and their distribution among soldiers who had sold it cheaply to merchants trading with the Levant and Russia.[127] The figures provided by the Dutch for 1634–36, by contrast, may have been unduly low owing to the plague that struck the Caspian region in this period. They claimed that in 1634 nothing was transported, and that the following year only eighty bales out of a reported total of 1,073 exported were carried north. The next year the plague again made all traffic impossible.[128] Though perhaps not as insignificant as suggested by the Dutch – who had no reliable way of monitoring the Volga trade – the traffic via Russia clearly remained modest compared to the volume carried with the ports of the Levant.

While marauders, disease, and rebellion blocked a real expansion of commercial traffic, another, more long-term obstacle to a flourishing Volga trade lay in the incongruity of commercial and political interests between Russia and several European states. The political dimension of the Russian transit trade is reflected in Moscow's reaction to the steps countries took to open up a transit route to Iran. Not only the major mercantile powers of western Europe – England, Holland, France, Sweden – but even smaller ones such as Holstein and Kurland in the course of the seventeenth century equipped commercial missions to this effect. The official Russian reaction to these initiatives combined a desire to increase customs receipts through the enhancement of foreign trade with efforts to find allies against the Ottomans. Moscow made the granting of privileges to merchants from foreign countries conditional upon the willingness of the latter to join its anti-Ottoman struggle. For their part, the Europeans were interested in trade relations, not political complications. Russian merchants meanwhile, concerned as they were about competitors, continually pressured the authorities

[124] Khodarosvsky, *Where Two Worlds Met*, 82–3.
[125] Dunlop, *Bronnen*, 566, Overschie, Gamron to Batavia, March 25, 1636.
[126] The first figure appears in Israel, *Dutch Primacy*, Table 5.10, 154. For the second figure, see Troebst, "Isfahan–Moskau–Amsterdam," 183–4.
[127] IOR, E/3/13/1379, Heynes, Isfahan to London, Sept. 26, 1630, fol. 70.
[128] Dunlop, *Bronnen*, 528, 547, 564, 587, 590, 599, 612.

against foreign participation in the market, and in 1627 petitioned the state to restrict the right of foreigners to trade in Russia.[129]

As a result, few foreign ventures designed to gain a foothold in the transit trade made it as far as Isfahan, and all eventually foundered. A Polish mission consisting of 300 men entered Qazvin in the fall of 1636, intent, according to rumors, on concluding a treaty that involved both silk and anti-Ottoman arrangements. The Poles arrived in Isfahan in early 1638 and left the Safavid capital in August of the same year. Their efforts do not seem to have had any concrete results.[130]

The best known of these ventures is the mission sent by Duke Frederic III of Holstein-Gottorf, in large part because it was immortalized by Olearius, whose travel account of Iran is the best of its kind for the early seventeenth century. Duke Frederic, hoping to turn his small state into a commercial rival of Holland, agreed to finance the venture upon being approached by Brüggeman, a lumber merchant from Hamburg. The initial preparations of the project go back to 1632, when Holstein supplied cannon and ammunition to Tsar Mikhail (who at that point was fighting the Poles). This was followed by an initially joint venture by Holstein and Sweden to gain transit rights through Russia.[131] Brüggeman and his companion, von Krusenstiern, first arrived in Moscow in 1634. There the mission managed to negotiate the right for ten years to engage in toll-free transit trade with Iran, using the Volga route to Astrakhan, in return for an annual subsidy of 600,000 *Reichstaler* (rix-dollars).[132] Delayed for more than a year by the need to have the Duke of Holstein countersign the accord, the mission only entered Iran in August 1637, accompanied by a Russian envoy, Aleksei Rumanchikov, who carried letters for the shah from the tsar and whose task it was to collect information about Iran.[133] Brüggeman proposed to Shah Safi the formation of an anti-Ottoman alliance in return for a monopoly on the export of Iranian silk and an annual payment of 200,000 rix-dollars for the right to transport silk through Iranian territory. The shah would also have to expel all Dutchmen from Iranian soil.[134] Shah Safi's reaction to these proposals has not survived, but the mission clearly failed to achieve its objectives and left again in December of the same year, to arrive in Moscow more than a year later. Brüggeman returned to Holstein with the message that the Iranians had offered nothing but "promises, politeness, and

---

[129] Zevakin, "Persidskii vopros," 132.
[130] Dunlop, *Bronnen*, 614, Overschie, Gamron to Batavia, March 25, 1637; and 655, van Oostende, Isfahan to Heren XVII, Aug. 10, 1638.
[131] Troebst, *Handelskontrolle*, 188ff.
[132] Mattiesen, "Versuche," 538–9; and Baron, "Vasilii Shorin," 512–13. According to Carol Bier, *Persian Velvets*, 70, the right was for eight years.
[133] Olearius, *Vermehrte newe Beschreibung*, 249; Tivadze, "Svedeniia russkogo diplomata," 101.
[134] IOR E/3/16/1646, Isfahan to London, Aug. 30, 1638, in Ferrier, "British–Persian Relations," 225; Olearius, *Vermehrte newe Beschreibung*, postscript by D. Lohmeier, 22.

hopes," and that the Russians demanded the first installment of the promised payments.[135]

Though documentary evidence is lacking, it is easy to see why Shah Safi refused to commit himself unambiguously to Brüggeman's proposals. There was the long history of European promises and proposals with regard to the forming of anti-Ottoman alliances with Iran. Moreover, it had never been and was not now in the shah's interest to tie himself to a single outside competitor for his country's silk by granting a route monopoly, much less to expel a group of foreign merchants who provided income for the crown. Shah Safi did send to Holstein a delegation, headed by one Imam-quli Beg Qajar, in response to the Brüggeman mission, but the letters this delegate took with him did not hint at Iran's readiness to conclude an accord and merely expressed the shah's hope for a continuation of mutual relations and an exchange of ambassadors.[136] In the ensuing period the Duke also sent a first commercial expedition to Iran. This delegation apparently reached Safavid territory but never returned to Holstein, as it was annihilated by Cossacks during its return voyage.[137] By that time the opening up of the Levant connection diminished Iran's need further to explore the Volga route.

The Levant connection

Benefiting from several periods of relative calm in the Iranian–Ottoman border area, the link to the Levant continued to expand in Shah 'Abbas's later reign and might be expected to have increased considerably in volume once the trade was "privatized" by Shah Safi. However, sedition and war prevented the Anatolian route from "taking off" in the 1620s and 30s. Eastern Anatolia and Mesopotamia, both situated at the extremity of Ottoman jurisdiction and populated by unruly Arab and Kurdish tribes and Celali bands, were unstable regions frequently plagued by internal unrest. The rebellion of Abaza Mehmet Pasha, the "robber vizier of Anatolia," who recruited a large number of mercenaries armed with firearms in his revolt against Istanbul, caused the spoliation of many caravans and halted traffic via Erzurum in 1624. Skirmishes between the Safavid army and Arab insurgents in early 1625 blocked the passage of caravans destined for Aleppo.[138] Of graver consequence was the protracted warfare in Mesopotamia. Shah 'Abbas's capture of Baghdad in 1623 left the city in ruins, at least according to Ottoman chroniclers, and immediately prompted the Porte to prepare for a counterattack. This came in the form of two (failed)

135 Bier, *Persian Velvets*, 71–2.
136 Vahman, "Three Safavid Documents."
137 Mattiesen, "Versuche," 539.
138 Dunlop, *Bronnen*, 149–50, van Laurens le Croy, Aleppo to Heren XVII, March 6, 1625; and Barkey, *Bandits and Bureaucrats*, 222–5.

sieges in 1625 and 1630, respectively.[139] War resumed in 1633–34, leading to fighting over Van and Baghdad and the blockage of roads through Anatolia and Mesopotamia.[140] The area was also hit by the ubiquitous plague in this period. Iraq continued to be the main battleground and hazardous terrain for merchants until the signing of the peace of Zuhab in late 1639, following the Ottomans' seizure of Baghdad the year before.[141]

Such instability could not but have an adverse impact on commercial traffic, even if interruptions were generally of short duration. Reliable information on the volume of Iranian silk carried to the Levantine ports is difficult to come by, either because only data from Aleppo are available, or because figures are given by company merchants in Iran who either had no interest in conveying more accurate information or, just as likely, had little insight in the tergiversations of this land-based connection. English silk exports from Aleppo are said to have amounted to 352 bales in 1619–20, 223 bales in 1620–21, and 295 bales in 1622–23. French imports from the entire Levant in 1621–22 were reportedly 137,000 kg or about 1,520 bales.[142] Venetian purchases seem to have leveled off by this period, despite the Republic's attempts to attract more Iranian silk by lowering and even abolishing various imposts on Iranian silk in Aleppo.[143] Annual Venetian imports for 1624–26 were a mere eighty-seven bales.[144] Dutch sources provide few clues to silk carried to the Levant at this time, and seem to confirm the problems caused by the prevailing unrest in Mesopotamia. Overschie's claim that in 1535–36 no more than 130 to 150 bales had been transported was a great underestimation, the result of ignorance about territory that fell outside the purview of the VOC, or perhaps a willful distortion of the facts that could be attributed to a devastating plague in Gilan.[145] At any rate, he failed to convince the Heren XVII, who quickly pointed out that his data were in error. They insisted that so much silk had arrived through Aleppo in 1637 that it had diminished the attractiveness of the silk imported by the VOC. An English ship carried 243 bales to England, while 200 to 300 bales arrived in Venice in the same period, quite aside from

[139] Niewöhner-Eberhard, "Machtspolitische Aspekte," 123; and Römer, "Die osmanische Belagerung."

[140] Dunlop, *Bronnen*, 431, Overschie, Qazvin to Batavia, June 30, 1633.

[141] ARA, VOC 1132, Surat to Batavia, Oct. 11, 1639, fol. 728b; ARA, VOC 1134, Taiwan to Gamron, Nov. 30, 1639, fol. 227.

[142] Steensgaard, *Asian Trade Revolution*, 161. It is not clear if the much higher figure of 118,000 lb or almost 900 bales as the volume of raw silk imported by England in 1621 is limited to Iranian silk or to silk imported via the Levant. See Davis, "England and the Mediterranean," 125.

[143] Berchet, *La Repubblica*, 67.

[144] Sella, *Commercie*, 111–13.

[145] Dunlop, *Bronnen*, 547, Overschie, Isfahan to Heren XVII, Dec. 15, 1635; and 564, idem to Batavia, March 15, 1636. As Herzig, "Volume of Iranian Raw Silk Exports," 78, notes, Overschie was hardly a disinterested observer of the Iranian silk scene. Eager to demonstrate to his superiors that his share of the silk trade was substantial, he probably downplayed the volume carried to the Levant.

the (relatively small) amount imported via Marseille that year. None of this included the silk that had arrived from Smyrna in England and Livorno.[146]

Sources from Aleppo suggest that the volume reaching that city was much greater than even the highest figures reported from Iran, even with the caveat that the information does not always distinguish between silk originating in Iran and silk arriving from Syria. In 1634, when Shah Safi's campaign brought the Safavid army before Van, it was said that the road through Mesopotamia had been opened and that Armenian merchants had carried 500 bales to Aleppo.[147] For the next two years the anonymous letter book kept by an agent of the English Levant Company provides us with the following figures. In late 1635, 640 bales arrived via Erzurum and Baghdad, respectively. In early 1636 some 440 bales came in from Diarbakr and Baghdad. In the summer of the same year a caravan arrived from Baghdad with 300 bales, while later in the season some 100 bales entered Aleppo from Van.[148]

Such figures should not blind us to the documented fact that the Aleppo link was often hazardous and that the threat of blockage as much as blockages themselves caused prices to go up and the transparency of the market to diminish. While some merchants made it through to Aleppo in 1635, others were unable to travel beyond Baghdad – either because of the plague or because the Ottoman army had confiscated draught animals – so that prices in Aleppo reached 80 *tumans* per load, exceeding what Iranian silk commanded in Holland at that time.[149] There are also suggestions that merchants faced with an impassable route often found alternative ways of reaching their destination. Indeed, the fall-out of the Safavid–Ottoman tug of war over Baghdad caused a long-term shift from the Mesopotamian to the Anatolian route. Accordingly, Aleppo, the main terminus of the Anatolian link, as of the 1620s began to be challenged by Izmir, which owed its tremendous growth in large part to a shift in the Iranian silk trade rather than a growing regional economy.[150] Higher dues en route to Aleppo and upon entering the city, and rising taxes on silk brought to Bursa also made Izmir more competitive.[151] The relative share of silk imports does not seem

[146] Dunlop, *Bronnen*, 632, Heren XVII to Batavia, Oct. 3, 1637; 634–5, idem, Dec. 6, 1637; and 639, report from Amsterdam concerning Persian silk, Dec. 31, 1637. Overschie later defended himself by repeating that no more silk had left Gilan for Aleppo than he had earlier indicated. He conceded, however, that some low-grade Shirvani silk might have been carried to the Levantine ports from the area of Shamakhi, which he admitted lay beyond the horizon of the VOC. See ibid., 666, report Overschie, Dec. 15, 1638.

[147] Ibid., 497, Batavia to Heren XVII, Aug. 15, 1634. Overschie, in ibid., 471, speaks of 250 bales, while a later estimate, given on p. 528, mentions 400.

[148] Steensgaard, *Asian Trade Revolution*, 50–1.

[149] Ibid., 51; and ARA, VOC 858, Batavia to Persia, Aug. 28, 1636, fol. 719.

[150] Goffman, *Izmir*, 75–6, claims that the flourishing of the Izmir route was mainly due to growth in the regional economy.

[151] Steensgaard, *Asian Trade Revolution*, 34, 186; and Frangakis-Syrett, *Commerce of Smyrna*, 24–5.

to have been a zero-sum-game, however. While Izmir grew in importance, the Aleppo connection in the 1630s continued to be the most heavily used for silk coming in from Iran.[152] After the Ottomans regained Baghdad in 1638 the Aleppo link resumed its former level of activity. Sebastião Manrique left Isfahan for Baghdad in late 1642 in the company of a caravan consisting of 700 horses and baggage-mules, "most of them laden with silk and the rest with cloth from Bengala and Indostan."[153] Yet Izmir continued to prosper as well. We have no data on the volume of silk arriving in Izmir in this period, but even from the fragmentary information available the conclusion must be that, war and unrest notwithstanding, the volume ferried across the established overland link to the Levantine ports far surpassed that of both the oceanic connection and the Volga route.

Conclusion

No sooner had Shah Safi come to power than the silk export monopoly lapsed, and merchants who previously had visited Isfahan to exchange their wares for silk quotas now transported silk directly from the Caspian provinces to ports inside and outside Iran.[154] The sources identify the Julfan Armenian merchants as the principal driving force behind this economic "decentralization." Though it remains unclear exactly how they benefited from the new situation, it seems likely that they worked together with members of the new political elite, the (Armenian) *ghulams*, who by this time had infiltrated the administration, assuming key positions in the bureaucracy, including the governorships of the silk-producing provinces, and who must have seen personal gain in the abolition of the monopoly.

While the loosening of state control must have offered private merchants and local officials great opportunities for personal gain, it by no means signaled a withdrawal of the state from the silk business. Anyone was now theoretically free to purchase raw silk on the open market, yet the Caspian provinces continued to be *khassah* land and the Safavid court retained fiscal control over the production and sale of the silk cultivated in its realm. The first to applaud diminished government control, the English and the Dutch were also quick to learn that free trade did not mean trade free of fees and obligations. Their ideal, to exchange silk for commodities, had never been accepted as a legitimate modus operandi by a cash-starved court which did not equate relaxing restrictions on silk exports with foregoing revenue, least of all from capital-rich foreign merchants. Instead, Shah Safi viewed the arrangement made with them in the same light as the traditional embassy trade, which only exempted royal wares from fees and charges.

---

[152] Dunlop, *Bronnen*, 451, instructions for v/d Trille, Nov. 4, 1633.
[153] Manrique, *Travels*, ii, 364.
[154] ARA, Coll. Gel. de Jongh 252, instructions Gel. de Jongh for Constant, April 20, 1643, unfol.

The foreign merchants also learned that trading in the open market created as many problems as it solved. Its small scale, fragmentation, and resulting limited absorption capacity hardly made it cost-effective. They also found it difficult to capitalize on this alternative for lack of logistical wherewithal, cash and, in the case of the English, vendible merchandise and the absence of a long-term investment policy. In addition, the vast amounts of cloth which the EIC began to import as of 1628 quickly oversupplied the Iranian market and led to a precipitous drop in prices and profits. Neither company ever managed to gain a foothold in the area of cultivation and both were thus forced to perpetuate their tenuous relationship with the Safavid court.

Following the relaxation of state involvement, the 1630s saw increasing diversification in the routing of Iranian raw silk. While the chartered companies began to transport a substantial volume via the maritime route, private traders were taking to the northern link in growing numbers. European states such as Holstein made efforts to acquire a share in this emerging route and to develop the Volga connection. For the time being, however, the northern flow appears to have been small, dwarfed as it was by the volume transported via the Levant route.

The growing competition for silk in the 1630s, finally, raises some important questions with regard to the cultivation system in the Caspian provinces. The difficulties experienced by the Dutch in procuring silk might suggest that Iran's silk production was unable to keep up with growing demand. If so, this may have been true for Gilan but not for all silk-producing regions. It may also have been a function of the fact, suggested by the dearth of royal silk following the Gharib Shah rebellion, that the shah relied heavily on Gilan for his silk. Was the court unable to honor its delivery commitments simply due to a lack of resources? Or was this deliberate, part of a strategy designed to maximize profits? We know too little about cultivation and its links to the political system to make categoric statements about these and other, related, questions, some of which will be further explored in the following chapter.

CHAPTER 6

Conflict and reorientation: silk to silver, 1640–1667

In 1639 Shah Safi concluded a peace treaty with the Ottomans that gave the latter definitive control over large parts of Iraq, including the Shiʻi shrine cities of Najaf and Kerbala. The peace of Zuhab did more than end nearly a century and a half of intermittent Safavid–Ottoman warfare. It also lessened Iran's military concerns and is thus as symptomatic of the "withdrawal" of the Safavid state from areas in which it had previously been deeply involved as was the cancellation of the silk export monopoly a decade earlier. Indeed, the two are linked inasmuch as permanent peace with the Ottomans decoupled silk exports from Iran's strategic calculations. The routing of silk no longer being politically sensitive, all obstacles to export through Ottoman territory were removed.

The improvement of relations with the Ottomans affected relations between the Safavids and the maritime companies as well. No longer tempted to seek military assistance from the European powers, Isfahan also lost an incentive to grant concessions and privileges to their merchants. The opening up of the Levant route widened Iran's export options and therefore ought to have increased Safavid leverage with the VOC and the EIC. Yet, paradoxically, this development did not translate into a vastly improved bargaining position for the Iranians, for simultaneously the Europeans lost their enthusiasm for Caspian silk. Responsible for this reorientation was the uneven quality of Iran's raw silk and its attendant low market price in Europe, combined with the growing attractiveness of silk originating elsewhere. While the English ceased to buy Iranian silk altogether in the 1640s, the Dutch, whose obligation to purchase a fixed amount remained in place, began to pursue minimal silk purchases and maximum cash exports. As the Iranians were as eager to maintain the status quo in their relationship with the VOC as the Dutch were to alter the terms of trade, conflict was inevitable.

Armed conflict: the VOC versus Iran

By 1639 the Dutch had become extremely unhappy about the terms of trade in Iran. They had been unable to recover the 4,006 *tumans* that Overschie had lost in 1637. They regarded the price of royal silk as too high. Expenditures on silk in excess of the proceeds on their import goods forced them to take out loans at annual interest rates of 15 to 20 percent. An even greater disadvantage was the fact that the merchants from whom they borrowed tended to be the very same ones who purchased their wares. Aware that the need to pay off the loans would sooner or later force the Dutch to sell their merchandise, these merchants naturally were in no hurry to pay exorbitant prices for it.[1] Such concerns grew as silk prices in Europe remained low, which in turn led the Heren XVII to reduce their silk orders from Iran. Underlying all of this, finally, were different interpretations of the original contract signed with Shah 'Abbas I. Whereas the Dutch believed that they had the right to export silk free of dues, the Iranians insisted that the VOC should pay toll over privately purchased silk, as such silk was cheaper for the Company and not profitable for the court.

To solve these problems as well as to reinstate the "freedoms enjoyed under Shah 'Abbas," Batavia in late 1638 sent Abraham Westerwolt to Iran. Westerwolt, however, died soon after receiving his first audience with Shah Safi.[2] He was succeeded by Adriaen van Oostende, who faced all the problems that Overschie had been unable to solve. The 1640 silk harvest had been abundant, but Mirza Taqi showed little willingness to grant silk for less than 50 *tumans*. Private silk was available for about 40 *tumans*. Yet foregoing official purchases would entail having to pay tolls on all incoming and outgoing goods at a rate of 10 and 13 percent, respectively. Van Oostende was thus forced to agree to a contract for 600 bales at 50 *tumans*, 400 of which he had to pay for in cash, so that a considerable loan proved unavoidable.[3]

When van Oostende requested to be discharged from duty in Iran, it fell to his successor, Wollebrand Geleynssen de Jongh, to continue the task of recovering all outstanding debts. Geleynssen de Jongh was specifically instructed to get the price of raw silk reduced and to ensure that the VOC would buy only as much of it as could be paid for with the proceeds of the wares it sold.[4] Arriving in Isfahan in the summer of 1641, Geleynssen de Jongh on August 11 had an audience with Shah Safi, who accepted some 150 *tumans* worth of gifts but otherwise showed little interest in the Dutch representative. Subsequent talks with Safavid officials convinced the new director that no royal silk could be had for under 50 *tumans*. Private buying, Geleynssen de Jongh argued, might be a feasible alternative; prices on the open market fluctuated between 38 and 42 *tumans* and interest rates had

[1] ARA, Coll. Gel. de Jongh, 158, Gel. de Jongh, Gamron to Batavia, May 9, 1641, unfol.; idem, Feb. 25, 1643, unfol.
[2] Coolhaas, *Generale missiven 1639–55*, 30–1, Dec. 18, 1639; and ARA, VOC 864, instructions for Gel. de Jongh, Aug. 28, 1640, fol. 487.
[3] ARA, VOC 1134, Isfahan to Heren XVII, Feb. 13, 1641, fol. 200.
[4] ARA, VOC 1137, Batavia to Gel. de Jongh, Gamron, Sept. 14, 1641, fol. 227.

fallen from 20 to 12 percent per annum.[5] Yet he estimated that to obtain permission to do so would necessitate a gift to the shah of up to Dfl. 3,000, or Dfl. 6,000 in case a VOC agent had to visit the shah's army camp to obtain a *raqam*. As for royal silk, Mirza Taqi rejected Geleynssen de Jongh's request for 200 to 300 bales at a discount, as well as his suggestion to pay for the silk in Bandar 'Abbas and following delivery, arguing that the court needed current coin to pay for its silk in Gilan. Geleynssen de Jongh therefore decided not to buy any silk until he sold the broadcloth in hand and unless concessions were forthcoming.[6]

This was the beginning of an acrimonious phase in the negotiations. Mirza Taqi warned the VOC agent that if the Dutch refused to buy silk they would have to pay tolls on all goods imported the previous year, to an estimated total of Dfl. 100,000. Geleynssen de Jongh, realizing how little time was left before the VOC caravan would have to leave Isfahan, decided to call the grand vizier's bluff. He submitted that the Dutch contributed a great deal to Bandar 'Abbas's commercial activity and that its revenue would fall drastically, indeed, that the port itself might fall to the Portuguese if the VOC took up and left. As this failed to impress his interlocutor, Geleynssen de Jongh thereupon openly threatened force. The favors the VOC enjoyed from the Safavid ruler, he explained, were of little consideration and certainly not commensurate with the power of the VOC. The Dutch were in a position to block the Persian Gulf to any incoming or outgoing ships, in which case Iran would forego the entire toll revenue of Bandar 'Abbas, or some 20,000 *tumans*.[7] Yet Mirza Taqi remained adamant: the Dutch had to convert all import proceeds into silk or else would have to pay tolls on them. Told by the *shahbandar* of Bandar 'Abbas that it would be prudent to abide by the grand vizier's wishes so as not to lose his favor and friendship, Geleynssen de Jongh agreed to a lowered volume of 300 bales.[8]

On May 11 the following year Shah Safi died. Contrary to expectations, the transfer of power to his pre-adolescent son, 'Abbas II, did not generate the turmoil that tended to accompany each royal succession. The strength of the troika in command, consisting of Saru Taqi, Muhammad 'Ali Beg, the *nazir* (supervisor of the royal workshops), and Jani Khan, the *qurchi-bashi* (head of the tribal guard), facilitated a smooth transition, and the new

[5] The fall in interest rates may have been caused by a drop in Iranian silver exports to India following a blockage of the Qandahar route. See Klein, "Trade in the Safavid Port City Bandar Abbas," 141.

[6] ARA, Coll. Gel. de Jongh, 157, Gel. de Jongh, Isfahan to Heren XVII, Oct. 5, 1641, unfol.; VOC 1137, fols. 134–42b and fols. 230–5b.

[7] ARA, Coll. Gel. de Jongh, 158, Gel. de Jongh, Gamron to Batavia, Feb. 25, 1643, unfol.; also in VOC 1144, fols. 536b–40.

[8] ARA, Coll. Gel. de Jongh 157, Gel. de Jongh, Isfahan to Heren XVII, Oct. 20, 1641, unfol.; idem. to Batavia, Oct. 25, 1641, unfol.

shah confirmed all political appointments, sending robes of honor to the incumbents.[9]

Relieved about the apparent stability and continuity, the Dutch were nevertheless apprehensive that the new ruler might reinstate the former silk monopoly, including the obligation to contract silk with Mulayim Beg – who was still alive – and to sell all their goods at Isfahan.[10] As the new shah, following his enthronement in Kashan, had moved to Qazvin, Geleynssen de Jongh decided to send two of his men, van Tuynen and Walckaert, to the former Safavid capital to congratulate him on his accession and to have existing privileges confirmed. The delegation was to request the renewal of the original agreement, but at 30 *tumans* per load – a price the Dutch thought they could justify on the basis of low current silk prices in Europe. The maximum amount to be negotiated was 350 bales, with permission to purchase up to thirty-five bales from private merchants.[11]

Having left Isfahan on August 21, 1642, van Tuynen and Walckaert reached Qazvin on September 5 and had their first audience with Mirza Taqi on the following day. The grand vizier agreed to listen to a long-standing VOC complaint about the habit of tying silk bales with rope, which was subsequently included in the weight of the bales, and promised to issue an order for the abandonment of rope as packing material. Before asking how much silk the Dutch intended to buy, he informed his visitors that the commodity was expensive that year.[12] The following week the agents held further talks, during which Mirza Taqi appeared adamant in his refusal to accept payment in broadcloth or to lower the price of royal silk. Indignant that they requested rebates instead of paying homage to the new monarch, he informed the Dutchmen that there might be room for negotiation if the VOC would send a proper ambassador to congratulate the new shah. At the same time he rejected their request for the restitution of the 4,006 *tumans* extorted from Overschie, reminding them that the shah continued to show the VOC his goodwill by not charging tolls over the merchandise that had yielded the cash with which the VOC paid for its silk – as the contract made with Shah 'Abbas I stipulated toll freedom only over the purchasing of *royal* silk. Finally, he rejected a request for exemption from two newly adopted measures. The first was an obligation to pay a 1 percent tax on goods sold in Isfahan, the second a rule that all goods destined for the southern ports were first to be inspected by the vizier, the

[9] ARA, Coll. Gel. de Jongh 157a, Gel. de Jongh, Isfahan to Vlasbloem, Aleppo, Sept. 13, 1642, unfol.; Coll. Gel. de Jongh 166, van Tuynen, Isfahan to Gel. de Jongh, Gamron, June 12, 1642, unfol.

[10] ARA, VOC 1144, Gel. de Jongh, Isfahan to Batavia, June 30, 1642, fol. 584.

[11] ARA, VOC 1141, resolution Gamron Council, Aug. 11, 1642, fols. 549–50; ibid., instruction for van Tuynen and Walckaert, Aug. 20, 1642, fols. 547–8.

[12] The high price, possibly caused by an outbreak of the plague in the north, was confirmed by Armenian merchants. See ARA, Coll. Gel. de Jongh 171a, van Tuynen, Qazvin to Gel. de Jongh, Gamron, Aug. 29, 1642, unfol.

kalantar and the *darughah* of the capital. Perhaps, a frustrated van Tuynen noted in one of his reports to Isfahan, it would help if the Dutch were to create such a noise in Bandar 'Abbas that the grand vizier would hear it in Qazvin. For the time being, however, he had no choice but to agree to the purchase of 400 bales, reduced to 360 after a gift to Mirza Taqi's vizier. He also received permission to purchase $66\frac{1}{8}$ bales from private merchants.[13] In mid-November the Dutch agents returned to Isfahan.

Negotiating silk, it was clear by now, was becoming an ever more complicated and frustrating process. None of the outstanding issues had been solved, none of the debts recovered, and new problems had arisen over the question of whether the Safavid authorities had the right to search VOC caravans for third-party goods. For Geleynssen de Jongh the conflict turned personal when, back in Bandar 'Abbas, a disagreement between him and the town's governor escalated into a scuffle and brief imprisonment. The only chance for better terms, he concluded on the basis of reports from Qazvin, would be to sign a new contract with the shah, and for that to happen it would be necessary to send an official Dutch embassy to the Safavid court. The alternative, free trade, would entail having to pay tolls on all imports. Any silk thus purchased would be burdened with further tolls. The only way to avoid this might be to contract silk with Armenian merchants willing to come to the coast. Alternatively, the exasperated director suggested to Batavia, the Dutch might choose to teach the Iranians a lesson with a show of force at Bandar 'Abbas. A blockade with two or three ships was all that was needed to prevent anyone from reaching or leaving that port.[14]

While Batavia would have endorsed the latter suggestion, the more dovish Heren XVII failed to see either the wisdom of sending an armed convoy to the Persian Gulf or the need to dispatch a full-fledged embassy, the cost of which was estimated at up to Dfl. 100,000. Instead, in 1642 they had taken a decision that was to have important repercussions, not just for the Company's relationship with Isfahan, but for its Asian operations at large. Aleppo, they noted, annually sent a considerable volume of silk that was cheaper than what arrived from Iran via the Cape. They therefore thought it advisable to concentrate on more profitable Chinese silk. Following suggestions made by Surat, they also sanctioned the practice of remitting Iranian cash proceeds to India.[15]

As long as the reverberations of this policy change had not reached the ears of Safavid policy makers, the Dutch were in a position to negotiate

[13] ARA, VOC 1141, van Tuynen, Qazvin, to Gel. de Jongh, Isfahan, Sept. 20, 1642, fols. 561–2b; Ibid., diary Walckaert, Aug. 21–Nov. 27, 1642, fols. 561–4b.

[14] ARA, Coll. Gel. de Jongh 166, van Tuynen, Isfahan to Gel. de Jongh, Bandar 'Abbas, Jan. 25, 1642, unfol.; Coll. Gel. de Jongh 158, Gel. de Jongh, Gamron to Batavia, Feb. 25, 1643, unfol.

[15] ARA, VOC 316, Heren XVII to Batavia, April 11, 1642, fol. 368.

more advantageous trading terms. The two agents who in the summer of 1643 traveled to the shah's camp in Qazvin for this purpose were Carel Constant, Geleynssen de Jongh's successor, and Willem Bastinck. Offering the Safavid ruler 600 gold ducats and an assortment of precious cloth, and Mirza Taqi 400 ducats and a smaller quantity of textiles, they submitted a petition with the following requests:

1 the right to purchase silk from private merchants
2 a price discount
3 restitution of the 4,006 *tumans* taken in 1637
4 official permission of exemption from tolls and *rahdari* throughout Iran
5 the extension of this exemption to silk purchased from private merchants
6 a prohibition for the *shahbandar* of Bandar 'Abbas to inspect VOC merchandise and exemption from any monopolization by the same official
7 redress for the injustice done to Geleynssen de Jongh in Bandar 'Abbas.

Following preliminary conversations with the *shahbandar*, who, having apologized for the effrontery suffered by Geleynssen de Jongh, acted as counselor and mediator in Qazvin, all of these requests were rejected. Mirza Taqi reiterated his previous position: the Dutch could either give up buying silk from the court and pay regular tolls, or take 600 to 800 bales at 50 *tumans* per load. The grand vizier also showed his irritation at Dutch bragging about their power and complaints that their Company's defensive capacity earned them few privileges, reminding them of the manner in which Iran had stood up to the mighty Ottomans. The latter, he averred in an apparent reference to the reign of Shah 'Abbas I, had demanded 200 bales of raw silk as Iran's tribute for peace. Iran had rejected this, after which war had resumed. The message was clear: military threats did not intimidate the Safavid crown.

During further talks Mirza Taqi showed his knowledge of the current market by informing the VOC agents that silk was expensive in Holland at the moment, and that the Dutch allegedly bought raw silk in Moscow for 70 to 90 *tumans* per load. The VOC representatives retorted by saying that if this were true, the Dutch and the English would be jockeying for Iran's silk. After this exchange, the positions hardened. A public disagreement between Mirza Taqi, Jani Khan, and Muhammad 'Ali Beg over the price the Dutch should be made to pay was won by the grand vizier, the most uncompromising of the three. Constant, meanwhile, emboldened by Batavia's willingness to contemplate armed force, was more confrontational than a foreign visitor at the Safavid court could afford to be. He argued that the Iranians would not have any spices in their food were it not for the VOC. Angered by this remark, Mirza Taqi told his interlocutors that the final offer was a 1,200-*tuman* discount on 700 bales, and briefly prevented Constant from leaving Qazvin. The latter finally suggested that the court deliver 700 bales of *legia* on time, at a price of 45 *tumans*, and that the VOC be exempted from the 1 percent transport duty.[16] This proposal was apparently accepted, supplemented with a clause that payment was due upon actual delivery, following reports that the Safavid authorities would be unable to procure more than half of the silk because of the prevailing scarcity.[17] The VOC delegation next returned to Isfahan.

If the VOC agents thought they had reached a solution of sorts to their immediate problems, they were soon to be disappointed. Returning to Isfahan in November, Mirza Taqi was informed that in the interim silk prices in Gilan had risen quite steeply. From the *shahbandar* he also received word that the Dutch had imported a greater value in goods than they had contracted in silk. Most importantly, he learned that the VOC had sent a large part of its cash proceeds to India instead of investing it in silk.[18]

The Iranian response to these developments was varied. The structural reaction to the Dutch (and English) cash remittances – which were to become standard procedure – was to allow officials in Isfahan to inspect all caravans heading for the coast.[19] In early 1644, moreover, a ban was issued on the export to India of *reals of eight* and ducats.[20] Following this, the Safavid authorities also began to keep track of the exact volume and value of goods imported and exported by the VOC.[21]

Mirza Taqi's immediate response to the news of increased silk prices was to renege on the verbal agreement that had just been made. Furious at the cash exports and the brazen manner of transportation – the Dutch had concealed 2,800 *tumans* in the eighty-five bales of silk that they had bought from private merchants – he also demanded 4,600 *tumans* – 1,900 in tolls over merchandise imported the previous year, and 2,700 for the value of goods imported in excess of silk purchases in the four preceding years. Threatening to take the money by force, he refused to grant the VOC caravan that was about to depart permission to leave, and made Iranian soldiers surround the Dutch compound. In subsequent negotiations, during which the grand vizier frequently lost his temper with the VOC agents, he informed them that he would accept just 1,900 *tumans* in payment if they would take 400 bales at 50 *tumans*. A Dutch counter-proposal of 700 bales at that price without further tolls was discussed in the royal Council but, with Mirza Taqi presiding over the assembly, rejected. The final settlement was 400 bales at 50 *tumans*, 900 *tumans* in tolls, and a provision that any

[16] ARA, VOC 1150, diary Constant and Bastinck, Aug. 4–Sept. 10, 1643, fols. 193–203b.
[17] ARA, VOC 1152, Constant, Gamron to Batavia, March 11, 1645, fol. 85b.
[18] ARA, VOC 1146, Constant, Gamron to Batavia, Feb. 12, 1644, fol. 902. The Dutch indeed had managed to send Dfl. 250,000 to Surat that year. See ARA, Coll. Gel. de Jongh 157a, Gel. de Jongh, Gamron to Batavia, March 23, 1643, unfol.
[19] The VOC sent its first cash to India in the 1641 season. See ARA, VOC 1138, Batavia to Heren XVII, November 1641, fol. 339. unfol.
[20] ARA, VOC 1150, Constant, Gamron to Batavia, March 10, 1644, fol. 136.
[21] ARA. VOC 1152. Constant, Gamron to Batavia, March 11, 1645, fol. 84b.

amount bought above the minimum would be subtracted from the remaining 1,000 *tumans*.[22]

The following season brought no relief. The VOC authorities expected 800 bales but wanted no more than 400 if the price exceeded 43 *tumans*.[23] The silk harvest was said to be small, though the quality was exceptionally good. Following reports about top quality, Mirza Taqi initially tried to sell the VOC 600 bales at 55 *tumans*. By handing out gifts Constant managed to bring this down to 550 bales at 50 *tumans*. Mirza Taqi also gave the Dutch permission to purchase 80 bales of toll-free private silk. This was an empty gesture, however, since no such silk was available because merchants feared the wrath of the grand vizier who, eager to have the royal warehouses supplied, had ordered all those who had bought silk in Gilan to hand it to the court at a fixed price.[24]

Meanwhile, the VOC authorities in Batavia had decided that the situation in Iran called for drastic action.[25] In late 1644 news reached Iran that around February an armed fleet from Goa or Ceylon could be expected in Bandar 'Abbas. The agents were instructed to send someone to explore the island of Qishm – the target of the naval expedition – on the pretext of organizing a hunting party.[26] A squadron of seven ships with 507 sailors and 452 soldiers indeed set sail from Ceylon in February, commissioned to occupy Qishm and to keep up a blockade of Bandar 'Abbas until the shah would honor the Dutch requests. Meanwhile commercial activity was to be transferred from Bandar 'Abbas to Qishm, and the VOC was to provide protection for shipping in the Persian Gulf in exchange for tolls.[27]

Secrecy in anticipation of the operation was not limited to the surreptitious exploration of Qishm. As the Dutch feared that the Iranians might take hostages, the plan also envisaged the immediate transportation of 527 bales of available silk to Bandar 'Abbas and the evacuation of all VOC personnel from Isfahan. The caravan's hasty departure without exit papers naturally aroused suspicion among the Iranians, who decided to halt it at Jahrum, south of Shiraz. All those accompanying the caravan were forcibly returned to Isfahan, where they effectively became hostages.

The VOC stratagem would have failed anyhow, for it was not until April 14 that commander Blocq arrived in Bandar 'Abbas with the first squadron of Dutch ships. The rest of the fleet having joined the force after another

[22] ARA, VOC 1150, diary Constant and Bastinck, Oct.1–Dec. 20, 1643, fols. 207–22; and VOC 1146, resolution taken at Isfahan concerning silk, December 1643, fols. 880–90.
[23] ARA, VOC 1151, Batavia to Iran, Aug. 9, 1644, fol. 842b.
[24] ARA, VOC 1146, Constant, Isfahan to Batavia, Sept. 15, 1644, fols. 985b, 987b; ibid., Constant, Isfahan to Heren XVII, Sept. 15, 1644, fol. 990; VOC 1152, Constant, Gamron to Batavia, March 11, 1645, fols. 78–80.
[25] VOC 317, Heren XVII to Batavia, Sept. 21, 1645, fol. 34.
[26] ARA, VOC 868, Batavia to Heren XVII, Aug. 9, 1644, fols. 531–2.
[27] ARA, VOC 1152, instructions Maetsuycker, Ceylon, for Blocq, sailing for the Persian Gulf, Feb. 2. 1645. fols. 167–72.

delay, the Dutch on June 10 proceeded to batter the fortress of Qishm, yet failed to take it because of its unexpected strength. Withdrawing to the tiny isle of Larak, they throttled Bandar 'Abbas with a naval blockade.[28] Bandar 'Abbas being inaccessible, they next decided to explore the market in Basra with goods that had remained unsold from the previous season, hoping to take advantage of low customs to lure private Iranian and Turkish merchants to this Ottoman port.[29]

The prospect of the southern trade's imminent ruin no doubt contributed to the speedy Iranian decision to make concessions to the Dutch. Informed that the shah was willing to agree to all Dutch conditions, Blocq in early July set out for the capital. When he arrived, Mirza Taqi announced that the shah would not receive him until the Dutch had lifted their blockade. This was accepted, and the Dutch on August 18 gave up their embargo of Bandar 'Abbas. Blocq never had his audience with Shah 'Abbas II: having fallen ill in Isfahan, he died on August 19.[30]

Blocq's death threw a big obstacle in the way of finalizing the new agreement. Left without instructions, Geleynssen de Jongh decided that it would be most prudent to wait for a new envoy from Batavia. While waiting, the Dutch on October 21 received a contract in which the shah offered them free trade for the duration of two years and also agreed to the restitution of 3,480 *tumans*.

This sudden mollification was related to dramatic developments that were simultaneously unfolding in Isfahan. While the Dutch were embroiled in their confrontation with the crown, Mirza Taqi fell victim to a conspiracy by a court cabal consisting of Qizilbash officials and led by the *qurchibashi*, Jani Khan. The final showdown unfolded in typical fashion. Courtiers who had witnessed how Mirza Taqi ruled virtually uncontested managed to persuade Shah 'Abbas II that his grand vizier had embezzled large sums of money during his tenure, that he was out to challenge royal authority, and that the state was severely weakened by these developments. The shah thereupon gave his fiat to the assassination of his octogenarian vizier. However, rather than signalling a triumphant revival of Qizilbash prestige, Mirza Taqi's death on October 11, 1645, symbolized the coming of age of Shah 'Abbas II, as the event was followed by the execution of the conspirators themselves and set the stage for a series of purges during which many officials lost their lives.[31] Although still no older than thirteen, Shah

---

[28] ARA, VOC 1152, Constant, aboard *de Vreede* before Larak, to Heren XVII, June 27, 1645, fol. 76. See also Floor, "Het Nederlands Iraanse conflict," 47.

[29] ARA, VOC 1146, Constant, Gamron to Batavia, Feb. 12, 1644, fols. 908b, 913b.

[30] ARA, VOC 1152, *farman*, Shah 'Abbas II to Blocq, fol. 77; and three resolutions, aboard *Reynsburgh*, off Bandar 'Abbas, Sept. 7, 1645, fol. 228.

[31] The most comprehensive contemporary account may be found in ARA, Coll. Gel. de Jongh 283, diary Winninx, October 1645, fols. 218–22; and VOC 1152, fols. 359–87. For a modern interpretation, see Floor, "Rise and Fall of Mirza Taqi."

'Abbas II now seemed ready to take power in his own hands. The management of commercial affairs was left to the new grand vizier, Sultan al-'Ulama Khalifah Sultan, a cleric with a reputation for piety and learning who had served Shah 'Abbas I in the same capacity.

Unresolved problems

The Dutch reacted with relief to the removal of Mirza Taqi and the subsequent granting of a new contract. Freed from the obligation to contract silk, they immediately resolved to remit a maximum percentage of available specie to India.[32] For the next seven years Dutch business in Iran flourished as never before, with the VOC exporting vast sums of cash without paying any imposts. While the Dutch bought no silk at all between 1645 and 1651, they sent some Dfl. 2.4 million to India from 1646 to 1649.[33]

Their relief was, however, shot through with anxiety. The concession they had won was only temporary and, though welcome, did not absolve the VOC from its long-term obligations vis-à-vis the Safavid crown. Nor did it obviate the need to dispatch a new embassy to Isfahan, especially since the plan to concentrate business in Bandar 'Abbas had proven a failure. Private merchants could not be enticed to come down to the coast, even with a promise of cash payments, as tolls added up to 3 *tumans* to the price of a bale.[34] Nor was the Dutch foray into the Basra market successful, despite welcoming gestures on the part of its *basha* and the promise of toll fees of $6\frac{1}{2}$ percent on imports ($7\frac{1}{2}$ percent on dry goods).[35] The very attention the port received soon led to fierce competition between merchants of different nationalities. Basra quickly became oversupplied with goods, few of which

---

[32] The Bandar 'Abbas Council took the decision to ship 300,000 *tumans* to Surat on Oct. 23, before news of temporary freedom of trade had arrived from Isfahan. See ARA, VOC 1152, Gel. de Jongh, Gamron to Heren XVII, Nov. 23, 1645, fols. 211–12.

[33] ARA, VOC 317, Heren XVII to Batavia, Oct. 4, 1647, fol. 83; VOC 1168, Verburgh, Lar to Heren XVII, June 19, 1648, fol. 608b. The only Dutch involvement with royal silk in these years occurred in 1646, when Shah 'Abbas II sent his factor Khajah Afrasiyab with forty-two bales of silk to Batavia (from where he was to go to Holland), ordering him to exchange the proceeds for wares varying from fine cloth to bulbs, dogs, and binoculars. The Heren XVII forbade transshipment to Holland, admonishing Batavia not to "encourage Oriental rulers in this," after which the silk was returned to Iran. See ARA, VOC 317, Heren XVII to Batavia, Nov. 9, 1647, fol. 96b; VOC 1170, Verburgh, Gamron to Shah 'Abbas, March 17, 1649, fol. 888. The silk returned, the shah's request to have it transported to Holland on Dutch or English ships was rejected. See VOC 1178, Sarcerius, Gamron to Batavia, Oct. 16, 1649, fol. 628. In 1652 Khajah Afrasiyab reappears in the sources in a similar scenario. This time the English had been forced to give him passage on one of their ships sailing for Masulipatnam in India, with ninety bales of silk. See ARA, VOC 1195, Schouten, Gamron to Batavia, May 22, 1652, fol. 819.

[34] ARA, VOC 1152, Constant, Gamron to Batavia, March 11, 1645, fol. 84b; VOC 1152, Bastincq, Isfahan to Heren XVII, Dec. 14, 1645, fol. 214.

[35] ARA, VOC 1152, Sarcerius, Basra to Heren XVII, Aug. 6, 1645, fols. 64–6; ibid., Sarcerius, Basra to Heren XVII. Jan. 9. 1646. fols. 254b–5.

could be sold at decent prices. To make matters worse, far fewer merchants than anticipated actually came down from Baghdad.[36] Most importantly, the Dutch realized that they would not be able to continue their profitable trade in Iran without eventually taking silk. The Heren XVII, in fact, continued to order between 300 and 400 bales for Europe after 1645.[37] Batavia, too, in 1645 ordered up to 150 bales from Iran, hoping to supply Japan after chaos had broken out in China.[38] Negotiations thus continued, conducted by Nicolaes Verburgh, the agent who in early 1647 was sent to Isfahan to resolve the remaining problems and who proposed that in return for protecting Bandar 'Abbas the VOC be allowed to buy up to 250 bales of royal silk at 40 *tumans*.[39] Verburgh was told that his proposals would have to be amended as the Safavid accounting department had found that the VOC still owed the shah 3,400 *tumans* for previously delivered silk. The dispute that ensued proved that the events of 1645 had done nothing to resolve the previous conflict. The Dutch, Khalifah Sultan noted, complained about being forced to pay 50 *tumans* for their silk. Yet the principle of free trade, he argued, made the vendor free to set his price as high as he wished. Rather than purchasing silk, the VOC could simply have chosen to pay tolls. To the counter-argument that private silk was much cheaper the grand vizier retorted that the Dutch had promised the shah greater profits than the tolls on their import and export wares. To Verburgh's surprise, the old argument about the VOC providing security in the Persian Gulf did not make much of an impression either. The grand vizier dismissed this out of hand by saying that the Iranians did not need the Dutch to protect them against the Portuguese. Nor did another standard argument – that the VOC had helped turn the sleepy town of Bandar 'Abbas into a flourishing port – convince the grand vizier, who responded that all the Dutch were doing these days was export vast sums of precious metal. The Dutch had to commit themselves to 600 bales a year at 45 *tumans* per load, for which they would receive permission to purchase 180 bales privately. The Dutch offered to take 400 bales at 42 *tumans* provided they were given the right to free trade. The Iranians, responding that free trade was out of the question, demanded 2,300 *tumans* and temporarily prevented Verburgh from leaving Isfahan.[40]

The following two years brought no fundamental change in this stand-

---

36 ARA, VOC 1152, Gel. de Jongh, Gamron, to Heren XVII, Nov. 23, 1645, fol. 212.

37 ARA, VOC 102, resolutions, 1644–50, fols. 12, 23, 44, 84, 100, 166, 246.

38 ARA, VOC 869, Batavia to Heren XVII, Oct. 25, 1645, fol. 520. Earlier that year a first consignment of ninety-five bales of Iranian silk had yielded a 50 percent profit in Japan. In time, Iranian silk proved less successful in Japan than silk from Bengal, which soon constituted four-fifths of total silk exports to Japan, and after 1647 no more Iranian silk was shipped to east Asia. See Prakash, *Dutch East India Company*, 123.

39 ARA, VOC 1162, Batavia to Gamron, Aug. 31, 1646, fols. 45b–6.

40 ARA, VOC 1162, diary Verburgh and Bastincq, April 6, 10, and May 4, 1647, fols. 210b–26b; ibid., Verburgh, Isfahan to Heren XVII, May 4, 1647, fols. 177–81.

off. The Dutch continued to request free trade and restitution, now claiming 12,800 *tumans* as the amount they had overpaid for silk since the days of Shah ʿAbbas I.[41] And again the reaction was the same: the VOC had no official permit to buy silk from third parties without paying tolls. The Iranian response to the monetary demand was equally clear: money taken from the VOC by the former grand vizier constituted no more than legitimate tolls on goods imported above the permitted volume.[42] Frustrated, the agents proposed a resumption of the blockade of Bandar ʿAbbas. Batavia approved and actually sent a fleet again, but the Heren XVII rejected this suggestion, arguing that it was better to take expensive silk than to wage war.[43]

The EIC: failed competition

The EIC, meanwhile, bought no silk in 1640 and 1641 and continued to be caught in a vicious cycle. As Geleynssen de Jongh noted, the English did not enjoy any respect at the Safavid court and continued to receive only a fraction of the toll revenue from Bandar ʿAbbas. This low standing, the Dutch director claimed, made merchants reluctant to lend money to the English, who thus were unable to purchase any silk.[44]

The low English prestige was not for lack of trying. Agents Adler and Codrington arrived in Qazvin on September 11, 1642, to congratulate Shah ʿAbbas II on his accession. Though they regaled the new monarch with 700 ducats, they were unable to secure an audience with him.[45] When they met Mirza Taqi, his blunt response to their request for a renewal of privileges was that "they were growne poore, bought noe more dear Silke of the King, and were not able to defend this port."[46] The two agents were also rebuffed in their request for exemption from the tax on the sale of goods in Isfahan.

Nor did the fortunes of the English improve in the next few years. Arguing that "their kingdom was not enriched" by them and that the reinstitution of former privileges would only "lead to disputes with the King's soldiers," Mirza Taqi continued to refuse making concessions.[47] Somewhat surprisingly, the EIC in 1645 did not even succeed in capitalizing

[41] The Dutch claimed that they had paid 8 *tumans* per bale more than the going private rate for a total of 1,600 bales since the reign of Shah ʿAbbas I. Adding to the resulting 12,800 *tumans* the 1,426 *tumans* they still claimed from the 4,906 taken in 1638, they arrived at a total sum of 14,226 *tumans*. See ARA, VOC 1170, Verburgh, Gamron to Shah ʿAbbas II, March 17, 1649, fols. 885–6b; and Coolhaas, *Generale missiven 1639–55*, 339–40.

[42] ARA, VOC 1165, petition Verburgh and Bastincq to Crown of Persia, and response, March 21, 1647, fols. 186–7, 266–8.

[43] ARA, VOC 317, Heren XVII to Batavia, Sept. 22, 1648, fol. 115.

[44] ARA, Coll. Gel. de Jongh 97a, Gel. de Jongh, Gamron to Garderijs, Pulicat, March 24, 1641, unfol.; VOC 1137, Gel. de Jongh, Gamron to Heren XVII, Jan. 18, 1642, fol. 260b.

[45] ARA, VOC 1141, van Tuynen, Qazvin to Gel. de Jongh, Sept. 20, 1642, fol. 562.

[46] Ferrier, "British–Persian Relations," 90–1.

[47] Foster, *English Factories 1642–45*, 169, Pitt, Gombroon to London, March 27, 1644.

on the abysmal standing of the Dutch. They did manage to be absolved from paying the 1 percent tax and also received some promises with regard to the toll receipts in Bandar 'Abbas, but failed to buy much silk. In their own words, they had an "excellent opportunity" of "purchasing a quantity at a reasonable price."[48] Despite the grand vizier's assurances of his goodwill, none of this materialized, however, and rumors continued to circulate that the English planned to abandon their factory in Isfahan and to concentrate their Iranian operation on the coast.[49] They certainly explored alternatives. In fact, the EIC preceded the VOC in deciding to seek its fortune in Basra. In 1643 the Company sent two ships to this port.[50] Initial returns were good, with profits on cloth of 45 to 50 percent. Yet Basra, the English found, was not the Eldorado it was made out to be. The Ottoman–Venetian conflict over Crete prevented a great influx of merchants. Armed conflict between the *basha* of Baghdad and the Basrans similarly impeded commercial traffic up and down the Euphrates. Nevertheless, the English continued to conduct a modest operation in Basra, even dealing in small amounts of Iranian silk. More and more confined to the Persian Gulf, they avoided Isfahan, preferring to sell all their goods in Bandar 'Abbas.[51]

Silk formed but a small part of these continued activities. Until 1647 London remained unenthusiastic about Iranian silk, and when the English resumed purchasing some the following year – in part for private accounts – they turned to the private market, warned that they should do so by their superiors who wished to avoid buying silk at unprofitable prices.[52] The volume they obtained was small, however, never exceeding more than eighty-six bales. Told that the shah would be willing to sell them "all his silk," Agent Lewis in the autumn of 1651 informed Khalifah Sultan that his Company had renounced its silk trading because of losses and long delays, adding that he would have to consult his superiors about a new contract. The Iranians, in turn, refused to explicate their conditions for such a new arrangement.[53] Lewis next approached Allah Virdi Khan, the "King's great favourite and our friend," with the suggestion that the EIC buy 200 bales of silk that year, and possibly a similar volume the following year, "paying cash if goods will not be taken in part satisfaction."[54] None of this had a lasting effect. The EIC never received the right to purchase silk at will.

[48] Foster, *English Factories 1646–50*, 42, Pitt, Gombroon to London, May 9, 1646.
[49] ARA, Coll. Gel. de Jongh 158, Gel. de Jongh, Gamron to Batavia, Feb. 25, 1643, unfol.; VOC 1146, Constant, Isfahan to Heren XVII, July 13, 1644, fol. 976.
[50] ARA, VOC 1141, Constant, Isfahan to Heren XVII, Oct. 16, 1643, fol. 518.
[51] Foster, *English Factories 1646–50*, 44, Cranmer, Basra to London, Aug. 3, 1646; ARA, VOC 1168, Verburgh, Gamron to Batavia, Dec. 19, 1647, fol. 775.
[52] Foster, *English Factories 1646–50*, 179, Merry, Swally Marine to London, Jan 3, 1648.
[53] Foster, *English Factories 1651–54*, 69, Lewis, Isfahan to Surat, Sept. 30, 1651.
[54] Ibid., 117, Lewis, Gombroon to Surat, March 20, 1652. A childhood friend and favorite of Shah 'Abbas II, Allah Virdi Khan was *amir-shikarbashi* and *qullar-aqasi*.

Instead, the English, like the Dutch, now preferred cash exports, spiriting money out of the country by hiding it inside silk bales.[55] In 1651–52, their last successful year in Iran, they are said to have shipped 800,000 'abbasis (16,000 tumans) to India.[56] Silk never again formed part of their activities in Iran. A proposal, made by the London Court during the Second Anglo-Dutch War (1652–54), to evade Dutch naval superiority by investing £20,000 in silk and having it transported overland to the Levant, remained unfulfilled.[57] In 1654, London enjoined its agents in Iran to refrain from buying silk, "it being here much declined in price by reason of the quantities now in towne."[58] This doubtless referred to the first Bengal silk that had been sold in London, at prices that were as good as or better than those paid for Iranian silk.[59] In 1657 Agent Matthew Andrews made one last attempt to conclude a new silk treaty with the Safavids. The price he offered, 45 tumans, made the endeavor doomed from the outset.[60]

The Cunaeus mission, 1651–52

It was seen earlier how, instead of buying silk, the VOC in the 1640s had begun to export increasing sums of specie, in defiance of an official ban on doing so. According to the Heren XVII, this made sense because cash in Surat generated more profit than Iranian silk. Yet, concerned as they were about the volume of goods transported to Holland, they urged their agents in Iran to purchase up to 400 bales of silk each year.[61] An annual gift to the grand vizier and other prominent courtiers, the thinking went, would ensure official connivance at a prolongation of free trade and the opportunity to buy freely from private merchants.[62]

Yet evading the court in this manner proved illusory. The Dutch prodded private entrepreneurs to sell silk to them in Isfahan, Shiraz, or Lar, but found these unwilling to do so as long as the VOC remained embroiled with the Safavid crown.[63] No more than fifty bales were privately contracted in 1651.[64] Nor were silk supplies guaranteed through the Basra connection, which the VOC resumed in the same period. Friendly treatment by the authorities and the port's location spoke of long-term profitability provided one could be patient. Short-term profits remained low, and though it

---

55 ARA, VOC 1178, Sarcerius, Gamron to Batavia, Oct. 16, 1649, fols. 630, 631b.
56 ARA, VOC 1195, Schouten, Gamron to Batavia, May 22, 1652, fol. 819; VOC 1188, overview of trade, Schouten, June 17, 1652, fol. 450b.
57 IOR E/3/84, London to Persia, Sept. 12, 1653, fol. 125.
58 IOR E/3/84, London to Persia, Aug. 24, 1654, fol. 144.
59 Ferrier, "British–Persian Relations," 383–4.
60 ARA, VOC 1226, Willemsz., Gamron to Batavia, Nov. 30, 1657, fol. 836b.
61 ARA, VOC 317, Heren XVII to Batavia, Sept. 10, 1650, fol. 193.
62 ARA, VOC 1185, Sarcerius, Gamron to Batavia, March 25, 1651, fols. 574b–5.
63 Ibid., fol. 585.
64 ARA, VOC 1195, Sarcerius, Gamron to Batavia, Nov. 27, 1651, fol. 780.

seemed that nice *legia* silk was available in Basra at 45 *tumans*, the VOC failed to buy any.[65]

A new phase in Dutch–Iranian relations announced itself when in 1652 the Heren XVII finally decided that no more silk should be purchased in Iran. It would be more profitable, they argued, to send all Iranian proceeds to India and to purchase Bengal silk, which was cheaper and in greater demand in Holland.[66] This, however, did not do away with the basic problem in the relationship with Iran, the absence of a final agreement specifying rights and obligations. It was with the aim of concluding such an agreement that Batavia in 1651 finally resolved to dispatch an official embassy to Iran. The head of the mission was an hitherto unremarkable VOC official by the name of Johan Cunaeus, who was accompanied by Cornelis Speelman, his secretary and the author of an invaluable diary of the journey and the subsequent negotiations in Isfahan.[67]

The mission having been agreed on in late July, Cunaeus left Batavia on September 15 and, after a few stops, arrived in Bandar ʿAbbas on December 24. From there he traveled to Isfahan, where he arrived on February 26, 1652. He had his first meetings with Khalifah Sultan on March 1 and 4, during which he reminded the vizier that it would be in the interest of both parties if they could reach an agreement before the beginning of April, the ultimate date of departure for the Dutch fleet.[68]

After these preliminaries, which included visits by prominent Armenian merchants, and following the Iranian New Year celebration on March 21, the Dutch opened the talks by presenting a list of requests. These included the oft-repeated desire for unrestricted trade throughout the country, the freedom to buy any quantity of raw silk from private merchants, and to export this free of tolls. In exchange Cunaeus declared himself willing to purchase 300 to 400 bales of *legia* silk at 40 or at the most 42 *tumans* per load, provided deliveries were made in Isfahan. A few days later, gifts were distributed among prominent Safavid officials.[69]

On March 28, just when Cunaeus began to fear that the projected deadline would not be met, a next meeting was convened. During this session the Iranians made it clear that the Dutch could not possibly expect free trade and total toll exemption throughout Iran, a request they would surely not make anywhere else. Besides, the Iranians claimed more than 16,000 *tumans* in back tolls, quite aside from the sum – yet to be determined – which the VOC would have to pay over the four years since 1647, during which they had not taken any silk at all. To this Cunaeus responded that the tolls in other ports were either non-existent or minimal compared with

---

[65] ARA, VOC 1188, Boudaens, Basra to Heren XVII, June 16, 1651, fol. 824.

[66] ARA, VOC 317, Heren XVII to Batavia, Oct. 14, 1651 and Oct. 4, 1652, fols. 238, 280.

[67] For the decision to dispatch the mission, see ARA, VOC 673, resolutions Batavia Council, July 28, 1651, unfol.

[68] Speelman, *Journaal*, 141.   [69] Ibid., 155–6, 160.

the ones levied in Iran. Besides, he argued, elsewhere the VOC was able to export wares in exchange for its imports, thereby greatly increasing its profits. In Iran, by contrast, a lack of goods desired outside the country made such enterprise impossible. The offer to purchase up to 400 bales was therefore meant to let the shah share in the profitability of toll-free trade.[70]

During the next round of discussions Cunaeus first brought up the permits which the VOC had received from Imam-quli Khan, the ruler of Fars, on behalf of Shah ʿAbbas I. The Safavid authorities responded by calling the commandments worthless, since they had been issued by a subaltern official. Cunaeus next submitted his Company's claim, which had its roots in the sum of 4,006 *tumans* extorted from Overschie as well as the 900 *tumans* taken from Constant. Since the shah had paid an installment of 3,480 *tumans* in the form of silk, a subtotal of 1,426.125 *tumans* was still outstanding. This, added to 12,800 *tumans* which the VOC had paid in excess over 3,200 bales, brought the total claim to 14,226.125 *tumans*. The Iranians not only disputed this, but instead claimed outstanding debts of 3,811 *tumans* over previously supplied silk – not 3,480 as the Dutch had it – and in addition kept insisting on a sum of 12,798.73 *tumans* in tolls for imports in excess of silk taken.[71]

Confident that, their pretensions nowithstanding, the Iranians were dependent on exports and would ultimately be forced to make concessions, Cunaeus on April 12 made a new offer: The VOC would be willing to pay 2 percent in tolls in Bandar ʿAbbas, provided its trade throughout Iran would be exempt from other imposts. This, Khalifah Sultan affirmed, was an unacceptable bid that could not possibly be presented to the shah. Only a Dutch willingness to take 600 to 800 bales at 44 *tumans* and to pay half the customary tolls, or 5 percent, might entice the shah to waive all outstanding debts. Cunaeus declared that the VOC would be willing to take 600 bales at that price in exchange for toll freedom.[72]

On April 22, Cunaeus and his suite met with the Safavid Council of State and received a negative response to this latest bid. The Dutch would have to pay 45 *tumans* and leave the decision about tolls to the discretion of the shah, who might be willing to grant a slight discount. Within its own ranks, the VOC delegation, by now anxious to receive permission to leave, had already decided that its final offer would be 45 *tumans*, provided an exemption from further dues was granted.[73]

Growing Dutch impatience marked the last phase of the negotiations. His eagerness to receive a final answer to their latest proposal made Cunaeus come dangerously close to breaking Safavid protocol according to which a foreign visitor had to wait until the shah gave him permission to depart. The Safavid authorities made it clear that leaving was out of the question

[70] Ibid., 163–5.   [71] Ibid., 176–8.
[72] Ibid., 202–5, 210–11.   [73] Ibid., 218–20.

until the toll fees were paid. Muhammad Beg, the *nazir*, informed Cunaeus that the shah might agree to 50 *tumans* per load, in which case the VOC would be allowed to purchase up to 100 bales privately. When Cunaeus rejected this, the price was reduced, first by 1, then by 2 *tumans* (though Khalifah Sultan insisted that the official accord should mention 50 *tumans* so that the English could be charged the same price should they wish to make their own contract).[74] The Dutch now had three options: they could either agree to the last offer, or pay 45 *tumans* per load and not buy silk from private merchants, or pay 3,400 *tumans* and leave. The final agreement was drafted after the arrival of a royal decree which stipulated 600 bales at 50 *tumans* per load – reduced to 48 as a "special" favor – in exchange for which the VOC received the right to import and export merchandise in the amount of 20,000 *tumans* – beyond the value of the silk, as Cunaeus understood it – per annum and free of tolls. In addition, the Dutch were prohibited from exporting Spanish *reals* and gold ducats.[75]

By now it was May, and the problems were not over yet, for the question of the outstanding payments remained unsolved. The Iranians, evidently desperate to fund the Qandahar war, insisted on immediate payment in cash, in the amount of 14,400 *tumans*, for the 600 bales that had been contracted (and 263 of which had meanwhile been delivered). Cunaeus was told that, until he paid the 3,811 *tumans* in arrears for earlier silk purchases, he would not be allowed to leave.[76] The issue was finally resolved with an agreement whereby the VOC was allowed to pay in Isfahan whatever it could afford, and to remit the rest in Bandar 'Abbas in the form of bills of exchange drawn on Isfahan.[77]

The result of the mission was clearly a victory for the Iranians. Cunaeus had contracted 121,500 pounds of silk, 40,000 more than planned, to be paid for in cash rather than merchandise. The price he had negotiated was not the 40 *tumans* per load initially proposed, but a full 48, a mere 2 *tumans* less than the Iranian opening bid of 50 – which, moreover, was touted by the court as a discount. While the Dutch committed themselves to taking silk, the Iranians were under no obligation to deliver any. Payments, finally, were to be made in Isfahan rather than in Bandar 'Abbas, so that personnel fees and the 2 percent charged on bills of exchange would further raise the price.

The Muhammad Beg vizierate, 1654–61

Despite their new contract, the Dutch after 1652 continued to aim for minimal silk purchases from Iran, focusing instead on Bengal. Their cash shipments to India, meanwhile, continued unabated. As for Iranian com-

---

[74] Ibid., 226–9.   [75] Ibid., 233–5.
[76] Ibid.. 247ff.   [77] Ibid.. 276–7.

modities, the VOC, like the English, had now set its eyes on goats' wool
from Kirman, for which a first official order was issued in 1657.[78]

This policy of eschewing (official) Iranian silk coincided with the tenure
of Muhammad Beg, who in 1654 succeeded Khalifah Sultan as grand vizier.
Muhammad Beg resembled Mirza Muhammad Taqi in more than one
respect. His appointment bespoke an urgent need to raise revenue for the
royal treasury. Like Muhammad Taqi he had a long-standing experience
with commerce, having represented the interests of the Julfan Armenians as
their *darughah*.[79] He also paired administrative skills with financial expertise, for prior to his appointment as *nazir* he had been assayer of the mint,
mu'ayyir al-mamalik. Successive appointments as *shahbandar* in Bandar
'Abbas and mint master intersected with the tenure of both offices within
the family of Muhammad Beg. In late 1651, when Muhammad Beg was
appointed *nazir*, his brother Ughan Beg, who had been *shahbandar*, became
mint master.[80] Husayn Beg, another of Muhammad Beg's brothers, was
shahbandar in 1649 and again in 1654, in which year he was made assayer of
the mint.[81] His son Muhammad Amin Beg, Muhammad Beg's nephew,
succeeded him as *shahbandar* in late 1653, and in 1658–59 served in the
same capacity for a second time.[82] In 1658, 'Isa Khan Beg, a cousin of
Muhammad Beg, briefly held the position of tollmaster.[83] In the same
period, one of Muhammad Beg's sons, Amin Beg, was the assayer of the
Isfahan Mint.[84] Ja'far Beg, one of Muhammad Beg's nephews, finally,
served as vizier of Lahijan in Gilan for as long as his uncle held the highest
administrative post.[85]

During his tenure as grand vizier Muhammad Beg took various measures
designed to increase the flow of revenue toward the shah's treasury, ranging
from the exploration of Iran's natural resources to increased taxation.[86]
While he was in office, the Safavid state also kept up its vigilance with
regard to the ever larger sums of money the VOC (and other parties)
siphoned out of the country. In 1657 Shah 'Abbas II issued a decree that
prohibited the exportation of gold coins and bullion. This was followed in

[78] ARA, VOC 104, resolutions Heren XVII, April 16, 1657, fol. 194. For this development, see
Matthee, "East India Company Trade."
[79] ARA, VOC 1150, diary Constant and Bastinck, December 1643, fol. 213.
[80] ARA, VOC 1195, Schouten, Gamron to Batavia, Feb. 20, 1652, fol. 798b.
[81] ARA, VOC 1203, Gamron to Surat, April 12, 1654, fol. 770.
[82] Foster, *English Factories 1651–54*, 65–6 and 201, Lewis, Isfahan, to Surat, Sept. 15, 1651,
and Spiller, Isfahan to Newland, Hurmuz, Sept. 16, 1653.
[83] ARA, VOC 1226, Willemsz., Gamron to Batavia, March 1, 1658, fol. 806; idem, April 19,
1658, 809b; Foster, *English Factories 1655–60*, 127.
[84] ARA, VOC 1210, Willemsz. to grand vizier, June 12, 1656, fol. 890; and VOC 1224,
Willemsz., Gamron to Batavia, March 1, 1658, fol. 800.
[85] Richard, *Raphaël du Mans*, ii, 61. According to Bafqi, *Jami'-i mufidi*, 199–203, Ja'far Beg
became governor of Yazd in 1656, after being deposed as vizier of Lahijan.
[86] For Muhammad Beg's economic policy, see Matthee, "Career of Mohammad Beg."

1659 by a survey of taxable income and, in the case of the companies, of their trading activity and the income they derived from it.

The Safavid state, these examples show, continued to be directly concerned with collecting revenue and with the loss of treasure through export. The ban on currency exports was said to be strictly monitored, and the VOC only managed to circumvent it through substantial bribery. The same is true for the question of imports and exports. The Dutch failed to convince the Iranians that the value of their imports was less than the maximum permitted 20,000 *tumans* or that their exports fell short of the entire proceeds of their imports. The ambiguous wording of the 1652 contract gave rise to a related dispute between the VOC and Muhammad Beg, since the Dutch maintained that the 20,000 *tumans* to which they were entitled did not include the silk they were obliged to take. Muhammad Beg disagreed.[87]

In reality, this remained something of a moot point since, their rhetoric notwithstanding, the Iranians continued to exert but little pressure on the Dutch to purchase silk. The new contract, in fact, barely interrupted the pattern begun in 1645 – the VOC in 1652 received 608 bales, the full quota – but in 1653 the quantity dropped to 454, after which the Iranians never forced the Dutch to take the maximum amount.[88]

How do we explain this low-key approach? The Dutch rightly suspected that it was not a matter of leniency on the part of the authorities. The continual disbursement of (monetary) gifts to high-ranking Safavid officials evidently contributed to minimal pressure, as it did to the conniving attitude toward the massive bullion exports of the VOC and, in general, the friendly treatment the Dutch continued to enjoy in Isfahan. The system of royal silk buying as explained in chapter 2 played into this as well. Administrative negligence and corruption ensured that only a fraction of the silk available in the north would reach Isfahan. Yet bribery alone would not have kept the Iranians from forcing greater quantities on the VOC. Some consideration must also be given to changes in the administration. While Shah 'Abbas II was said to be increasingly given to drinking, Khalifah Sultan at first was minimally involved in the issues that his predecessor had pursued so assiduously. Not too much should be made of this either, however, for the grand vizier proved to be an effective negotiator in talks with Cunaeus. Besides, little changed under Muhammad Beg, despite the latter's keenness to enhance revenue and his hands-on approach to collecting it.

Crucial to the issue is Iran's involvement in a new military venture in the late 1640s, when the Safavid army set out to recapture Qandahar, the frontier city that had been lost to the Mughals in 1637. As well as removing

---

[87] See the discussion between van Wijck and Muhammad Beg in ARA, VOC 1226, Willemsz., Gamron to Batavia, Nov. 30, 1657, fol. 835.

[88] ARA, VOC 1201, Sarcerius, Gamron to Batavia, Sept. 30, 1653, fol. 840.

key administrators from Isfahan, this operation also shifted the court's focus away from its dealings with the Western merchants. Once the Qandahar war was won, soldiers were needed in the north, where Lezgi attacks and Uzbeg irruptions wrought great havoc. The Iranians may therefore have been reluctant to create problems in the south by antagonizing the VOC.[89]

The other aspect of the Qandahar conflict was its enormous burden on the fisc. Reports speak of underfed and ill-equipped soldiers deserting from the army for lack of pay. The urgent need for cash is seen in the eagerness with which the court solicited money from the VOC, ostensibly to recruit and pay its soldiers.[90] The state further sought to enhance revenue by imposing extraordinary taxes (*ahdas*).[91] The Mint around this time also tampered with the value of the currency, issuing *'abbasis* that were between 5 and 10 percent lighter in weight than the current ones.[92]

All things being equal, the Safavid appetite for ready money should have led the shah to maximize silk supplies to the VOC. Unusual circumstances, however, had a paradoxical effect on the very availability of silk. Whereas in normal times at least part of Gilan's tax revenue was paid in raw silk, Shah 'Abbas II in the late 1640s reportedly had ordered payments in cash. The silk itself, meanwhile, was being transported to the Levant and Russia.[93] Great quantities, Verburgh noted in 1647, had been carried to the Ottoman ports, as a result of which very little was left for sale in Isfahan.[94] Two years later Verburgh insisted that of the entire 1648 harvest of 8,000 bales, 6,000 had been taken to the Levant and Russia, with 2,000 used for the manufacturing of precious cloth inside Iran. The shah, Verburgh concluded, had not received any silk that year.[95]

Two interrelated factors seem crucial for an understanding of this phenomenon. One is the inability of the Safavid court to procure silk at will. It was seen earlier that, for all his power, the shah for silk purchases still depended on the goodwill of local forces in Gilan, honest brokers and political authorities and, above all, on market principles. This relates to the second factor, extending the scope, following the peace of Zuhab, of the land-based silk outlets. The Anatolian trade link was further energized by a follow-up Ottoman–Safavid agreement in 1657 which provided for the free

[89] Barendse, "Zijde, zambouqs, zilver," 72. According to the English, the Iranians lost 12,000 soldiers in their war against the Lezghis.

[90] Speelman, *Journaal*, 211–12; Foster, *English Factories 1646–50*, 266–7, Lewis, Isfahan to London, July 26, 1649; and de Chinon, *Relations nouvelles*, 73.

[91] Zabihi and Situdah, *Az Astara ta Astarabad*, vi, 34.

[92] Foster, *English Factories 1646–1650*, 123, Heynes, Gombroon to Surat, April 25?, 1647; ARA, VOC 1170, Verburgh, Gamron to Batavia, May 15, 1648, fol. 738.

[93] ARA, VOC 1170, Barenssen, Gamron to Heren XVII, Jan. 29, 1649, fol. 868.

[94] ARA, VOC 1162, Verburgh, Isfahan to Heren XVII, May 4, 1647, fol. 180b.

[95] ARA, VOC 1170, Verburgh, Gamron to Heren XVII, Feb. 12, 1649, fol. 871b. In the course of 1649, up to 800 bales of silk arrived in Isfahan for the shah's account, presumably destined for the VOC; in ibid., Verburgh, Gamron to Heren XVII, May 7, 1649, fol. 881.

movement of subjects from both countries and abolished escheat in case of death.[96] The court's failure to provide the VOC with regular silk consignments was doubtless related to the fact that it was more profitable to channel it through Anatolia. It remains unclear if in this the state acted in collusion with the Julfan merchants, or whether the latter simply outbid the court. A Dutch observation to the effect that most silk was purchased by Armenian merchants and that silk was therefore scarce and too expensive for the authorities suggests the latter.[97]

This situation continued for years and was left unaffected by Muhammad Beg's dismissal as grand vizier in 1661. Nor did the accession of Mirza Muhammad Mahdi, a cleric whose appointment reflected the growing prominence of the religious estate in late Safavid times, seem to portend major changes. Iran's Armenian merchants, mindful of a recent governmental campaign against non-Muslims organized at the behest of the Shi'i 'ulama, at first were said to fear the allegedly hard-line 'alim. In time, however, his rather weak performance proved to be a boon for all merchants, who received an even freer hand in their activities. Yet it was under Muhammad Mahdi that the court intensified its scrutiny of the VOC, demanding greater accountability for the huge currency exports. In 1664 an official was sent to Bandar 'Abbas to investigate the reasons why the port's toll revenue had declined so dramatically. The Dutch may have been right in suspecting a connection between this and the death of 'Avaz Beg, the governor of Lar, who, in their words, was their last good friend and intermediary in Isfahan.[98] A loss of influence at the court combined with a (temporary) slump in silk exports via the Levant and Russia may also have been responsible for a renewed insistence on VOC silk purchases.[99] Regardless of the cause, in 1665 the viziers of the silk-producing regions received orders to deliver the exact amount of silk they were obliged to procure for the state, or else to pay the shah 50 *tumans* for each load short of the mandatory quota.[100] In early 1666 it was reported that 400 bales were in preparation for delivery to the VOC.[101] Worried that this unexpected consignment might jeopardize the shipment of specie to India, VOC Agent Roothals wrote a letter to Muhammad Mahdi requesting a reduction to 300 bales.[102] The vizier's reponse was that, since for years the Dutch had been allowed to take little silk, complaints were uncalled for. A flexible payment schedule was the only concession granted.[103] The VOC was forced to take 518 bales.

[96] ARA, VOC 1229, Willemsz., Gamron to Heren XVII, Nov. 30, 1657, fol. 834.
[97] ARA, VOC 1210, Gamron to Batavia, Nov. 21, 1656, fol. 918b; and IOR, G/36/103, Weale, Isfahan to Surat, Aug. 11, 1656, fol. 182.
[98] Heeringa, *Bronnen*, 163–4, Warnerus, Istanbul, Feb. 22, 1663.
[99] ARA, VOC 888, Batavia to Persia, Oct. 20, 1664, fol. 548.
[100] ARA, VOC 1255, Resident Isfahan to Roothals, Gamron, July 9, 1667, fols. 915–17.
[101] ARA, VOC 1251, Bosem, Gamron to Heren XVII, April 6, 1666, fol. 1327.
[102] ARA, VOC 1255, Roothals to Muhammad Mahdi, April 13, 1666, fol. 833.
[103] Ibid., response Muhammad Mahdi to Roothals, received May 15, 1666, fol. 831.

By that time Batavia had also resolved to dispatch an embassy to Iran, charged to investigate the activities of its agents in the country and to upgrade the Company's standing in Isfahan. The decision, coming as it did after much temporizing, remained a halfhearted one. Huybert de Lairesse, the mission's leader, was first and foremost sent to Iran as the new VOC director; visiting the shah was his secondary concern, and one that, for the sake of saving money, was certainly not to be advertised as his main objective. De Lairesse therefore received rather vague instructions as to the nature of his mission and the results that his superiors expected from it.[104]

After much delay, de Lairesse reached Bandar ʿAbbas in January 1666. Upon arriving in Isfahan and learning that Shah ʿAbbas had left the city, he decided to follow the royal retinue to Mazandaran. Brief talks with the shah led to a promise of ownership of the factory in Bandar ʿAbbas with certain extraterritorial rights, but did not solve the question of tolls and silk. De Lairesse left the royal camp in late September. Upon returning to Isfahan in November he learned that Shah ʿAbbas II had died.[105] After receiving confirmation of Dutch privileges by the new ruler, Shah Safi II, de Lairesse himself expired in early 1667.

The alternative routes

Russia

Following the success of Holland and England in opening up an Asian trade link, European Baltic nations made efforts to establish a foothold on the Volga route. Among these was the small state of Kurland, whose ruler, Duke Jacob (r. 1642–81), was eager to turn his principality into a "second Holland."[106] Sweden, too, in the 1640s again decided to explore the possibility of diverting Iranian silk from the passage through Archangel to the Baltic, and to that effect lowered toll tariffs in its ports.[107] In 1651 a Swedish Russia Company was created and endowed with a charter that included toll freedom for the export of Swedish wares to Russia and the importation of various commodities, including silk, via Russia. The English, finally, whose relations with Russia had been severed in 1649, were eager to regain their trading privileges once they had a new king on the throne. To that effect an English mission visited Moscow in 1663–64.

None of these efforts bore much fruit. Duke Jacob's request was rejected by the Russians, who considered Kurland a mere appendage to their Polish

---

[104] ARA, VOC 889, Batavia to Persia, Sept. 13, 1665, fols. 504–9.
[105] ARA, VOC 1255, de Lairesse, Gamron to Heren XVII, Dec. 30, 1666, fol. 808.
[106] Mattiesen, *Die Kolonial- und Überseepolitik*, 32.
[107] Sartor, "Die Wolga," 55.

enemies.[108] The success of the Swedish Company was modest, despite the fact that the Second Anglo-Dutch War closed the White Sea outlet: with some 300 bales of Iranian silk finding their way to Europe via Sweden it managed to divert no more than a small percentage of the silk that passed through Russia in transit. Besides, the rupture in Swedish–Russian diplomatic and commercial relations in 1656 spelt the end to its activities.[109] And the English, too, were rebuffed by the Russians.[110]

Behind Russia's unwillingness to let outsiders take a share in the transit trade was a closer cooperation between the state and the *gosti*, whose assistance Tsar Alexis Mikhailovich sought in his attempt to stem a crisis in state finances. Bowing to the demands of the *gosti*, Moscow as of 1646 began to curtail the rights of foreign merchants, abolishing toll-free trade and imposing a surtax on goods they bought and sold in Russia. In 1649 the government institutionalized this new policy by issuing a series of economic regulations knows as *Ulozhenie*, which included new restrictions on foreigners. Those wishing to trade in Russia had to do so in Archangel on the White Sea.

Direct Russo-Iranian contacts in this period were somewhat intermittent as well. The trend of diminished official contacts, begun under Shah Safi, continued in the early part of 'Abbas II's reign, when Russia's renewed anti-Ottomanism failed to resonate with the Iranians, who had just made peace with their western neighbors. Between 1647 and 1653, moreover, relations between the two countries deteriorated sharply over a series of caravan robberies in the Caucasus, the detention of Russian merchants in Iran, and the construction of a Russian garrison town on the Iranian side of the river Terek. The conflict briefly turned violent when Khusraw Khan of Shirvan torched the town in 1652. Negotiations over the outstanding issues were to continue for a full ten years, with missions going back and forth between Moscow and Isfahan.[111]

Yet tensions never stood in the way of official commerce, which continued through diplomatic traffic. The Safavid envoy who set out for Russia in 1658 carried a large amount of silk with him.[112] And when ambassador Lobanov-Rostovsky visited Isfahan in 1654 with a suite of 200 to 300 persons, he was accompanied by as many camel loads of fur and other valuable merchandise and gifts. As well as making peace with the shah, he

[108] Following the official rebuttal, Jacob continued to pursue his plan, albeit as a private enterprise rather than through official embassies, and as of 1651 managed to conduct a modest silk trade with the market in Moscow. See Mattiesen, *Die Kolonial- und Überseepolitik*, 77–87; and idem, "Versuche."

[109] De Rodes, "Beskrivning"; Troebst, "Narva und der Aussenhandel Persiens," 164; and idem, "Stockholm und Riga."

[110] For these attempts, see Konovalov, "England and Russia," 60–104.

[111] Zevakin, "Konflikt Rossii s Persiei."

[112] IOR E/3/21/2089. Lewis and Best. Gombroon to London. Dec. 4, 1648. fol. 42b.

was said to be charged with the task of negotiating the establishment of a sustained silk trade between the two countries.[113]

The main Russian initiative in this period took the form of joint ventures between the state and the *gosti* and was led by Vasilii Shorin, one of Russia's most successful *gosti* merchants. Working in close cooperation with the government, Shorin was allowed to build warehouses for the storage of furs and wares imported from the east. In 1651, he managed to get the tsar to underwrite a mission to Iran by granting its leaders the title of official messengers. Shorin in 1660 again dispatched an expedition to Iran. He launched a third attempt in 1664, again in the form of a joint political and commercial venture. Headed by F. Y. Miloslavski, this mission was accompanied by a suite of 350 people and some prominent merchants, who brought goods of a total value of 76,749 *rubles*.[114] In exchange, the merchants apparently bought a substantial amount of silk, so much in fact that the Dutch attributed the small volume they had received that year to large Russian purchases.[115] Shorin's ventures mixed success with failure. His first one seems to have ended in disaster. Having suffered extortion, harassment, arrest and even torture, he is said to have lost 17,000 *rubles* in the process.[116] In subsequent years, Shorin imported some silk, 303 *puds* (about 50 bales), valued at 11,300 *rubles*, in 1654, and 126 *puds* in 1655.[117] His third mission, though commercially profitable, failed in its objective of opening free trade between Russia and Iran. An initially friendly reception turned sour when the Iranians discovered that the embassy was just a trading mission in diplomatic disguise. Shah 'Abbas II rejected a proposal for free trade when he learned that the Russians intended to build a military stronghold instead of a trading post on the Caspian shore.[118]

Iranian initiatives in this period resembled Russian ones in their semi-private character. In Iran's case it was the Julfan merchants who entered into negotiations with Moscow. A mission led by Zakhariya Shahrimanean arrived in Russia's capital in 1659, set to convince Russian officials of the advantage of closer trade links with Iran. While the precise standing of this mission remains obscure, it appears that its representatives behaved in Russia as quasi-official merchants and were treated as such by the authorities. The richness of the gifts they offered to the tsar reflects Julfan interest

---

[113] ARA, VOC 1203, Gamron to Batavia, 16 May 1654; Foster, *English Factories 1651–54*, 271, Spiller, Isfahan to London, April 10, 1654.

[114] Quoted in Attman, *Russian and Polish Markets*, 190–1.

[115] Coolhaas, *Generale missiven*, iii, 502.

[116] Baron, "Vasilii Shorin."

[117] Ermolaeva, "Krupnoe kupechestvo," 309.

[118] ARA, VOC 1245, van Wyck, Gamron to Heren XVII, Jan. 9, 1665, fol. 366a; ibid., March 8, 1665, fol. 468b; ibid., April 29, 1665, fol. 514b; de Thévenot, *Suite du voyage*, 202–4; Chardin, *Voyages*, x, 112ff. In 1664, the Dutch reported that the diplomatic contact had resulted in the reopening of the borders between Iran and Russia. See ARA, VOC 1242, Gamron to Heren XVII. June 20, 1664, fol. 1090.

in Russia as a transit route but may also have been meant to emphasize that, rather than being just royal merchants, they operated as private entrepreneurs as well.[119] While the mission does not seem to have achieved any tangible results, it did foreshadow more fruitful future contacts between the Russians and the Julfan merchant community.

Specific information on the silk trade to Russia in this period is spotty. The Dutch in 1644 noted that broadcloth was very inexpensive in Isfahan because the shah's factor had imported a great volume from Moscow and Aleppo. Since silk was generally the return merchandise, the implication is that a large official silk transport had gone to Russia in exchange.[120] Explicit information to the same effect comes from the English agents in Bandar 'Abbas, who in 1648 noted that earlier that year an Iranian envoy had gone to Moscow. The fact that he had taken a large volume of raw silk with him, in addition to the high prices paid in the Ottoman ports, had made silk scarce in Iran.[121] As mentioned earlier, the merchants accompanying the Russian mission of 1664 took a great deal of silk with them back to Russia.[122] Yet, overall, the traffic in silk at this point was still an intermittent flow that was frequently interrupted by unrest in the Caucasus and along the Volga. In 1650–51, 138 bales of Iranian silk lay in storage in Astrakhan for lack of buyers.[123] How little silk was ferried through Russia in this period is illustrated in Johann de Rodes's report on the Russian trade, written for the Swedish king in 1653, in which he estimated the volume of Iranian silk transshipped through Archangel every three years to be 120 to 150 bales.[124] Equally suggestive is a figure of 372 bales as the total amount carried to the Baltic port of Reval, modern Tallin, between 1649 and 1653.[125]

The Levant route

In the wake of the treaty of Zuhab, the Anatolian route appears to have witnessed a tremendous upsurge in commercial traffic. Zuhab, stipulating that trade should be immune from hostilities, also caused a lowering of the

[119] Kukanova, "Rol' armianskogo kupechestva," 23–4. See also Baiburtian, *Armianskaia koloniia*, 94–6; and Rahmani, *Azerbaidzhan*, 185. Herzig, "Armenian Merchants," 189–90, notes the ambiguity of the Armenian position and suggests that their presentation of the so-called Diamond Throne might have been an effort to gain standing as private merchants. That they saw themselves as more than commercial agents of the shah is illustrated in their complaint in 1672 to the tsar that Iranian merchants were in the habit of bribing the treasurer to have their wares classified as royal wares in order to avoid having to pay tolls. See Bushev, "Iranskii kuptsina," 169.
[120] ARA, VOC 1146, Constant, Gamron to Batavia, May 24, 1644, fol. 929b.
[121] IOR E/3/21/2089, Lewis and Best, Gombroon to London, Dec. 4, 1648, fol. 42b.
[122] IOR G/36/104, Flower, Gombroon to Surat, Sept. 9, 1664, fol. 121.
[123] Baiburtian, *Armianskaia koloniia*, 93–4.
[124] De Rodes, "Beskrivning," 114.
[125] Hundt, >>*Woraus nichts geworden*<<, 9.

high taxes paid by Armenians in Izmir.[126] The Heren XVII in 1644 complained that so much Iranian silk was brought to Europe via Aleppo that little profit could be made on it in Holland.[127] A year later a VOC report averred that the silk traffic from Iran to Aleppo greatly exceeded the volume transported via Moscow.[128] To be sure, the Candia War between Venice and the Ottomans briefly interrupted this trend, making Mediterranean shipping lanes unsafe and causing fewer merchants to come to Iran.[129] Following the termination of hostilities, however, traffic resumed, as is evidenced in the report that such great quantities had been carried to the Levant that little silk was available for the Safavid court in 1647. The same was true a year later, when high prices in the Ottoman Empire "induced Armenians all they could light on."[130] With the shah demanding his taxes from Gilan in cash, all the more silk was available for transport to the Levant.[131] When the French declared war on the English in 1649 and sent a fleet to the Mediterranean, silk prices in Iran fell.[132] In the same year many "Turkish, Persian, and Armenian" merchants came to Gilan to make their purchases.[133] Anglo-French hostilities in the next few years did not leave silk shipments unaffected, yet they do not seem to have caused a crisis in the silk market.[134]

The upgrading of the peace of Zuhab with a clause stipulating that if a merchant died on Ottoman soil, his assets would fall to his relatives at home rather than to the sultan, further invigorated the Anatolian link.[135] The results were soon apparent: in early 1660 merchants from Izmir and Aleppo were said to have put "so much broadcloth in bartar that these marketts continnued cloyed therewith and most of the drapers or sellers thereoff in Spahaune are either broke and uterly ruined or their credit suspected."[136]

In Iran, the main entrepôt for the caravans to and from the Levant now had become Tabriz. According to a French missionary writing in the 1660s, Tabriz was a

great commercial city and one of the largest approaches of Persia for all sorts of merchandise that is offered in Persia. People arrive there from Constantinople, Smyrna, Bursa, Tokat, Erzurum, Erevan, Nakhjavan, Aleppo, Diarbakr, Mardin, Urfa, Bitlis, Van, Khursa, Agulis, Egis, and Tiflis ... from Kurdistan, Ganja, Shamakhi, Gilan and Ardabil ... Merchants pass through on their way to Gilan,

[126] Baiburtian, *Armianskaia koloniia*, 65–6.
[127] ARA, VOC 317, Heren XVII to Batavia, Sept. 21, 1644, fol. 6.
[128] ARA, VOC 1152, Constant, Gamron to Batavia, March 11, 1645, fol. 83.
[129] ARA, VOC 1162, diary Verburgh and Bastincq, March 22, 1647, fols. 207b–8.
[130] Foster, *English Factories 1646–50*, 223, Lewis, Gombroon to Surat, Dec. 4, 1648.
[131] ARA, VOC 1170, Barenssen, Gamron to Heren XVII, Jan. 29, 1649, fol. 868.
[132] Foster, *English Factories 1646–50*, 268, Lewis, Isfahan to London, Nov. 21, 1649.
[133] ARA, VOC 1178, Sarcerius, Gamron to Batavia, Oct. 16, 1649, fol. 630.
[134] Foster, *English Factories 1651–54*, 66, Lewis, Isfahan to Surat, Sept. 15, 1651.
[135] ARA, VOC 1226, Willemsz., Gamron to Batavia, Nov. 30, 1657, fol. 834.
[136] IOR E/3/26 2868, Buckeridge, Isfahan to London, Jan. 25, 1660, unfol.

Shamakhi, and Ganja, the three towns where the silk of Iran is traded. The Julfan Armenians have their factories and shops there for the caravans that come from Smyrna and Aleppo[137]

Izmir accordingly had become the undisputed main terminus in the Levant, growing apace despite a series of devastating earthquakes in the seventeenth century. Better equipped for trade than Aleppo, the city also was situated closer to the Ottoman capital, thus rendering instances of extortion and abuse less frequent than in the Syrian port.

These years also witnessed a shift in the routing of silk in the Mediterranean basin. Following the French decision of 1629 to reopen the trade of Marseille and Toulon to Armenian merchants, much of the silk leaving the Levant ports found its way to southern France. The imposition of hefty tolls in 1634 and 1650, however, stymied these imports in the 1650s. Subsequently, Marseille ceded its position as Europe's main entrepôt for west Asian silk to Livorno, whose ruler attracted more and more foreigners by turning his port into a franchise.[138] In 1665 a convoy of five Dutch ships leaving Izmir for Livorno carried almost 500 bales of silk.[139] In 1668 some 2,500 bales arrived in Livorno from the Levant, mostly originating in Iran.[140] Not surprisingly, the city at this point became home to an Armenian–Iranian consul.[141]

Conclusion

The 1640s witnessed several changes in the configuration of Iran's silk exports. Most important was the growing attractiveness of the Levant, which, following the peace of Zuhab, became the single most profitable destination for Iranian silk and hence the focus of Safavid efforts to optimize revenue. At the same time, the maritime companies all but abandoned the Iranian silk market. Frustrated with the complications of procuring royal silk, the VOC and EIC also reached the conclusion that Iran's raw silk was uncompetitive, that nothing substituted for silk, and that profits earned in the country might be better used to finance operations elsewhere in Asia. Having decided to switch to silk from Bengal, they now set out to export their excess cash to India. The Dutch in particular experienced a veritable bonanza in this regard, exporting millions of guilders as specie to the subcontinent.

To be sure, the decision to minimize silk purchases did not spell an end to political relations with Isfahan, since the need to negotiate commercial rights and privileges remained unchanged. The English, not beholden to the

---

[137] Du Mans, *Estat de la Perse*, 332, de Bourges to Colbert.
[138] Tékéian, "Marseille," 18; and Bayburdyan, *Naqsh-i Aramanah*, 82, 100–1.
[139] BN, Mélanges Colbert 129b, fols. 732–3b, de Poussainpierre to Colbert, May 26, 1665.
[140] Masson, *Histoire du commerce français*, 416–17; and Anderson, *English Consul*, 160.
[141] Bayburdyan, *Naqsh-i Aramanah*, 97–8.

court by a commercial contract, were little affected. No longer militarily relevant, short on cash, and importer of undesirable goods, they ceased to purchase any silk in Iran and entered a long period of decline in the country. The VOC, by contrast, continued to be bound by a contract that granted toll freedom in exchange for an obligation to buy silk. Its evasion of this obligation inevitably created problems with the Iranians, who, regarding toll exemption as a royal favor, not an inherent right, argued that the Dutch would only be exempt from paying tolls over the amount they bought in royal silk and that they would have to pay regular tolls if they wished to switch to private silk. The Dutch remonstrated that their contribution to Iran's prosperity and royal profits justified toll freedom. They balked at the idea of having to pay tolls over goods the proceeds of which had to be used to pay the interest on loans they were forced to take out in order to pay in advance for silk. The Iranians disagreed. According to them, the VOC made huge profits in part because of its toll freedom, in addition to siphoning enormous quantities of treasure out of the country. It would therefore be reasonable to plow some of the gain back into the coffers of the agency that allowed them to make such nice profits.

In reality, and measures such as bans on bullion exports notwithstanding, little was done to thwart the Dutch in their commercial activity. Given the growing impecuniousness of the Safavid state, it is at first glance surprising that Isfahan did not put more effort into forcing silk on the VOC with its contractual obligation to take a fixed amount. Though contributing factors, corruption and a lack of firm leadership do not adequately explain why the shah's desperate need for revenue did not translate into a strict enforcement of the silk contract with the Dutch, especially after it had been renewed under terms favorable to the Iranians. Most compelling as an explanation is a combination of fiscal urgency and limited government capacity to take advantage of market forces. Desperate for quick cash yet unable to coordinate the lucrative Levant route with the maritime outlet, the Safavid state taxed sericulture and reneged on complying with its own contract. Some of the questions this raises about the ability of the central state to command its economic resources and the nature of the Safavid approach to commerce will be examined further in the following chapter.

CHAPTER 7

Renewed regulation and the rise of the Russian connection, 1660s–1690s

The period from the 1660s to the 1690s, coinciding with the reign of Shah Sulayman (1666–94), saw a deepening of Iran's financial crisis and various unmistakable signs of economic retrenchment. A thorough analysis of this development, which was not limited to Iran or even west Asia, lies outside the scope of this study. Even a cursory overview, however, points to a convergence of structural weaknesses and conjunctural factors. The former center on an inherently fragile economy marked by low productivity and chronically dependent on outside sources of bullion and thus vulnerable to external pressure. Among the latter are the exhausting Safavid–Ottoman wars of the early century, a loss of revenue due to territorial contraction, a restructuring of landed property, and other counterproductive policies. All this may have been exacerbated by an unusual series of epidemics and natural disasters.

Severe financial woes are the clearest manifestation of Iran's worsening economic climate in the second half of the seventeenth century. Symptomatic of this is a reported decrease in the volume of trade between Iran and the Levantine ports in the 1660s. The Dutch consul in Istanbul in 1663 wrote that the caravans coming from Iran were no longer as numerous and frequent as they used to be.[1] Though this was little more than a temporary slump, the arrival of an unusually small number of merchants from Anatolia in the 1670s and diminishing commercial activity in the Persian Gulf ports similarly point up the country's impoverishment to which the Dutch alluded.[2] As important – and related – was a reduced inflow of silver into the country. Spurred on by a 1667 Russian ban on bullion exports, war in Europe, and renewed Ottoman–Safavid tension, this phenomenon ultimately reflected a long-term silver shortage in all of west and south Asia that in the second half of the 1600s led to lower silver supplies to India and a considerable decrease in the number of active mints in Iran, the Ottoman

[1] Heeringa, *Bronnen*, 163–4, Warnerus, Istanbul, Feb. 22, 1663.
[2] ARA, VOC 1349, Bent, Gamron, to Batavia, Nov. 25, 1679, fols. 1717b–19a.

Empire, and Central Asia.[3] Though the fact that few mints closed in the country's northwest suggests that silk exports via the Levant and Russia were not directly affected by the silver famine, numerous bankruptcies among Iran's merchants between 1665 and 1675 underscore the severity of the crisis.[4]

Internal causes, centering on the effects of warfare and excessive taxation, played an important role in Iran's economic malaise. The wars of 1623–38, fought in Azerbaijan and Mesopotamia, left western Iran impoverished.[5] The very measures taken by the state in response to fiscal exigency had a mostly negative impact as well. These include the acceleration of the conversion of state land to crown land that took place under Shah Safi I, something that was cited by contemporary observers as a main cause of Iran's long-term financial ruin. Culminating under Shah 'Abbas II, this practice enhanced immediate state income but contributed to a gradual depletion of productive forces, since it removed an incentive for governors to pay attention to the long-term productivity of the lands they adminis-tered.[6] The conversion of road tolls to *khassah* property and the farming out of key offices had the same effect.[7] Speelman in the 1650s described Fars as overtaxed, an opinion echoed by Chardin and corroborated in the Persian sources.[8] Tavernier referred to the decline of irrigation and fertility in Azerbaijan.[9] Armenia in the 1650s suffered the exactions of Muhammad Khan, a governor who imposed numerous new taxes on economic activity and its fruits.[10] Currency manipulation by the state had pernicious long-term effects as well. A prevalence of adulterated coins in circulation reduced the purchasing power of people living on fixed incomes and made life miserable for the urban masses. A halfhearted monetary reform initiated by the state in 1684 only made matters worse.[11]

Natural disaster in the form of drought and pestilence, finally, had an adverse effect on harvests and export activity, especially since the areas of cultivation and transit were invariably among the stricken parts. The frequency and severity of the cycles of drought, bad harvests, and famine as of the 1660s seem to suggest a long-term pattern rather than random weather fluctuations; however, the present state of knowledge about long-

---

[3] The number of Iranian mints decreased from about thirty in 1625 to about fifteen in 1685. For the Ottoman Empire, see Pamuk, "Disintegration"; and idem, "Money in the Ottoman Empire." The shortfall in Indian silver imports is discussed in Haidar, "Precious Metal Flows," 336ff.

[4] ARA, VOC, Generale Missiven, Jan. 30, 1666, fol. 205; [Chick], *Chronicle*, i, 442.

[5] Tucci, "Emissioni," 310.

[6] Chardin, *Voyages*, v, 250–3. In the 1660s, the need to confront nomadic attacks in the north led to a temporary reversal of this process.

[7] Kaempfer, *Am Hofe*, 121.

[8] Speelman, *Journaal*, 101–2; Chardin, *Voyages*, iii, 270–2; Qazvini, '*Abbasnamah*, 318–19.

[9] Tavernier, *Les six voyages*, i, 415–16.

[10] Arak'el Davrizhets'i, *Girk' patmut'eants'*, trans. in Brosset, *Collection*, ii, 87.

[11] Matthee. "Politics and Trade." 290ff.

itudinal climatic change – especially in the eighteenth century – is insufficient for us to be categorical on this issue. In 1663 no snow or rain fell for six months from Nakhjavan to Tabriz in the northwest. Wells dried up and crops withered.[12] Between 1666 and 1669 large parts of Iran suffered locust swarms followed by poor harvests, famine, and the plague.[13] Drought and epidemics at this point may have afflicted an area stretching all the way from Mesopotamia to the Persian Gulf coast.[14] The early 1670s saw a drought, locust swarms, and a bad famine, which set food prices soaring and reduced many in the north to a state of begging.[15] In the later part of the decade the staggering cost of living and growing deprivation caused bread riots in Isfahan when people pelted political officials with rocks.[16] From early 1678 until mid-1679 in Isfahan alone more than 70,000 people are said to have died from a terrible famine.[17] In 1681, Armenia and Azerbaijan again were stricken with starvation.[18] The mid-1680s and the early 1690s once again witnessed a prolonged outbreak of the plague, this time in the western and the northern regions. Instances of the plague are recorded as early as 1684–85 when parts of Gilan, always prone to epidemics, were affected. In 1685, more than 80,000 people may have died in and around Ardabil.[19] In the latter year the disease raged in the area of Hamadan as well.[20] In 1686–87 there were outbreaks in Azerbaijan, in Mazandaran, Astarabad, and Isfahan.[21] In 1689 the epidemic surfaced in

[12] Geidarov, *Remeslennoe proizvodstvo*, 174.

[13] Chardin, *Voyages*, ix, 571; x, 2–4; and ARA, VOC 1266, Surat to Heren XVII, Nov. 8, 1668, fols. 155, 941.

[14] IOR, G/36/105, Isfahan to Surat, Aug. 14, 1668, fol. 36. The only source that mentions the incidence of the plague about the time of Safi II's accession is Kaempfer, *Am Hofe*, 59, who was not in Iran at that time. However, an outbreak of the plague in western Iran around this time is quite conceivable given the mention of the plague in Aleppo in early 1669. See IOR, G/36/105, Isfahan to Surat, Sept. 5, 1669, fol. 86b. For the situation in Kung, see ARA, VOC 1266, Surat to Heren XVII, Nov. 8, 1668, fols. 155, 941. For Kirman, see Bardsiri, *Tazkirah-i Safaviyah-i Kirman*, 352–3.

   The problems caused by the lack of food continued into 1669 despite that year's abundant winter rains. See Chardin, *Voyages*, viii, 130; ARA, VOC 1266, Gamron to Heren XVII, 28 Feb. 1669, fol. 923b. Chardin suggests that in 1669 a new famine broke out. The exceptional rainfall is mentioned in Chardin, *Voyages*, viii, 435; and IOR, G/36/105, Gombroon to Surat, Jan. 21, 1669, fol. 55. In Shiraz more than 2,000 houses were destroyed by the torrential rains, which were said to be the worst in living memory.

[15] Geidarov, *Remeslennoe proizvodstvo*, 174–5, quoting Agulets'i, *Oragrut'yune*, 94.

[16] ARA, VOC 1323, Bent, Gamron to Batavia, April 18, 1678, fol. 656a.

[17] [Chick], *Chronicle*, i, 407–08; ARA, VOC 1351, Casembroot, Gamron to Heren XVII, Sept. 1, 1679, fol. 2588b.

[18] Geidarov, *Remeslennoe proizvodstvo*, 174–5, quoting Agulets'i, *Oragrut'yune*, 125–6.

[19] Khatunabadi, *Vaqa'i' al-sannin*, 537.

[20] AME, vol. 351, Roch, Hamadan to Paris, Oct. 31, 1686, fol. 223. This missionary, referring to an outbreak the year before, foresaw a possible recurrence as a result of the extraordinary amount of rain that had fallen. The abundant rainfall in the winter of 1685–86 and the resulting spread of the plague is confirmed in a letter by Sanson written from Hamadan on April 19, 1686, in ibid., fols. 186–8.

[21] Khatunabadi, *Vaqa'i' al-sannin*, 538–40, 543–4, claims 20,000 deaths in Tabriz; see also Witsen, *Noord- en oost Tartarye*, 694. Parts of India, too, were hit by drought and famine in

Shiraz, where it was said to have killed thousands.[22] At about the same time the plague extended over the entire arc that connects Baku with Basra via Mosul and Baghdad. A French missionary in 1690 visiting several villages in the vicinity of Baku commented on the great ravages the plague had caused in that area. When the epidemic struck Tiflis in 1691 it caused many Armenians to leave the city.[23] Mesopotamia, possibly the original of the disease, suffered in particular. Two French missionaries, traveling through eastern Anatolia and along the Euphrates in 1690, noted that from Diarbakr to Mosul the epidemic had raged for three years, causing many thousands of deaths.[24] Said to have started in Basra – where as many as 80,000 people may have perished – the disease at its height in 1691 killed between 1,000 and 1,100 people a day in Baghdad alone. Qazvin, Kirman-shah, Erzurum, and Erevan were also afflicted.[25] Whether the incidence of the plague in Kirman in 1692 was in any way related to the epidemic in the west is unclear. Reports about Surat being stricken in the same period, however, suggest that southeastern Iran was affected as well.[26] In 1696, finally, Fars again suffered a severe period of drought and famine.[27]

Shaykh 'Ali Khan and the reorganization of silk

Desperate and ill-conceived as they may appear, the various measures taken by the Safavid state in this period belie the widely believed image of a system in paralysis headed by a monarch given only to the pleasures of the harem. It is true that Shah Sulayman reigned rather than ruled; following a trend begun under his predecessors, he left the day-to-day affairs of the realm to his officials. Yet, like them, he knew how to select capable administrators and, just as importantly, periodically reminded them who

the same period, though there may not have been a connection. See Martineau, *Mémoires de François Martin*, ii, 448–50.

[22] Carmelite Archives, Rome, O.C.D. 237h, Elia de S. Alberto, Isfahan to Rome, June 18, 1689.

[23] Propaganda Fide Archives, Rome, S.C. Giorgia 1, Giulio da Cremona Capp., Oct. 22, 1691, fol. 429; ibid., Nov. 26, 1691, fol. 438.

[24] AME, vol. 348, Relation du voyage de M. Gaudereau, fols. 451–2; and BN, Mss. Fr. 24516, [Vachet], "Journal du voyage de Perse commencé au mois de décembre de l'année 1689," fols. 185–6.

[25] This figure is given by Hamilton, *New Account*, i, 82–3. Al-'Azzawi, *Tarikh al-'Iraq*, v, 129, 131, speaks of 100,000 deaths in Baghdad in 1689 and of up to 1,000 casualties a day for 1690. Other references to the plague in Basra and Khuzistan in 1691 are found in Carmelite Archives, O.C.D. 184a, annales de la mission de Bassorah, 1691, fols. 54–5; ARA, VOC 1476, Renshagen, Kung to Heren XVII, May 19, 1691, fol. 633a; VOC 1493, van Leene, Isfahan to Batavia, Oct. 13, 1691, fol. 283b; and in Ja'fariyan, *'Ilal-i bar uftadan-i Safaviyan*, 331. For other cities, see AME, vol. 347, Vachet, "Journal," fols. 561–2, 574, 578.

[26] The occurrence in Kirman is mentioned in IOR, G/40/4, Gladman, Gombroon to London, July 25, 1692. The Surat reference is found in AN, Coll. Colonies C², 64, Le Sr. Roques, Suratte, Jan. 28, 1692, fol. 26a. See also Ovington, *Voyage to Suratt*, 347.

[27] Nasiri, *Dastur-i shahriyaran*, 153.

was the realm's final arbiter. There is no better example of this than his choice of Shaykh 'Ali Khan, who in 1669 succeeded Mirza Muhammad Mahdi as grand vizier.

Shaykh 'Ali Khan acceded to the highest executive post at a moment when the signs of an acute crisis were everywhere visible. In Isfahan, shortages occurred when, following the enthronement, the shah and his enormous entourage returned to the capital before adequate measures for its provisioning were taken. Hoarding and overcharging by grain merchants and bakers is said to have led to a threefold rise in food prices.[28] This flux of drought and famine coincided with domestic instability and external military threats. The incidence of a series of spectacular caravan robberies along major caravan routes suggests weakening central authority.[29] A wave of Uzbeg incursions into Khurasan threatened the northeastern border lands.[30] The most serious threat was posed by rebel Cossacks who did great damage in the lands around the Caspian Sea. They not only captured Astrakhan and almost seized Darband but also ravaged the western and southern littoral, where Iran's most productive silk-growing areas were located.[31] Following the devastation of parts of Gilan and Mazandaran, including the towns of Farahabad and Astarabad, silk harvests for years remained low. These events, combined with the excessive expenses incurred by the new shah, had by 1668 nearly depleted the royal treasury. The EIC agents in that year opined that the country "was never in a poorer condition to defend itselfe having neither men nor moneys."[32] A year later their Dutch colleagues noted that orders had gone out for the recruitment of troops to be sent against the Uzbegs but that the operation proceeded very slowly for lack of money.[33]

Known for his integrity, the new grand vizier lost no time in tackling the question of royal income. He immediately embarked on a policy that combined cutting expenses with increasing revenue. The shah gave him a free hand in this: less than a year after his installation, Shaykh 'Ali Khan was said to be in sole charge of the affairs of state.[34]

---

[28] Chardin, *Voyages*, x, 2–4. The famine is also mentioned in AME, vol. 349, du Mans, Isfahan to Baron, Aleppo, April 23, 1668, fols. 161–4.

[29] Matthee, "Politics and Trade," 132–3.

[30] Chardin, *Voyages*, ix, 65ff.

[31] ARA, VOC 1266, Goske, Gamron to Heren XVII, Feb. 28, 1669, fols. 916–17b, 929b; Chardin, *Voyages*, x, 135–8; and Borob'eva, "K voprosu prebyvanii." Goske and Chardin tell the well-known story of how the Cossacks raided the town of Farahabad disguised as merchants.

[32] IOR, G/36/105, Flower, Gombroon to Surat, Nov. 26, 1668, fol. 41. Similar remarks about the poor state of the country and the army are found in AME, vol. 349, fols. 259–62, Père J.-B. de la Maze, Isfahan to Aleppo, Nov. 7, 1667.

[33] ARA, VOC 1266, Goske, Gamron to Heren XVII, Feb. 28, 1669, fol. 930.

[34] ARA, VOC 1284, van Dussen, Gamron to Batavia, Aug. 26, 1670, fol. 2278a.

Dealing with the grand vizier

The Dutch may have been the first foreigners to notice a new direction in the state's economic management with the accession of Shaykh 'Ali Khan. For years, the VOC had succeeded in taking no more than 400 bales of silk by bribing the *nazir* and the *tahvildar* with annual monetary gifts, and nothing seemed to indicate that this situation might change in the near future.[35] Director Goske in early 1668 speculated that, due to the Cossack ruination of the Caspian provinces, he would not have to accept more than 100 bales.[36]

Developments the next season forced Goske to revise his estimate upward to 600 bales. The governors of Gilan and Lahijan, it transpired, had managed to rescue all the silk in their charge from marauding Cossacks by sending it to Isfahan.[37] A great deal of silk had also fallen into the shah's hands because the unrest had kept silk merchants away from the Caspian region. However, the main catalyst, Goske noted, had been the new grand vizier who, as soon as he had learned of the terms of the silk contract, had realized its potential profitability for the crown. Informed about the meager volume that was about to arrive in Isfahan, Shaykh 'Ali Khan had reportedly exploded in rage against the *tahvildar* responsible for deliveries, berating him for failing to get the northern governors to remit the full VOC quota. He had also written to the khans themselves, asking them to account for their failure to comply with royal orders, and had moreover demanded delivery of the entire amount before the end of the season.[38]

Shaykh 'Ali Khan's severity struck fear in the hearts of those around him. Immune to monetary inducements himself, he frowned upon others taking bribes, leaving the Dutch to fret that the *nazir* would not dare accept the 200 to 250 ducats they offered him for a minimal silk consignment.[39] As active exporters of bullion, they were also directly affected when in 1670 a 5 percent tax was slapped on all money transported from Isfahan to the coast. Most disturbingly, Shaykh 'Ali Khan, an official who had earned his credentials in the military, did not seem to have any great interest in commerce, much less in maritime trade.

It is unknown how much silk arrived in Isfahan for the VOC in 1669 and 1670. In 1671, the Dutch anticipated a huge volume and were especially dismayed by the rumor that Shaykh 'Ali Khan, in a desire to institute a silk export monopoly reminiscent of the one that had existed under Shah

[35] ARA, VOC 1255, Roothals, Gamron to Heren XVII, Sept. 23, 1667, fol. 1134; VOC 1264, Gamron Council to Batavia, April 9, 1667, fol. 665; and VOC 1261, Goske, Gamron to Heren XVII, July 12, 1668, fols. 781b–2a.
[36] ARA, VOC 1266, Goske, Gamron to Heren XVII, Feb. 28, 1669, fol. 917b.
[37] ARA, VOC 1270, Goske, Gamron to Batavia, June 18, 1669, fol. 961b.
[38] ARA, VOC 1266, Goske, Gamron to Heren XVII, July 20, 1669, fols. 951a–2b.
[39] ARA, VOC 1270, Goske, Gamron, to Heren XVII, April 24, 1670, fol. 877.

'Abbas I, had issued an order prohibiting the sale of silk to anyone but the shah. They also feared that the grand vizier would do his utmost to force a maximum amount on them because prices in Europe were low and market competition minimal. In the event, however, only 368 bales were sent down. Even for a determined grand vizier, it seemed, procuring raw silk at the place of origin was not easy. The reason for the lower than expected volume was said to be the inadequate capital carried by the royal agent who had been dispatched to Gilan. The man died an accidental death en route, and when it was discovered that he had insufficient funds on him the silk producers had refused to deliver the full amount requested by Isfahan. To avoid any more deliveries later in the season, the Dutch decided to send their silk caravan to Bandar 'Abbas early and to use its departure as an excuse for refusing to accept more silk later in the season.[40]

In later years Shaykh 'Ali Khan was more successful in summoning silk to Isfahan. Possibly taking advantage of newly strained Ottoman–Safavid relations and the attendant slackening of trade through Anatolia, he continued to keep a watchful eye on the silk supply, and each season sent government agents to Gilan and Mazandaran. The officials in charge of those provinces made sure to deliver a large amount punctually around *Nawruz*, fearing punishment for failing to comply.[41] The Dutch, accordingly, were forced to accept a large volume as well throughout the 1670s (see appendix).

Nor was the grand vizier's silk policy limited to attempts at maximizing deliveries from the north. His hand can be recognized in an order, issued in 1670, which stipulated that silk payments were henceforth to be handed directly to the chief eunuch and royal treasurer, Agha Kafur. Until then, the money had always been handled by the *tahvildars*, who received an annual fee of 200 to 300 *tumans* for their services.[42] Aside from reflecting a shift from the *divan* to the *khassah* administration, this was clearly a cost-cutting measure, for the vizier of Isfahan with responsibility for the payment duties did not receive a penny for his service. The *mustawfi khassah*, by contrast, was to receive a bonus of six *pays* on every *tuman* that would flow into the treasury, presumably as a way to encourage diligent supervision.[43] The *mustawfi* continued to receive the silk payments until 1675, when the

[40] ARA, VOC 1284, Van Dussen, Shiraz to Batavia, July 28, 1671, fol. 2371a; VOC 1274, van Dussen, Gamron to Heren XVII, Sept. 10, 1671, fol. 746b; VOC 1288, de Haeze, Gamron to Heren XVII, May 16, 1672, fol. 924a.

[41] ARA, VOC 1360, memorandum Casembroot to v/d Heuvel, March 4, 1679, fol. 1902a. It is perhaps significant in this regard that Shaykh 'Ali Khan's vizier, Mirza Riza, was a former *mustawfi* of Mazandaran. See Nasrabadi, *Tazkirah-i Nasrabadi*, 80.

[42] ARA, VOC 1288, van Dussen, Gamron to Batavia, Jan. 31, 1672, fol. 887a; VOC 1360, Memorandum Casembroot to v/d Heuvel, March 4, 1679, fol. 1906b.

[43] The *pays* was a copper coin that was current among the poor. Workers were often paid in *pays*.

assignment was given to the vizier of Isfahan.[44] It was only under Shaykh 'Ali Khan's successor, Mirza Tahir, that the custom of annually appointing a new *tahvildar* was resumed.[45]

In spring 1672 Shaykh 'Ali Khan temporarily fell out of grace with Shah Sulayman.[46] Yet even his fourteen-month discomfiture made little difference as far as silk was concerned. The Dutch in 1673 requested a small supply, invoking the French invasion of their country the previous year and the ruin it had brought to the silk market at home. They received a sympathetic hearing from the *nazir*, who agreed that their request was reasonable and who may have considered that it was ultimately better to sell to a party that could be counted on for payment. The *tufangchi-aqasi* (riflemen commander), however, on whom Shaykh 'Ali Khan's authority had devolved, insisted on a full acceptance of the quota. In the event, a full 776 bales arrived in Isfahan.[47]

In the same year Shaykh 'Ali Khan was reinstated in his former position. Rather than resuming his task with the same vigor and energy that he had displayed before his dismissal, he now chose to keep a low profile, handing letters unopened to the shah and leaving much of the daily management of affairs to subordinates. In economic matters, however, the grand vizier continued to be in charge and just as adamant as before. Opportunities for resistance were limited. In their attempts to circumvent the grand vizier, the Dutch continually sought to persuade lesser officials to reduce silk consignments. Despite the prospect of bribes, however, the latter chose to execute the grand vizier's orders, afraid as they were of the consequences if they contravened them.[48] Returning dirty silk, as the Dutch did in 1679, was an option but, rather than lessening the total amount, it simply resulted in the delivery of alternative silk.[49] They tried other stratagems as well. In 1674 the VOC received 292 bales and, when it transpired that more was on the way, decided immediately to transport these to the coast so as to have the excuse that their caravan had left.[50] Yet overall, Shaykh 'Ali Khan's vigilance was such that they rarely succeeded, and if they did it was usually because of low silk harvests. Thus in 1675 the VOC received no more than 390 bales, apparently because of a meager yield in the Caspian provinces.[51] The following year Shaykh 'Ali Khan, accompanying Shah Sulayman on a journey to Mazandaran, was able personally to supervise the governor's silk dealings and, as if to demonstrate that the low volume of the previous year

[44] ARA, VOC 1349, Bent, Gamron to Batavia, Nov. 25, 1679, fol. 1709b.
[45] ARA, VOC 1611, memorandum Hoogcamer to Casteleyn, May 31, 1698, fol. 55.
[46] For this, see Matthee, "Administrative Stability."
[47] ARA, VOC 1285, de Haeze, Gamron to Heren XVII, May 6, 1673, fol. 385; ibid., de Haeze, Shiraz to Heren XVII, July 31, 1673, fol. 380b.
[48] ARA, VOC 1351, Casembroot, Gamron to Heren XVII, Sept. 1, 1679, fol. 2584b.
[49] ARA, VOC 1360, Casembroot, Gamron to Batavia, March 4, 1680, fols. 1881a–2a.
[50] ARA, VOC 1304, Bent, Gamron to Batavia, Sept. 4, 1674, fols. 510a, 518a.
[51] ARA, VOC 1297, Bent, Gamron to Heren XVII, July 12, 1675, fol. 1018a.

had been an aberration, forced the VOC to take 588 bales.[52] Shaykh 'Ali Khan's personal supervision of silk affairs translated into equally large supplies during the next few years. In response, the Dutch could do little more than protest and delay payments, for they realized that a refusal to take the silk might jeopardize their entire contract. In the early 1670s, the Heren XVII, faced with a disastrous silk market in Holland, had suggested that it might be preferable to pay tolls than to be tied to an unprofitable contract. Now that silk again made money at home, they encouraged their agents in Iran not to risk its abolition.[53]

Shaykh 'Ali Khan, no doubt aware of the state of the silk market in Europe, proved adept at playing this very game. According to information passed on by the vizier of Isfahan, the grand vizier in 1679 gave orders to hand the silk destined for the Dutch to the *malik al-tujjar*, who in turn was to sell it to Armenian merchants at a price equal to that paid by the VOC.[54] Director Bent later confirmed that the grand vizier had threatened to force the silk on the Armenians. However, he reassured his superiors, this was pure bluff, since the Iranians would not be the first to give up the contract. As for the Armenians, they would not be so gullible as to take expensive silk that would only increase in price with transportation.[55] Although nothing seems to have come of this, it reminded the Dutch just how dependent on the court they were.

Toward renewed armed confrontation

For the Dutch in Iran, the early 1680s resembled the early 1640s to a remarkable degree: they were not just unhappy with the price they paid for silk but also extremely displeased with the conditions under which they conducted their trade. The officials in Bandar 'Abbas treated them with contempt. In Isfahan they had become involved in a dispute about a newly instituted 1 percent fee on merchandise that tax farmers claimed for storage.[56] Forced to pay for their silk in Isfahan instead of Bandar 'Abbas, they were burdened with interest payments on bills of exchange. And they found no relief from large silk consignments at a time when profits in Europe were once again falling. In 1679 yet another large volume was

52 ARA, VOC 1315, Bent, Gamron to Batavia, Jan. 20, 1677, fol. 638a; ibid., Bent, Gamron to Heren XVII, July 17, 1677, fol. 725a.
53 ARA, VOC 319, Heren XVII to Batavia, Aug. 27, 1671; and VOC 320, Heren XVII to Batavia, Aug. 31, 1678, unfol. With Surat and Malabar, Iran formed an exception to the general tendency of falling VOC profits in Asia in the 1670s. While only 1 percent of the Company's expenses went to Iran, the country yielded 6.2 percent of its revenue. See Gaastra, *Bewind en beleid*, 81, 85.
54 ARA, VOC 1323, Casembroot, Isfahan to Bent, Gamron, May 26, 1678, fol. 662a.
55 ARA, VOC 1323, Bent, Gamron to Heren XVII, July 30, 1678, fol. 652a.
56 ARA, VOC 1343, resolution Gamron Council, March 18, 1680, fol. 603a; VOC 1370, request Casembroot to grand vizier, Feb. 6, 1681, fols. 2523a–5a; VOC 1379, Casembroot, Gamron to Batavia, March 6, 1682, fol. 2652a.

delivered, 528 bales in all. The following year they faced a similar prospect. Pleading and cajoling had even less effect than usual, for court officials could ill afford to be accused of aiding and abetting foreign merchants. Increasingly unpredictable in his behavior, the shah had blinded the *divanbegi* while treating Shaykh 'Ali Khan and the *nazir* to the bastinado.[57]

To modify the silk contract thus once again became Dutch priority. Changing the terms of trade, the argument went, was justified because the original contract had been made at a time of low competition in the Iranian market. With the entry of rivals such as the French, opportunities had become more limited and import wares had fallen in price.[58] As always, the Dutch viewed freedom of trade as the ideal. They realized, however, that the Iranians would only accept complete freedom, including toll exemption, in return for an annual fee to the shah equal to the court's loss in silk and toll revenues. They also anticipated that giving up the trade accord would mean having to pay tolls of 15 to 16 percent, a loss of sovereignty – they would be unable to fly their flag over their factory, and the Iranians would inspect their warehouses and search their caravans – and an increase in the *shahbandar's* farming fees.[59] An alternative option might be a structural reduction to 300–400 bales of good *kadkhuda pasand* quality, as opposed to the inferior *kharvari* which made up much of current supplies, even at the risk of causing a price increase.[60]

Short-term policy as of 1680 was to be based on the second option, with the understanding that an Iranian refusal to cooperate might justify more drastic action. In that year the Heren XVII ordered their subordinates not to take any more silk than could be paid for with proceeds in Iran, an estimated 300 to 340 bales.[61] Justus van den Heuvel, chief merchant in Isfahan, also received permission to grease the palms of various officials responsible for the silk transfers.[62]

All such efforts were in vain. Neither multiple requests for a reduction in silk and exemption from newly instituted road taxes, nor threats that the VOC would leave Iran altogether, had any effect.[63] Shaykh 'Ali Khan, highly irritated at the Dutch persistence, at times declined even to read their petitions. Whenever the VOC interpreter accosted him, he refused to listen and simply stated that, since the Dutch were not at war with any nation, they had no reason not to accept the full quota. The Dutch, he argued, were mistaken in thinking that they were dealing with a peddler instead of a powerful monarch, and should withdraw from Iran if they did not like their

[57] ARA, VOC 1343, Casembroot, Gamron to Batavia, April 13, 1680, fol. 610.
[58] ARA, VOC 1370, v/d Heuvel to Heren XVII, Feb. 26, 1681, fol. 2516.
[59] ARA, VOC 1355, Casembroot, Gamron to Batavia, March 5, 1681, fols. 396b–7a.
[60] ARA, VOC 1343, resolution Gamron Council, Feb. 13, 1680, fol. 601.
[61] ARA, VOC 1355, Casembroot, Gamron to Heren XVII, April 17, 1681, fol. 394a.
[62] ARA, VOC 1355, resolutions Gamron Council, Jan. 27 and March 24, 1681, fols. 408a–9a.
[63] The various petitions appear in ARA, VOC 1370, fols. 2523a–5a; and VOC 1379, fols. 2623a–25, 2669b.

contract. Tensions rose further as the grand vizier ordered the *rahdars* to halt all VOC transports between Isfahan and the coast. The *mustawfi khassah*, who received 100 ducats to intercede for the Dutch, was of little help, despite his great influence at the court. Noting the gravity of the situation and Shaykh 'Ali Khan's impatience, he advised van den Heuvel not to challenge the grand vizier any longer and to accept the silk that was being offered, lest all VOC trading rights would be annulled.[64] In 1681 and 1682 the Dutch had no choice but to accept close to the full quota.

Frustrated with Shaykh 'Ali Khan's intransigence and the increasingly uncivil manner in which he felt he and his men were treated, Reynier Casembroot, since 1680 VOC director in Iran and long a hardliner, now succeeded in convincing his superiors in Batavia that drastic action was unavoidable. A new naval blockade of Bandar 'Abbas had been suggested with some frequency as of the mid-1670s. Recent French and English examples, it was argued, had shown that attempts at persuasion were useless. Resorting to force might be a more effective strategy, as had been demonstrated by the Portuguese, who had secured their share in the tolls of Kung by appearing with a naval force in 1674.[65] The initial response from the Heren XVII to this had been negative: the VOC simply did not have enough ships available. Batavia, too, at first was reluctant to authorize force, but in 1676 underwent a change of mood with the appointment of Rijkloff van Goens, a noted hawk, as governor-general. After Casembroot became director in Iran, plans gradually evolved from a blockade to an attack.[66] In 1682 Casembroot was summoned to Batavia for consultation, and the following year the decision was taken to teach the Iranians a lesson by sending an expeditionary force to the Persian Gulf, similar to the one dispatched in 1645.

The mission was supposed to be secret, yet news of its coming had spread to Iran long before the VOC fleet appeared before Bandar 'Abbas on June 3, 1684.[67] The Iranians had thus had ample time to fortify the port in advance. As Hurmuz and Qishm were in the process of being strengthened, the Dutch decided to engage in a naval blockade. Cruising in the waters off the Iranian coast, they sequestered some ten vessels belonging to indigenous traders with merchandise for Iran. Meanwhile, a letter containing Dutch grievances written by the Batavia Council was handed to local officials in Bandar 'Abbas for transmission to Isfahan.[68] When after one and a half months no response had arrived, the Dutch, observing how contingents of

[64] ARA, VOC 1355, Casembroot, Gamron to Heren XVII, Aug. 21, 1681, fol. 426.
[65] ARA, VOC 1343, resolution Gamron Council, Feb. 13, 1680, fol. 601.
[66] VOC 1355, Casembroot, Gamron to Batavia, March 5, fol. 397a; ibid., idem, April 17, fol. 394b; VOC 1379, idem, Sept. 17, 1681, fols. 2628b–29a.
[67] ARA, VOC 1406, Casembroot, Cochin to Batavia, March 12, 1684, fol. 1201b.
[68] ARA, VOC 1383, Casembroot, aboard *Blauwe Hulck* to Batavia Aug. 28, 1684, fols. 712ff; also in VOC 1406, fols. 1210–12.

200 to 300 troops daily arrived from the interior, suspected deliberate procrastination on the part of Isfahan. They thus contemplated occupying Hurmuz. Hurmuz, however, was short of water and firewood, and was also deemed too strong by that time, so that in late July it was decided to attack the fortress of Qishm. Neither party won a decisive victory in the ensuing battle. After several more skirmishes, the Iranians sued for peace and, following an agreement concluded on August 3, 1684, evacuated the stronghold.[69]

Isfahan, meanwhile, continued its policy – apparently orchestrated by Shaykh 'Ali Khan – of confounding the Dutch through dilatoriness and mixed signals. Instead of sending a representative, the court authorized the khan of Bandar 'Abbas to solve the dispute. This official informed the Dutch that the shah had absolved them from buying any silk, allowing them to engage in toll-free trade until a final agreement was reached. They were, however, not allowed to inspect the sealed message to that effect, which was addressed to the Batavia Council. Frustrated, the Dutch agents once again requested a representative mission from Isfahan.[70] Weighing political versus economic interests and consequences, they released the ships in their possession, after confiscating the goods destined for Iran, and ordered them to proceed to Basra. In a replay of the events of 1645, they also decided to explore the trading opportunities in the latter port.[71]

When the VOC agents in Bandar 'Abbas next opened the letter (with permission from their superiors in Batavia), they were disappointed at its contents: canceling the silk contract would mean losing all commercial privileges. The shah furthermore expressed his readiness to renew the silk contract and requested Batavia to send an embassy for that purpose.[72] Under the impression that the court was biding its time and that Shaykh 'Ali Khan kept Shah Sulayman in the dark about developments, the Dutch could do little more than wait while holding on to Qishm. For the time being their multiple requests for serious negotiators from Isfahan remained unanswered. Neither the fact that they held Qishm nor their repeated warnings that they might leave Iran altogether seemed to have much effect on the grand vizier, who no doubt knew that the Dutch stood to lose the most from abandoning their lucrative trade in Iran.[73]

A breakthrough occurred on October 20, when news arrived from Isfahan that, given the distance to Batavia, the shah had asked Casembroot

[69] ARA, VOC 1406, fols. 1279a–80a for the terms of the capitulation of Qishm.
[70] ARA, VOC 1383, Casembroot, aboard *Blauwe Hulck* to Batavia, Aug. 28, 1684, fols. 712b–18b; also in VOC 1406, fols. 1206b–21a; and ibid., resolutions Gamron Council, fols. 1265b–71b; and Casembroot to Shah, Aug. 20, 1684, fols. 1288b–90a.
[71] Ibid., fols. 718b–9a; 1221b–22a; 1273a–76b.
[72] ARA, VOC 1416, Shah Sulayman to Speelman, July 1684, fols. 1660–4a. The Persian text of this missive appears in Nava'i, *Asnad va mukatibat 1038 ta 1105 h.q.*, 294–6.
[73] ARA, VOC 1406, Casembroot, aboard *Blauwe Hulck* to Batavia, Aug. 29, 1684, fol. 1265b. VOC 1416, Casembroot, aboard *Blauwe Hulck* to Batavia, Oct. 20, 1684, fols. 1607b–14b.

to come to Isfahan for negotiations. As Casembroot had fallen ill, it was van den Heuvel and Herbert de Jager who set out from the coast on November 3 and arrived in Isfahan on December 13, authorized to distribute up to 1,200 *tumans* in gifts to the shah and his courtiers.[74] The instructions they brought with them comprised thirty-nine points, the most important of which were requests to annul the 1652 silk treaty, to have absolute freedom of trade in all of Iran, and to be exempted from all tolls.[75]

Upon arrival in Isfahan, the VOC delegates were quickly disabused of any illusions about the mood at the court. The shah, they learned, was extremely displeased with the Dutch. Shaykh 'Ali Khan, no less angry and determined to humiliate the arrogant Hollanders, forbade anyone to welcome the delegates and took no initiative to grant them an audience. After being shunned and snubbed for weeks, van den Heuvel and de Jager learned from the French cleric and court confidant Raphael du Mans that, instead of Shaykh 'Ali Khan, the court registrar, *vaqa'i' nivis*, Mirza Muhsin, had been put in charge of the negotiations. Though welcome inasmuch as Mirza Muhsin belonged to a court faction that was rather favorably inclined to the VOC, this choice complicated rather than facilitated matters, since Shaykh 'Ali Khan, marginalized but not eliminated from the discussions, continually attempted to regain control and did everything possible to obstruct communication with the shah.[76]

All through February and March preliminary talks took place between Mirza Muhsin and the Dutch envoys, when the latter attempted to dispel rumors about their intentions so as to create a more congenial atmosphere. Asked about their offer, they floated the idea of paying an annual *pishkash* (enforced giving) of 800 *tumans* in exchange for free trade. When the Iranians rejected this gambit as ridiculous, van den Heuvel wrote for new instructions to Casembroot, who raised the offer to 1,200 *tumans*, provided that the amount of toll-free trade would go up to 35,000 *tumans*. To this the Iranians objected that under the old contract the amount had been 20,000 *tumans*. After further discussions, the two parties provisionally agreed on the latter sum, with the stipulation that any shortfall in a given year could be carried over to the next trading season.[77]

Further progress proved difficult. The shah, the Dutch were told, refused to enter into any kind of agreement unless and until Qishm was restored to Safavid sovereignty. This message was also relayed to the VOC command in Bandar 'Abbas. Though reluctant to give up their only bargaining chip, the

[74] Ibid., fols. 1622b–3b.
[75] ARA, VOC 1416, memorandum Casembroot to v/d Heuvel, Oct. 30, 1684, fols. 1685a–95b; ibid., Casembroot to Mirza Muhammad Riza, Jan. 18, 1685, fols. 1704a–16b.
[76] ARA, VOC 1410, v/d Heuvel, Isfahan to Casembroot, aboard *Blauwe Hulck*, Aug. 31, 1685, fols. 405a–12a.
[77] ARA, VOC 1416, Casembroot, aboard *Blauwe Hulck* to Batavia, April 9, 1685, fols. 1669a–72a; VOC 1398, v/d Heuvel, Isfahan to Heren XVII, Oct. 13, 1685, fols. 604b–20b.

VOC agents recognized that holding on to Qishm had its price: The English, taking advantage of the Dutch–Iranian enmity, had already captured much of the trade with India and were undermining the Dutch threat to leave Iran with a suggestion to Isfahan to transport all merchandise between Bandar 'Abbas and Surat in their ships. In addition, the merchandise stored in the VOC warehouse in Bandar 'Abbas was deteriorating, and it was feared that any further delay might force the indigenous merchants to move elsewhere. The Dutch therefore decided to relinquish Qishm, and the island was restored to Iranian control on June 27.[78]

The governor of Bandar 'Abbas and Casembroot, negotiating separately, next reached an agreement that would serve as the basis of the interim accord that was later confirmed by the shah: the VOC was permitted to conduct its trade provided a record would be kept of its imports and exports, so that at a later date the appropriate tolls and fees could be assessed.[79] The decree was signed by Shaykh 'Ali Khan, who at this point was officially reinstated as chief negotiator. His return caused talks in Isfahan to continue in an atmosphere of recrimination. Not only did the grand vizier announce that the VOC would have to pay tolls after all, but he also brought up the question of silk, which hitherto had been left undiscussed.[80] As van den Heuvel declared that he had no mandate from his superiors to accept any silk, the talks dragged on until early 1686, when the earlier agreement was reiterated: pending a definitive new agreement, for the conclusion of which van den Heuvel promised the sending of an ambassador, the Dutch were allowed to conduct their trade without having to pay tolls. In June the shah issued a *farman*, ordering the coastal officials to keep a detailed list of all VOC imports and exports.[81] It took until the late summer before the shah signed the *farmans*, another delay for which the Dutch blamed Shaykh 'Ali Khan's machinations. The talks, van den Heuvel smugly concluded, had proved that the loss of income hurt the Iranians, that the Gulf was prosperous because of Dutch commercial activity, and that Safavid officials feared that trade might relocate to Basra.[82] He left Isfahan on November 21, 1686. Shortly thereafter it transpired that he had abused his position for personal gain.

---

[78] ARA, VOC 1416, resolution aboard *Blauwe Hulck*, June 22, 1685, fol. 1736b; VOC 1416, Casembroot, Gamron to Batavia, July 16, 1685, fols. 1719b–23b; VOC 1398, Casembroot, Gamron to Batavia, July 16, 1685, fol. 648b; VOC 1430, v/d Heuvel, Isfahan to Heren XVII, Oct. 13, 1685, fols. 1514a–21b; VOC 1439, v/d Heuvel, Isfahan to Batavia, Jan. 4, 1687, fols. 1617b–18a. The English proposal fell through because the Iranians refused to agree to the demand that the shah pay for damages incurred during war with other European nations.

[79] ARA, VOC 1398, Casembroot, Gamron to Batavia, July 16, 1685, fol. 629.

[80] ARA, VOC 1398, v/d Heuvel, Isfahan to Batavia, Sept. 30, 1685, fol. 643b.

[81] ARA, VOC 1425, trans. royal *farman*, Rajab 1097/June 1686, fols. 327a–8b; and VOC 1430, v/d Heuvel, Isfahan to Batavia, July 5, 1686, fols. 1550b–1a.

[82] ARA, VOC 1425, v/d Heuvel, Isfahan to Heren XVII, July 28, 1686, fol. 451; ibid., v/d Heuvel, Gamron to Batavia, Jan. 18, 1687, fol. 454a.

The van Leene mission

In the first few years following the 1684–85 confrontation the VOC was left in peace by the Safavid court. As no definitive commercial protocol had been established, however, it was inevitable that problems would arise again as soon as the Dutch resumed their trading. When they did so in 1687, the country's toll masters received orders to scrutinize all their incoming and outgoing wares, for the purpose of which special officials were appointed.[83] This lent new urgency to the need for the official mission promised by van den Heuvel. Such a mission, the Dutch thought, was indispensable for a definitive settling of differences and possibly a new accord that would guarantee cheaper silk.[84] They had not purchased any silk since 1683 and the commodity had long ceased to be a priority for them, but it had not lost its relevance altogether. The worsening quality of the Iranian currency greatly lowered the profits made on money transports to India. Kirman wool by now absorbed some of the Dutch profits on imports. The VOC had also entered the pearl market at Kung, in the expectation that this might be a profitable alternative.[85] Neither, however, was able to fill the vacuum left by silk.

For their part, Safavid officials also seemed amenable to a resumption of negotiations. By 1687 the court had three years' worth of unsold silk stored in its warehouses. As the Iranians had intended to sell these remainders for as much as the Dutch customarily paid for their silk, no buyers had come forward. Shaykh 'Ali Khan had even summoned Armenian merchants to gauge their willingness to buy the silk, but these had refused to agree to any purchases. Wondering why the Iranians had not lowered the price, the Dutch speculated that perhaps they still anticipated that the VOC would agree to purchase the silk.[86] In 1688 Shaykh 'Ali Khan also ordered a closer scrutiny of the silk business in the Caspian provinces, as a result of which the governors were once again paying more attention to the shah's interests.[87]

Huybert Jan van Leene, the ambassador charged with the task of renegotiating the silk treaty, arrived in Isfahan on July 13, 1690. A French missionary who witnessed his entry into the capital commented that the splendor of his entourage was such as the Iranians "had hardly ever seen." Among the gifts he especially noted the four elephants "of exceptional beauty" that accompanied the delegation.[88]

From September 14, when van Leene had his first, purely ceremonial

[83] ARA, VOC 1582, memorandum Verdonck for Bergaigne, May 15, 1696, fol. 146.
[84] ARA, VOC 1448, Verdonck, Gamron to Heren XVII, July 16, 1689, fol. 429a.
[85] ARA, VOC 1416, Casembroot, Gamron to Batavia, July 16, 1685, fol. 1726a.
[86] ARA, VOC 1455, v/d Heuvel, Gamron to Batavia, Nov. 25, 1687, fol. 1412a.
[87] ARA, VOC 1559, Hoogcamer, Isfahan to Verdonck, Gamron, July 8, 1693, fol. 800.
[88] Villotte, *Voyages*, 161–2.

audience with Shah Sulayman,[89] until *Nawruz* of 1102 (March 21, 1691), the occasion of the appointment of a new grand vizier, Mirza Tahir Vahid,[90] van Leene was able to do little more than submit a series of written requests listing the terms of a new contract as desired by the VOC. These included the restoration of all former trading privileges, the annulment of the previous silk contract, and the right to engage in toll-free trade throughout Iran. In return the VOC would commit itself to the annual payment of a substantial present.[91] The negotiations that took place between March and the end of Ramadan on June 28, when van Leene was again invited to attend a royal ceremony, were slow and tortuous, hampered as they were by court factionalism and the need for the new grand vizier to consult on the most trifling of matters with a monarch to whom access was ever more difficult. The position of both parties impeded quick progress as well. While van Leene argued for free trade, proposing to pay an annual tribute of 800–1,000 *tumans* and a 3 percent customs fee on all import and export goods in return, Mirza Tahir maintained that any arrangement would have to include silk, that no concessions could be made on its price and volume, and that if the Dutch no longer wished to take silk, compensation would have to be commensurate.[92] Van Leene, sensing that he would not receive permission to leave until a new silk contract was drawn up, and convinced that the grand vizier would persuade the shah to make reciprocal concessions, gradually increased his offer to an annual tribute of 1,600 *tumans* while agreeing to raise the customs fee on imports to 5 percent.[93] On silk the Dutch representative relented as well. Mollified by the shah's promise of a speedy conclusion during the *'Ayd al-fitr* audience, van Leene agreed to accept 300 bales of *kadkhuda pasand* at 40 *tumans* per load. He also expressed a willingness to exceed his mandate and pay a 6 percent toll on imports and 3 percent on exports (noting that this was his final offer, since Basra charged 5 percent).[94]

Following this, the talks dragged on for another two months in an atmosphere of intimidation and intrigue, with the grand vizier claiming that he had little room for maneuver because he was new to his post and had a great many enemies who would suspect Dutch bribery if he made any concessions. The Iranians also made the most of the shah's ambiguous position as a ruler who, though absent from the talks, exercised ultimate authority and could not be presented with displeasing proposals. The monarch, van Leene suspected, was completely left in the dark about the

[89] ARA, VOC 1459, van Leene, Isfahan to Heren XVII, Dec. 20, 1690, fol. 1014b.
[90] ARA, VOC 1501, diary van Leene, March 20, 1690, fols. 505b–6a. The position of grand vizier had been vacant since October, 1689, the date of Shaykh 'Ali Khan's death.
[91] ARA, VOC 1476, diary van Leene, Isfahan, Oct. 21, 1690, fols. 392a–3b.
[92] Ibid., March 28–May 29, fols. 512–47.
[93] Ibid., June 19, fols. 552–3.
[94] Ibid., June 29–July 1, fols. 559b–67b.

state of the talks and the Dutch letters never even seemed to reach him. While van Leene declared that silk from Bengal and China had cornered the market at home, where Iranian silk was left unsold on account of its bad quality, and that the Dutch were ready to leave Iran, the Iranians kept insisting on a written acceptance of 600 bales at 46 *tumans*. In the end, resigned to the idea of contracting silk, van Leene agreed to take 400 bales at 44 *tumans*.[95]

Rather than giving van Leene permission to leave, the Iranians next raised the issue of the Dutch failure to purchase silk in the 1684–91 period, arguing that they would have to pay tolls for their operations in those years. Van Leene rejected this out of hand, insisting that the VOC would rather leave Iran immediately.[96] Before long, however, a list arrived, drawn up by the *shahbandar*, with an overview of Dutch import and export goods over the previous seven years. The VOC, it was estimated, owed the shah 11,000 *tumans* in back tolls.[97] To evade this imposition, van Leene hereupon offered the grand vizier 2,000 ducats and Mirza Yahya, his son-in-law and vizier, 350. At the same time he proposed to cancel all loss of income for the court against the injustice and damage suffered by the VOC.[98] Yet Mirza Tahir deemed this insufficient compensation and notified van Leene that without a "gift" in the amount of $7\frac{3}{4}$ percent of the toll fees these could not be written off. Protests were to no avail, and in the end van Leene had no choice but to pay Mirza Tahir a reduced $6\frac{1}{2}$ percent over 10,000 *tumans*, or 650 *tumans*, in addition to 600 ducats to Mirza Yahya.[99] Further delays were caused by the Shi'i celebration of the sacred month of *Muharram* and the fact that the shah's drinking habits and his bad temper with the grand vizier complicated communications. On September 13 van Leene finally received letters for Batavia, as well as a promise that the royal decrees would be sent to Bandar 'Abbas after his departure from Isfahan.[100] On October 18, after a stay of nearly eighteen months, van Leene, having promised that a new ambassador would be sent to Isfahan, finally left the Safavid capital. Traveling via Shiraz, Jahrum, and Lar, he reached Bandar 'Abbas on November 29.

Days before van Leene left Isfahan, 'Isa Beg, the *ishikaqasi-bashi* (master of ceremony) apprized him of the real reason why the Iranians had insisted on a new silk treaty with the Dutch. Aside from the shah's profit, he explained, the contract ensured that the Dutch would do more with their profits than drain Iran of specie. The VOC's enormous gains, he added, suggested how much Iran's trade meant to the Dutch.[101]

Once in Bandar 'Abbas, van Leene proceeded to write his last letter to the

---

[95] ARA, VOC 1501, diary van Leene, July 14, fol. 608.
[96] Ibid., July 25, fol. 622b.
[97] Ibid., Aug. 9, 10, and 15, fols. 636b, 651.
[98] Ibid., Aug. 16, fol. 655.   [99] Ibid., Sept. 21, fol. 695b.
[100] Ibid., Oct. 12, fol. 707b.   [101] Ibid., Oct. 17, fol. 711b.

shah. In it he announced that his acceptance of 600 bales had been for one year only; beyond that the Dutch did not feel obliged to take that much at the same price. Instead, they aimed at 400 bales at 40 *tumans*, coupled with trade freedom and toll exemption.[102] The royal decree that arrived at about the same time contained the germs of future conflict: it absolved the VOC from paying tolls over the period from 1684 to 1691, but held the Company to an annual purchase of 600 bales at 46 *tumans* per load.[103]

The northern link

The treaties of 1667 and 1673

The most striking aspect of trade via Russia in the 1660s is the growing share of private, or rather, semi-official Russo-Iranian ventures. Despite various, mostly Russian, initiatives, commercial exchange via the Volga route was still not subject to a formal "bilateral" agreement between the two countries. All efforts to regularize trade links had failed in their long-term objectives, either because of Iranian suspiciousness of Russia's motives or because of Moscow's unwillingness to grant concessions to foreign merchants. Neither Iran's political sensitivity nor Russia's protectionist impulses would ever disappear, but a reordering of the economic, and especially geopolitical landscape in the 1660s, encompassing Russia, Iran, the Ottoman state, and the Armenian merchants who plied their trade through all three states, at least opened up prospects for substantial change in this regard.

At first glance little changed in Moscow's preoccupation with its domestic economy. A crisis of the country's copper money in 1662–63 and a disturbing outflow of precious metal prompted the Russian state to take measures aimed at an increase in state revenue as well as the protection of its domestic merchant class.[104] Both goals are reflected in the New Trade Charter (*Noviy Torgoviy Ustav*), promulgated in 1667, which forbade the export of precious metals and restricted the rights of foreign merchants in Russia to operate in border trading centers such as Archangel, Pskov, and Novgorod in the north, and Kazan and Astrakhan in the south. Non-domestic merchants were prohibited from engaging in transit trade, which became a monopoly of the *gosti*.[105]

This decree, however, was almost immediately negated, allowed to be overridden by interests of greater force and consequence. What prompted the Russian authorities to ignore the *gosti* and to grant transit privileges to

---

[102] Ibid., Dec. 29, fols. 734–7b.
[103] Ibid., royal decree, late Dec. 1691–early Jan. 1692, fols. 776–80.
[104] Baron, "A.L. Ordin-Nashchokin," 4.
[105] Andreev, "Novotorgovyi ustav 1667." This Russian policy was supervised by a new and energetic chancellor of foreign affairs, Ordin-Nashchokin.

outsiders again may have been a combination of an urgent need to counter the Ottoman threat, a lack of credit, and the fact that the outsiders possessed what the Russians did not: the logistical and financial ability to take on the transit trade between Iran and western Europe.[106] A new Ottoman thrust into the heart of Europe caused the Romanovs to launch a fresh initiative toward anti-Turkish coalition-building. Desirous to secure its northwest flank, Russia in 1661 concluded the peace of Kardis with Sweden-Finland, and in 1667 signed the treaty of Andrusovo with Poland-Lithuania, an indispensable ally in the anti-Ottoman struggle. New initiatives toward Iran followed the same rationale.

The outsiders were the Julfan Armenians, who had their own good reasons to entertain the northern alternative as an option and who, as was seen earlier, had long probed the Russian authorities for concessions. It was not the inherent convenience or safety of the Russia route which made the Armenians change their attitude toward the Volga route in the 1660s. True, the route was shorter than the maritime itinerary but, as Armenian merchants noted, it was plagued by high tolls and poor security, and it therefore was hardly preferable over the Ottoman link.[107] However, similarly high tolls and a growing number of robberies in Ottoman territory as well as the threat of a new round of Ottoman–Safavid warfare at this point made the Julfans inclined to seek an alternative outlet for their silk trade.[108]

Strengthened in their motivation to turn to Russia by the outbreak in 1665 of a new episode in the Turco-Venetian war, a Julfan mission, led by P'anos Eramadanents and Grigor Lusikents, in 1666 once again engaged in talks with Tsar Alexis Mikhailovich. They suggested the establishment of a fully-fledged transit route between Iran and western Europe through Russia, and a series of privileges for the Julfans as the ones who would ply this route. Their proposals included an Armenian role in the routes to Europe beyond Russian territory, and made mention of various itineraries, such as those via the White Sea and via Novgorod and the Finnish Sea, as well as the route through Poland and Lithuania. In exchange, the delegates proposed to dispatch the entire Iranian silk yield – said to amount to 8,000 bales – via Russia.[109]

The 1666 mission resulted a year later in an agreement between Russia and the Julfans that violated both the letter and the spirit of the newly

---

[106] Troebst, "Isfahan–Moskau–Amsterdam," 188, emphasizes the financial and organizational weakness of the Russian merchants from Moscow, Kazan, and Astrakhan as the reason for the choice of the Armenians.

[107] Parsamian et al., *Armiano-russkie otnosheniia v XVII veke*, 73, in Armenian, quoted in Herzig, "Armenian Merchants," 103.

[108] Zevakin, "Persidskii vopros," 158; Kukanova, "Rol' armianskogo kupechestva," 23.

[109] Parsamian et al., *Armiano-russkie otnosheniia v XVII veke*, 34–41; and Troebst, "Isfahan–Moskau–Amsterdam," 189–90.

concluded New Trade Charter. The Armenian merchants not only received permission to conduct their trade in all of Russia but also acquired a monopoly over the transportation of silk beyond Astrakhan. Aside from road taxes, they were required to pay a (reduced) 5 percent ad valorem toll in Astrakhan and Moscow. Silk that could not be sold in Moscow might be exported to western Europe at the payment of another 5 percent. The Russians promised to provide security for cargoes shipped on the Caspian Sea and the Volga. They also made preparations for the building of ships that would be used on the Caspian Sea. In return, the Armenians committed themselves to the exclusive use of Russia as their transit route. Russian merchants received permission to conduct their trade in Iran.[110]

Iran's role and motivation in this entire episode, by contrast, are harder to fathom and cannot be arrived at on the basis of explicit documentation. For one thing, it remains unclear how and to what extent the Safavid court was involved and represented in the 1666–67 negotiations and the agreement that followed. The Armenians may have presented themselves as a regular trading company in Moscow in order to gain status and legitimacy.[111] At the same time they conceivably operated under some mandate of the Safavid court. After all, in 1671, when Lusikents visited Moscow again, he did so both as the shah's envoy and as the agent of the Julfan merchants.[112] Yet Shah Sulayman, scrupulous in avoiding any action that might give the Ottomans an excuse to annul the Zuhab peace accord, may have wanted to create the impression that the Armenians visited Moscow as mere private merchants.

Iran was equally ambiguous in its reaction to the Russian political initiative, sending the usual vague signals about its interest in joining its northern neighbor in the anti-Ottoman struggle. Such ambiguity, while not unusual in the atmosphere of prevarication prevalent at the court of Shah Sulayman, probably stemmed from a complex set of specific interests and objectives. On the one hand, Russo-Iranian political relations at this point were strained, with both parties accusing each other of improperly handling the Sten'ka Razin revolt that had rocked the lower Volga and Caspian Sea region in the late 1660s. More fundamentally, the Iranians harbored deep suspicions about Russia's role in the uprising itself, believing that it had stirred up the unrest to suit its own expansionist designs.[113] This would explain why Ambassador F. Voznictsyn in 1672 received such a chilly welcome at the Safavid court and why he was humiliatingly forced to approach the shah on his knees. His colleague, the Greek K. Khristoforov,

---

[110] Parsamian et al., *Armiano-russkie otnosheniia v XVII veke*, 44–64; Voskanian, "Novo-torgoviy ustav"; Troebst, "Isfahan–Moskau–Amsterdam," 190.

[111] Herzig, "Armenian Merchants," 192.

[112] Bayburdyan, *Naqsh-i Aramanah*, 140.

[113] Vorob'eva, "K voprosu," 35.

visiting Iran in 1673 as Moscow's representative, similarly found that anti-Russian sentiments were running high in Isfahan, and that no one was more outspoken in this regard than Shaykh 'Ali Khan.[114]

On the other hand, the Iranians were no doubt mindful of their political and commercial interests and objectives, something that involved balancing parties ranging from the Dutch and the English to the Ottomans. Hence Shaykh 'Ali Khan's decision that same year to accord Khristoforov and his suite preferential treatment over missions from western Europe – while granting an audience to a delegation from Russia he postponed seeing English and French envoys with the argument that "the Muscovites are our neighbors and friends and our trade relations go back a long time and have never been interrupted."[115] Tensions with Istanbul were on the rise at that point, Persian Gulf exports were dwindling, and the Dutch kept refusing to take their full share of silk. The grand vizier had therefore good reason to keep his options open and to lend a willing ear to the commercial aspects of Russian initiatives.

The actual short-term effect of the 1667 agreement was negligible. Not only were trade links severely disrupted by the Sten'ka Razin rebellion, but the Armenian merchants with their vested interests in the Ottoman trade also failed to follow up on their commitment to reroute their trade. Yet none of this prevented those with a stake in the transit trade via Russia from continuing to pursue the issue. In fact, Russia within days after concluding the peace of Andrusovo sought to enlist its new ally in a diplomatic and commercial initiative toward Iran. The Poles agreed, and in 1668 they sent a mission to Isfahan, led by Bohdan Gurdziecki, with the aim of persuading Shah Sulayman to join the new Russo-Polish anti-Ottoman alliance and of getting the Iranians to ratify the Russo-Armenian commercial treaty of 1667, provided that part of Iran's exports would be directed to Poland. Gurdziecki arrived in Iran in late 1669 and was received by Shah Sulayman in March the following year. Speaking for the Polish and the Russian authorities as much as on behalf of the Armenian merchants, he ostensibly convinced the Safavid ruler of the advantages of channeling Iran's trade via the northern route, for the result of his mission was a royal *farman* ordering Iran's Armenian merchants to stay away from the Ottoman route and to direct their silk exports henceforth to Russia and Poland. The Polish envoy embarked on his return voyage in June 1670, accompanied by an Iranian emissary, but got no further than Shamakhi,

---

[114] Matthee, "Iran's Ottoman Policy"; and Bayburdyan, *Naqsh-i Aramanah*, 140–2. The latter claims that there was also a pro-Russian faction at the Safavid court, led by Zaynal Khan, the "aqasi bashi" (*qullar-aqasi*?) and Mirza Mu'min "mamalik" (*mustawfi al-mamalik*?). Neither name appears in any of the sources consulted for this study.

[115] ARA, VOC 1285, de Haeze, Gamron to Heren XVII, Oct. 19, 1673, fol. 406; and Chardin, *Voyages*, iii, 171–2, and 191ff.

Sten'ka Razin having meanwhile seized Astrakhan. He stayed on in Shirvan for the next three years, to return to Poland in 1675.[116]

It is unclear why Gurdziecki did not resume his homeward voyage as soon as the Razin rebellion was quelled in 1671. The person who set out for Moscow instead in that year was Grigor Lusikents, heading a mission that represented both the shah and the Shahrimanean family. In the first capacity he was to discuss matters pertaining to Georgia, while as commercial envoy he was also to demand compensation for losses suffered by Iranian merchants during the Razin rebellion and to negotiate the confirmation of the 1667 treaty.[117] The outcome of this mission, a new treaty concluded in 1673, showed the effects of pressure exerted by Russian merchants who feared competition in their lucrative transit trade which yielded them profits of up to 50 percent on silk. The Russians used the frequent incidence of robberies and oppression of their merchants in Iran as a pretext to curtail the right of Armenians to carry transit goods through Russia. The latter were no longer allowed to transport merchandise beyond Astrakhan and Moscow (although they retained an important privilege and an edge over their main competitors, merchants from the Indian subcontinent, in being the only eastern merchants with permission to carry goods beyond Astrakhan).[118] They were only allowed to carry silk in transit if it could not be sold in Russia, silk transshipped through Russia could only be sold to countries with which Russia was at peace, and transit rights were only valid provided they did not conflict with Russian state interests. In the case of such conflict, the Armenians would have the right to sell any silk brought as far as the borders back to the state or its merchants at a minimum price (which was, however, set considerably lower than the market prices at Archangel). They also needed special permission to leave Russian soil. In return for the rights they did receive, the Armenian merchants promised that they would henceforth transport Iranian silk only via Russia.[119]

Not surprisingly, the 1673 treaty with its new restrictions on Armenian transit trade led to an immediate slump in the transit of silk. Only 24 *puds* (about 390 kg or four bales) appears to have been transported to Russia in 1673, followed by less than 100 *puds* (1,630 kg., seventeen bales) the next year.[120] The appearance of a rather frugal Russian mission in Isfahan in the same year further seemed to suggest that the Russians no longer accorded a

---

[116] Zedginidze, "Iz istorii," 12–19. In 1676 Gurdziecki returned to Iran as permanent resident representing the Polish crown. In that capacity he stayed in Isfahan until 1699.

[117] Bayburdyan, *Naqsh-i Aramanah*, 140.

[118] Troebst, "Isfahan–Moskau–Amsterdam," 197.

[119] Baiburtian, *Armianskaia koloniia*, 104–5; Zevakin, "Persidskii vopros," 159; Kukanova, "'Rol' armianskogo kupechestva," 26. Troebst, "Isfahan–Moskau–Amsterdam," 197–8, argues that the partial reversal of Moscow's policy marked a compromise between the state, keen on fiscal gain, and the *gosti*, concerned about market share.

[120] Baiburtian. *Armianskaia koloniia.* 105.

high priority to relations with Iran.[121] Yet it soon became evident that this was a temporary state of affairs. In 1675 the tsar created a post of silk factor, no doubt "in response to what was expected to be a massive expansion of the silk trade [with Iran]."[122] He also ordered the governor of Astrakhan to send as many mulberry trees as would be needed to transplant the silk cultivation to Russia, so that the Russians might become acquainted with the art of sericulture.[123] In 1676 the Russians reinstated the Armenian right to carry their goods via Russia to Europe.[124]

The following years saw an upsurge in the passage of Iranian silk through Russia to Europe, though the volume at all times was far lower than the more than 8,000 bales to which the Armenians, eager to inflate their potential, committed themselves in 1679.[125] In 1676 Armenian merchants moved 1,170 *puds* (about 195 bales) of Iranian silk through Archangel, in 1690 they transported 1,305 *puds* (about 220 bales), and in 1691 1,107 *puds* (about 185 bales, via Novgorod), a volume that doubled to 2,232 *puds* (about 370 bales) in 1695.[126] In 1696 quantities shot up to 5,119 *puds* (about 855 bales).[127]

The Fabritius missions

In 1676, the Dutch diplomat-cum-merchant Coenraad van Klenck obtained the right for European merchants to trade directly with Armenians in Archangel without Russian mediation. Following this, the Armenians began to transport considerable amounts of their silk through Archangel, which became the point of passage of the bulk of Iranian silk going north. As of 1687, however, Archangel lost its leading position to the port of Narva. The rise of Narva was part of a Swedish campaign to divert the flourishing transit trade away from the White Sea to the Baltic. To that effect the Swedes in 1679 decided to establish diplomatic relations with Iran. The man chosen to lead the delegation dispatched for that purpose, Ludvig Fabritius, was a Brazilian-born Dutchman who had made a career in the Russian military. Captured during the Sten'ka Razin rebellion in 1670, he had managed to escape to Iran, spending some time in Isfahan.[128]

Little is known about this first of Fabritius's three missions to Iran. He must have arrived in Isfahan sometime in late 1680, but was only received in

[121] Chardin, *Voyages*, iii, 113–15, noted that the envoy's suite included only nine people.
[122] Baron, "Who were the Gosti?" 14.
[123] Von Nasackin, "Die kaukasische Seidencultur," 30.
[124] Bayburdyan, *Naqsh-i Aramanah*, 145.
[125] Parsamian et al., *Armiano-russkie otnosheniia v XVII veke*, 157–8.
[126] Kukanova, *Ocherki*, 96.
[127] Herzig, "Volume of Iranian Silk Exports," 72; based on Parsamian et al., *Armiano-russkie otnosheniia XVII veke*, 213–24.
[128] David Butler, "Extract uyt den brief geschreven in den stadt Ispahan, 6 March 1671," in Struys, *Drie aanmerkelijke en seer rampspoedige reysen*, 5–34.

audience the following year, together with missions from Poland and Russia, both of which seem to have been designed to gauge Safavid willingness to engage in an anti-Ottoman coalition.[129] In September 1681 Fabritius presented his memorandum to Shah Sulayman. Its main points were permission for Iranian merchants to enter Swedish soil, a two-year toll exemption, and a Swedish offer to build ships in the Caspian Sea. The precise nature of the Iranian response to the idea of diverting the trade to the northern route remains unclear. Fabritius's biographer maintains that the Iranians showed themselves to be ignorant of Sweden's location and its commercial significance.[130] This sounds hardly plausible given the fact that the Safavids had dealt with Scandinavian states, including Sweden, since the days of Shah 'Abbas I. VOC Agent Casembroot spoke of a positive reaction but added that Shah Sulayman insisted that the Armenian merchants themselves would have to consent to the idea.[131] The shah's official response to Fabritius's visit was limited to a letter to his Swedish colleague in which he thanked him for the mission and the proposals it had conveyed. The reaction of the Armenian merchant body, on the other hand, was rather enthusiastic. Grigor Lusikents addressed a letter to King Charles of Sweden in which he expressed his willingness to try the alternative route via Novgorod and Narva, the *kalantar* of Julfa joined him in expressing his interest in the ship-building project and promised that he would urge his fellow Armenians to ply the new route, and various silk merchants decided to accompany Fabritius on his return voyage. Arriving in Moscow, they are said to have been dissuaded by local as well as foreign merchants with the argument that no one in Sweden would be ready to purchase their silk.[132]

Almost as soon as Fabritius returned to Sweden, Charles XI began to make preparations for a second, more elaborate and weightier mission to inform Iran's Armenians merchants about the privileges that awaited them in his country. Fabritius, once more chosen to lead the mission, again was to suggest ship-building facilities on the Caspian, albeit at the shah's expense. Arriving in Isfahan in spring 1684, he was received by Shaykh 'Ali Khan but, in an illustration of the continued importance of the Armenian merchants to the Safavid court, mostly negotiated with a trade council consisting of Julfan representatives that had been instituted by the grand vizier. They solicited suggestions about the ways in which Armenian merchants might conduct their trade with Sweden. Fabritius reminded them of the dangers of the Archangel connection, mentioning the catastrophic loss of 400 bales of silk to French pirates who had attacked a Dutch ship in

---

[129] ARA, VOC 1355, Casembroot, Gamron to Heren XVII, April 17, 1681, fol. 395a.
[130] Johan Kempe, *Konigl. Swenska Envoijen Ludwich Fabritii Lefwerne* (Stockholm, 1762), 101; quoted in Troebst, "Die Kaspi–Volga–Ostsee Route," 143.
[131] ARA, VOC 1364, Casembroot, Gamron to Heren XVII, March 6, 1682, fol. 357.
[132] Konovalev, "Ludvig Fabritius's Account," 95–6.

1678, and on behalf of the Swedish king promised them a two-year toll exemption in Sweden.[133]

Fabritius's stay in the Safavid capital was prolonged into 1685, when he was received by Shah Sulayman during the *Nawruz* audience. According to Engelbert Kaempfer, who accompanied Fabritius and whose well-known travelogue recounts the mission, the shah accorded the Swedish envoy preferential treatment because of the distance he had traveled and the favorable personal impression he made compared with the other envoys present in Isfahan, most of whom were clergy members or officials of lesser rank.[134] Yet what really prompted the Safavid court to pay special attention to the Swedish mission may have been the prospect of an alternative outlet in case the current conflict with the VOC was not solved satisfactorily.

However that may be, Fabritius stayed for a total of three years and four months and, in his own words, in this period submitted ten petitions and saw the shah eleven times. He never received a clear answer from the Safavid ruler. It did not help that at this point Sulayman was often incommunicado. Ensconced in his harem, the shah in the last decade of his life often spent weeks without leaving his palace.[135] Fabritius was finally informed that the shah would be happy to grant his Swedish colleague all of his requests, except for the suggestion to resume war with the Ottomans. This, he was told, the Safavid monarch could not do since his predecessors had made peace with their erstwhile enemy. Leaving Isfahan in autumn 1686 with two royal letters for Charles XI, Fabritius was again accompanied by a number of Armenian merchants, who took thirty bales of silk with them.

Fabritius and his entourage arrived in Stockholm in the summer of 1687. Keen to secure raw material for the silk manufacture industry it hoped to establish, the Swedish immediately embarked on negotiations with the Armenian merchants. The outcome of these was an agreement that was highly favorable to the Armenians. They were to receive royal protection, a low 2 percent toll rate on goods carried to or through Sweden, an even lower 1 percent fee on return goods from Europe destined for Iran, total freedom from tolls for a period of three years, a number of transport facilities, and a hostel-cum-storage depot in Narva. In exchange, the Armenians promised a diversion of their trade line from Archangel to Narva, which they painted as a future Amsterdam in terms of commercial allure.[136]

---

[133] Ibid., 97–8. See also Raphael du Mans, *Estat de la Perse*, LIX–LX.

[134] Kaempfer, *Am Hofe*, 262. Fabritius himself also refers to the preferential seating arrangement. See Konovalov, "Ludvig Fabritius's Account," 99.

[135] After its initial audience, the Fabritius embassy in 1684 had to wait four months before being received again by the shah, who, having lost his favorite wife, had been advised by his astrologers not to engage in state affairs lest more bad luck befall him. See Meier-Lemgo, *Die Briefe Engelbert Kaempfers*, 276, Fabritius to Steno Bjelke, July 3, 1684.

[136] Troebst, "Narva und der Aussenhandel," 166–7; idem, "Die Kaspi–Volga–Ostsee Route," 157, 161–2.

Table 7.1 *Iranian silk carried in transit through Narva, 1683–1697*

Year	No. of bales	Year	No. of bales
1683	165	1691	200
1686	21	1695	400
1687	30	1696	536
1689	200	1697	196
1690	230		

Source: Troebst, "Die Kaspi–Volga–Ostsee Route," 175.

Despite numerous start-up problems, the privileges accorded to the Armenians caused the Narva connection to become a significant outlet for Iranian raw silk destined for western Europe, especially after a new Armenian delegation visiting Stockholm in 1692 managed to renew the privileges obtained in 1687.[137] In the last decade of the seventeenth century Armenian merchants wishing to use the Baltic outlet continually requested and obtained exceptions and special privileges from the Swedish crown. As a result, the Narva route in the 1690s became a much-used alternative outlet for Iranian silk. Stefan Troebst has calculated that, between 1690 and 1697, an average of 272 bales were carried through in transit to western Europe each year (see Table 7.1).[138] The hostel, built in the city after much delay at that time, was said to be home to fifty Armenian merchants, a number that overburdened the available translators and interpreters.[139]

The Narva link did not remain uncontested. A Swedish failure to meet all the Armenian conditions – Stockholm never granted them freedom of religion on Swedish territory – and a never-ending quest for diversification led the Armenian merchant houses to search for an alternative Baltic outlet. A prominent, though somewhat obscure role in this search was played by Khajah Philip'os, a colorful Iranian Armenian who, upon converting to Catholicism, had adopted the name of Comte de Siry and who in 1681, posing as Husayn Beg Talish, had managed to interest the ruler of Brandenburg-Prussia in setting up a transit trade in Iranian silk for Baltic amber.[140] In 1695, operating under yet another name, Philippe de Zagly, he appeared in Stockholm, where his offer to travel to Isfahan to further Swedish commercial interests was accepted. He got no further than

[137] Ibid., 171–2.
[138] Kukanova, *Ocherki*, Table 2, pp. 90–9, gives figures of 200–300. In 1698 the Heren XVII claimed that the Armenians had imported more than 1,000 bales via Moscow and Narva in the previous two years. See Glamann, *Dutch-Asiatic Trade*, 126.
[139] Troebst, "Narva und der Aussenhandel," 168–9.
[140] He next traveled to Isfahan with a letter from the ruler of Brandenburg. The response from Shah Sulayman that he brought back from Iran showed that it was the Julfan merchant houses who were most interested in a transit arrangement. See Hundt, >>*Woraus nichts geworden*<<, 12–13.

Moscow, however, having become embroiled in double dealing and financial difficulties. Representing the Shahrimanean family, he next approached the ruler of neighboring Kurland with the idea of diverting Iran's silk trade via that principality. Frederic Casimir offered the Armenians toll freedom for a period of four years, extremely favorable rates thereafter, commercial rights in his domain, and freedom of religion. Following this, de Zagly in 1697–98 pursued similar arrangements with Poland and Brandenburg. None of these seems to have had any concrete result, however.[141]

More importantly, the Russian authorities, put under pressure by their own merchants and heeding English and Dutch concerns about the White Sea trade, were naturally keen to direct the transit flow back to the Archangel outlet. Its desire to attract Armenians traders in 1689 caused Moscow to prohibit all Western merchants from engaging in a transit trade that excluded Julfan Armenians. In the east, Indian, Bukharan, and (non-Armenian) Iranian merchants were banned from traveling beyond Astrakhan. Here too the Armenians were exempted.[142] In 1692 Moscow forced all (non-Armenian) Iranian merchants to make use of the Archangel connection, as it did the merchants who accompanied the Safavid envoy Muhammad Husayn Khan Beg in 1691–92. One of them, Agha Karim Murad Khan, who carried forty-five bales of raw silk and a certain volume of manufactured silk from Tabriz and Shamakhi, requested and obtained the right to transship his wares to western Europe after the prices offered for them were not to his satisfaction. However, instead of being allowed to travel via Narva, he was forced to take his wares to the White Sea.[143] As for the Narva link, it was effectively disrupted by the outbreak of the Great Northern War between Russia and Sweden in 1701.

Despite its incontrovertible expansion, the volume of silk carried via the Volga route should not be overestimated, at least not when compared with the quantities that continued to be transported elsewhere. The Armenians naturally took advantage of the opportunities offered to them, but failed to live up to their earlier commitment to transport all of their silk through Russia. Russian and Iranian inability to alter this situation became clear in 1692, when Moscow complained about the Armenian behavior to Muhammad Husayn Khan Beg. With the complaint came a demand for compliance. However, no change was ever effected in the direction of the bulk of Armenian-borne silk. In all likelihood the Safavid authorities never pressed the Armenians to follow up on the arrangement. One suspects that, even if they had wanted to persuade the Armenians, they would not have been able to do so.[144]

---

[141] Ibid., 16–20; Gulbenkian, "Philippe de Zagly"; and Troebst, "Die Kaspi–Volga–Ostsee Route," 176–92.

[142] Antonova et al., *Russko-Indiiskie otnosheniia v XVII veke*, 347, doc. 242.

[143] Bushev, "Puteshestvie Mokhammada Khosein-Khan Beka," 166–9.

[144] Ibid., 162; Baiburtian, *Armianskaia koloniia*, 116–19.

Conclusion

The early years of Shah Sulayman's reign confronted the Safavid state with an empty treasury, the combined result of protracted wars, a long-standing policy of converting state land into crown domain, and a diminishing influx of silver from abroad. This acute insolvency prompted the state to search for new sources of revenue. Shaykh 'Ali Khan's appointment as grand vizier and a closer attention to silk and the profits derived from it must be seen in this light.

His energy notwithstanding, the grand vizier's power to impose new and comprehensive terms on the silk trade was limited. Although Shaykh 'Ali Khan belies the image of late Safavid Iran as a hotbed of indolence and incompetence, his tenure also suggests that individual initiative is no match for systemic hypostasis. Ministerial energy and diligence were insufficient weapons against the vested interests of a corrupt political elite, the elusiveness of control over the Caspian littoral and, most intractably, the working of the market. Though it remains unclear whether the state was unable or unwilling to apply enough resources to the procurement of Caspian silk, it was the supply and demand of the market that set prices. The irony of the period 1670–90 is that while the financial wherewithal of the Safavid state hit a new low and the need for sustained silk exports at stable prices was greater than ever, growing supplies of especially Indian silk caused prices in Europe to fall precipitously. The most affected was Iranian silk, which was considered relatively low in quality.

The most significant transregional development in this period was the rise to prominence of the Russian link. The emergence of the Volga connection was in part a function of a new direction in Russia's commercial policy. The Russian state, finally emerging from the turbulence of the early century, adopted a policy designed to increase commercial revenue and to isolate the Ottoman Empire. Iran served both goals. Politically, Russia and Iran remained suspicious of each other. Commercially, however, they drew closer. The 1667 and 1673 treaties marked the beginning of a more regulated and active silk trade between the two countries. Significantly, however, the stimulus behind intensified commercial exchange was private rather than governmental. Though they must have acted under the auspices or at least with the approval of the Safavid state, the Julfan Armenians essentially served their own interests. Persistent Russian merchant opposition notwithstanding, they began to frequent Archangel and, as soon as the Baltic route opened up to them, the city of Narva. Yet for all their new rights and privileges, they never completely redirected their trade from the Levant route, which offered them free trade, to the Russian route, where they still faced restrictions on their movements and activities.

CHAPTER 8

Contraction and continuity, 1690–1730

The turn of the eighteenth century witnessed important shifts in the movement of silk between Iran and Europe. Part of this reflects longitudinal trends, such as the expansion of an indigenous sericulture in southern Europe, and its corollary, a diminishing Western dependence on Iranian raw silk. Italian silk especially, popular since the 1630s, became a sought-after commodity, with exports from Sicily growing year after year. Most importantly, the EIC and VOC in the late 1600s definitively shifted their attention to the Indian subcontinent and more particularly to Coromandel and Bengal, the origin of the decorative cloth for which Europe developed a craze at the time. For silk, they more and more relied on the *tanny* grade from Bengal, the demand for which accelerated in the later part of the century.[1] Whereas in 1676–77 the 81,501 lb of Iranian silk sold in Amsterdam still dwarfed the 14,227 lb from Bengal, as of the 1690s raw silk from Iran typically accounted for 6 percent of sales in volume and 4 percent in value, while Bengal silk comprised 88 percent and 90 percent, respectively.[2]

It remains unclear whether this shift to alternative sources signaled a dramatic decrease in the total volume of Iran's silk exports, or whether the country's raw silk merely diminished as a proportion of a growing supply to European markets. The dwindling volume carried via the maritime route is not a good measure of change, for this channel had probably never represented more than a small proportion of total exports. The reduction in volume of specie entering Iran from the Ottoman Empire as of the 1660s suggests a diminishing counterflow of silk. Yet the fragmentary state of our knowledge of the actual silk traffic via the Levant makes it impossible to be categorical about any long-term retrenchment before 1700. The Russia link, in turn, saw a great upsurge as of the 1670s. Around the turn of the eighteenth century Iranian silk transported north was no longer just taken

---

[1] In England the ban on silk by Parliament in 1700 greatly diminished silk imports of any kind. See IOR E/3/93, London to Persia, May 4, 1700, fol. 149.

[2] These figures appear in Prakash, *Dutch East India Company*, tables on pp. 217–18.

in transit to western Europe but also began to be used in Russia's fledgling manufacturing industry.

Given the minor share of the maritime silk exports, it is not the economic importance that warrants a continued examination of the companies' participation in silk. What makes following the dealings of especially the VOC in Iran interesting is rather the light the Dutch documentation continues to shed on Iran's changing political and economic climate, and in particular the response of Safavid officialdom to the country's growing fiscal and governmental crisis.

By the time Shah Sultan Husayn acceded to the Safavid throne in 1694 the stability that Iran had enjoyed for over half a century was unraveling. Highway brigands plagued the country's roads, outside invaders threatened the borders, and internal sedition and rebellion were on the rise. The Uzbegs staged a series of incursions into Khurasan, while Baluchi tribesmen raided caravans in the area around Kirman and Yazd. Unrest also erupted in places as diverse as Kurdistan, Georgia, 'Arabistan (Khuzistan), Astarabad, and Qandahar.[3]

These developments must be seen and analyzed in the context of long-term changes in the make-up and exercise of power in the late Safavid state. Following Shah 'Abbas I's military and administrative reforms, the state's viability hinged on the effectiveness of a central bureaucratic apparatus capable of keeping the country's centrifugal forces in check. Periodic territorial expansion of the realm, actual or promised, had long contained or deflected these forces. Once frontier activity came to an end after 1648, centrifugality turned inward and began to undermine stability inside the realm. Order and control more than ever came to depend on territorial surveillance and the deterrent effect of military sanction. It is precisely in this area that Shah Sulayman failed. Whereas his predecessors had been ambulant warriors, forever vigilant in patrolling their realm and its frontiers to quell revolts, pacify unruly tribes and repel border raiders, Shah Sulayman reigned as a stationary monarch who, aside from occasional hunting or pleasure outings, preferred to live ensconced in his capital and never participated himself in the few military campaigns launched during his reign. The price of such sedentary rule was a loss of infrastructural power.

Shah Sultan Husayn resembled his father in his aloofness from administrative concerns and his relative neglect of the military. He took the process of retreating into seclusion one step further, however. Whereas Shah Sulayman had maintained the balance between benevolence and severity that had traditionally underpinned the shah's authority, Sultan Husayn's reluctance to intervene directly in the intrigues of his courtiers weakened his immediate "punishing" power as well. Weak-willed and disconnected,

[3] Nasiri, *Dastur-i shahriyaran*, 70; Sanandaji, *Tuhfah-i Nasiri*, 127–8.

Sultan Husayn reneged on the primary task of a Safavid ruler, that of preventing partisan interests from solidifying into a challenge to the established order. A weak center inevitably unleashed rivalry and faction-alism between and among divan officials and court eunuchs and allowed corruption and peculation to flourish as never before.[4] It is no exaggeration to say that, in the early 1700s, not the shah but his immediate entourage was in control of policy making.

The financial realm is where existing problems continued to be manifest most dramatically. Massive bullion exports by domestic and foreign mer-chants caused a veritable hemorrhaging of precious metal. The state tried to stem this outflow by imposing bans or fees on specie leaving via the southern ports. However, if corruption and bribery reduced the practical effect of such measures, their very intention was gainsaid by the simulta-neous official encouragement of the annual hajj – a mass exodus that drained huge amounts of gold from the country via the overland routes. Meanwhile court panoply and the construction of royal pleasure gardens absorbed an ever-greater portion of a shrinking revenue base. The result was excessive taxation on the part of the central government matched by similar behavior on the part of provincial authorities who heeded Isfahan's strictures less and less.[5] As of the 1710s a desperate drive for revenue set in motion a vicious cycle of venality, expropriation and extortion that under-mined economic initiative and profitability. Formerly restrained in its urge to amass wealth by fear of sanctions, the Safavid elite now exacted revenue indiscriminately and mostly with impunity. Yet the results still fell short of the needs. Shortages reached such critical proportions that by 1717 his inability to pay his troops led the shah to order gold from the shrine in Mashhad to be melted and minted into coinage and even to have the precious metals removed from his ancestors' graves in Qum.[6]

As counterproductive as the financial administration was the growing emphasis on the Shi'i character of the Safavid polity, a policy that bred a great deal of resentment among Iran's peripheral population, from Sunni Kurds in the western border regions to the Christians of the Caucasus, whose loyalty to the Safavid state was crucial in this period of external threats. Higher taxes were imposed on Banian Indians and Armenians, groups whose wealth was paired with vulnerability.[7] The increase in fiscal pressure on non-Shi'i subjects was a long-term and incremental process that went back as far as the tenure of Muhammad Saru Taqi.[8] Julfan merchants

---

[4] See the vivid description in Mar'ashi Safavi, *Majma' al-tavarikh*, 48–9. Details about the venality of the court eunuchs may also be found in Ja'fariyan, *'Ilal-i bar uftadan*, 46–7.

[5] Geidarov, *Remeslennoe proizvodstvo*, 167–8, quoting Aguiets'i, *Dnevnik*, 68, 92–3, 114; and Yerevantsi, *Dzhambr*, 39.

[6] Mustawfi, "Zubdat al-tavarikh," fol. 204a; Bushev, *Posol'stvo Artemiia Volynskogo*, 257.

[7] Chardin, *Voyages*, viii, 114; and x, 20. See also Herzig, "Armenian Merchants," 100–1.

[8] Chardin, *Voyages*, vii, 315, claims that Mirza Muhammad Saru Taqi taxed the inhabitants of New Julfa ten times their annual dues in a period of five months.

continued to thrive and may in fact have reached their acme toward the end of the seventeenth century.[9] Yet by this time their privileges began to erode, in a process that accelerated in the early 1700s, when the community lost the advantages of royal patronage and was brought under the jurisdiction of the court eunuchs. State officials were allowed to interfere in Julfa's internal affairs and instances of arbitrary levies and extortion became widespread.[10] Growing manifestations of outward religiosity and with it the ascendance of a doctrinaire strand of Shi'ism, epitomized by the appointment of Muhammad Baqir Majlisi as *shaykh al-Islam* of Isfahan in 1687, sanctioned this increased pressure on non-Muslims.[11]

These conditions had a direct impact on the interaction between the state and producers and, to a lesser extent, merchants. Their lack of mobility naturally exposed the former most directly to corruption and excessive taxation. For merchants the results were mixed. While the loss of central state control entailed diminishing road security and enabled local powers to exact larger fees and bribes, it also left more room for mobile entrepreneurs to circumvent control and evade restrictions. Least affected were the maritime companies. Though they suffered, they had the power, including the power of the purse, to turn dwindling central control to their benefit. Most importantly, they had options besides Iran.

The VOC: the Hoogcamer embassy

In the years following van Leene's departure from Iran, the VOC did not purchase any silk. Owing to low prices in Europe and the profits they made on exporting specie from Iran, the Dutch were little interested in a resumption of silk deliveries. In this they were forced to walk a fine line. While keeping a low profile so as not to create the impression that they were ready to buy silk, the VOC agents could not simply reject offers, for this might prompt the Iranians to raise the issue of tolls. The Dutch dilemma is epitomized in two somewhat contradictory statements from 1696, a year in which great Dutch and English consignments of Chinese silk to Europe caused prices to drop sharply. While the Heren XVII urged Bandar 'Abbas to minimize its silk shipments, Batavia sent a secret missive to Iran

---

9   Fryer in the 1670s claimed that many of the New Julfa merchants were worth 100,000 *tumans*. A decade later the wealth of the shahrimaneans, one of the most prominent Julfan merchant families, was estimated at 70,000 *tumans*. Fryer, *New Account*, i, 258; and [Chick], *Chronicle*, i, 459.

10 The overlordship of the eunuchs was mixed in quality and effect. The tenure of Ja'far-quli Khan as *mirshikar-bashi* until 1713 is said to have caused the ruin of many Armenians, while his successor, Isma'il Agha, was much more benevolent. See ARA, VOC 1856, Oets, Isfahan to Schorer, Gamron, Aug. 1, 1713, fol. 408; ibid., Schorer, Gamron to Oets, Isfahan, Sept. 10, 1713, fol. 891; and ibid., Oets, Isfahan to Backer Jacobsz., Gamron, Oct. 19, 1713, fol. 476.

11 ARA, VOC 1455, v/d Heuvel, Gamron to Batavia, Nov. 25, 1687, fol. 1413a; Khatunabadi, *Vaqa'i' al-sannin*, 540–1.

expressing a preference for 300 bales at 46 *tumans* per load over a cancellation of trade privileges.[12]

The typical Dutch response to this quandary was to pay Iranian officials off, negotiating a sum that was acceptable to both parties. In early 1693, for instance, Agent Hoogcamer was told on behalf of Mirza Tahir that he could expect 600 bales of silk. After protests, the *mustawfi khassah* suggested that a solution might be found if the Dutch agreed to pay a 1,800-*tuman* "gift" in cases of future non-delivery. A written request to this effect, accompanied by a minimum payment of 300 *tumans* to both him and the *nazir*, would suffice. Hoogcamer's response – that he had no authority to disburse gifts without explicit permission from Batavia but that, if the amount would be reduced to 1,300 or 1,400 *tumans*, a letter might be sent to Batavia – epitomizes the ambivalence of the Dutch in their dealings with the Safavid court. When the Iranians kept insisting on 1,800 *tumans*, the negotiations came to a temporary halt.[13] Yet the following year the VOC agents set aside 5,000 *tumans* to stave off demands for compensation for their failure to purchase silk during the previous three years.[14]

Fortunately for the Dutch, their reluctance to buy silk was matched by an abiding Iranian inability to deliver the commodity. Adriaen Verdonck in 1693 expressed his willingness to buy an annual amount of 600 bales of *kadkhuda pasand* but simultaneously voiced his skepticism about Iran's capacity to deliver that much consistently. VOC agents speculated that the Iranians would hardly be able to procure the kind of silk they preferred as long as the shah's control over the silk-producing regions remained weak and good-quality silk was sold to private merchants rather than to the court.[15]

Under these conditions, the 1691 contract proved to be more advantageous for the VOC than for the shah. If no silk was offered, the former kept their money and still enjoyed freedom of trade up to 20,000 *tumans*. The court, by contrast, enjoyed neither silk proceeds nor toll income.[16] It is therefore not surprising that the Dutch were quite content with the status quo. In three years, director Verdonck argued in 1695, they had a turnover of more than 2.2 million guilders, a sum on which a 15 percent toll would have cost them over 300,000 guilders. An additional 2-*tuman* reduction on 600 bales of silk meant an extra profit of 600 *tumans*.[17]

Continuity under even more favorable conditions seemed guaranteed when Shah Sultan Husayn in 1695 ordered all *farmans* granted by his predecessor to be copied in his name. The *farman* involving silk was held up

[12] ARA, VOC 112, resolutions Heren XVII, Nov. 15, 1696, unfol.; VOC 1582, memorandum Verdonck for Bergaigne, May 15, 1696, fol. 149.

[13] ARA, VOC 1507, Verdonck, Gamron to Heren XVII, Oct. 21, 1693, fol. 448b.

[14] ARA, VOC 1559, Hoogcamer, Isfahan to Verdonck, Gamron, Jan. 31, 1694, fol. 865b; VOC 1549, Verdonck, Gamron to Heren XVII, Dec. 9, 1994, fol. 617b.

[15] ARA, VOC 1507, Verdonck, Gamron to Batavia, Sept. 3, 1693, fol. 478.

[16] Stapel, *Corpus diplomaticum, 1691–1725*, 152.

[17] ARA, VOC 1549, Verdonck, Gamron to Heren XVII, July 19, 1695, fol. 585.

by discussions concerning the question of whether the 2-*tuman* reduction obtained by van Leene might not be doubled. The shah, propitiated by an additional Dutch gift on the occasion of Ramadan, seemed favorably inclined to such an additional concession as well as to a cancellation of the toll fees for the previous three years. The *vaqa'i nivis*, brandishing a report concerning the costs and benefits of silk for the court, suggested that the ruler should not let himself be bullied by the Dutch and that they should be made to pay 46 *tumans*. Yet the VOC also won the support of Mirza Tahir, his son and spokesman, Mirza Isma'il, and Mirza Rabi'ah, a rising star at the court who after returning as envoy to Siam had been made secretary to the grand vizier, in addition to being appointed *mustawfi* of the silk-producing provinces. Needless to say, their mediation came at a price: in 1695 the Dutch distributed 1,500 *tumans* among the most influential courtiers, including the grand vizier and two court eunuchs who had opposed the VOC in its requests.[18] In the summer they finally received their new *farmans* and *raqams*, which included the debt cancellation over the previous three years and the 2-*tuman* reduction. Following this they received 559 bales of varying weight, some of it in good-quality *sha'rbafi* silk.[19]

This large volume, the first supply since 1691, was not the beginning of a trend, and not just because the VOC continued to spend money to have future supplies reduced.[20] Following Shah Sultan Husayn's succession, an increase in demand on the part of the court made high-grade silk a scarce commodity. Shah Sultan Husayn was a great builder of pleasure gardens and palaces, all of which required considerable amounts of fine wool and silk for upholstery and draperies.[21] After 1693 silk prices also skyrocketed due to the Nine Years' War (1689–97), a conflict that impeded Italian silk supplies and thus caused a dramatic increase in the European demand for Asian silk.[22] In these circumstances the court was either unable to procure silk or in a position to have silk transported most profitably via other outlets; in either case, it would not have been willing to set aside any for the

[18] ARA, VOC 1549, Verdonck, Gamron to Hoogcamer, Isfahan, May 31, 1695, fol. 590; and Hoogcamer, Isfahan to Verdonck, Gamron, June 17, 1695, fol. 593a; and ibid., Verdonck, Gamron to Heren XVII, July 19, 1695, fol. 585a.

[19] ARA, VOC 1582, Hoogcamer, Isfahan to Heren XVII, Sept. 10, 1695, fols. 67–8. According to Coolhaas, ed., *Generale missiven*, v, 810, the Dutch exported a total of 783 bales that year.

[20] In 1696 Hoogcamer was authorized to hand out 200 to 300 gold ducats in gifts to the grand vizier if silk supplies were lowered and a similar amount if the quality would improve as well. Only sixty-two bales were dispatched with the caravan of 1696. See ARA, VOC 1582, Verdonck, Gamron to Batavia, May 15, 1696, fol. 128.

[21] ARA, VOC 1598, Bergaigne, Gamron to Batavia, June 8, 1697, fols. 77–8; VOC 1611, Hoogcamer, Gamron to Batavia, Nov. 27, 1697, fol. 53. In 1710 the shah ordered the authorities in Kirman to buy up all available wool and send it to Isfahan, where it was needed for the upholstery and decoration of the ruler's palace. See Matthee, "East India Company Trade," 371.

[22] IOR, E/3/51/6065, Brangwin, Isfahan to London, Aug. 6, 1695, unfol.; and Chaudhuri, *Trading World of Asia*, 346ff.

Dutch. It is surely no coincidence that in 1693 Armenian merchants offered to take to the Levant all royal silk that had not been sold to the Dutch since 1683.[23]

The Dutch did not immediately react to this turn of events, keen as they were to expand their Bengal connection. However, concerns about quality and unrest in India once again made them turn to Iranian silk. In the 1696–97 season, the Heren XVII ordered a large quantity of raw silk from Bengal, but also expressed an interest in 1,200 bales of Iranian silk, said to be eminently suitable as sewing silk.[24] By then a silkworm disease in Gilan had made silk so expensive that the shah was said to be unable to make purchases even for his own needs. The royal warehouses were reportedly empty in 1698, and prices paid by private merchants in Gilan rose to 160 *mahmudis* per *mann-i shah* for *sha'rbafi* silk (28.8 *tumans* per bale), 140 *mahmudis* for *kadkhuda pasand* (25.2 *tumans* per bale), and 110 to 120 *mahmudis* for *kharvari* quality (19.8–21.6 *tumans* per bale). In Isfahan 30 *mahmudis* more was paid per *mann-i shah*. In Aleppo Iranian silk in 1699 was offered at 10.8 guilders per Dutch pound, or more than 50 *tumans* per bale![25]

The VOC agents in Iran reacted to the new circumstances in time-honored fashion: they tried to coax the court into acceding to a new silk contract, offering money as an incentive.[26] As for the Iranians, they used the price increase as an excuse to cancel the 1691 contract, invoking the pestilence in the Caspian region and the unfairness of forcing the local population to sell at prices that had been fixed in advance. In return for continued freedom of trade, the VOC would have to pay an annual "recognition" of between 150,000 guilders (3,529 *tumans*) and 127,500 guilders (3,000 *tumans*) for every year that no silk was bought or supplied.[27] Batavia, finally, was worried enough to dispatch the embassy to which van Leene had committed the Dutch when he left Iran in 1692. The mission, led by Jacobus Hoogcamer, reached Iran in early 1701, arrived in Isfahan on June 7 the same year, and stayed in the Safavid capital until February 18,

---

[23] ARA, VOC 1559, Verdonck, Gamron to Batavia, Sept. 3, 1693, fol. 791; idem in VOC 1507, fol. 471a.

[24] ARA, VOC 112, resolutions Heren XVII, Nov. 15, 1696, and March 27, 1697, unfol. For the problems in Bengal, see Prakash, *Dutch East India Company*, 217.

[25] ARA, VOC 1603, Damensen, Isfahan to Hoogcamer, Gamron, June 5, 1698, fol. 1885b; ibid., Hoogcamer, Gamron to Batavia, Feb. 6, 1699, fol. 1851b; VOC 1611, Hoogcamer, Gamron to Heren XVII, June 5, 1698, fols. 41–2.

[26] Mirza Rabi'ah encouraged the Dutch to think about obtaining a new silk contract as well, reminding them that Mirza Tahir was in his nineties and that his death might have adverse consequences for their standing in Iran. See ARA, VOC 1626, Casteleyn, Isfahan to Hoogcamer, Gamron, Feb. 22, 1699, fol. 95.

[27] ARA, VOC 1614, Castelijn, Isfahan to Heren XVII, July 8, 1700, fol. 1120; VOC 1630, Hoogcamer, Gamron to Batavia, Dec. 11, 1700, fol. 1860; ibid., Hoogcamer, Gamron to Batavia, Feb. 3, 1701, fol. 1861b. The *raqam* of Muharram 1111/July 1699 appears in VOC 1603, fols. 1883–84, and is reproduced in Stapel, *Corpus diplomaticum 1691–1725*, 153–4.

1702.[28] Hoogcamer's request was simple: the Dutch wished to see the Iranians comply with the terms of the silk treaty concluded by van Leene. In the negotiations that followed – talks in which, significantly, the Iranians were not represented by the as yet inexperienced grand vizier, Muhammad Mu'min Khan (who in 1699 had succeeded Mirza Tahir) but by the *mustawfi khassah*, Mirza Rabi'ah, the court master of ceremony, *ishikaqasibashi*, 'Ali Mardan Khan, and the former *shahbandar* of Bandar 'Abbas, Mirza Sharif – Hoogcamer was told that, due to the high mortality in the Caspian region silk was very scarce and could not be supplied according to the wishes of the VOC. Instead, the Iranians proposed a fuller version of what they had already proclaimed in 1699:

1 Each year the shah would send his servants to the Caspian provinces at the expense of the VOC in order to buy silk at market rates, which would subsequently be transferred to the Dutch provided the latter would pay tolls and fees on their exports and imports.
2 The price would be adjusted so that the shah would benefit from the tolls on silk.
3 The silk contract would be canceled, but the Dutch would have the right to send their own people to the silk-cultivating areas, with the understanding that the shah would receive an annual sum in compensation.[29]

Hoogcamer reacted to this proposal by insisting that he had not come to cancel the silk contract. The Iranians responded that the official silk price would have to be as high as 150 *mahmudis* per *mann* (54 *tumans* per load).[30] Hoogcamer countered that the references to the plague were mere excuses not to have to supply silk to the Dutch so that, instead, great quantities of it could be sent to Moscow and Aleppo. The viziers of the silk-producing provinces, he contended, did not buy *kadkhuda pasand* silk at 130 *mahmudis*, but low-grade varieties at 50 to 80 *mahmudis*. Purchasing good silk on the shah's account, they resold this to private merchants, using the proceeds to buy silk of lesser quality, which then was supplied to the VOC. Now that the silk contract had been set at 44 *tumans* and a silk sample had been sent to the Caspian area, all avenues for fraud were blocked and the Iranians brought up the plague as an excuse.[31]

Liberally distributing money among the principal courtiers, Hoogcamer managed to conclude an agreement whereby the Iranians would each year deliver 200 bales of *kadkhuda pasand* silk at a price of 44 *tumans* per load. In return, the VOC would be allowed to continue its trading activities in Iran

---

[28] ARA 1667, Hoogcamer, Isfahan to Batavia, Aug. 21, 1701, fol. 287. See also Valentyn, *Oud en nieuw Oost-Indien*, v, 276, 284.
[29] ARA, VOC 1667, Hoogcamer, Isfahan to Batavia, Aug. 21, 1701, fols. 290–1.
[30] Ibid., fol. 292.
[31] ARA, VOC 1667, Hoogcamer's points of request to the Safavid court, Aug. 13, 1701, fols. 366–7.

and to import and export a volume of toll-free goods to the value of 20,000 *tumans* per annum. In addition, the Dutch committed themselves to the annual supply of an assortment of wares, mostly condiments and spices such as sugar, cardamom, cloves, cinnamon, pepper, nutmeg, and mace, to the shah. In case the court failed to supply the stipulated amount of silk, the Dutch were not held to the delivery of these wares. If, on the other hand, they decided to take less than the 200 bales of silk, they still had to furnish the goods.[32]

The new contract resulted in a first consignment of fewer than 200 bales in the spring of 1702, yet did not lead to the resumption of steady deliveries.[33] The Iranians made sure to supply the Dutch with just enough silk to make the latter reciprocate with half the stipulated "recognition." In early 1703 the VOC received sixty-four bales.[34] In 1704 an extra gift to Muhammad Mu'min brought forth forty bales.[35] The court kept justifying its failure to supply a greater volume by referring to the scarcity in the Caspian region. Delivering expensive silk to the Dutch, the Iranians argued, would mean a financial loss for the shah.[36] Even the royal workshops received meager amounts at this point.[37] The Dutch, however, suspected that what kept silk from being sent down was less its scarcity than the self-interest of the governors of the Caspian provinces who found excuses to withhold supplies to the court.[38] In this context they singled out the appointment in 1704 of Ja'far-quli Khan, the *mirshikar-bashi*, as governor of Gilan. This official apparently saw to it that little silk made it to Isfahan, reaping the profits for himself. Since, as a favorite of the shah, he was very influential, no one dared incur his displeasure by protesting about the small deliveries of silk.[39]

Subsequent developments suggest that the Dutch may have been right in their analysis. By the time that Hoogcamer reached his agreement prices were falling again in Europe, following expectations of abundant harvests of Italian silk and the supply of a great deal of silk from Bengal and China. At first this had little effect on the Dutch appetite for silk. Iranian silk, the Heren XVII insisted, continued to be much in demand in Dutch factories.[40] A continuing drop in prices lessened the urgency of buying in Iran, however, so that the Heren XVII ordered their agents no longer to insist on

---

[32] The text of the agreement appears in Valentyn, *Oud en nieuw Oost-Indien*, v, 271ff.; and in Stapel, *Corpus diplomaticum 1691–1725*, 209–13.

[33] ARA, VOC 1679, Wichelman, Gamron to Casteleyn, Isfahan, May 29, 1702, fol. 39.

[34] ARA, VOC 1679, Casteleyn, Isfahan to Wichelman, Gamron, Feb. 10, 1703, fol. 246.

[35] ARA, VOC 1694, Wichelman, Gamron to Batavia, May 25, 1704, fols. 268–9.

[36] ARA, VOC 1679, Casteleyn, Isfahan to Wichelman, Gamron, Jan. 21, 1703, fol. 234; ibid., Wichelman, Gamron to Batavia, March 25, 1703, fols. 173, 184.

[37] ARA, VOC 1694, Casteleyn, Isfahan to Wichelman, Gamron, Aug. 24, 1703, fol. 154.

[38] ARA, VOC 1679, Casteleyn, Isfahan to Wichelman, Gamron, Feb. 10, 1703, fol. 247.

[39] ARA, VOC 1694, Wichelman, Gamron to Batavia, March 29, 1704, fol. 130; VOC 1732, Backer Jacobsz., Isfahan to Heren XVII, Sept. 30, 1705, fol. 236.

[40] ARA, VOC 324, Heren XVII to Batavia, July 23, 1701, unfol.

compliance with the contract.[41] The agents, meanwhile, speculated that more Caspian silk might soon become available, given its diminishing profitability.[42] However, the Iranian court produced little more than hundreds of bales of inferior silk from Shirvan, which were taken to the royal manufactories in Yazd after the Dutch rejected them.[43]

Crisis and the quest for revenue

After 1710 the profound crisis that had been simmering for decades intensified and became manifest on various levels. As pressure on Iran's borders increased, the political order rapidly degenerated into unchecked factionalism, mismanagement, and abuse. The son of the Kurdish rebel Sulayman Baba wreaked havoc on Kurdistan, the people of Luristan deposed their governor, while the inhabitants of Mashhad imprisoned their ruler and his vizier. Shirvan as of 1708 suffered from the uprising of Jaro-Belokanski. Four years later insurgents from Daghistan marched on Shamakhi.[44] Baluchis continued their incursions deep into the Kirman area; Arabs revolted in 'Arabistan; Qandahar was threatened by Afghan forces, and Uzbegs laid siege to Mashhad.[45] Diminishing central control gave provincial rulers a free hand to extort money from their wretched subjects. Some even filled their pockets by aiding and abetting highway robbery, or enriched themselves by hoarding grain. The result was internecine strife and food shortages in Tabriz and Isfahan, followed by bread riots.[46] The shah meanwhile, unaware of or indifferent to, the developments in his realm, built new pleasure gardens and ordered the construction of a new central square for Farahabad, the funds for which were extorted from courtiers and domestic merchants.[47]

Not only were available funds not put to the most urgent task at hand, the assembling of a fighting force, but the collecting of revenue was offset by the opposite phenomenon, the country's virtual hemorrhaging of precious metal. Indigenous and foreign merchants continued to siphon huge sums off to India. Iran's Armenian merchants, hard pressed by the

[41] ARA, VOC 324, Heren XVII to Batavia, July 24, 1704, unfol.; VOC 1714, Wichelman, Gamron to Casteleyn, Isfahan, Jan. 31, 1705, fols. 259–60.
[42] ARA, VOC 1719, Casteleyn, Isfahan to Heren XVII, Nov. 30, 1706, fol. 2157b.
[43] ARA, VOC 1747, Backer, Isfahan to Casteleyn, Gamron, June 15, 1706, fols. 218–19; idem, July 25, fol. 227; idem, Oct. 6, 1706, fol. 269; and VOC 1700, Casteleyn, Gamron to Heren XVII, July 31, 1706, fols. 2418–21. After the Dutch rejected the Shirvan silk in 1706, the EIC unsuccessfully tried to get hold of it as payment in kind for their toll entitlements.
[44] Sotavov, *Severniy Kavkaz*, 46–7.
[45] ARA, VOC 1856, Oets, Isfahan to Backer Jacobsz., Gamron, Nov. 23, 1713, fol. 541.
[46] Krusinski, *History of the Revolutions of Persia*, i, 108, 113, 116–19, 132. In 1711 internecine strife in Tabriz is said to have taken 3,000 lives. See [Chick], *Chronicle*, i, 519. For bread riots in Tabriz and Isfahan in 1717, see Bushev, *Posol'stvo Artemiia Volynskogo*, 83, 106; and Worm, *Ost-Indian- und persianische Reisen*, 272, 293.
[47] ARA, VOC 1856, Oets, Isfahan to Backer Jacobsz., Gamron, April 15, 1714, fol. 714; VOC 1848, Backer Jacobsz., Gamron to Batavia, April 13, 1715, fol. 2280b.

increasing tax burden and growing insecurity, began to invest part of their capital abroad. The Shahrimaneans are thus said to have taken 200,000 *scudi* (13,330 *tumans*) to Venice and 100,000 to Rome in the 1690s.[48] But it was no longer only merchants who carried off money; hundreds of thousands of gold ducats were drained from the country by an ever-growing number of Iranians of high rank who, in a state-sponsored operation, went abroad each year to perform the hajj.[49]

The foreign companies were not spared in the Safavid search for revenue. The VOC in 1706 received a decree whereby the shah allowed his court merchants to purchase all Dutch import goods, to resell these to private merchants. Other problems arose over the issue that had never been satisfactorily settled between the two parties, the continued VOC export of specie. An initially intra-Dutch quarrel between Director Backer Jacobsz. and his deputy, Pieter Macare, concerning their private profit-making in the bullion trade, set off an acrimonious dispute between the VOC and Isfahan when Macare turned to the Safavid authorities, accusing his colleague of malversation and providing the Iranians with VOC account books. This resulted in a decree that authorized the inspection for ducats of all Dutch caravans prior to departure for the coast.[50] Macare sowed the seeds for further problems by lending 14,000 *tumans* to the grand vizier, Shah-quli Khan, who in 1713 succeeded Muhammad Mu'min Khan.

Silk, too, became entangled in the drive to raise revenue. The Dutch received no silk until 1712, when fifty-five bales were delivered to them.[51] Seventy bales followed in 1713.[52] The Iranians, taking the VOC to task for its refusal to pay tolls over its considerable gold exports, argued that if no silk was supplied, no specie could be taken out free of tolls.[53] The issue was the old one: if the Dutch did not buy silk they were not to enjoy unlimited trade and certainly could not export gold. The Dutch argued that they should not be penalized for the non-delivery of silk. Following further claims and counterclaims, the Iranians demanded that the VOC pay toll arrears, calculated at 14,695 *tumans*. The Dutch, in turn, insisted on restitution of the money that Macare had loaned to the court, suggesting that silk deliveries be subtracted from the amount. For the Iranians this was contingent upon the Dutch paying the shah's claim.

In August 1713, a ban was issued on the exportation of ducats without

[48] [Chick], *Chronicle*, i, 485.
[49] This phenomenon is noted in the Persian sources as well as in the maritime ones. See Mustawfi, "Zubdat al-tavarikh," fol. 203r. Gold ducats were the only accepted currency. According to one report, the main court eunuch going on hajj in 1714 took 200,000 ducats with him. ARA, VOC 1870, Oets, Isfahan to Batavia, Dec. 27, 1714, fol. 38. See also Matthee, "Between Venice and Surat."
[50] Floor, *Commercial Conflict*, 11ff.
[51] ARA, VOC 1843, Backer Jacobsz., Gamron to Batavia, March 15, 1713, fol. 21.
[52] ARA, VOC 1843, Backer Jacobsz., Gamron to Batavia, June 22, 1713, fol. 294.
[53] ARA, VOC 1843, Oets, Isfahan to Backer Jacobsz., Gamron, April 27, 1713, fols. 111–12.

the *mustawfi khassah*'s permission. This measure bore the imprint of Shah-quli Khan, a son of Shaykh 'Ali Khan who was said to be as obstinate as his father and to be opposed to all English and Dutch privileges. He raised the question of the unpaid tolls and fees during the years in which the Dutch had failed to purchase silk.[54] It was also found that for years the VOC had harmed the royal treasury by including merchandise belonging to third parties in its own toll-free exports. Intra-elite divisions complicated Shah-quli Khan's task. The grand vizier's main competitor was Safi-quli Khan, the *divanbegi*, who in 1712 had been put in charge of dealing with the VOC.[55] Authority over the silk provinces, including the issue of revenue, was conferred on another of Shah-quli Khan's rivals, the formidable Fath 'Ali Khan Daghistani, who combined the functions of *qullar-aqasi* and *qurchibashi* and who was a protégé of the all-powerful eunuchs, to whom everyone, including the grand vizier, was beholden at this point.[56] Shah-quli Khan pressed the shah to maximize the silk supply for the Dutch. Fath 'Ali Khan had, however, no desire to assist his rival by sending silk on which, anyhow, little or no profit could be made on account of its high price.[57] He insisted on cash payments, encouraged in this demand by the *mustawfi khassah*, who tried to link silk deliveries and payments to the issue of the Dutch export of ducats. As the newly appointed farmer of gold exports, the latter sought to tap the trade for profit by levying a fee on the coins.[58]

Rivalries notwithstanding, the Safavid court in the summer of 1714 presented the VOC with a cancellation of the silk contract as it had been agreed on in 1701. A *raqam* stipulated that, in keeping with the *farmans* issued by the shahs 'Abbas I, Safi, and 'Abbas II, the Dutch were held to purchase 600 bales at 48 *tumans* per load, in return for which they would have the freedom to trade in the amount of 20,000 *tumans*. The *raqam* went on to state that no automatic exemption from road tolls was granted, that all wares transported would have to be inspected, that no Spanish *reals* and uncoined gold could be exported, and that the VOC would have to pay a fee on gold ducats that it wished to take out of the country.[59] A letter with the same content accompanied Muhammad Ja'far Beg, who simultaneously was sent to Batavia with the task of settling the shah's claim on the Dutch and to request the dispatch of an official mission in case the Dutch authorities did not agree to the new terms.

When in July 1715, following Shah-quli Khan's death, Fath 'Ali Khan

---

[54] ARA, VOC 1763, Backer Jacobsz., Isfahan to Casteleyn, Gamron, Dec. 15, 1707, fol. 46.

[55] ARA, VOC 1843, Oets, Isfahan to Heren XVII, Nov. 14, 1712, fol. 191.

[56] ARA, VOC 1856, Oets, Isfahan to Backer Jacobsz., Gamron, July 17, 1713, fol. 351; idem, Sept. 30, fol. 471.

[57] ARA, VOC 1870, Oets, Isfahan to Backer Jacobsz., Gamron, Aug. 6, 1714, fol. 217.

[58] ARA, VOC 1856, Backer Jacobsz., Gamron to Heren XVII, April 23, 1714, fols. 168–9; VOC 1870, Backer Jacobsz., Gamron to Batavia, April 13, 1715, fol. 446.

[59] ARA, VOC 1870, Oets, Isfahan to Backer Jacobsz., Gamron, Sept. 1, 1714, fols. 256–8. The text also appears in Stapel, *Corpus diplomaticum 1691–1725*, 448ff.

was appointed grand vizier, the pressure for immediate revenue grew even more intense. Fath 'Ali Khan lowered the salaries of courtiers, had all the retainers of his predecessor dismissed and started an investigation into their financial dealings, as a result of which several were forced to pay considerable fines. According to the Dutch not a day passed without some official's property being confiscated. Other groups in society suffered as well. Merchants were forced to collect large sums of money to pay for the shah's architectural projects as well as for halfhearted attempts at mustering troops.[60] The urban masses suffered from a steep increase in the official price of wheat and flour, a measure ascribed to the machinations of the grand vizier and other officials including prominent members of the clergy, and famine soon followed.[61] Pressure began to be exerted on non-Muslim subjects to pay the poll tax, *jizya*. Banian traders bore the brunt of this, but even the influential Armenian Sharimanean family, who since the reign of Shah 'Abbas II had been exempted from paying the *jizya*, lost this privilege.[62] The one to benefit most from such policies was apparently the grand vizier himself. During his five years in office, the French envoy Padery noted in 1720, Fath 'Ali Khan had amassed seven times as much in wealth as the royal treasury.[63]

The Dutch, already familiar with Fath 'Ali Khan's avarice, paid the new grand vizier 1,000 *tumans* in the expectation that this might buy them a new lease of life on their untrammeled operations. This, however, did little to mollify Fath 'Ali Khan, who immediately accused the Dutch of massive bullion exports and the "coloring" of goods. Rather than waiting for the return of Muhammad Ja'far Beg – whose mission he dismissed as having been dispatched under his predecessor – he announced that the shah had declared all existing *farmans* invalid and wished to conclude a new agreement, the terms of which were similar to those relayed to the Dutch by Muhammad Ja'far Beg prior to his departure for Batavia. On account of the Dutch bullion exports he claimed the staggering sum of 26,000 *tumans*.

[60] ARA, VOC 1886, Oets, Isfahan to Backer Jacobsz., Gamron, Sept. 29, 1715, fol. 230; VOC 1886, Oets, Isfahan to Backer Jacobsz., Gamron, Feb. 2, 1716, fol. 43; VOC 1897, 4th fasc., Backer Jacobsz., Gamron to Batavia, Nov. 30, 1716, fol. 4; VOC 1913, Schorer, Isfahan to van Biesum, Gamron, April 9, 1718, fol. 286.

[61] Ja'fariyan, "Adabiyat," 246; Bushev, *Posol'stvo Artemiia Volynskogo*, 106–7; Worm, *Ost-Indian- und persianische Reisen*, 272, 293; Krusinski, *History of the Revolutions of Persia*, i, 132.

[62] Fath 'Ali Khan is said to have torn up the *raqam*, stating that the family would have to pay the tax retrospectively for the duration of Shah Sultan Husayn's reign. Following an outpouring of petitions and money the term was reduced to the previous few years. See ARA, VOC 1886, Oets, Isfahan to Backer Jacobsz., Gamron, Oct. 23, 1715, fol. 278. For the pressure on the Banyan to pay the poll tax, see ARA, VOC 1928, Oets, Gamron to van Biesum, Isfahan, Jan. 1719, fols. 330–1; VOC 1947, 3d fasc., trans. letter grand vizier to van Biesum, recd. May 16, 1719, and trans. letter Lutf 'Ali Khan to van Biesum, recd. Sept. 28, 1719, fols. 110–20.

[63] AE, Perse 5, Padery, Shamakhi to Paris, Jan. 5, 1720, fols. 258–60. This was no doubt an exaggeration, the stuff of rumors that tended to swell the illegal enrichment of high officials to unbelievable proportions following their fall from grace.

The VOC received a grace period of thirty days to respond to this and other claims. Only by offering him the considerable sum of 6,000 ducats did Director Oets succeed in placating the Safavid official.

None of this oppressive behavior had any effect on silk supplies: in 1715 no pressure was exerted on the VOC to take silk, which sold in Isfahan at the exorbitant price of 190 *mahmudis* per *mann-i shah* for the *sha'rbafi* grade and up to 160 *mahmudis* for *kadkhuda pasand* (34.2 and 28.8 *tumans* per bale, respectively). The prospects for the next silk harvest were not good either, for the abuse and violence of the governors of the silk-producing areas had caused the cultivators to refrain from cultivating silkworms.[64] In 1716 a terrible pestilence broke out in the silk-producing areas, especially in Shirvan. The epidemic turned even more virulent the following year, when it reportedly caused the death of 60,000 people.[65] In the same period Gilan's peasantry erupted in revolt against the Safavid authorities.[66]

Batavia, meanwhile, in receipt of Muhammad Ja'far Beg's message, had decided that it could not abide by the new terms, and resolved to send an official embassy to Iran. Chosen to lead the mission was Joan Joshua Ketelaar, a German-born VOC official who in 1711 had headed a delegation to the Mughal court.[67] Ketelaar arrived in Bandar 'Abbas on October 4, 1716, left the coast on March 27, 1717 and arrived in the capital on May 16.[68] His *istiqbal* (reception) was pleasant enough, not least because Shah Sultan Husayn showed himself immensely pleased with the six elephants which the Dutch envoy had brought with him. During the next official meeting, however, the gloves came off. The grand vizier asked Ketelaar to which of the two alternatives he would be willing to agree: taking 600 bales each year with 20,000 *tumans* in toll-free trade, or paying tolls on imports and exports. When the Dutchman responded that he did not intend to agree to either but wished to have the 1701 contract arranged by Hoogcamer reinstated, Fath 'Ali Khan replied that this would be impossible, since that accord, having been arranged in a devious manner and with the assistance of courtiers, had been inattentively signed by the shah. The contract, he clarified, had proved harmful for the monarch. If the Dutch wished to accept neither alternative they would have to leave Iran, especially since the wares they supplied consisted of little more than rags, wood, fruit, and tree bark, stuff that others would be able to furnish just as well. When Ketelaar replied that he had no mandate and would have to seek counsel with

---

[64] ARA, VOC 1886, Jacobsz, Gamron to Batavia, March 24, 1716, fol. 11.
[65] ARA, VOC 1862, Oets, Isfahan to Heren XVII, July 20, 1716, fol. 2564; Bushev, *Posol'stvo Artemiia Volynskogo*, 186; and Bell of Antermony, *Travels*, 91–2, 97.
[66] Bushev, *Posol'stvo Artemiia Volynskogo*, 106–7.
[67] For Ketelaar and his mission to Agra, see Vogel, *Journaal*.
[68] ARA, VOC 1913, 2d fasc., report Ketelaar to Batavia, March 31, 1718, fols. 453–61. For a description of Ketelaar's ceremonial reception by Shah Sultan Husayn, see Worm, *Ost-Indian- und persianische Reisen*, 267–71.

Plate 7 Entry into Isfahan of Dutch envoy Johan Joshua Ketelaar and his suite, 16 May 1717, drawing in J. G. Worm, *Ost-Indian- und persianische Reisen*, 1737. Courtesy of Thüringer Universitäts und Landesbibliothek.

Batavia, Fath ʿAli Khan angrily referred to the unambiguous message Jaʿfar Beg had taken to Batavia.[69]

After ascertaining that the shah was pleased with his elephants and did not harbor the Dutch any personal grudge, Ketelaar regaled Fath ʿAli Khan with another 6,000 *tumans*. This proved sufficient to have the 1701 accord reactivated, with the exception of the free export of ducats, a privilege that had never been unambiguously granted. Following disagreement over details, the shah issued a new *farman* to that effect.[70] A *raqam* issued in August 1717 listed the wares the VOC was held to furnish, even in years in which no silk would be offered.[71]

The consequences for silk of this new contract were negligible. The Dutch dutifully requested silk until 1722, anticipating that little or none would be forthcoming. Invariably, the Iranian reaction was that silk was so expensive

[69] ARA, VOC 1913, 2d fasc., report Ketelaar to Batavia, March 31, 1718, fols. 453–61.

[70] Ibid., fols. 471–8.

[71] ARA, VOC 1913, 2d fasc., *raqam* of Shah Sultan Husayn, Ramadan 1129/August 1717, fols. 137–8.

that it would not be profitable to the shah to supply any to the Dutch.[72] Until the eclipse of Safavid rule none ever materialized.

The Russian link

The last quarter of the seventeenth century witnessed a great expansion of trade between Iran and Russia via the Caspian and Volga artery. A shorter route and safer roads helped make the Russian transit route an attractive alternative to the Anatolian link, the eastern stretch of which was increasingly beset with security problems in the late 1600s. Reports about the flourishing state of the main cities of Shirvan corroborate this. Shamakhi, observers claimed, was a commercial hub, the entrepôt between Russia and Iran, and home to some 30,000 Armenians, in addition to Russian merchants, who had their own caravanserai in town, Georgians, Greeks, Turks, Circassians, and other foreigners. Several visitors claimed that Ganja boasted the most magnificent bazaars of the Orient.[73] The settlement of numerous Russian and Indian merchants in Azerbaijan as well as the increasing presence of Armenian merchants in Russian cities on the trade route to the north similarly bear witness to a flourishing trade.[74] The Armenians at this time are said to have captured 70–76 percent of the Russia trade,[75] but participants also included the *gosti*, as well as independent Russian merchants, individuals such as S. Luzin and P. Pushnikov, whose trading networks spanned numerous Russian cities.[76]

An active role continued to be played by third parties keen on utilizing the northern route. The Dutch, reacting to the threat to their maritime trade posed by the war with France, toyed with the idea of redirecting their commercial operations to the land-based Russian route. The famous burgomaster of Amsterdam, Nicolaes Witsen, visiting Moscow in 1690–91, suggested reorienting his country's commerce from the Indies and the Levant to the Archangel link.[77] A similar objective may have underlain the voyage to Iran via Russia undertaken in 1703–04 by the well-known Dutch traveler Cornelis de Bruyn.[78]

The Dutch were not alone. In 1696 the Swedish king, concerned about Philippe de Zaghly's initiative toward Kurland, decided to dispatch Ludvig

---

[72] ARA, VOC 1947, 3d fasc., trans. request van Biesum to grand vizier, March 10, 1719; and response, recd June 3, 1719, fols. 187–9; ibid., van Biesum, Isfahan to Oets, Gamron, May 20, 1719, fol. 173; VOC 1999, 6th fasc., memorandum Oets for Krouse, Nov. 15, 1722, fol. 274.

[73] [de la Maze], "Mémoire," 27; and Avril, *Voyage*, 79, 84.

[74] Rahmani, *Azerbaidzhan*, 179

[75] Tadjirian and Karapétian, "Les voies de transit," 160.

[76] Ermolaeva, "Krupnoe kupechestvo Rossii," 311–13.

[77] Uhlenbeck, *Verslag*, 51.

[78] De Bruyn may have been commissioned by the Amsterdam merchant house of Witsen and de Hoochepied. See Scheltema, *Rusland en de Nederlanden*, iii, 119–30.

Fabritius a third time to Iran, where he was to request reciprocal rights for Swedish merchants, including a hostel and lighter tolls. Fabritius was also to see if Shah Sultan Husayn would be willing to ask the tsar to grant free transit for Swedish merchants on their way to and from Sweden. As Charles XI died before Fabritius left, the latter's mission took on the additional task of informing the Safavid court of the change of power in Sweden.

Fabritius left Stockholm in May 1697 and only arrived in Isfahan in November the following year. Following a rather brief round of meetings with the grand vizier, Mirza Tahir, and Shah Sultan Husayn himself, he seems to have achieved little more in Iran than the expression of friendship on the part of Shah Sultan Husayn, though the Safavid ruler did dispatch an envoy, Saru Khan Beg, with the returning emissary.[79] Shortly after Fabritius returned to Stockholm in 1700 the outbreak of the Great Northern War between Russia and Sweden effectively scuttled the chances of a viable transit trade between Iran and Sweden through the tsar's realm.

With this, the initiative shifted back to Moscow, where in 1689 Tsar Peter I (Peter the Great) had come to power. Under him Russia embarked on an active policy designed to lessen the country's dependence on the outside world by promoting the cultivation of crops and securing raw materials for its incipient manufacturing industry. Peter also dreamed of turning Russia into the conduit for overland trade between Asia and Europe. To this end he conceived a grandiose project to connect the Baltic and the Caspian seas via a series of canals, and undertook the development of a strong Caspian fleet. Ultimately, the Russian ruler hoped to extend trade links to Central Asia and India, a design that led him to dispatch two exploratory missions to the khanates of Khiva and Bukhara.[80]

Peter was equally as interested in the rich resources of the Caucasus and the Caspian Sea region. These included metal, oil, saltpeter, wool, cotton, saffron and, of course, silk. He saw the country as a source of silk for the textile manufacturing industry he had in mind for Russia.[81] Anxious to prevent the Ottoman cities from becoming exclusive entrepôts for Iranian

[79] Troebst, "Die Kaspi–Volga–Ostsee Route," 192–200. Saru Khan Beg cannot have been the same person as Saru Khan Sahandlu, as Troebst surmises, for Saru Khan Sahandlu had been executed in 1691. The shah's letter to the Swedish King is reproduced in Zettersteen, *Türkische, tatarische und persische Urkunden*, 131, doc. 216.

[80] The Bekovich–Cherkasski mission, sent to Khiva in 1716, was annihilated by the Khivans the following year. In 1718 Peter dispatched the Italian Florio Beneveni to Bukhara via northern Iran. For his mission, see Volovnikova et al., *Poslannik Petra I*.

[81] Lystsov, *Persidskii pokhod*, 16ff, 52; and Kukanova, "Russkoe-iranskie torgovlye otnoshe-niia," 232. The first mention of indigenous silk manufacturing in Russia dates from the 1620s, when a "brocade court," was established in Moscow. Further manufacturing establishments are recorded in the 1650s and 1680s. In the 1660s, the Russians began to experiment with an indigenous sericulture. Peter's initial encouragement of a local sericulture in the regions of Terek and Astrakhan failed, since the local population refused to cultivate more than the amount needed for local consumption. The establishment of manufacturing industry only took off after 1714. See Sartor, "Die Wolga," 25ff., 262, 282.

commerce, he also envisioned a redirection of Iran's silk exports through Russia. With this in mind the Russian ruler engaged in a policy designed to maximize the flow of Iranian raw silk to and through Russia. In 1696 and 1697 official orders were issued to assist Iran's Armenian merchants in transporting their wares via Russia to Europe.[82] A specific effort was made to get the Armenians to abide by their commitment, made in 1667 and 1673, to carry all of their silk via Russia. To that effect their previously granted privileges were confirmed, while new ones, such as the right to travel abroad via Moscow and Archangel, were added in 1711.[83]

As always, this failed to achieve the desired goal: the Armenians continued to carry their silk through Ottoman territory. Peter thereupon decided to turn to the Safavid authorities by sending an official mission to Isfahan in 1715. The official appointed to lead the mission was the young Artemii Petrovich Volynskii. It was Volynskii's task to gather intelligence on the political and economic situation in Iran, including the access routes to and from the silk-producing provinces via the Caspian Sea, Iran's military strength, and the country's main agricultural and mineral resources. He was also to persuade the shah of the advantages of the Volga route over the Ottoman link for commercial traffic between Iran and Europe, and to awaken Iranian interest in a commercial agreement centering on this route. Such an agreement would have to include permission for Russian merchants to conduct their trade without obstacles in all of Iran and to be free to purchase any merchandise, including silk, and transport it to Russia. A related issue to be raised by Volynskii was the plight of Russian merchants in Iran. Abused by local authorities who often confiscated their goods without payment, they also suffered from the intrigues of merchants, especially the Julfans. In addition, Russian traders had to contend with robbers in Daghistan, and a number of them had been taken captive by raiding Lezgis. Last but not least, Volynskii was to make the Safavid court put pressure on the Julfan Armenian merchants to honor their commitment.[84]

Volynskii set out from St. Petersburg in the summer of 1715, took a full year to reach Astrakhan, and arrived in Niazabad in autumn 1716. It took him another six months to reach Isfahan, as he was held up in Shamakhi and Tabriz. In both places he became entangled in acrimonious disputes with quasi-autonomous local officials about *mihmandari*, the daily allowance to which he was entitled as a foreign envoy.[85] Volynskii's journal suggests that the treatment he enjoyed in Isfahan was little better. He became further embroiled in disagreements over protocol, turning on the question of whether he would be allowed to follow the Russian custom of riding his horse all the way to the shah's quarters and whether he would be

---

[82] Parsamian et al., *Armiano-russkie otnosheniia*, 244–5, docs. 93 and 94.
[83] Ibid., 249.
[84] Bushev, *Posol'stvo Artemiia Volynskogo*, 23–9, 123–4.
[85] Ibid.. chs. 2–4.

able to hand his credentials to the Safavid ruler in person and in full regalia. He also became the object of endless humiliations by the Iranians, who had long despised Russians for their uncouthness. Long-standing Iranian fears of Russia's military designs grew acute when it was discovered that the Bekovich–Cherkassky expedition, sent to Central Asia as an exploratory mission, had constructed fortresses on the eastern shore of the Caspian Sea.[86] Rumor also had it that Russian ships had been spotted near Gilan. Apprehensive and suspicious, the Iranians queried Volynskii about the motives behind the Bekovich–Cherkassky mission, the strength of the Russian fleet in the Caspian Sea, and the intentions behind the building of fortifications.[87]

Nervous paranoia continued to mark the ensuing negotiations between Volynskii and Fath ʿAli Khan Daghistani, negotiations that, in terms of the stratagems employed by the Iranians, bear a striking resemblance to the experience of VOC envoy van Leene twenty-five years earlier. While the Iranians continually assured Volynskii that they did their utmost to accommodate him, they hid behind the shah, insisting that the monarch could not be told what to do and how to decide. Days after the two parties had agreed on a particular point the grand vizier would report to Volynskii that the shah had had a change of mind.[88] Unlike van Leene's, however, Volynskii's stay in Isfahan was brief. Convinced that he was a spy and afraid that a long stay in the capital might enable the Russian envoy to gain a full picture of Iran's lamentable military state, the Iranians kept the negotiations relatively short.

Some of the Russian concerns voiced by Volynskii met with Iranian resistance or disinterest. In keeping with a position held since the 1640s, Safavid officials rejected the Russian suggestion to form an anti-Ottoman alliance. When Volynskii raised the issue of Russian commercial losses and requested reimbursement, Fath ʿAli Khan refused retroactive compensation but promised protection for Russian merchants in the future. The raids, he said, fell outside the jurisdiction of the Safavid court. The Lezgis were the shah's subjects, yet did not obey his laws.[89] A related topic of discussion was the restrictions to which Russian merchants were subjected. The Iranians agreed to offer them the right to buy silk in Gilan and Shirvan and to export that to Russia while paying regular tolls and fees, but did not accede to Volynskii's request that the Russians be granted special rights in purchasing silk. This, Fath ʿAli Khan insisted during one of their last and most crucial meetings, on July 28, would prevent merchants from the

---

[86] Lockhart, *Fall of the Safavi Dynasty*, 105.

[87] Bushev, *Posol'stvo Artemiia Volynskogo*, 58.

[88] Ibid., 102–6. Lockhart, *Fall of the Safavi Dynasty*, 105–6, relying on John Bell's description, paints a picture of Volynskii's stay in Iran that is distinctly more positive than what emerges from Volynskii's own account as rendered by Bushev.

[89] Bushev, *Posol'stvo Artemiia Volynskogo*, 165–6.

Ottoman lands and other countries to come to Iran and was therefore not in Iran's interest. Volynskii's suggestion to find a harbor that would be more accommodating than Niazabad also fell on deaf ears. According to the Russian envoy, the Iranians failed to see how they might benefit from this project.[90] They no doubt also feared that the Russians had a strategic interest in a new harbor.

Despite the tension and the obstacles, the talks resulted in a Russo-Iranian commercial arrangement, concluded in late July 1717, and ratified by the tsar in July 1719 and by Shah Sultan Husayn in 1720. This accord gave the Russians the right to conduct their trade in all of Iran in security and to purchase silk in Gilan and Shirvan. It also envisioned Iranian convoys for Russian merchants on the dangerous route between Shamakhi and Niazabad. A final point was the stationing of resident Russian consuls in Iran, something that was effected in 1720 when Russia sent its first consul, Semeon Avramov, to Isfahan, and a vice-consul, Alexei Baskakov, to Shamakhi.[91] Not included in the treaty were provisions about the Armenian merchants and the routes they used. Armenian scheming against Volynskii may have helped keep the question of Julfan trade practices off the agenda.[92] The Julfans are said to have jealously guarded their monopoly through Anatolia. According to Volynskii they put obstacles up to safeguard their profits, out of which they paid political leaders, such as the rulers of Shirvan and Gilan, to make sure that others would not export to Russia.[93] However that may be, Fath 'Ali Khan told the Russian envoy that he would be unable to force the Armenians to transport all their wares via Russia.

Following the Russian inability to persuade them to change their habits, but mostly under pressure from the *gosti*, new measures were taken against the Armenian merchants. In 1719 their rights were revoked; henceforth they could trade alongside other merchants and had to pay regular tolls. When the Armenians next reiterated their promise to transport their silk through Russia, the Russian authorities reinstated some of their privileges, most particularly those concerning reduced taxes.[94]

Otherwise the treaty had few direct results. Its terms were widely disregarded and ignored, mostly because by this time Iran's central authorities had lost the means to make local rulers abide by them. The massive unrest in Iran that followed shortly made practical implementation utterly impossible. In 1717, while Volynskii was still in Isfahan, Gilan witnessed an uprising against heavy taxation.[95] Outright rebellion threatened much of Shirvan as of 1718, when the Lezgis raided villages around Niazabad and

---

[90] Lystsov, *Persidskii pokhod*, 79.
[91] Ibid., 62–5, 74; and Bushev, *Posol'stvo Artemiia Volynskogo,*
[92] Ibid., 140.   [93] Ibid., 253.
[94] Soimonov, "Auszug aus dem Tage-Buch," 506–7; and Lystsov, *Persidskii pokhod*, 54–9.
[95] Bushev, *Posol'stvo Artemiia Volynskogo*, 107, 161–2.

Shamakhi and attacked passing caravans. Further raids followed in early 1720.[96] The turmoil and devastation culminated in 1721, when the Daghistani rebel Hajji Da'ud Beg and his men seized Shamakhi and terrorized the surrounding countryside. Russian merchants in the city are said to have lost between 70,000 and 100,000 *tumans* during these events.[97] The episode brought trade between Iran and Russia to a standstill and turned Astrakhan into the terminus for the Volga route.[98] It also provided Tsar Peter with an excuse to launch his Caspian campaign.[99]

The Levant connection

Until more information comes to light from Ottoman archives, the Levant route remains the least well documented for this period as well. One continuing trend was the rise of Izmir as the principal terminus for Iranian silk. In the last years of the seventeenth century, when war in Europe and the disruption of the silk industry in Italy made supply scarce and caused prices to rise, most silk from Iran was sent by private merchants and the Safavid court had problems getting its share from the northern provinces. The movement of silk and other merchandise to the Ottoman Empire is likely to have shifted towards the northern routes across Azerbaijan with the recurrent outbreaks of the plague and unrest in Mesopotamia.[100] Thus in the early 1690s the insecurity of roads in Kurdistan caused many caravans to go north and enter Iran via the Erzurum road. In 1701 de Tournefort reported that, due to the occupation by rebellious Arabs of the shorter desert route via Baghdad, all caravans passed through Erzurum, whence caravans left weekly for Ganja, Tiflis, Tabriz, Trabzon, Tokat, and Aleppo.[101]

Few export figures are available for the last quarter of the seventeenth century. For the period around 1675 the annual flow of Iranian silk through Izmir is given as about 2,900 bales, of which the bulk, about 2,400 bales, consisted of *ardas*.[102] Extant sources permit no comparison in volume with the preceding period but leave no doubt that in the last decade of the century silk continued to be carried in considerable volume through the

[96] Ibid., 215–16, 219–20; AE, Perse 5, Padery, Shamakhi, Jan. 5, 1720, fols. 258–60; Lystsov, *Persidskii pokhod*, 103.

[97] Bachoud, "Lettre de Chamakié," 99, cites 70,000 *tumans*. The Russian consul Avramov mentions a sum of 100,000 *tumans*. See Mamedova, *Russkie konsuly*, 19.

[98] Lystsov, *Persidskii pokhod*, 67–8.

[99] Ibid., 119–20. A good Soviet historian, Lystsov criticizes "bourgeois" historians for focusing on a presumed Russian "cultural mission" and in particular Russia's defense of fellow-Christian Armenians suffering under the Irano-Turkish yoke as the real causes of Peter's invasion. See especially p. 8.

[100] Erzurum itself was not spared an outbreak of the plague, however. See *Lettres édifiantes et curieuses*, iii, 361, Mémoire de la mission d'Erzeron.

[101] De Tournefort, *Relation*, ii, 266–7.

[102] Savary, *Le parfait négociant*, v/2, 716–18.

Ottoman Empire. In 1691 the French consul in Izmir reported that almost all the merchandise bought by the French in the city consisted of Iranian *ardas* silk, whose value was more than five times as high as all other purchases combined. Each year, he noted, 400 to 500 bales were transported to Marseille.[103] In 1698, 618 bales of Iranian silk, 576 *ardas* and 42 *sha'rbafi*, were carried to Marseille.[104] In 1699 an English report from Aleppo called that year's silk harvest from Gilan plentiful, noting that silk was coming in almost daily.[105] In March of the same year a caravan with 450 bales of Iranian silk arrived in Izmir, while an even larger supply was anticipated.[106]

Even when prices fell at about the same time, quantities remained impressive. In March 1700 more than 800 bales were carried to Izmir from Iran, while in August of the same year more than 300 bales arrived in Aleppo.[107] In the records of Marseille's Chambre de Commerce 1701 is shown as the year with the highest importation of *ardas* in the first four decades of the eighteenth century, worth 268,182 *livres*.[108] In January 1702, finally, two caravans brought more than 600 bales to Izmir.[109] It is difficult to extrapolate a trend from such scattered information. Since the figures fail to suggest an aggregate volume, it is impossible to say whether the traffic through Anatolia increased or even sustained its previous level. What is clear, however, is that the transit route between Iran and the Ottoman Empire was far from undergoing a steep decline prior to the eighteenth century. The period around 1700 may in fact have witnessed the greatest volume of Iranian silk exports to Izmir. As for Aleppo, it is estimated that around the turn of the century the Armenians transported between 1,200 and 1,800 bales a year from Ganja to that city.[110] Unfortunately it remains unclear whether this only represents silk from the area or accounts for all of Iran's silk exports to Aleppo.

By the first decade of the eighteenth century, the volume of silk carried through Anatolia began to level off and then diminish. In 1705 the customs inspector at Erzurum reported that the volume of silk coming from Iran was decreasing.[111] To be sure, this was a gradual process. Silk continued to be brought to Aleppo from Iran until the 1720s, when it was replaced by Syrian silk, supplemented by an occasional consignment from the Bursa

[103] AN, Coll. Affaires Etrangères, B¹, vol. 1042, Blondet, Smyrna to Paris, March 18, 1691, fol. 149a.
[104] AN, Coll. Affaires Etrangères, B³, vol. 235, Mémoire sur les monnaies et sur les manufactures de drap, de soie et de coton, fol. 6.
[105] PRO, SP, 110/21, Aleppo to London, Nov. 1699, fol. 29.
[106] ARA, Smyrna a², Hochepiet, Smyrna to Staten Generaal, March 5, 1699, fol. 428.
[107] ARA, Smyrna a², Smyrna to Amsterdam, March 31, 1700, fol. 650; PRO, SP 110/21, Aleppo to London, Aug. 14, 1700, fol. 96.
[108] Ülker, "Rise of Izmir," 83–4; and Erim, "Trade, Traders and the State," 129.
[109] ARA, Smyrna a³, Hochepiet, Smyrna to Staten Generaal, Jan. 24, 1702, fol. 95.
[110] Lystsov, *Persidskii pokhod*, 51; and Bushev, *Posol'stvo Artemiia Volynskogo*, 227. For similar figures, see Frangakys-Syrett, *Commerce of Smyrna*, 29.
[111] Masters, *Origins*, 194–5.

area.[112] Izmir continued to receive considerable quantities of Iranian silk as well. In fact, for most of the 1710s silk was still the most important export product of Izmir, on average representing one-third of total exports to Marseille. By 1716 more than half of Izmir's export volume consisted of silk.[113] An estimate from the same year holds that about 1,400 bales of silk, *sha'rbafi*, *ardas*, and *ardassin*, were annually transported from Iran to Aleppo. Two hundred of these were used in the city's local manufactories.[114] After 1719, the percentage in exports to Marseille dropped to an insignificant figure that rarely exceeded 10 percent.[115] By 1720 the export via Izmir was only a fraction of what it had been at the turn of the century. The trade temporarily collapsed altogether in the 1720s, following the chaos in Iran caused by the Afghan invasion and, just as importantly, the Russian conquest of Gilan.[116]

The Ottomans responded to this falling volume of silk transit by lowering import duties, but as the decline was mostly due to problems at the source this had little effect.[117] The Porte took other measures as well to stem the decline in revenue. In 1716 an Ottoman envoy visited Isfahan with the request that the Safavid state send all of its silk via the Levant route. Durri Efendi, the Ottoman ambassador who in 1721 visited Isfahan with the aim of gathering information about the state of the Safavid realm, brought a letter with him in which the authorities in Isfahan were assured that Iranian merchants ferrying their wares to the West would enjoy protection and full liberty of commerce under Ottoman jurisdiction. Through him the Porte also requested that all maritime trade henceforth be carried through Ottoman territory and that silk should no longer be transported via Russia.[118] The response of the Safavid grand vizier, Muhammad-quli Khan, to this request was reportedly similar to what his predecessor had told Volynskii: he was not in a position to force merchants to follow a particular route.[119]

After the fall of Isfahan

In 1722 the invading Afghans defeated the Safavid army and laid siege to Isfahan. In an apt metaphor, the *Majma' al-tavarikh*, describing the

---

[112] Marcus, *Middle East*, 147, 149.
[113] Frangakis-Syrett, *Commerce of Smyrna*, 225.
[114] AE, Perse 5, Commerce d'Alep, fol. 22.
[115] Frangakis-Syrett, "Ottoman Port of Izmir," 150, 161.
[116] Frangakis-Syrett, *Commerce of Smyrna*, 225.
[117] Masters, *Origins*, 194–5.
[118] In a further sign of concern over the Levant trade, the Ottomans asked the shah not to grant the French trading privileges in the Persian Gulf. See Durri Efendi, *Relation*, 67–8; Volovnikova, *Poslannik Petra I*, 56; and Mamedova, *Russkie konsuly*, 19. According to Bayburdyan, *Naqsh-i Aramanah*, 157, the Ottoman request included a ban on all European shipping in the Persian Gulf and Iranian control of Russian shipping in the Caspian Sea.
[119] Volovnikova, *Poslannik Petra I*, 56.

desperate state of the beleaguered city, states that "people who used to dress in silk clothing had to resort to leaf eating like the silkworm."[120] After six months and horrible scenes of starvation and cannibalism, the city on October 23 fell to the forces of the Afghan commander Mahmud Ghalzai. Shah Sultan Husayn was captured and imprisoned in his harem, while one of his sons, Tahmasp II, managed to escape to the north where he proclaimed himself Shah in the old Safavid capital of Qazvin.[121]

The Afghans never reached the silk-producing parts of Iran, though they at one point threatened Gilan. The Caspian littoral and the Transcaucasian region of Shirvan escaped the Afghan invasion as well, but were not left untouched by the chaos that accompanied the fall of Isfahan. Peter the Great, prompted to move by the turmoil in Iran and the fall of Shamakhi to Hajji Da'ud Beg, in 1722 launched an invasion that won him possession of the western Caspian littoral as far as Darband. Logistical difficulties made it impossible for the Russians to continue their march that same year despite pleas by Shah Tahmasp II, who promised to cede Rasht, Shamakhi, and Baku in return for assistance against the Afghans.[122] The following year the Russians continued their thrust by landing troops in Gilan. This aggression changed the minds of Tahmasp and the local authorities in Gilan, who now saw the Russians as a greater threat than the Afghans. Their armed resistance did not, however, prevent the Russians from taking control over the entire Caspian coastal area, from Baku to Astarabad, encompassing the provinces of Talish, Gilan, and Mazandaran.

The Ottomans, meanwhile, threatened Azerbaijan and Shirvan. Their appetite for the latter region, awakened by Iran's weakness, was further sharpened when Da'ud Beg, the master of Shamakhi, solicited their protection against the Russians. The result was a 1723 Russo–Turkish agreement that protected borders and established spheres of influence in the area between the Black and Caspian Seas, leaving Shamakhi as a buffer, albeit under Ottoman protection and influence. The Ottomans subsequently launched their attack on northwestern Iran, taking Erevan in 1724 and, after a season of unsuccessful campaigning, Tabriz in 1725. In the same year they captured Ganja and, taking advantage of the death of Peter the Great, pushed as far as Ardabil. In the end they managed to establish control over all of Georgia, Armenia, Azerbaijan, and Shirvan.[123]

Sericulture and the silk trade naturally suffered heavily from these events. As usual, little information is available about the vicissitudes of the Levant connection. The Aleppo link was clearly adversely affected, for as of early

---

[120] Mar'ashi Safavi, *Majma' al-tavarikh*, 58.
[121] He subsequently moved to Tabriz and, when the Ottoman army threatened Azerbaijan, relocated to Ardabil. Chased from the latter place by the Ottomans, he returned to Qazvin in 1725, to end up in Tehran.
[122] Lockhart, *Fall of the Safavi Dynasty*, 186.
[123] Ibid.. 265–6.

1725 the English factors in Aleppo reported that little or no Iranian silk was reaching the city.[124] Other outlets may have fared better in light of alleged Ottoman attempts to increase revenue by stimulating the export trade from the areas under their control. Fariba Zarinebaf-Shahr claims that the trade in "kinar" silk showed "clear signs of recovery" under the Ottomans, but, in the absence of figures for the period between 1720 and 1727, only offers evidence for long-term continuity and stability in low volume. Thus in 1719, 23,505 *mann-i Tabriz* or some 700 bales were officially moved through Erzurum. This volume in 1728–29 increased but little to 24,010 *mann*, some 720 bales.[125] Gilan, occupied by the Russians and cut off from the Levant channels, cannot have sent much silk east in this period. Overall, there appears to have been a significant drop in exports through Erzurum following the Ottoman withdrawal from Tabriz, though we have no way of knowing if this was due to the turmoil in Iran or to the termination of Ottoman jurisdiction.[126]

More is known about the fate of the Caspian region. The Iranian chronicler Muhammad ʿAli Hazin paints a vivid picture of the ruination of the province of Gilan following the Russian invasion of the province.[127] By 1723, all Armenians are said to have fled Gilan and Mazandaran.[128] The Russian officer Soimonov, describing the decline of silk cultivation and northern trade in the early 1720s, noted that, though there was still money around in the villages, there was no more profit "because buyers no longer came for the available silk." Caravans arriving from Anatolia, Soimonov claimed, were robbed by Hajji Daʾud Beg, while the Afghan lust for plunder had made all roads in Iran and the routes from India unsafe. As a result, the reputedly fifty caravanserais of Rasht had been empty for years. There was also the fear of the Russians, whose invasion had been followed by the emigration of the city's principal merchants. As Soimonov put it, the "pretty trading town had turned into a place of arms."[129]

Following the demise of Safavid rule silk continued to go through Astrakhan, albeit in small quantities. While in 1712 Armenian merchants had transported 2,660 *puds* (475 bales) via Astrakhan, in 1726 a total of 999 *puds*, or fewer than 200 bales, worth 41,741 *rubles* is said to have been carried through. In 1733–34 no more than 1,600 *puds* (about 250 bales) were carried from Iran to Russia.[130] For 1735 the numbers are 1273 *puds* (about 250 bales) at 66,905 *rubles*, and for 1745 738 *puds* at 55,124 *rubles*.[131]

124 Masters, *Origins*, 30.
125 Zarinebaf-Shahr, "Tabriz under Ottoman Rule," 174.
126 Iukht, *Torgovlia s vostochnymi stranami*, 174–5.
127 Hazin, *Tarikh-i Hazin*, 50–1.
128 Ghougassian, *Emergence*, 46.
129 Soimonov, "Auszug aus dem Tage-Buch," 354–5.
130 Iukht, *Torgovlia s vostochnymi stranami*, 46–7.
131 For the figures for 1712, see Kukanova, *Ocherki*, 110. The other figures appear in Iukht, "Torgovye sviazi Rossie," 142–3.

Increasingly, Iranian silk was used for domestic manufacturing purposes in Russia. Beginning in 1710, the Russians had lured Iranian silk weavers to Russia to help set up a domestic weaving industry.[132] Between 1714 and 1725 fourteen silk weaveries had been established, seven of which were located in Moscow and four in St. Petersburg.[133] In 1725 thirteen such factories existed, a number that went up to thirty-two in 1745.[134] There was also considerable growth in Armenian silk weaving in Astrakhan from 1724 to 1747, activated by a massive Armenian migration to Russia during the tumultuous 1720s.[135]

The Treaty of Rasht, concluded in 1732, returned Gilan to Iranian sovereignty. Under the Treaty of Ganja which followed three years later, Russia relinquished control over the region and city of Baku as well as over Darband. In exchange Russian merchants won specific privileges, including the right to engage in toll-free trade throughout Iran and to use the country as a transit route to India without paying tolls and customs.[136] The episode was marked by Nadir Shah's destruction of Shamakhi and the slaughter of many of its people – he built a new town nearby – and followed by a dreadful pestilence that engulfed all of northwestern Iran in 1737.[137] Yet trade gradually picked up again and indeed reached its highest level in the 1740s, when the Russians plied the Caspian Sea with a commercial fleet consisting of thirty ships. In one year, 1744–45, more than 9,000 *puds* (1,500 bales) of silk seem to have been imported into Russia.[138] A. I. Iukht has calculated that between 1733 and 1739 an annual average of 116,700 *rubles* worth of silk in transit was carried through Astrakhan, while between 1740 and 1748 the corresponding figure was 292,100, an increase of nearly 250 percent. Assuming, as he does, an average price of 70 *rubles* per *pud*, this translates into an annual average of 1,667 *puds* or some 275 bales in the 1730s and of 4,172 *puds* or almost 700 bales in the 1740s.[139] That the trade continued amid severe insecurity and lawlessness is illustrated by the fact that between 1745 and 1748 Russian merchants lost 158,079 *rubles* in stolen and destroyed goods in Iran.[140]

Conclusion

Early eighteenth-century Iran suffered a combination of economic contraction and political impotence. As internal rebellion surged and outside

---

[132] Bayburdyan, *Naqsh-i Aramanah*, 154.
[133] Lystsov, *Persidskii pokhod*, 26, 28.
[134] Sartor, "Die Wolga," 262, 282.
[135] Iukht, "Armianskie remeslenniki."
[136] Sotavov, *Severniy Kavkaz*, 23; and Iukht, *Torgovlia s vostochnymi stranami*, 32.
[137] The epidemic is described in Marvi, *'Alam-ara-yi Nadiri*, ii, 657–60.
[138] Iukht, *Torgovlia s vostochnymi stranami*, 30, 46–7.
[139] Ibid., 89.   [140] Ibid., 35.

attacks multiplied, growing unrest and insecurity posed a grave challenge to those engaged in economic activity. The state, approaching paralysis under a reclusive shah, and fragmenting into a series of competing factions, only exacerbated this situation. Despite its empty coffers, the political elite aided and abetted a massive and growing monetary drain via the annual pilgrim traffic to the Arabian peninsula, while the shah himself, rather than strengthening the military, indulged in the construction of pleasure gardens. The necessary funds were squeezed from any source available.

While the last decades of Safavid rule clearly saw neither an increase in productive state revenue nor in merchant capital, it is important not to exaggerate the magnitude of the immediate effects of this downward cycle by extrapolating from a few dramatic examples. The episode calls for a balanced assessment of how various symptoms that suggest a decline in security and prosperity affected economic vitality. Rather than stifling entrepreneurial activity, decreasing government control may encourage it. Diminishing central control did not just invite local abuse but also gave merchants opportunities for circumventing rules and regulations through bribery and evasion. Merchants, always keen to stay out of the state's orbit, took full advantage of this. The Dutch were surely not the only ones to thrive in the face of worsening economic conditions. In spite of the growing tax burden imposed on it, New Julfa continued to grow until the end of the seventeenth century and did not suffer a significant decline until the end of Safavid rule.[141] Peasants lacked the mobility of merchants and the deteriorating conditions were therefore much harder on them. There are signs that the recurrent cycles of pestilence decimated their numbers, at least in the Caspian region, and that the growing incidence of abuse and extortion caused many of the survivors to abandon cultivation.

Overland silk exports continued to flourish right through to the end of the 1600s, but afterwards began to decrease. A serious decline had set in by the 1710s, continuing through the Afghan invasion of Iran proper and the Russian seizure of the Caspian littoral. It is possible that the Ottoman incorporation of Azerbaijan stabilized silk exports to the Levant but, in the absence of sequential figures, nothing definitive can be said about this.

The volume of silk transports via the Volga route continued to be higher than ever in the early eighteenth century, though the Russians never succeeded in their goal of diverting the trade away from the Ottoman routes. Several developments favored the vitality of the transit trade. Among them were the opening up of the Baltic route, the granting of new toll privileges to the Julfan merchants, and the worsening Ottoman–Safavid relations in the 1720s. The ravages of lawlessness in Shirvan and of war in Gilan, however, prevented this route from reaching its full potential.

---

[141] Julfa's real ruin did not even occur with the fall of Isfahan but under the extortionate rule of Nadir Shah. See Herzig, "Armenian Merchants," 81, 100–104.

Though the cessation of commercial traffic in the early 1720s was only temporary, the troubled aftermath of the Safavid eclipse made it impossible for silk exports to attain their former levels, let alone increase in volume. Least of all were the silk-producing provinces ever in a position to break away from the disintegrating center to become part of a "rising" periphery.

Conclusion

This study has viewed the network of economic, social and political relations within the Safavid realm, between Iran and its neighbors, and between Iran and the world at large, through the prism of the late Safavid silk trade. Disproportionately important to state revenue, the only commodity that spanned Iran's entire economic space, and the main target of outside commercial interest in the country at the turn of the seventeenth century, silk has been treated as emblematic of various aspects of late Safavid society. Four were singled out and examined in detail: the Safavid political economy, the interaction between the Safavid court and foreign merchants, the matrix of Iranian export routes and longitudinal changes therein, and the political and economic problems contributing to the collapse of the Safavid state in the early 1700s. All of these have been traced as processes.

The reign of the Safavids was a crucial episode in Iran's history. Under their aegis a state evolved that continued to be rooted in but was no longer solely beholden to, the traditional mainstay of Iranian statecraft: tribal power. Though not a nation-state, Safavid Iran contained the elements that would later spawn one by generating many enduring bureaucratic features and by initiating a polity of overlapping religious and territorial boundaries. The Safavid era also saw the beginning of Iran's inexorable incorporation into a wider and increasingly interconnected world. This was a reciprocal process. As Safavid rulers dispatched diplomatic and commercial missions to the courts of European and Asian rulers, their realm became the object of numerous outside ventures, political and above all, commercial, of unprecedented frequency and intensity. The ensuing interaction had several consequences. One was the dovetailing of expanding trade relations with the outside world and a growing imprint of commercial concerns on policy making. Safavid Iran was one of many early modern Eurasian states in which long-distance trade not only figured prominently but seemed to be part of a domestic economic agenda. Another was the growth in scope and intensity of transregional commercial routes and networks. Land-based trade between Iran and the Mediterranean ports of the Ottoman Empire expanded considerably in volume, a northern route linking Iran and north-western Europe via Russia emerged as a significant commercial artery, and, alongside these, a maritime trade link developed connecting Iran with the Atlantic world via the Persian Gulf and the Indian Ocean.

In its analysis of the state and its interaction with society, this study has made an effort to avoid teleological assumptions. Rather than as a realm ruled by progressively weaker monarchs overseeing a steady slide toward political decline and economic ruination, late Safavid Iran is best analyzed as a perpetually shifting amalgam of centripetal and centrifugal forces. Centralizing features such as a shared core religion, a long legacy of strong personalized authority, and a governmental tradition centering on royal justice and commercial activism were offset by decentralizing forces – formidable mountain ranges, fearsome deserts, a harsh climate, long distances, and a thinly spread and largely nomadic population, all of which constituted strong pull factors that limited the scope and range of effective "infrastructural" state power.

Within these parameters, the Safavid state operated as a military fiscal state bent on maximizing surplus and power but constrained in its ability to do so by economic, social, and political forces. Unable to administer the realm effectively, the central government had to rely on the assistance of intermediate agents and on negotiation with local forces, to whom it granted varying degrees of autonomy in return for tax, tribute, and military colla-boration. Rulers thus optimized their power and wealth not simply through coercion but by way of a negotiation process that included accommodation, inclusion, and manipulation. Negotiations over power, status, and money produced the balance itself between state and society. Equilibrium was found not in the centrality of institutions but in bargaining and its outcome, tributary reciprocity, epitomized in *pishkash* (forced gift-giving) and dis-counted merchandise traded for robes of honor, favors, and emoluments.

No ruler was as successful in gaining autonomy of political action by tipping the balance toward centralized and concentrated power as Shah 'Abbas I, who paired the customary despotic power of Safavid rulers with a relatively high degree of "infrastructural" control. Shah 'Abbas's approach to economic issues was congruent with this in combining a traditional royal penchant for direct control over productive and distributive forces with far-reaching measures designed to harness the resources of the realm. The building of numerous caravanserais and the exploration of new trade routes are good examples. Silk occupied a pivotal role in many of these measures. Shah 'Abbas conquered and pacified Iran's main silk-producing regions and turned them into crown domain, thus securing a flow of revenue from sericulture. He included silk in his embassy trade and enlisted the Julfan Armenians, Iran's preeminent exporters of raw silk, as a service elite of the crown. Capitalizing on an increase in competition for his country's most vital resource, the shah also instituted a silk export monopoly.

While grounded in traditional methods and procedures, these initiatives and ventures were unusual in their scope, coherence, and consistency. They did not, however, add up to a comprehensive commercial policy. 'Abbas's overall economic practice cannot be dismissed as sheer parasitic fiscalism. Yet the revolt in Gilan following his death suggests that commercial solicitation did not preclude excessive taxation at the source of production and was, even under Shah 'Abbas, not above exploitative practices.

Ultimately, 'Abbas's economic practice answered to the imperatives of the military fiscal state: silk revenue was applied to the state's vital functions guaranteeing its war-making capacity, maintaining public order and securing the reproduction of power – but equally served the dynastic objectives of increasing the shah's personal power and income. These converged in the shah's primary concerns: to overcome the single most formidable obstacle to personal royal power, the Qizilbash warrior elite, and to counter the threat posed by his external adversaries, the Ottomans. Reducing Qizilbash power and fighting the Ottomans were strategically complex and costly ventures. Silk played a role in both, either as a source of income or as an economic weapon.

Shah 'Abbas's dealings with silk underline the fact that the lasting management of economic resources was beyond the capacity of the Safavid state apparatus. This was a natural outgrowth of a peripatetic royal life style and the absence of the notion of a national economy, both of which militated against a concerted state-directed economic policy. It was also a function of the rebarbative nature of Iran's natural and social environment. Though hardly constrained by the kind of institutional and procedural arrangements that had begun to curb contemporaneous Western rulers in their freedom to act, Safavid shahs saw their effective power circumscribed by environmental obstacles, custom and tradition, and human recalcitrance. It is clear that even under Shah 'Abbas I the state by no means "controlled" silk. In its efforts to supervise and regulate the mechanisms and practices involved in its production, distribution, and export, the Safavid court had to defer to market principles, which included the advance purchasing system based on cash outlays. The below market prices paid by the court invited concealment and underreporting by cultivators. Shah 'Abbas turned the Julfans into his "court merchants," but they did not thereby become mere appendages of the state. Shah 'Abbas's silk export monopoly, finally, was a commodity monopoly, not a route monopoly, and in effect amounted to little more than a tax on silk destined for export.

If treasure was the objective of the Safavids, commercial profit was the motive of the outsiders who came to Iran to purchase silk. Keen to exchange commodities for silk, they aspired toward achieving maximum profit with a minimum of political interference. They succeeded in neither. Khalifah Sultan's reminder to the Dutch that they had promised the shah greater profits than the tolls on their import and export wares epitomizes the Safavid position on dealing with the Europeans who came to buy Iran's raw silk. No rights would be granted without a guarantee that the shah would profit from the arrangement. The Safavids thus never obliged themselves to supply the Europeans with silk if it could be sold more profitably elsewhere. The price to be paid for silk, moreover, had economic as much as political significence. While the Europeans envisioned the integration of Iran in an intra-Asian operation based on an exchange of commodities, the Iranians desired cash. The fluctuations of the market soon left the court in Isfahan with growing quantities of unvendible import wares, even as the shah himself was forced to make cash payments to procure silk. Over time, the need for ready money, always in short supply in Iran, only increased. Favored status, finally, involved more than cash payments and guaranteed quotas at fixed prices; it also entailed obligations. Shah 'Abbas reached out to the Spanish and the Russians as potential allies against the Ottomans. He granted toll receipts to the English in return for their assistance in ejecting the Portuguese from Hurmuz. The price the Dutch paid for commercial privilege was an obligation to contract a set amount of silk at above-market rates and the understanding that VOC naval power would be at the disposal of the Safavids.

It is in the bargaining over silk and commercial advantage that the late Safavid state most clearly manifests itself as a forum for negotiation. The very same elements found in the interaction between the Safavid state and domestic societal groups marked the relationship between the government and the European merchants. Procuring silk involved continual negotiation over volume, price, and the proportion between court-supplied silk and private dealings and between payment in cash or commodities. Agreements were no more than temporary, for contracts expired with the death of each ruler and had to be renegotiated on the accession of his successor.

These negotiations reveal a complex encounter between two parties which brought their own interests, techniques, and cultural assumptions to the table. The Safavid state was represented by a shifting circle of government functionaries and mediators who used the opacity of court ritual and the fluidity of the chain of command to create an atmosphere of ambiguity which regularly left their interlocutors confused and even baffled. The "secret weapon" remained the shah, the sole but mostly unseen source of legitimate power whose authority subordinates frequently invoked to stall talks, to retract previously made promises, and to manipulate the outcome of discussions for their personal objectives. Though less elliptical in their modus operandi, the company agents had their own ways of deflecting issues and confounding their opponents. They spoke on behalf of distant directors and often hid behind their superiors to claim a lack of negotiation flexibility and to evade requests for naval assistance.

At bottom, though, the stakes were clear, at least in the case of the VOC: for the Safavid crown the cost of trading privileges was silk at official prices. If the Dutch wished to be absolved from this arrangement they could choose to pay regular road tolls and custom fees, or leave Iran. The Westerners had no choice but to respect Iranian sensibilities and even suffer humiliating treatment for the sake of commercial gain. Lacking political clout, they were unable to maneuver their own personnel into strategic court positions in order to gain influence and control, let alone apply their own legal system, as they managed to do in other parts of Asia. They tried to compensate for these disadvantages with money. However, money, though necessary in facilitating business, was not sufficient. It often wrought miracles but it generally bought no more than temporary advantage and it did not make the Europeans structural players in the political arena. Just as importantly, the European merchants were not backed up by a credible threat in the form of armed force. For all their naval power, the Dutch could do little more than block trade, including their own, by taking the island of Qishm.

Iranian silk never fulfilled the promise of the maritime outlet, and their "victory over the ocean"[1] did not enable the chartered companies to appropriate a significant share in Iran's silk trade. Bert Fragner preempts the process of history by stating that "When at last the country was consolidated under the Safavids, and the internal preconditions for the commercial recuperation of Iran were restored, it was already too late: world trade was now running along new tracks,"[2] but not by much. Ultimately, Iranian silk was a mere interlude in European commercial and manufacturing history.[3] The EIC gave up buying silk in the 1640s, and failed in its effort to recapture some market share in the 1680s. As for the Dutch, they continued to export silk throughout the seventeenth century, but as of the 1640s did all they could to minimize their purchases. That the VOC never pulled out of the Iranian silk market altogether had less to do with a continued Dutch demand for the commodity than an awareness that buying silk remained an essential ingredient of a commercial agreement that enabled the Company to engage in toll-free trade and, most notably, the export of vast sums of specie from Iran.

Why did the maritime merchants fail in their attempt to capture the Iranian export trade in silk? There is no question that political factors provide a large part of the answer. The Safavids were clearly not interested in allowing outside merchants to acquire a majority share in the export of their country's most valuable commodity. There is little doubt that they were actively encouraged in this by Iran's Armenian merchants, who used their influence and money to protect their dominance in the trade by inciting state officials against foreign interlopers.

As important were the environmental and logistical obstacles. Gilan and

---

[1] Braudel, *Civilization and Capitalism*, i, 415.
[2] Fragner, "Social and Internal Economic Affairs," 526.
[3] Herzig, "Iranian Silk Trade," 89.

the other northern provinces were remote from the Europeans' coastal bases, difficult of access, and climatologically treacherous. As the English put it, the disease-ridden north would "cost more mens lives than 'tis worth."[4] The very lack of information in the maritime sources on rural conditions in the silk-producing regions reflects the absence of Western contact with the productive sector.

The Europeans, finally, were poorly equipped to compete for silk with Iran's indigenous merchants. Large and thinly stretched enterprises burdened with huge overhead costs, the maritime companies lacked the flexibility adequately to respond to price and supply fluctuations of the market. In this they could never match the Armenian merchants. Nor were they in a position to follow the latter in penetrating the production process. As in China, in Iran they were unable to establish a firm position at the beginning of the line that connected producers with consumers. They never managed to do with silk in northern Iran what they did with indigo and cloth weaving in India, where the Dutch gained control over a system of rural workshops producing for the VOC. They were not even in a position to establish a solid interlocking network of advance purchases through a credit system, as they had done with great success all over Asia. Staunchly committed to the principle of free trade, they would have preferred to deal with private merchants. As long as the silk export monopoly was in place, they were prevented from doing so. Even after its abolition, however, private silk buying proved difficult and hardly more cost-effective than dealing with the shah, which at least offered the advantage of a concentration of capital and goods.

The Europeans had never craved Iranian silk at any cost. Their frustration with a lack of control over production, an inelastic price structure following their continued dependence on the court, and interminable and often desultory negotiations over quantity and price, ultimately prompted them to explore sources of silk outside Iran. Steensgaard's observation that too much force and too many conditions would simply prompt the merchant to seek other routes, ultimately applied to the Europeans as much as to Iran's indigenous merchants.[5] The difference was that the former were in a position to bypass Iran altogether. The Safavid elite miscalculated this very fact. Assuming that the Westerners were dependent on Iran and were eager to buy its silk, the country's rulers failed to realize that alternative sources of silk existed elsewhere in Asia.

A substitute for better quality silk from other parts of Asia, Iranian silk was only attractive inasmuch and so long as it was cheap and relatively easy to obtain. In time dealing in the commodity became too complicated for the maritime companies, too unattractive given the ratio between relatively high

[4] Ferrier, "British–Persian Relations," 79–80.
[5] Ibid. 66.

(political) cost and uneven quality. Ultimately, silk was a commodity by default for the EIC and VOC: time and again their agents noted that Iran had no other viable export product. By the early eighteenth century, the Europeans had honed their practices and with the rise of China and India and the emergence of the Americas as suppliers of raw materials and consumption goods, the Far East and the Atlantic trade began to prevail at the expense of the Middle East.

Could Iran's silk trade have turned into a capitalistic enterprise had not Europe turned its back on Iranian silk? The scenario is counterfactual and the question flawed in its negative assumptions and implications. However, since the outcome should perhaps not determine the potential, a few observations are in order.

It is true that the silk trade, supported by strong exogenous demand, was fully monetized and that its production and handling infused the system with much commercial capital. Our lack of knowledge about production precludes a categorical verdict in this regard, but nothing suggests that the external demand stimulus for silk had a discernible impact on production, much less coerced labor, to produce cash crops. Moreover, this book has argued, to answer affirmatively would be artificially to divorce silk production, sale, and distribution from the ambient Safavid physical environment and political economy. Caspian silk was integrated in a wider environment of limited productive capacity. Natural circumstance joined with a political system that operated on thoroughly traditional principles and practices to create conditions in which profits were insufficiently plowed back into the system, especially after the reign of Shah 'Abbas I. Much state revenue was used unproductively, squandered or hoarded by the political elite. Most commercial surplus left the country, thus negating the multiplier effect of foreign trade activity. The Dutch decision to export specie to India rather than spend their import proceeds on Iranian commodities epitomizes the weakness of the Safavid economy vis-à-vis that of its neighbors. Making sizeable profits on the money trade, the Dutch (and other merchants) were also unable to find any commodity other than silk that could profitably be exchanged for their import goods.

Finally and famously, commercialization does not necessarily entail further economic, let alone social and political development. Iran's Armenian merchants had many of the characteristics of an incipient commercial bourgeoisie. As an aggregate merchant body they certainly were not small-scale peddlers, though the agents they hired to carry out the actual business ventures often were, traveling as they did with small amounts of merchandise and little capital. Yet, in spite of the symbiotic relationship they developed with the state, the Julfans lacked the clout to make their interests synonymous with that of the political order. Like all merchant capital theirs was assimilated into prevailing premodern structure rather than transforming it. Especially after 1650, when growing financial instability encour-

aged the rich to hoard their wealth and rich merchants to export their
profits, the potentially transformative role of fixed capital rapidly dwindled.
Hence silk, embedded as it was in a complex web of social, political, and
economic relations, could not, by itself have emerged as the engine of
economic growth and expansion.

Though insufficient for a detailed exploration of the activities of the
Armenians, the information marshaled in this study bears testimony to their
strength and resilience. They were the main force behind the revocation of
the silk export monopoly, using their access to members of the newly
established *ghulam* elite, who are likely to have been interested in commercial decentralization themselves. Their ties to the court as well as their
ability to choose between two land-based itineraries – the Levantine and the
Russian – enabled them to outmaneuver their maritime competitors, who
were confined in their activities to the Persian Gulf. The Armenians may
individually have dealt in smaller volume than the Europeans, but the
ability of the latter to internalize protection costs only concerned the
maritime stretch of the journey. If, as Ashin das Gupta has argued, the
position of the peddler was inherently insecure,[6] this applied to the
individual Armenian merchant as much as to the maritime companies
which, in Iran at least, were hardly in a position to lessen price fluctuations
and to enhance control over supply and demand by improving communication between market and producer. The silk market never became more
predictable and more predictably profitable and, if anyone, it was the
merchant with the more solid grip on production who stood to benefit the
most from prevailing conditions. Not only did the indigenous merchant
communicate between markets and consumers through the network provided by the family firm, but he also compensated for his inability to alter
the non-transparency of the traditional market with greater nimbleness. The
chartered companies, moreover, faced their own non-transparent market in
complicated relations with Isfahan. As Steensgaard acknowledges, maritime
superiority did not translate into overall commercial advantage, at least not
in Iran.

The result of the commercial energy and the political acumen of the
Julfan Armenians was the continued viability and vitality of the overland
trade. Scattered figures and circumstantial evidence suggest that, over time,
the Levant route expanded rather than contracted in a process that began as
early as the 1550s and that accelerated after 1639. The same is true for the
Volga trade. Due to political and logistical obstacles, the latter connection
long remained a trickle rather than a stream. Its moment came in 1667,
when the Russian government accorded the Julfan merchant houses special
rights to ferry silk and other commodities in transit to western Europe.
Unfortunately it remains unclear in what capacity the Julfans negotiated the

---

[6] Das Gupta, *Indian Merchants*, 11–12.

terms of these treaties. Further research will have to answer this important question. In any case, the many attempts at invigoration notwithstanding, the stream never turned into a flood. Aside from the route's climatic limitations, the Armenian merchants themselves seem to have had too much of a stake in the Levant trade to divert their entire trade to the Volga route. The volume carried along the Anatolian connection therefore continued to surpass that of the Russian transit trade.

Both routes continued to thrive into the first decade of the eighteenth century, when worsening political and economic conditions, in Iran itself and, to a lesser extent, in the Ottoman Empire, created a less hospitable climate for commerce. Neither came to a complete halt, however, even during the worst moments of turmoil in Iran in the early 1720s. In fact, the Russian connection seems to have carried its highest volume sometime in the 1730s.

Rather than endorsing conventional views by viewing the period after 1629 as an unrelieved falling away from the ideal of Shah 'Abbas "the Great", this study has attempted to bring out process and continuity alongside rupture and retrenchment. The period following Shah 'Abbas's reign cannot be seen as one of unmitigated decline. In fact, the entire seventeenth century in Iran is one of remarkable stability. Iran neither was racked by the equivalent of the Ottoman Celali revolts, nor did it have to contend with unrest on the scale of the Shivaji insurgency in Mughal India. No production and distribution network on the scale of that of silk could have maintained itself without the facilities that the Safavid administrative and logistical apparatus continued to provide.

Yet it is also true that Shah 'Abbas's successors showed a diminished concern in balancing commercial revenue with facilitating and encouraging trading activity. This was in part the outcome of peace with the Ottomans, which obviated the strategic search for alternative outlets. At bottom, it also reflects a diminished interest in matters of trade on the part of the only force which could harness resources to common ends, the shah himself. It is no exaggeration to say that Shah Safi's reign introduced a new geopolitical orientation in Safavid policy. Shah 'Abbas's policy had centered on strategies that included (failed) initiatives to the outside world with the aim of building political coalitions, military alliances, and commercial ties. With Shah Safi the Safavid polity entered a different phase. Expansionism gave way to consolidation, growing intra-elite factionalism fostered inward-looking tendencies, and the manipulation of foreign representatives increasingly served immediate and particular interests rather than broader, long-term geopolitical objectives. As well as in politics, this changing climate manifested itself in economic management. Shah Safi gave up his grandfather's policy of building up stocks of silk as a mechanism designed to ensure availability and to influence prices. A shift in the balance between the state with its desire for power and revenue and those who accumulated and engendered private wealth is also seen in the abolition of the silk export monopoly in 1629. A defining moment in the process of Safavid political and economic decentralization, this measure testifies to the power special interests brought to bear on the state. The Crown-land status of the silk-producing provinces, finally, cannot be overlooked either. The heavy tax burden imposed by Shah 'Abbas is unlikely to have been lifted under his successors, and the loss of central control no doubt exacerbated the exploitation of the cultivators.

None of this means that the Safavid state relinquished its quest for silk revenue. It remained a powerful and complex mediator between production and the (international) market, both in its continued control over the maritime companies and in its habit of dispatching diplomatic-cum-trade missions to foreign lands. Efforts to tax sericulture, either in kind or in cash, also continued. Most of these were now led by the grand vizier, on whom executive power devolved as the shah's public profile diminished. The seventeenth century saw a series of capable grand viziers make great efforts to tackle the pressing budgetary problems by finding new and better methods to enhance revenue.

They failed, mostly because their policies contravened too many vested interests, including those of the market, which at this point successfully resisted the commanding power of the central state. Strapped for cash, the latter at times even failed to collect enough silk for its own needs. Though the role of Iran's Armenian merchants in this remains unclear, it appears that, far from being subordinated to the political authorities, they competed with the court for silk and were in a position to spurn the latter's offers to purchase the commodity at fixed prices.

Nothing illustrates the state's decreasing commanding power at this point better than its frequent inability to collect enough raw silk to fulfill the Dutch quota even at times when it was less profitable to export the commodity to the Levantine ports. Demanding tax payments in cash instead of kind, as a cash-starved government did in the 1640s, made little difference. A growing tax burden combined with a proliferation of corrupt practices and lax control over the silk-producing regions invited subterfuge and evasion. Collecting revenue, never easy, became progressively more difficult as the need for it became more acute.

In the later seventeenth century Iran's inherently precarious economic base was seriously undermined in a process that combined natural disaster and external circumstances, but that was rooted in long-term internal changes attending Iran's continuing transformation from a nomadic to a military–fiscal polity. The latter was only viable with the type of strong central control and direction that only a shah, the sole source of legitimacy, could provide. Neither Shah Sulayman nor Shah Sultan Husayn was able to provide such leadership. Under the former the state's "infrastructural" power decreased, while the mild-mannered inertia of the latter contributed to the additional undermining of absolute, "punishing" authority. Especially under Shah Sultan Husayn, diminishing revenue and misguided attempts to rectify the shortfall reinforced each other in a vicious cycle. Productivity declined as a result of long-term neglect following changes in landholding. As external money flows dried up, capital flight intensified; while available funds were utilized unproductively, increasingly crippling taxes fell on those who generated the wealth, peasants and merchants. As the central government retreated, local powers stepped up abuse and violence, forcing peasants to give up production and to abandon the land. The result was bankruptcies, the consolidation of mints, currency debasement, a growing incidence of highway robbery, famine and revolt and, ultimately, the breakdown of central authority and the country's exposure to outside attack. Neither outside aggression nor "tribal resurgence" were at the root of this process; both were the effect rather than the cause of a disintegrating center.[7]

The late Safavid state bears little resemblance to the contemporary Mughal state, a "patchwork rather than a uniform structure,"[8] where imperial decline was paralleled by the rise of regional successor states, or the Ottoman Empire, where, in revisionist terminology, royal inertia could not prevent the emergence of new forms of bureaucratic responsibility and accountability.[9] Iran's relative political uniformity and its limited economic resources circumscribed the potential for local forces of productive and constructive capacity to emerge and thrive. Those centers that had a potentially independent economic base of international import, the northwest, comprising Azerbaijan, Shirvan and the Caspian provinces, and the Kirman region in the southeast, suffered invasion and occupation. Shirvan and the Caspian littoral were seized by the Russians and, in the process, suffered terrible loss and destruction. The Kirman area bore the brunt of Baluchi raids and the subsequent Afghan invasion. The administrative order, far from becoming autonomous and institutionalized, broke down into a series of feuding factions. While the loss of central control did unleash a great deal of entrepreneurial energy, its more pernicious consequence was the rise of local abuse, translated in excessive taxation and lawlessness. Its drawbacks therefore were more deleterious than its advantages were beneficial. Foreign merchants complained about stern and uncompromising bureaucrats such as Mirza Taqi and Shaykh 'Ali Khan, who dictated terms and made them abide by quotas, but fared little better under weak ones who were less able to check subordinate officials in their abuse of power.

---

[7] For the argument that Iran's decline was the result of a tribal resurgence, see Lambton, "Tribal Resurgence." John Foran, *Fragile Resistance*, 99, rightly stresses the "largely *internal* determinants of the Safavid crisis."

[8] Alam and Subrahmaniyam, "L'Etat moghol," 210.

[9] Murphey, "Continuity and Discontinuity."

As Subrahmanyam has pointed out, it is ironic that scholars rarely hail the collapse of the very same state that they often accuse of stifling initiative and dynamism.[10] Of course, it all depends on what aspect of the state we choose to highlight. A strong central state was necessary for sustained productivity, but its absence did not necessarily unleash productive private initiative. State interference could be as helpful as it might be counter-productive. This study bears out Mann's contention that strong states, even militaristic ones, tend to increase the possibilities of production and trade as long as they do not overtax and they simultaneously maintain communication systems, and that states which only exploit economic mechanisms of production and circulation may create the conditions for their own demise.[11]

[10] Subrahmanyam, "Introduction," in idem, *Merchants, Markets*, 12.
[11] Mann, *Sources of Social Power*, i, 147, 153.

Appendix

VOC and EIC silk exports from Iran 1618–1715

	Bales	
	VOC	EIC
1618	0	71
1619	0	0
1620	0	523
1621	0	772
1622	0	820
1623	0	0
1624	370	160
1625	311	105
1626	534	60
1627	338	938
1628	761	93
1629	225	582
1630	200	200
1631	0	350
1632	410	224
1633	195	110
1634	325	371
1635	200	325
1636	1000	373
1637	1120	281
1638	400	470
1639	370	594
1640	593	43
1641	300	0
1642	426	0
1643	432	0
1644	566	0
1645	0	0

VOC and EIC silk exports from Iran 1618–1715 (contd)

	Bales	
	VOC	EIC
1646	0	0
1647	0	0
1648	0	0
1649	0	0
1650	0	0
1651	0	0
1652	608	0
1653	454	0
1654	234	0
1655	216	0
1656	167	0
1657	201	0
1658	290	0
1659	230	0
1660	182	0
1661	268	0
1662	208	0
1663	234	0
1664	233	0
1665	218	0
1666	518	0
1667	366	0
1668	212	0
1669	456	0
1670	502	0
1671	419	0
1672	545	0
1673	776	0
1674	329	0
1675	390	0
1676	588	0
1677	618	0
1678	590	0
1679	528	0
1680	639	0
1681	594	0
1682	570	0
1683	366	0
1684–90	0	0
1691	675	0
1692–94	0	0

1695	783	0
1696	149	0
1697–1702	0	0
1703	64	0
1704	80	0
1705–10	0	0
1710	?	0
1712	55	0
1713	70	0
1714	252	0

Sources: ARA, Coll. Gel. de Jongh, 157a; VOC 1150, fol. 184b; VOC 863, fol. 557; VOC 1134, fol. 202; VOC 1146, fols. 933b, 973b; VOC 1152, fol. 69; VOC 1201, fol. 840; VOC 1210, fol. 850b; VOC 1217, fol. 403; VOC 1236, fol. 7; VOC 1229, fol. 870; VOC 1234, fol. 189; VOC 1245, fols. 373, 364, 693; VOC 1251, fol. 1327; VOC 1255, fol. 917; VOC 1285, fols. 380b, 385; VOC 1297, fol. 1018a; VOC 1315, fols. 638a, 725a; VOC 1323, fol. 660b; VOC 1324, fol. 694; VOC 1355, fol. 426; VOC 1364, fols. 357, 390b; VOC 1379, fols. 2630b–2a; VOC 1818, fol. 241b; VOC 1843, fol. 21; Dunlop, *Bronnen*, 139, 173, 213, 226, 255, 269, 276, 280, 317, 329, 357, 371, 420–1, 467–70, 472, 517–18, 523, 527–8, 547–8, 611–12, 615, 640, 653, 569. Speelman, *Journaal*, introd. Hotz, pp. XXX, 308; Coolhaas, *Generale missiven*, ii, 32, 112, 141, 163, 204, 247, 293; iii, 443, 571, 662, 703, 717, 749, 775, 871, 923; iv, 18, 154, 204, 260, 397, 572, 581, 637, 669; v, 559, 604, 810, 858; vi, 727; van Dam, *Beschryvinge*, ii/3, 313; de Rodes, "Beskrivning," 110; Ferrier, "British–Persian Relations," 69, 347, 350; Steensgaard, *Asian Trade Revolution*, 395–7.

Currency rates

Iranian currency

1 tuman = 50 'abbasis
100 mahmudis
200 shahis
2,000 qazbegis
3,200 pays

Foreign currency equivalents

1 tuman was equivalent to 40 guilders (Dfl.); 20 stuivers; ca. 14 rix-dollars (Dutch)
£6 6s 8d. (English)
15 écus (1675); 45 livres (1694) (French)
15 scudi (Italian)
15–16 piasters (1669); 20 piasters (1719) (Ottoman)
10 rubles (1615); 8 rubles (1674) (Russian)

Weight equivalents

1 pud	ca. 16.38 kg
1 mann-i Tabriz	ca. 2.9 kg
1 mann-i shah	ca. 5.8 kg
1 bale	6 puds (ca. 98 kg)
1 load	2 bales (36 mann-i shah)
1 ansyr	1 pound avoirdupois

Sources: IOR E/3/97, fol. 289b; Chardin, *Voyages*, v, 432; [Chick, ed.], *Chronicle*, i 777; Fryer, *New Account*, ii, 126, iii, 152; de Thévenot, *Travels*, 89; Sanson, *Voyage* 98–9; Ferrand, "Les poids, mesures et monnaies"; Hinz, *Islamische Masse*; Bushev *Istoriia posol'stv 1613–21*, 153; Buskovitch, *Merchants of Moscow*, 54.

Glossary

'abbasi. A unit in the Safavid monetary system. The silver *'abbasi,* introduced by Shah 'Abbas I as a 4-shahi coin, was the most common currency in the late Safavid state. Originally struck according to a 2-*misqal* standard (9.22 gr.), *'abbasis* in the seventeenth century were reduced in weight, first to 7.68 gr., later to 7.39 gr. One *'abbasi* equaled 2 *mahmudis* or 4 *shahis,* and 50 *'abbasis* made up 1 *tuman,* the Iranian money of account.

abrisham. Persian for silk.

ahdas. Extraordinary taxes.

'alim, pl. *'ulama.* Religious scholar, member of the religious class.

ansyr. A measure of weight from Bukhara, equaling 1 lb in the seventeenth century.

apareshum (or *apreshum*). The Pahlavi (Old-Persian) word for silk.

ardas. A rather low-quality grade of Iranian silk.

ardasset. See *ardassin.*

ardassin. A fine grade of Iranian silk, only slightly inferior to *sha'rbafi,* the best quality.

'Ayd al-fitr. The festival that concludes the Islamic month of fasting, Ramadan, when Muslims celebrate the breaking of the fast.

baj. Tribute, customs fee or toll.

barat. A bill of exchange or an assignment on revenue.

basha. A pasha or ruler, or toll master.

bayt al-tiraz. The textile workshops of the 'Abbasid empire.

beglerbeg. A provincial governor; the highest-ranking title for a provincial magistrate.

buyutat-i saltanati. The royal workshops in the Safavid state, which produced mostly, but not exclusively, for the royal court.

canarsie (or *kanari*). A grade of Iranian silk, possibly derived from the town of Kanar in Armenia.

chappar. An express messenger – a long-distance runner delivering news.

commenda. A trading partnership between an investor and a merchant in which the participants share the risk of loss and also divide the eventual profits.

connorsee. See *canarsie.*

dah-yik. Literally, "ten-one": the tithe, a tax of 10 percent.

darughah. The police prefect of a town in Safavid Iran. In some towns the *darughah* was also the mayor.

dhimmi. Literally, "a client": a term used for Christians and Jews (and in practice often Zoroastrians) who enjoyed protection under Islam and who, in exchange for being allowed to practice their religion, had to pay a special tax, the *jizya*.

dinar. An accounting unit going back to a gold coin used in the eastern Roman Empire and, later, in the eastern half of the Islamic Empire. A unit of account since Mongol times, the *dinar* does not figure prominently in the Safavid sources, its function having been overtaken by the *tuman*, which was valued at 10,000 *dinars*.

divan. The chancery; the state administration.

divanbegi. The supreme justice in the Safavid judicial system.

écu. A French coin, originally, first produced in the thirteenth century, struck in gold. As of 1643 a silver *écu* (*écu blanc*) made its entry. One *tuman* was the equivalent of about 15 *écus*.

farman. A royal decree.

garmsir. A warm region, more specifically the name given to the region in southern Iran along the Persian Gulf coast.

ghulam. Slave: the term for the Georgians, Circassians, and Armenians who after being captured were made to convert to Islam and were trained for military and administrative positions in the Safavid state.

gosti. Russian state merchants, select groups who conducted their trade in close association and cooperation with the Russian state.

ishikaqasi-bashi. "Head of the masters of the threshold": the master of ceremony and protocol at the Safavid court who was also in charge of the doorkeepers and palace guards.

istiqbal. Reception (of an envoy).

jizya. The poll tax that non-Muslims tolerated by Islam, mostly Christians and Jews, were made to pay.

kadkhuda pasand. A high-grade Iranian silk.

kalantar. The head-man or mayor of a town or a community.

kanari. See *canarsie*.

karkhanah. Factory.

kharaj. Land tax.

kharvar. An ass-load; the measure of 100 *mann-i Tabrizi* or some 600 lb.

kharvari. A rather low grade of Iranian silk.

khassah. A term used to denote the sector of the administration belonging to and responding to the crown, as opposed to the state sector of the administration (*mamalik*).

khil'at. A "robe of honor," handed by the shah as a gift to visiting envoys. Subordinates received a *khil'at* on an annual basis as a token of royal favor and a symbol of continued service. The *khil'at* always consisted of an actual robe but typically included other items, such as other textiles, a sword or a horse.

kirm. (Silk)worm.

laji. The most common grade of Iranian silk, referring either to Lahijan in Gilan or, less likely, to the town of Lahij near Shamakhi in Shirvan.

las. A low-grade silk from Mazandaran, known in Europe as *salvatica*.

legia. See *laji*.

litra, pl. *litry*. A Russian measure of weight, equaling 0.75 lb, or about 340 gr.

livre (*tournois*). A French money of account valued at one-third of an *écu*; 1 *tuman* was worth 45 *livres*.

mahmudi (*muhammadi*). A Safavid currency unit. The silver *muhammadi* is assumed to have been introduced by Shah Muhammad Khudabandah (r. 1578–87) but the story of its origin is probably a good deal more complicated. One *mahmudi* was worth half an *'abbasi*, and 1 *tuman*, the Iranian currency standard, was worth 100 *mahmudis*.

majlis-nivis (also known as *vaqa'i'-nivis*). The official recorder of the shah. This was a very important function in the Safavid bureaucracy. The *majlis-nivis* often acted for the grand vizier during the latter's absence.

malik al-tujjar. Chief of merchants. Appointed by the shah, the *malik al-tujjar* was a government official who at the same time represented the country's merchant community, acting as an intermediary between the merchants and the state. He engaged in trade for the shah in his capacity as royal factor, and also supervised the royal textile workshops.

mamalik (pl. of *mamlakat*). Realm. The term is used to denote the state sector of the administration as opposed to the sector belonging to the crown (*khassah*).

mann. A Safavid measure of weight. Different regional types existed and were used.

mann-i sang-i Gilan. Measure of weight, perhaps equal to the *mann* of Lahijan, a medieval weight used in Gilan, equaling 18.2 kg.

mann-i shah. Equivalent to about 5.8 kg, i.e. twice the weight of the *mann-i Tabriz*.

mann-i Tabriz. Equivalent to about 2.9 kg (seventeenth century).

mihmandar. Host: the official who was assigned to a visiting foreign envoy as his guide and caretaker.

mirshikar-bashi (or *amirshikar-bashi*). Master of the hunt. Hunting being an important part of royal life, the *mirshikar-bashi* was a prominent official in the Safavid bureaucracy. The *mirshikar-bashi* was also the court liaison with the Armenian community of New Julfa.

misqal. A currency weight standard which varied, according to age and locality, from about 67.5 grains to 90.7 grains In Safavid Iran, 1 *misqal* equaled 72 grains, or 4.608 grams.

mu'ayyir al-mamalik. The controller of the assay; the head of the mint.

Muharram. The first month of the Islamic calendar. On 10 Muharram, Shi'i Muslims commemorate the death of Imam Husayn on the battlefield of Kerbala in 680.

muhtasib. The market inspector, a state-appointed official who was in charge of the bazaar and who was also responsible for the proper state of weights and measures.

musalisa (*muthallatha*). A sharecropping system involving landowners, peasants, and merchants who invested raw material and money (landlords and merchants), or labor (peasant), and shared in the profits.

mustawfi. The comptroller or revenue officer. The *mustawfi khassah* supervised the revenue of the crown domain; the *mustawfi al-mamalik* was in charge of state lands.

nasihat-namah. A book of advice or counsel for rulers; a genre of literature designed to instruct the incoming ruler in the art of statecraft.

Nawruz. The Iranian New Year, celebrated on March 20 or 21, the date of the vernal equinox.

nazir. The supervisor of the shah's household and the head of the royal workshops.

nuqandar. A silk cultivator.

pays. Small flat copper coins, used as currency by the poor, who were also paid in *pays*. There were 4,000 *pays* in one *tuman*.

piaster. See *real of eight*.

pish-furush. Advance selling; the practice of selling a commodity on the basis of outstanding credit, involving the payment of money in anticipation of a future harvest.

pishkash. A present; a term covering different forms of gifts offered and received in a political setting, often indistinguishable from tribute, a regular tax, or a bribe.

pud. A Russian measure of weight, equaling 16.38 kg.

qafilah-bashi. The leader of a caravan.

qazbegi (*qazbaki*, also called *qaz*). A copper coin in Safavid Iran, used by the poor, and worth one-fortieth of an *'abbasi*. There were 2,000 *qazbegis* to 1 *tuman*.

qishlaq. Winter quarters of nomadic groups or of the shah and his retinue.

Qizilbash. The Turkoman tribesmen who had been the main supporters of the Safavid dynasty and who for a long time were the mainstay of the Safavid army.

qullar-aqasi. The head of the *qullar* or *ghulams*, slave soldiers.

qurchibashi. The head of the *qurchi* corps, one of the most important positions in the Safavid hierarchy.

qurchis. Special forces recruited from the Qizilbash and used as royal guards.

rahdari. A road toll.

rahdars. Toll masters along the roads.

raqam. A decree issued from the royal council, written by the *majlis-nivis*, the royal clerk, and sealed with the shah's seal.

real of eight. The *real de ocho*, or piece of eight, a Spanish currency widely used in west Asia in the sixteenth and seventeenth centuries. One *tuman* was equal to 15 *reals* in the seventeenth century.

Reichstaler (*rix-dollar, rijksdaalder*). A large silver coin that made its first appearance in the 1520s as the *Joachims Taler*, struck from Bohemian silver. In 1566 the Holy Roman Empire adopted a taler standard, proclaiming the *Reichstaler* the imperial silver coin. The provinces and cities of the Dutch Republic began to strike equivalent *rijksdaalder* as of 1581. In the mid-seventeenth century 1 *tuman* equaled around 14 *talers*.

ruble. A Russian coin. In the mid- to late seventeenth century 1 *tuman* was equal to 8–10 *rubles*.

salvatica. The term used in Europe for a coarse and irregular grade of Iranian silk also known as *las*.

sarkar-i khassah-i sharifah. The supervisor of the crown domain.

scudo. A large Italian silver coin, first struck in the early sixteenth century. One *tuman* was worth 15 *scudi*.

seta canare. Silk from Kanar; see *canarsie*.

sha'rbafi. Weaving silk, the finest grade of Iranian silk, mostly manufactured domestically.

sha'rbaf-khanah. Silk weavery.

shahbandar. A harbor master.

shahi. A currency unit in Safavid Iran. Two silver *shahis* were equal to 1 *mahmudi*, and 1 *tuman* contained 200 *shahis*.

shaykh al-Islam. The highest religious functionary of a town. The *shaykh al-Islam* of Isfahan was the most prominent religious functionary in Safavid Iran.

shirvani. Referring to silk from Shirvan, a region in northwestern Iran.

sipahsalar. The commander-in-chief of the Safavid army.

strugi. Flat vessels used to transport goods across the Caspian Sea.

stuiver. Dutch currency unit. One Dutch *guilder* was divided into 20 *stuivers*.

sughat. A gift, more specifically a gift or curiosity sent or brought by a traveler.

suyursat (or *sursat*). Purveyance, the practice of supplying food or providing services for the royal court and the state. This included the provisioning and billeting of troops and the upkeep of passing foreign envoys.

tahvildar. Collector for the royal workshops, in this case the department involving silk. This official supervised the silk brought to Isfahan for the maritime companies.

tamgha. A tax on trade commodities, a customs fee.

tanny. A grade of Bengal silk.

tarh. Commodity monopolization; the practice of forcing producers or merchants to sell to or to purchase from the royal court.

tilimbar. The rectangular sheds in which silkworms were reared.

tufanghchi-aqasi. A riflemen commander.

tuman. The unit of account in the Safavid currency system. The *tuman* did not represent an actual coin, but served as a ghost money, with all coins being reckoned as its multiples.

tuyuldar. A landholder.

'ulama. See *'alim*.

ulozhenie. A series of economic regulations issued by the Russian state in 1649.

vaqa'i' nivis. See *majlis-nivis*.

vazir-i kull. Vizier-general.

Voorcompagnieën. A series of ad hoc trading companies established in Holland in the 1590s in response to the first Dutch trading expeditions to Asia. In 1602 they merged to become the Verenigde Oostindische Compagnie (Dutch East India Company).

warshum (or *warshüm*). Pamir dialect words for silk.

wresham. Afghan for silk.

zapovedenye torgovy. "Forbidden wares": special goods on whose export the Russian government imposed restrictions.

zarbaft. Brocade.

zarrab-bashi. Mintmaster; head of the technical operation of the mint.

Bibliography

Archival sources

Netherlands

Algemeen Rijksarchief (ARA), The Hague. Eerste afdeling (first section)

Records of the Verenigde Oostindische Compagnie (VOC) (Dutch East India Company)

Overgekomen brieven en papieren (Letters and papers received), vols. 1130–1999 (1639–1722). Papers relating to the VOC factories in Isfahan, Shiraz, Kirman, Gamron (Bandar 'Abbas), and Surat, written from these factories to the VOC Asian headquarters in Batavia and its general headquarters in Amsterdam, respectively.

Bataviasch uitgaand brievenboek (Batavia's outgoing Letterbook), vols. 850–974 (1623–1721). Letters relating to Iran, written from the VOC headquarters in Batavia to the factory in Gamron.

Resoluties van de Heren XVII (Resolutions of the Heren XVII), vols. 106–11 (1660–1695). Resolutions taken by the VOC directors in Holland.

Copieboek van brieven (Copy book of letters), vols. 315–22 (1627–1696). Copies of letters, instructions, and other papers sent by the Heren XVII and the Amsterdam Chamber to the Indies and the Cape).

Collectie Geleynssen de Jongh, vols. 28, 92, 97, 97a, 141, 142, 148, 157, 157a, 158, 166, 283, 296, 296a.

ARA, Hoge Regering Batavia, 877. Radicale beschrijving van 's Compagnies handel in Perzië, Dec. 1756.

Archief consulaat Smyrna, vols. a[1–3].

Archief consulaat Aleppo, vols. 162[1–2].

Great Britain

India Office Records (IOR), London

Records of the English East India Company (EIC).
Letters from Persia, Original Correspondence, vols. E/3/6–E/3/51 (1618–1695).
Despatch Books (Letters from the London Council to Asia), vols. E/3/84–E/3/92 (1653–1695).

Factory Records Persia and Persian Gulf G/29/1.
Factory Records Surat G/36/84–G/36/110 (1653–1694).
Factory Records Miscellaneous G/40/2–5; G/40/30
Abstract Letters Bombay G/40/7–7a.

Public Record Office, London

State Papers (SP), vols. 110–18, 16, 18, 19, 20, 21 (1688–1697).

British Library, London

Junabadi, Mirza b. Hasan Husayni, "Rawzat al-Safaviyah," ms. Or. 3388.
Vali, Qazvini, Muhammad Yusuf , "Khuld-i barin," Ms. Or. 4132.

Cambridge University

Khuzani Isfahani, Fazli, "Afzal al-tavarikh," vol. 3, Christ's College, ms. Dd.5.6
Mustawfi, Muhammad Muhsin, "Zubdat al-tavarikh," ms. Browne G.15 (13).

France

Archives des Affaires Etrangères (AE), Paris.

Coll. Perse, vols. 5–6.

Archives Nationales (AN), Paris

Coll. Affaires Etrangères, B^3, vol. 235. "Mémoire sur les monnaies et sur les manufactures de drap, de soie et de coton."
Coll. Colonies, C^2. Correspondance générale, 1674–1698, nos. 62–64.
Coll. Marine et outre-mer, III. Commerce aux colonies, FB^2 II. Nos. 134, 178, 215, 233.

Archives de la Société des Missions Etrangères (AME), Paris

Vol. 347. Vachet, Bénigne, "Journal d'un voyage en Perse."
Vol. 348. Gaudereau, M., "Relation du voyage de M. Gaudereau à Ispahan adressée aux supérieurs et directeurs du séminaire de Tours, le 22 janvier 1691."
Vols. 349–53.

Bibliothèque Nationale (BN), Paris

Mélanges Colbert, 129b.
[Vachet, Bénigne], "Journal du Voyage de Perse commencé au mois de décembre de l'année 1689." Mss. Fr. 24516.

Italy

Carmelite Archives, Rome
O.C.D. series, vols. 184a, 236, 237, 238, 241, 242, 243.

Propaganda Fide Archives, Rome

Scritture referite nei Congressi (S.C).
Mesopotamia, Persia, Caldei. Vol. 1 (1614–1690). Vol. 2 (1691–1707).
Giorgia. Vol. 1 (1626–1707).

Germany

Staatsbibliothek Berlin

Shirazi, Muhammad Mahdi b. Muhammad Hadi. "Tarikh-i Tahmaspiyah," ms. Or.
Sprenger 204.

United States

Minnesota, Minneapolis, University of Minnesota

James Ford Bell Library

Bembo, Ambrosio. "Viaggio e giornale per parte dell'Asia di quattro anni incirc
fatto da me Ambrosio Bembo Nob. Veneto."

Primary sources

Afushtah'i Natanzi, Mahmud b. Hidayat Allah. *Naqavat al-asar fi zikr al-akhyar.*
    Ed. Ihsan Ishraqi. Tehran, 2nd edn 1373/1994.
Agulets'i, Zakariia, *Dnevnik Zakariia Aguletsi.* Ed. S. V. Ter-Avetsyan. Erevan, 1938.
'Alam-ara-yi Shah Tahmasp. Zindigani-dastani-yi divummin padshah-i dawrah-i
    Safavi. Ed. Iraj Afshar. Tehran, 1370/1991.
Albuquerque, Afonso. *The Commentaries of the Great Afonso Dalboquerque, Second
    Viceroy of India.* Ed. Walter de Gray Birch, 4 vols. London, 1875–95.
Alonso, Carlos, O.S.A. "Cartas del P. Melchior de los Angeles, OSA, y otros
    documentos sobre su actividad en Persia (1610–1619)." *Analecta Augustiniana,*
    64 (1981), 251–98.
    "La embajada persa de Denguiz-Beg y Antonio de Gouvea, osa, a la luz de
    nuevos documentos." *Archivo Augustiniano,* 64 (1980), 49–115.
    Missioneros agustinos en Georgia (siglo XVII). Valladolid, 1978.
Andersen, Jürgen and Iversen, Volquard. *Orientalische Reise-Beschreibungen.*
    Schleswig, 1669; repr. ed. Dieter Lohmeier, Tübingen, 1980.
Ange de St. Joseph. *Souvenirs de la Perse safavide et autres lieux de l'Orient
    (1664–1678).* Trans. and annotated Michel Bastiaensen. Brussels, 1985.

Antonova, K. A., Gold'berg, N. M. and Lavrenkov, T. D., eds. *Russko-Indiiskie otnosheniia v XVII veke. Sbornik dokumentov.* Moscow, 1958.

Arak'el Davrizhets'i. *Girk' patmut'eants'.* Trans. "Livre d'historien," in Brosset, *Collection d'historiens arméniens,* 269–553.

Astarabadi, Sayyid Hasan Murtaza Husayni. *Tarikh-i sultani: Az Shaykh Safi ta Shah Safi.* Ed. Ihsan Ishraqi, Tehran, 1364/1985.

Attman, Artur, et al., eds. *Ekonomiska förbindelser mellan Sverige och Ryssland under 1600-talet. Dokument ur svenska arkiv.* Stockholm, 1978.

Aubin, Jean, ed. *L'ambassade de Gregório Pereira Fidalgo à la cour de Châh Soltân Hosseyn 1696–1697.* Lisbon, 1971.

Avril, Ph., SJ, *Voyage en divers Etats d'Europe et d'Asie entrepris pour découvrir un nouveau chemin à la Chine.* Paris, 1692.

Bachoud, Père. "Lettre de Chamakié, le 25 septembre 1712, au Père Fleuriau." In *Lettres Edifiantes,* iv, 91–100.

Bafqi, Muhammad Mufid Mustawfi. *Jami'-i mufidi va tarikh-i Yazd.* Ed. Iraj Afshar. Tehran, 1342/1963.

Barbosa, Duarte. *The Book of Duarte Barbosa.* Trans. and ed. M. Longworth Dames, 2 vols. London, 1918.

Bardsiri, Mir Muhammad Sa'id. *Tazkirah-i Safaviyah-i Kirman.* Ed. Muh. Ibrahim Bastani- Parizi. Tehran, 1369/1990.

Baulant, Micheline, ed. *Lettres de négociants marseillais, les Frères Hermite (1570–1612).* Paris, 1953.

Bedik, Bedros. *Cehil Sutun, seu explicatio utriusque celeberrimi, ac prettiosissimi theatri quadraginta columnarum in Perside orientis, cum adjecta fusiori narratione de religione, moribus.* Vienna, 1678.

Bell of Antermony, John. *Travels from St Petersburg to Various Parts of Asia.* Edinburgh, new edn in 1 vol., 1805.

Berchet, Gugliemo, ed. *Relazioni dei consoli veneti nella Siria.* Turin, 1866.

La Repubblica di Venezia e la Persia. Turin, 1865.

Boullaye-le-Gouz. *Les voyages et observations du Sieur Boullaye-le Gouz.* Paris, 1657.

Brosset, M.-F., trans. and ed. *Chronique géorgienne.* Paris, 1830.

Collection d'historiens arméniens. 2 vols. St. Petersburg, 1874–76.

Histoire de la Géorgie depuis l'antiquité jusqu'au XIXe siècle. 2 vols. St. Petersburg, 1856.

Des historiens arméniens des XVIIe et XVIIIe siècles: Arakel de Tauriz, registre chronologique. St. Petersburg, 1873

"Itinéraire du très-révérend frère Augustin Badjetsi, évêque arménien de Nakhid-chévan, de l'ordre des Frères-Prêcheurs, à travers l'Europe." *JA,* 3rd ser., 3 (1837), 209–45, 401–21.

Cartwright, John. *The Preachers Travels.* London, 1611; facs. repr. Amsterdam, 1977.

Chardin, Jean. *Voyages du chevalier Chardin, en Perse, et autres lieux de l'Orient.* Ed. L. Langlès. 10 vols. and map. Paris, 1810–11.

Chesneau, J. *Voyage de Monsieur d'Aramon ambassadeur pour le roy en Levant.* Ed. C. Schefer. Paris, 1887.

[Chick, ed.]. *A Chronicle of the Carmelites in Persia and the Papal Mission of the XVIIth and XVIIIth Centuries.* 2 vols. London, 1939.

Clark, G. N. and W. J. M. Eysinga, eds. *Les conférences anglo-néerlandaises de 1613 et 1615.* Leiden. 1940. 1951.

Colenbrander, H. T., ed. *Daghregister gehouden int Casteel Batavia 1631–34, 1635, 1636, 1641–42*. The Hague, 1898–1900.

Coolhaas, W. Ph., ed. *Generale missiven van Gouverneurs-Generaal en Raden aan Heren XVII der Verenigde Oost-Indische Compagnie*. 9 vols. The Hague, 1960–88.

   ed. *Pieter van den Broecke in Azië*, 2 vols. The Hague, 1962–63.

Courbé, Augustin. "Relation d'un voyage en Perse faict es années 1598 & 99 par un gentilhomme de la suite du Seigneur Scierley Ambassadeur du Roy d'Angleterre." In *Relations véritables et curieuses de l'isle de Madagascar et du Brésil*. Paris, 1651.

De Bourge, M. *Relation du voyage de monseigneur l'évêque de Beryte vicaire apostolique du royaume de la Cochinchine par la Turquie, la Perse, les Indes etc ... jusqu'au royaume de Siam*. Paris, 1666.

De Bruyn, Cornelis. *Reizen over Moskovie, door Persie en Indie: Verrykt met driehondert konstplaten, vertoonende de beroemdste lantschappen en steden, ook de byzondere dragten, beesten, gewassen en planten die daer gevonden worden: Voor al derzelver oudheden en wel voornamentlyk heel uitvoerig die van heerlyke en van oudts de geheele werrelt door befaemde hof van Persepolis, by de Persianen Tchilminar genaemt*. Amsterdam, 1711; 2nd edn, 1714.

De Bulhão Pato, Raymundo Antonio, ed. *Cartas de Affonso de Albuquerque*. 2 vols. Lisbon, 1898.

De Chinon, Gabriel. *Relations nouvelles du Levant ou traités de la religion, du gouvernement et des coûtumes des Perses, des Arméniens, et des Gaures*, Lyon, 1671.

De Clavijo, R. G. *Narrative of the Embassy of Ruy Gonzalez de Clavijo to the Court of Timour at Samarcand A.D. 1403–06*. Trans. and ed. C. R. Markham. London, 1859.

De Gouvea, A. *Relation des grandes guerres et victoires obtenues par le roy de Perse*. Trans. de Meneses. Rouen, 1646.

De la Maze, Jean-Baptiste, SJ, "Journal du Père de la Maze, de Chamakie à Ispahan, par la province du Guilan." In *Lettres édifiantes et curieuses*, iv, 43–90.

[De la Maze, Jean Baptiste], SJ, "Mémoire de la province de Sirvan, en forme de lettre adressée au Père Fleuriau." In *Lettres édifiantes et curieuses* iv, 11–42.

Della Valle, Pietro. *Delle conditioni di Abbàs Rè di Persia*. Venice, 1628.

   Viaggi di Pietro della Valle. Il pellegrino descritti da lui medesimo in lettere familiari all- erudito suo amico Mario Schipano divisi in tre parti cioè: la Turchia, la Persia e l'India. 2 vols. Brighton, 1843.

De Rodes, Johan. "Beskrivning av handelsförhållandena i Ryssland." In Attman et al., eds., *Ekonomika förbindsler*, 106–30.

De Thévenot, Jean. *Relation d'un voyage fait au Levant*. Vol. II, *Suite du voyage de Levant*. Paris, 1674.

   Voyage de Mr. de Thevenot au Levant. Paris, 1689.

De Tournefort, J. Pitton. *Relation d'un voyage du Levant*. 2 vols. Paris, 1717.

Don Juan. *Don Juan of Persia. A Shi'ah Catholic 1560–1604*. Trans. and ed. G. le Strange. London, 1926.

Durri Efendi, Ahmad. *Relation de Dourry Efendy, ambassadeur de la Porthe Otomane auprès du roy de Perse*. Ed. L. Langlès. Paris, 1810.

Du Mans, Raphael. *Estat de la Perse en 1660*. Ed. Ch. Schefer. Paris, 1890.

Dunlop, H., ed. *Bronnen tot de geschiedenis der Oostindische Compagnie in Perzië, 1611–1638*. The Hague, 1930.

Efendi, Evliya. *Narrative of Travels in Europe, Asia, and Africa in the Seventeenth Century*. Trans. Joseph von Hammer. 2 vols. London, 1834; repr. New York. London, 1968.

Elton, John and Greame, A. *A Journey through Russia into Persia by two English Gentlemen*. London, 1742.

Ezov, G. A., ed. *Snosheniia Petra Velikogo s armianskim narodom*. St. Petersburg, 1898.

Fekete, L., ed. *Einführung in die persische Paläographie: 101 persische Dokumente*. Ed. G. Hazai, Budapest, 1977.

Ferrier, R. W. "An English View of Persian Trade in 1618." *JESHO*, 19 (1976), 182–214.

Fletcher, Giles, "Of the Russe Commonwealth." In Lloyd E. Berry and Robert O'Crummey, eds., *Rude and Barbarous Kingdom: Russia in the Accounts of Sixteenth-Century English Voyagers*, 109–246. Madison, 1968.

Florencio del Niño Jesús, P. Fr. *Biblioteca Carmelitano-Teresiana de Misiones*. 3 vols. Vol. 3, *En Persia (1608–1624). Su fundación-Sus embajadas-Su apostolado*. Pamplona, 1928–30.

Flur, Vilim (Floor, Willem), ed. *Bar uftadan-i Safaviyan, bar amadan-i Mahmud Afghan*. Trans. Abu'l Qasim Sirri. Tehran, 1365/1986.

Foster, Sir William, ed. *The Embassy of Sir Thomas Roe to India 1615–1619*. 2 vols. Oxford, 1926.

The English Factories in India, 1618–1669. 13 vols. Oxford, 1906–27.

Letters Received by the East India Company. London, 1901.

The Travels of John Sanderson in the Levant 1584–1602. London, 1931.

Fryer, John A. *A New Account of East India and Persia, Being 9 Years' Travels, 1672–1681*. Ed. W. Crooke. 3 vols. London, 1909–15.

Fumani, 'Abd al-Fattah Gilani. *Tarikh-i Gilan dar vaqa'i'-i salha-yi 923–1038 h.q.* Ed. Manuchihr Situdah. Tehran, 1349/1970.

Gemelli Careri, Giovanni. *Giro del Mondo del dottor D. Gio. Francesco Gemelli Careri*. 6 vols. Naples, 1699.

Gilani, Mulla Shaykh 'Ali. *Tarikh-i Mazandaran*. Ed. Manuchihr Situdah. Tehran, 1352/1973.

Gmelin, Johann Georg. *Reise nach Russland zur Untersuchung der drey Natur-Reiche*. 4 vols. St. Petersburg, 1770–84.

Godinho, Manuel. *Relação do novo caminho que fêz por terra e mar vindo da India para Portugal, no ano de 1633 o Padre Manuel Godinho* Ed. A. Reis Machado. Lisbon, 1944.

Grey, Charles, ed. *A Narrative of Italian Travels in Persia*. London, 1873.

Gulbenkian, Robert, ed. *L'Ambassade en Perse de Luis Pereira de Lacerda et des Pères Portugais de l'Ordre de Saint-Augustin, Belchior dos Anjos et Guiherme de Santo Agostinho 1604–1605*. Lisbon, 1972.

Hakluyt, Richard. *The Principal Navigations Voyages Traffiques and Discoveries of the English Nation*. 12 vols. Glasgow, 1903.

Hamilton, Alexander. *A New Account of the East Indies*. 2 vols. Edinburgh, 1727.

Hanway, Jonas. *An Historical Account of the British Trade over the Caspian Sea: With a Journal of Travels through Russia into Persia ... to which are added, The*

Revolutions of Persia during the Present Century, with the Particular History of the Great Usurper Nadir Kouli. 4 vols. London, 1753.

Harris, P. R. "An Aleppo Merchant's Letterbook." *British Museum Quarterly*, 22 (1960), 64–9.

Hazin, Muhammad Ali. *The Life of Sheikh Muhammad Ali Hazin.* Trans. and ed. F. C. Belfour. London, 1830.

Hedges, William. *The Diary of William Hedges, Esq., during his Agency in Bengal; as well as on his Voyage Out and Return Overland (1681–1687).* Ed. R. Barlow and H. Yule. 3 vols. London, 1887–89.

Heeres, J. E., and Stapel, F. W., eds. *Corpus diplomaticum Neerlando-Indicum.* 5 vols. of *Bijdragen tot de Taal-, Land- en Volkenkunde van Nederlandsch-Indië.* The Hague, 1907–55.

Heeringa, K., ed. *Bronnen tot de geschiedenis van de Levantsche handel.* 2 vols. The Hague, 1910–17.

Herbert, Thomas. *Some Yeares Travel into Divers Parts of Africa and Asia the Great.* London, 1638.

Isfahani, Muhammad Ma'sum b. Khvajigi. *Khulasat al-siyar. Tarikh-i ruzgar-i Shah Safi Safavi.* Tehran, 1368/1989.

Ja'fariyan, Rasul, ed. *'Ilal-i bar uftadan-i Safaviyan. Mukafat namah.* Tehran, 1372/1993.

Kaempfer, Engelbert. *Am Hofe des persischen Grosskönigs 1684–1685.* Trans. Walther Hinz, Leipzig, 1940; new edn, Tübingen, 1977.

Katib, Ahmad b. Husayn b. 'Ali. *Tarikh-i jadid-i Yazd.* Ed. Iraj Afshar. Tehran, 1345/1966.

Khatunabadi, Sayyid 'Abd al-Husayn. *Vaqa'i' al-sannin va al-a'vam: ya guzarishha-yi salyanah az ibtida-yi khilqat ta sal-i 1195 hijri.* Tehran, 1352/1973.

Kilburger, Johann Philipp. "Kurzer Unterricht von dem russischen Handel, wie selbiger mit aus- und eingehenden Waaren 1674 durch ganz Russland getrieben worden." *Magazin für die Neue Historie und Geographie,* 3 (1769), 243–342.

Konovalev, S. "Ludvig Fabritius's Account of the Razin Rebellion." *Oxford Slavonic Papers,* 6 (1955), 72–101.

Kotov, F. *Khozhenie kuptsa Feodora Kotova v Persiiu.* Ed. A. A. Kuznetsov. Moscow,1958.

Krusinski, Judasz Tadeusz. *The History of the Revolutions of Persia.* 2 vols. London, 1728.

Lettres édifiantes et curieuses, écrites des missions étrangères. 8 vols. Toulouse, new edn, 1810.

Leupe, P. A. "Stukken over den handel van Perzië en den Golf van Bengalen, 1633." *Kronijk van het Historisch Genootschap gevestigd te Utrecht,* 2nd ser., 10 (1854), 168–208.

Manucci, Nicolao. *Storia do Mogor or Mugul India 1653–1708.* Trans. William Irvine. 4 vols. London, 1907.

Manrique, Sebastien. *Travels of Fray Sebastien Manrique 1629–1643.* Trans. C. Eckford Luard and Father H. Hosten SJ. 2 vols. Oxford, 1927.

Mar'ashi, Mir Taymur. Tarikh-i khandan-i Mar'ashi-yi Mazandaran. Ed. Manuchihr Situdah. Tehran, 1364/1985.

Mar'ashi Safavi, Mirza Muhammad Khalil. *Majma' al-tavarikh dar tarikh-i inqiraz-i Safaviyah va vaqa'i'-i ba'd ta sal-i 1207 h.q.* Ed. 'Abbas Iqbal Ashtiyani. Tehran, 1362/1983.

Marvi, Muhammad Kazim. *'Alam-ara-yi Nadiri*. Ed. Muh. Amin Riyahi. 3 vols. Tehran, 2nd edn, 1369/1990.

Meier-Lemgo, Karl, ed. *Die Briefe Engelbert Kaempfers. Akademie der Wissenschaften und der Literatur. Abhandlungen der Mathematisch-Naturwissenschaftliche Klasse* 6. Wiesbaden, 1965.

Membré, Michele. *Mission to the Lord Sophy of Persia (1539–1542)*. Trans. and ed. A. H. Morton. London, 1993.

Minorsky, Vladimir, trans. and ed. *Tadhkirat al-Muluk. A Manual of Safavid Administration*. London, 1943; repr. 1980.

Morgan, E. Delmar, and Coote, C. H., eds. *Early Voyages and Travels to Russia and Persia by Anthony Jenkinson and other Englishmen*. 2 vols. London, 1886.

Munajjim, Mulla Jalal al-Din. *Tarikh-i 'Abbasi ya ruznamah-i Mulla Jalal*. Ed. S. A. Vahid Niya. Tehran, 1366/1987.

Nasiri, Muhammad Ibrahim b. Zayn al-'Abidin. *Dastur-i shahriyaran*. Ed. Muh. Nadir Nasiri Muqaddam. Tehran, 1373/1994.

Nasrabadi, Muhammad Tahir. *Tazkirah-i Nasrabadi*. Ed. Vahid Dastgirdi. Tehran, 1317/1938.

Natanzi, Mu'in al-Din. *Muntakhab al-tavarikh-i mu'ini*. Ed. Jean Aubin. Tehran, 1336/1957.

Nawzad, Firaydun, ed. *Namahha-yi Khan Ahmad Khan Gilani. Nimah-i divvum-i sadah-i dihum-i hijri*. Tehran, 1373/1994.

Nava'i, 'Abd al-Husayn, ed. *Asnad va mukatibat-i siyasi-yi Iran az sal-i 1038 ta 1105 h.q.* Tehran, 1360/1981.

Olearius, Adam. *Vermehrte newe Beschreibung der Muscowitischen und Persischen Reyse sodurch gelegenheit einer holsteinischen Gesandschaft an den Russischen Zaar und König in Persien geschehen*. Schleswig, 1656; facs. repr. Tübingen, 1971.

Ovington, John. *A Voyage to Suratt in the Year 1689*. London, 1696.

Pacifique de Provins, Père. *Relation d'un voyage de Perse faict par le R.P. Pacifique de Provins prédicateur capucin*. Paris, 1631.

Parsamian, V. A.,Voskanian, V. K., and Ter-Arakimova, S. A., eds. *Armiano-russkie otnosheniia v VXII veke*. Erevan, 1953.

Pegolotti, F.B. *La pratica della mercatura*. Ed. A. Evans. Cambridge, Mass., 1938.

Pelsaert, Francisco. *De geschriften van Francisco Pelsaert, 1627: Kroniek en remonstrantie*. Ed. D. H. A. Kolff and H. W. van Santen. The Hague, 1979.

Petis Fils, Sieur. *Extrait du journal du Sieur Petis, Fils*. In L. Langlès, ed., *Relation de Dourry Efendy ambassadeur de la Porte Othomane auprès du roy de Perse*. Paris, 1810.

Pires, Tomé. *The Suma Oriental of Tomé Pires*. Trans. and ed. A. Cortesao. 2 vols. London, 1944.

Poullet (d'Armainville). *Nouvelles relations du Levant. Avec une exacte description ... du royaume de Perse*. 2 vols. Paris, 1668.

Purchas, Samuel. *Hakluytus Posthumus or Purchas his Pilgrimes*. 20 vols. Glasgow, 1905–07.

Qazvini, Abu'l Hasan. *Fava'id al-Safaviyah. Tarikh-i salatin va umara-yi Safavi pas az suqut-i dawlat-i Safaviyah*. Ed. Maryam Mir-Ahmadi. Tehran, 1367/1988.

Qazvini, Mirza Muhammad Tahir Vahid. *'Abbasnamah, ya sharh-i zindigani-yi 22 salah-i Shah 'Abbas sani (1052–1073)*. Ed. Dihqan. Arak, 1329/1951.

Rafi'ah, Mirza. *Dastur al-muluk-i Mirza Rafi'ah*. Ed. M. T. Danishpazhuh. *Majallah-i Danishkadah-i Adabiyat va 'Ulum-i Insani-yi Danishgah-i Tihran* 15 (1347/1968), 504–75; 16 (1347–48/1968), 62–93, 198–322, 416–40, 540–64.

Richard, Francis. *Raphaël du Mans missionnaire en Perse au XVIIe s.* 2 vols. Paris, 1995.

Rumlu, Hasan Big. *Ahsan al-tavarikh*. Ed. 'Abbas Husayn Nava'i. Tehran, 1357/1978.

Sainsbury, W. Noel., ed. *Calendar of State Papers, Colonial Series, East Indies, China and Japan, 1617–1621*. London, 1870; repr. Vaduz, 1964.

Sanandaji, Mirza Shukr Allah. *Tuhfah-i Nasiri dar tarikh va jughrafiya-yi Kurdistan*. Ed. Hishmat Allah Tabibi. Tehran, 1366/1987.

Sanson, N. *Voyage ou Etat présent du Royaume de Perse*. Paris, 1694.

Savary, Jacques. *Le parfait négociant, ou instruction génerale pour ce qui regarde le commerce des marchandises de France, & de pays étrangers*. Paris, 7th edn, 1713.

Scarcia-Amoretti, Biancamaria, ed. *Šāh Ismā'īl I nei <<Diarii>> di Marin Sanudo*. Rome, 1979.

Schillinger, Père Franz Caspar. *Persianische und Ost-Indianische Reise*. Nuremberg, 1707.

Shami, Nizammudin. *Tarikh-i futuhat-i Amir Taymur Gurgan ma'ruf bih Zafarnamah*. Ed. Felix Tauer. Prague, 1937.

Sherley, Antony. *Sir Antony Sherley His Relation of His Travels into Persia*. London, 1613; facs. repr. 1972.

Silva y Figueora, Don Garcia de. *Comentarios de D. Garcia de Silva y Figueroa de la embajada que de parte del Rey de España don Felipe III hize al Rey Xa Abas de Persia*. 2 vols. Madrid, 1903–05.

Soimonov, Fedor I. "Auszug aus dem Tage-Buch des ehemahligen Schiff-Hauptmanns und jetzigen geheimen Raths und Gouverneurs von Siberien, Herrn Fedor Iwanowitsch Soimonov, von seiner Schiffahrt der Caspische See." In G. F. Müller, ed., *Sammlung russischer Geschichte*. 10 vols. Vol. 7, 155–530. St. Petersburg, 1762.

Speelman, Cornelis. *Journaal der reis van den gezant der O.I. Compagnie Joan Cunaeus naar Perzië in 1651–1652*. Ed. A. Hotz. Amsterdam, 1908.

Spilman, James A. *A Journey through Russia into Persia in the Year 1739*. London, 1742.

Stanley of Alderley, ed. *Travels to Tana and Persia by Josafa Barbaro and Ambrogio Contarini*. Trans. Thomas and S. A. Roy. London, 1873.

Stapel, F.W., ed. *Corpus diplomaticum, 1691–1725*. See Heeres.

Stodart, Robert. *The Journal of Robert Stodart being an Account of his Experiences as a Member of Sir Dodmore Cotton's Mission to Persia in 1628–29*. Ed. Sir E. Dennison Ross. London, 1935.

Struys, J. J. *Drie aanmerkelijke en seer rampspoedige reysen door Italie, Griekenlandt, Lijflandt, Moscovien, Tartarijen, Meden, Persien, Oost-Indien, Japan, en verscheyden andere gewesten*. Amsterdam, 1676.

Tajbakhsh, Ahmad. *Tarikh-i Safaviyah. Asnad va tarikh*. Shiraz, 1372/1994.

Tavernier, Jean Baptiste. *Les six voyages de Jean Bapt. Tavernier en Turquie, en Perse, et aux Indes*. 2 vols. Utrecht, 1712.

Tenreiro, Antonio. *Itinerarios da India a Portugal por terra*. Ed. Antonio Baiao. Coimbra, 1923.

"Testamento di Pietro Vioni Veneziano fatto a Tauris (Persia) MCCLXIV, X dicembre." *Archivio Veneto*, 26 (1883), 161–5.

Texeira, Pedro. *The Travels of Pedro Texeira*. Trans. and ed. W. F. Sinclair. London, 1902.

Tucci, Ugo, ed. *Lettres d'un marchand vénitien Andrea Berengo (1553–1556)*. Paris, 1957.

Iskandar Munshi. *Tarikh-i 'alam-ara-yi 'Abbasi*, ed. Iraj Afshar. 2 vols. Tehran, 1350/1971.

Iskandar Munshi and Valah Isfahani. *Zayl-i tarikh-i 'alam-ara-yi 'Abbasi*. Ed. Suhayli Khvansari. Tehran, 1317/1938.

Vahman, Faridun. "Three Safavid Documents in the Record Office of Denmark." In K. Eslami, ed., *Iran and Iranian Studies: Papers in Honor of Iraj Afshar*, 178–90. Princeton, 1998.

Valentyn, François. *Oud en nieuw Oost-Indiën*. 5 vols. Vol. 5, *Keurlyke beschryving van Choromandel, Pegu, Arrakan, Bengale, Mocha, van 't Nederlandsch comptoir in Persien en zaken overblyvzlen; een net beschryving van Malacca ... Sumatra ... Malabar ... Japan ... Kaap der goede hoope ... Mauritius*. Dordrecht-Amsterdam, 1726.

Van Dam, Pieter. *Beschryvinge van de Oostindische Compagnie*. Ed. F. W. Stapel and C. W. van Boetzelaer. 7 vols. The Hague, 1927–54.

Van Ghistele, Joos. *'T voyage van Mher Joos van Ghistele*. Gent, 1557.

Villotte, Père Jacques (attributed to). *Voyages d'un missionnaire de la Compagnie du Jésus en Iran, aux Indes, en Arabie et en Barbarie*. Paris, 1730.

Vogel, J. Ph., ed. *Journaal van J.J. Ketelaar's hofreis naar de Groot Mogol te Lahore 1711–1713*. The Hague, 1937.

Witsen, Nicolaas. *Noord- en oost Tartarye; behelzende eene beschryving van verscheidene Tartersche en nabuurige gewesten in de noorder en oostelijkste deelen van Aziën en Europa*. Amsterdam, 1705.

Worm, Johan Gottlieb. *Ost-Indian- und persianische Reisen, oder: zehenjärige auf Gross-Java, Bengala, und im Gefolge Herrn Joann Josua Kötelär, holländischen Abgesandtens an den Sophi in Persien geleistete Kriegsdienste*. Dresden-Leipzig, 1737.

Yerevantsi, Simeon. *Dzhambr. Pamiatnaia kniga zertsalo i sbornik vsekh obstoiatel'stv sviatogo prestola Echmiadzina i okrestnykh monastyrei*. Moscow, 1958.

Zabihi, Masih, and Manuchihr Situdah, eds. *Az Astara ta Astarabad*. 7 vols. Tehran, n.d.

Zettersteen, K. V., ed. *Türkische, tatarische und persische Urkunden im schwedischen Reichsarchiv*. Uppsala, 1945.

Modern studies

Ahmedov, Ia. Z. "The Export of Iranian Silk to Western Europe from the 16th to the Beginning of the 18th Century." *The Annual of the Society for the Study of Caucasia*, 6–7 (1994–96), 39–49.

Alam, Muzaffar and Sanjay Subrahmanyam. "L'Etat moghol et sa fiscalité XVIe-XVIIIe siècles." *Annales HSS* (1994), 189–217.

Alexandrowicz, C. H. *An Introduction to the History of the Law of Nations in the East Indies (16th, 17th and 18th Centuries)*. Oxford, 1967.

Allen, W. E. D. *Problems of Turkish Power in the Sixteenth Century*. London, 1963.
Ames, Glen J. *Colbert, Mercantilism, and the French Quest for Asian Trade*. De Kalb, 1996.
Anderson, Lisa. *An English Consul in Turkey: Paul Rycaut at Smyrna 1667–1678*. Oxford, 1989.
Andreev, A. I. "Novotorgovyi ustav 1667 g. (k istorii ego sostavleniia)." *IZ*, 13 (1942), 303–07.
Arasaratnam, A. *Merchants, Companies, and Commerce on the Coromandel Coast*. Delhi and New York, 1986.
Ashtor, Eliyahu. *Levant Trade in the Later Middle Ages*. Princeton, 1983.
——— "Observations on Venetian Trade in the Levant in the XIVth Century." *JEH*, 5 (1976), 533–86.
Ashurbeili, Sara. *Gosudarstvo Shirvanshakhov (VI–XVI veka)*. Baku, 1983.
Attman, Artur. *The Russian and Polish Markets in International Trade 1500–1650*. Göteburg, 1973.
Aubin, Jean. "L'avènement des Safavides reconsidéré." *MOOI*, 5 (1988), 1–130.
——— "Le royaume d'Ormuz au début du XVIe siècle." *Mare Luso Indicum*, 2 (1973), 77–179.
Al-'Azzawi, 'Abbas. *Tarikh al-'Iraq bayn al-ihtilalayn*. 7 vols. Baghdad, 1372/1953.
Babayan, Kathryn. "The Waning of the Qizilbash: The Temporal and The Spiritual in Seventeenth-Century Iran." Ph.D. dissertation. Princeton University, 1993.
Bacqué-Grammont, Jean-Louis. "Notes et documents sur les Ottomans, les Safavides et la Géorgie 1516–1521." *CMR(S)* 20 (1979), 239–72.
——— "Notes sur le blocus du commerce iranien par Selîm Ier." *Turcica*, 6 (1975), 69–88.
——— "Notes sur une saisie de soies d'Iran en 1518." *Turcica*, 8 (1976), 237–53.
——— *Les Ottomans, les Safavides et leurs voisins, Contributions à l'histoire des relations internationales dans l'Orient islamique de 1514 à 1524*. Leiden, 1987.
Baghdiantz, Ina. "The Armenian Merchants of New Julfa: Some Aspects of Their International Trade in the Late Seventeenth Century." Ph.D. dissertation. Columbia University, 1993.
Baiburtian, V. A. *Armianskaia koloniia Novoi Dzhul'fy v XVII veke: Rol' Novoi' Dzhul'fy v irano-evropeiskikh politicheskikh i ekonomicheskikh sviaziakh*. Erevan, 1969.
——— "Posrednichaia rol' novo-dzhul'finskikh kuptsov v diplomaticheskikh otnosheniiakh Irana s zapadno-evropeiskimi stranami v nachale XVII veka." *KSINA*, 77 (1964), 20–30.
——— (Bayburdyan, Vahan). *Naqsh-i Aramanah-i Irani dar tijarat bayn al-milali ta payan-i sadah-i 17 miladi*. Trans. Adik Baghdasariyan. Tehran, 1375/1996.
Banani, A. "Reflections on the Social and Economic Structure of Safavid Persia at Its Zenith." *IS*, 11 (1978), 83–116.
Barendse, René Jan. *The Arabian Seas 1640–1700*. Leiden, 1998.
——— "Zijde, Zambouqs, Zilver: De Verenigde Oost-Indische Compagnie en Iran 1623–1693." M.A. thesis. University of Leiden, 1985.
Barkey, Karen. *Bandits and Bureaucrats: The Ottoman Road to State Centralization*. Ithaca, 1994.
Baron, Samuel H. "A.L. Ordin-Nashchokin and the *Orel* Affair." In idem, *Explorations in Muscovite History*, 1–22. Aldershot, 1991.

"Ivan the Terrible, Giles Fletcher and the Muscovite Merchantry: A Reconsideration." *The Slavonic and East European Review*, 56 (1978), 563–85.

"The Muscovy Company, the Muscovite Merchants and the Problem of Reciprocity in Russian Foreign Trade." *FOG*, 27 (1980), 133–55.

"Vasilii Shorin: Seventeenth-Century Russian Merchant Extraordinary." *Canadian-American Slavic Studies*, 6 (1972), 503–48.

"Who Were the Gosti?" *California Slavic Studies* 7 (1973), 1–40.

Barthold, W. *An Historical Geography of Iran*. Trans. Svat Soucek. Princeton, 1984.

Bastani-Parizi, Muhammad Ibrahim. "Sha'r-i gulnar." In idem, *Farmanfarma-yi 'alam*, 163–303. Tehran, 2nd edn, 1367/1988.

Siyasat va iqtisad dar 'asr-i Safavi. Tehran, 3rd edn, 1362/1983.

Bautier, Robert-Henri. "Les relations économiques des occidentaux avec les pays d'Orient, au Moyen Age. Points de vue et documents." In M. Mollat, ed., *Sociétés et compagnies de commerce en Orient et dans l'Océan Indien*, 280–6. Paris, 1970.

Bayly, Christopher. *Rulers, Townsmen and Bazaars: North Indian Society in the Age of British Expansion 1770–1870*. Cambridge, 1983.

Bazin M. and Bromberger, C. "Abrišam." *EIr* 1. London, Boston and Henley, 1985, 229–32.

Bennigsen, Alexandre. "L'expédition turque contre Astrakhan en 1569 d'après les registres des 'affaires importantes' des archives ottomanes." *CMRS*, 8 (1967), 427–46.

"La poussée vers les mers chaudes et la barrière du Caucase. La rivalité Ottomano-Moscovite dans la seconde moitié du XVIe siècle." *Journal of Turkish Studies*, 10 (1986), 15–46.

Bier, Carol. *The Persian Velvets at Rosenborg*. Copenhagen, 1995.

Boxer, C. P. "Anglo-Portuguese Rivalry in the Persian Gulf 1603–1635." In E. Prestage, ed., *Chapters in Anglo-Portuguese Relations*. 46–130. Waterford, 1935.

Braudel, Fernand. *Civilization and Capitalism 15th–18th Century*. Trans. S. Reynolds. Vol. 1. *The Structures of Everyday Life*. Vol 2, *The Wheels of Commerce*. New York, 1981–82.

The Mediterranean and the Mediterranean World in the Age of Philip II. Trans. S. Reynolds. 2 vols. New York, 1976.

Braun, Hellmut. "Ein iranischer Grosswesir des 17. Jahrhunderts: Mirza Muhammad-Taqi." In W. Eilers, ed., *Festgabe deutscher Iranisten zur 2500 Jahresfeier Irans*, 1–7. Stuttgart, 1971.

Brewer, John. *The Sinews of Power: War, Money and the English State, 1688–1783*. Cambridge, Mass., 1990.

Bromberger, Christian. "Changements techniques et transformation des rapports sociaux. La sériculture au Gilan dans la seconde moitié du XIXe siècle." In Y. Richard, ed., *Entre l'Iran et l'Occident. Adaptation et assimilation des idées et techniques occidentales en Iran*, 71–90. Paris, 1989.

Brummett, Palmira. *Ottoman Seapower and Levantine Diplomacy in the Age of Discovery*. Albany, 1994.

Burton, Audrey. *The Bukharans: A Dynastic, Diplomatic and Commercial History 1550–1702*. New York, 1997.

Bushev, P. P. "Iranskii kuptsina Kazim -Beg v Rossii, 1706–1709 gg." In *Iran: Sbornik statei*. 166–80. Moscow, 1973.

264   Bibliography

Istoriia posol'stv i diplomaticheskikh otnoshenii russkogo i iranskogo gosudarstv v 1586–1612 gg. Moscow, 1976.
Istoriia posol'stv i diplomaticheskikh otnoshenii russkogo i iranskogo gosudarstv v 1613–1621. Moscow, 1987.
Posol'stvo Artemii Volynskogo v Iran v 1715–1718 gg. Moscow, 1978.
"Posol'stvo V. G. Korob'ina i A. Kuvshinova v Iran v 1621–1624 gg." In *Iran: Ekonomika, istoriia, istoriografiia, literatura (Sbornik statei)*, 124–55. Moscow, 1976.
"Puteshestvie Mokhammada Khosein-Khan Beka v Moskvu v 1690–1692 gg." *Strany i Narody Vostoka*, 18 (1976), 135–72.
Buskovitch, Paul. *The Merchants of Moscow, 1580–1650.* Cambridge, 1980.
Calmard, Jean, ed. *Etudes Safavides.* Paris-Tehran, 1993.
Chaudhuri, K. N. "The East India Company and the Export of Treasure in the Early Seventeenth Century." *EHR*, 2nd ser., 16 (1963–64), 23–38.
The English East India Company: A Study of the Early Joint Stock Company 1600–1640. London, 1965.
Trade and Civilisation in the Indian Ocean: An Economic History from the Rise of Islam to 1750. Cambridge, 1985.
The Trading World of Asia and the English East India Company 1660–1760. Cambridge, 1978.
Christensen, Peter. *The Decline of Iranshahr: Irrigation and Environment in the History of the Middle East, 500 BC to AD 1500.* Copenhagen, 1993.
Çizakça, Murat. "Price History and the Bursa Silk Industry: A Study in Ottoman Industrial Decline, 1550–1650." *JEH*, 40 (1980), 533–50.
"Sixteenth–Seventeenth Century Inflation and the Bursa Silk Industry: A Pattern for Ottoman Decline?" Ph.D. dissertation, University of Pennyslvania, 1978.
Clifford, W. W. "Some Observations on the Course of Mamluk–Safavi Relations (1502–1516/908–922)." *Der Islam*, 70 (1993), 245–78.
Coleman, D. C., ed. *Revisions in Mercantilism.* London, 1969.
Dale, Stephen Frederic. *Indian Merchants and Eurasian Trade, 1600–1750.* Cambridge, 1994.
Dalsar, Fahri. *Türk sanayi ve ticaret tarihinde Bursada ipekçilik.* Istanbul, 1960.
Das Gupta, Ashin. *Indian Merchants and the Decline of Surat c. 1700–1750.* Wiesbaden, 1979; repr. Delhi 1994.
Davis, D. W. *Elizabethans Errant.* New York, 1967.
Davis, Ralph. *Aleppo and Devonshire Square: English Traders in the Levant in the Eighteenth Century.* London, 1976.
"England and the Mediterranean, 1570–1670." In F. J. Fisher, ed., *Essays in the Economic and Social History of Tudor and Stuart England*, 117–37. Cambridge, 1961.
De Roover, Florence Edler. "Andrea Banchi, Florentine Silk Manufacturer and Merchant in the Fifteenth Century." *Studies in Medieval and Renaissance History* 3 (Lincoln, 1966), 223–85.
Dickson, Martin. "The Fall of the Safavi Dynasty." *Journal of the American Oriental Society*, 82 (1962), 503–17.
"Shah Tahmasp and the Uzbeks (The Duel for Khurasan with 'Ubayd Khan)." Ph.D. dissertation, Princeton University, 1958.
Dorn, Bernhard. "Beiträge zur Geschichte der kaukasischen Länder und Völker, aus

morgenländischen Quellen. II. Geschichte Schirwans unter den Statthaltern und Chanen von 1538–1820." In *Mémoires de l'Académie Impériale des Sciences de Saint Pétersbourg*, 6th ser., vol. 4, 317–434. St. Pétersburg, 1840.

Eilers, W., "Abrišam." *EIr* 1. London, Boston and Henley, 1985, 229.

Emerson, John. "Ex Oriente Lux: Some European Sources on the Economic Structure of Persia between about 1630 and 1690." Ph.D. dissertation. Cambridge University, 1969.

—— "Some General Accounts of the Safavid and Afsharid Period, Primarily in English." In Charles Melville, ed., *Persian and Islamic Studies in Honour of P. W. Avery*, 27–41. Cambridge, 1990.

Emerson, John and Floor, Willem. "Rahdars and their Tolls in Safavid and Afsharid Iran." *JESHO*, 30 (1987), 318–27.

Erim, Neşe. "Trade, Traders and the State in Eighteenth-Century Erzurum." *New Perspectives on Turkey*, 5–6 (1991), 123–50.

Ermolaeva, L. K. "Krupnoe kupechestvo Rossii v XVII-pervoi chetverti XVIII v. (po materialam astrakhanskoi torgovli)." *IZ*, 114 (1986), 303–25.

Falsafi, Nasr Allah. "Dastha-yi khun-alud." In idem, *Chand maqalah-i tarikhi va adabi*, 211–22. Tehran, 1342/1963.

—— "Sarguzasht-i 'Saru Taqi'." In idem, *Chand maqalah-i tarikhi va adabi*, 285–310. Tehran, 1342/1963.

—— *Zindigani-yi Shah 'Abbas-i avval*. 5 vols. Tehran, 4th ed., 1369/1990.

Faroqhi, Suraya. "Bursa at the Crossroads: Iranian Silk, European Competition and the Local Economy 1470–1700." In idem, *Making a Living in the Ottoman Lands 1480 to 1820*, 113–48. Istanbul, 1995.

Fekhner, M. V. *Torgovlia russkogo gosudarstva so stranami vostoka v XVI veke*. Moscow, 1956.

Feltwell, John. *The Story of Silk*. New York, 1990.

Ferrand, Gabriel. "Les poids, mesures et monnaies des mers du Sud aux XVIe et XVIIe siècles." *JA*, 2nd ser., 16 (1920), 5–150; 193–311.

Ferrier, R. W. "The Agreement of the East India Company with the Armenian Nation 22nd June 1688." *REA*, new ser., 7 (1970), 427–43.

—— "The Armenians and the East India Company in Persia in the Seventeenth and Early Eighteenth Centuries." *EHR*, 2nd ser., 26 (1973), 38–62.

—— "British–Persian Relations in the 17th Century." Ph.D. dissertation. Cambridge University, 1970.

—— "The European Diplomacy of Shah 'Abbas I and the First Persian Embassy to England." *Iran*, 11 (1973), 75–92.

—— "The Terms and Conditions under which English Trade was Transacted with Safavid Persia." *BSOAS*, 49 (1986), 48–66.

Floor, Willem M.. *Commercial Conflict between Persia and the Netherlands 1712–1718*, Durham, 1988.

—— "The Dutch and the Persian Silk Trade." In Charles Melville, ed., *Safavid Persia: The History and Politics of an Islamic Society*, 323–68. London, 1996.

—— "Het Nederlands-Iraanse conflict van 1645." *Stichting cultuurgeschiedenis van de Nederlanders overzee. Verslagen en aanwinsten 1978–1979*, 46–51. Amsterdam, 1980.

—— "New Facts on the Holstein Embassy to Iran (1637)." *Der Islam*, 60 (1983), 302–8.

"The Rise and Fall of Mirza Taqi, the Eunuch Grand Vizier (1043–55/1633–45) Makhdum al-Omara va Khadem al-Foqara." *Studia Iranica*, 26 (1997), 237–66.

(Flur, Vilim). *Avvalin sufara-yi Iran va Holand: Sharh-i safar-i 'Musa Bik' safir-i Shah 'Abbas bih Huland v safarnamah-i 'Yan Esmit' safir-i Huland dar Iran.* Ed. D. Majlisi and H. Turabiyan. Tehran, 2536/1978.

Foran, John. *Fragile Resistance: Social Transformation in Iran from 1500 to the Revolution.* Boulder, 1993.

Foster, Sir William. *England's Quest of Eastern Trade.* London, 1933.

Fragner, Bert G. "Social and Internal Economic Affairs." *Cambridge History of Iran,* 6 (1986), 491–567.

Frangakis-Syrett, Elena. *The Commerce of Smyrna in the Eighteenth Century (1700–1820).* Athens, 1992.

"The Ottoman Port of Izmir in the Eighteenth and Early Nineteenth Centuries, 1695–1820." *Revue de l'Occident Musulman et de la Méditerranée,* 39 (1985), 149–62.

Gaastra, Femme S. *Bewind en beleid bij de VOC 1672–1702.* Zutphen, 1989.

De geschiedenis van de VOC. Zutphen, 1991.

Gardella, Robert P. "Qing Administration of the Tea Trade: Four Facets over Three Centuries." In J. Kate Leonard and J. R. Watt, eds., *To Achieve Security and Wealth: The Qing Imperial State and the Economy 1644–1911,* 97–118. Ithaca, 1993.

Gaube, Heinz and Wirth, Eugen. *Aleppo: Historische und geographische Beiträge zur baulichen Gestaltung, zur sozialen Organisation und zur wirtschaftlichen Dynamik einer vorderasiatischen Fernhandelsmetropole.* Wiesbaden, 1984.

Geidarov, M. Kh. *Goroda i gorodskoe remeslo Azerbaidzhana XIII-XVII vekov. Remeslo i remeslennyi tsentry.* Baku, 1982.

Remeslennoe proizvodstvo v gorodakh Azerbaidzhana v XVII v. Baku, 1967.

Ghougassian, Vazken Sarki. *The Emergence of the Armenian Diocese of New Julfa in the Seventeenth Century.* Atlanta, 1998.

Glamann, Kristof. *Dutch-Asiatic Trade, 1620–1740.* Copenhagen, 1958.

Goffman, Daniel. *Izmir and the Levantine World, 1550–1650.* Seattle, 1990.

Goitein, S. D. "Minority Self-Rule and Government Control in Islam." *Studia Islamica,* 31 (1970), 101–16.

Gökbilgin, M. Tayyib. "Rapports d'Ibrahim Paša sur la campagne d'Anatolie orientale et d'Azerbaidjan." *Anatolia Moderna,* 1 (1991), 187–229.

Gommans, Jos J. L. *The Rise of the Indo-Afghan Empire c. 1710–1780.* Leiden, 1995.

Grampp, William. "An Appraisal of Mercantilism." In Lars Magnuson, ed., *Mercantilist Economics,* 59–85. Boston, 1993.

Gregorian, Vartan. "Minorities of Isfahan: The Armenian Community of Isfahan 1587–1722." *IS,* 7 (1974), 652–80.

Gulbenkian, R. "Philippe de Zagly, marchand arménien de Julfa et l'établissement du commerce persan en Courlande en 1696." *REA,* new ser., 7 (1970), 361–99.

Haneda, Masashi. "L'Evolution de la garde royale des Safavides." *MOOI,* 1 (1984), 41–64.

Haussig, Hans Wilhelm. *Die Geschichte Zentralasiens und der Seidenstrasse in vorislamischer Zeit.* Darmstadt, 1983.

Die Geschichte Zentralasiens und der Seidenstrasse in islamischer Zeit. Darmstadt, 1988.

Haidar, Najaf. "Precious Metal Flows and Currency Circulation in the Mughal Empire." *JESHO*, 39 (1996), 298–364.

Heimpel, H. "Seide aus Regensburg." *Mitteilungen des Instituts für Österreichische Geschichtsforschung*, 62 (1954), 270–98.

Heller, Klaus. "Zur Entwicklung der Handelsbeziehungen des moskauer Reiches mit Persien und Mittelasien im 16. und 17. Jahrhundert." *FOG*, 51 (1996), 35–43.

Herrmann, Albert. *Die alten Seidenstrassen zwischen China und Syrien*. Berlin, 1910.

Herzig, Edmund. "The Armenian Merchants of New Julfa, Isfahan: A Study in Pre-Modern Asian Trade." Ph.D. dissertation. Oxford University, 1991.

"The Deportation of the Armenians in 1604–1605 and Europe's Myth of Shah 'Abbas I." In Charles Melville, ed., *Persian and Islamic Studies in Honour of P. W. Avery*, 59–71. Cambridge, 1990.

"The Family Firm in the Commercial Organisation of the Julfa Armenians." In Jean Calmard, ed., *Etudes Safavides*, 287–304. Paris and Tehran, 1993.

"The Iranian Raw Silk Trade and European Manufacture in the Seventeenth and Eighteenth Centuries." *JEEH*, 19 (1990), 73–89.

"The Rise of the Julfa Merchants in the Late Sixteenth Century." In Charles Melville, ed., *Safavid Persia: The History and Politics of an Islamic Society*, 305–23. London, 1996.

"The Volume of Iranian Raw Silk Exports in the Safavid Period." *IS*, 25 (1992), 61–80.

Heyd, Wilhelm. *Geschichte des Levantehandels*. 2 vols. Stuttgart, 1879.

Hicks, John. *A Theory of Economic History*. Oxford, 1969.

Hill, Christopher. *The Century of Revolution 1603–1714*. London, 1961.

Hinz, Walther. *Islamische Masse und Gewichte*. Handbuch der Orientalistik. Ergänzungsband 1, Heft 1. Leiden, 1955.

"Schah Esma'il II. Ein Beitrag zur Geschichte der Safaviden." *Mitteilungen des Seminars für Orientalische Sprachen an der Friedrich-Wilhelms-Universität zu Berlin*, 2. Abt., *Westasiatische Studien* 36 (1933), 19–99.

Hodgson, Marshal. *The Venture of Islam*. 3 vols. Chicago, 1974.

Höffner, Joseph. *Wirtschaftsethik und Monopole im 15. und 16. Jahrhundert*. Darmstadt, 1969.

Hoppe, Hans. "Die diplomatische Missionen des schwedischen Gesandten Ludwig Fabritius nach Moskau und Isfahan gegen Ende des 17. Jahrhunderts." In Hans Hüls and Hans Hoppe, eds., *Engelbert Kaempfer zum 330. Geburtstag*, 155–66. Lemgo, 1982.

Hundt, Michael. >>*Woraus nichts geworden.*<< *Brandenburg-Preussens Handel mit Persien (1668–1720)*. Hamburg, 1997.

Inalcik, Halil. "Bursa and the Commerce of the Levant." *JESHO*, 3 (1960), 131–47.

"Osmanli imperatorlugunun kuruluş ve inkisafl devrinde Türki, e'nin iktisadi vaziyeti üzerinde bir tektik münasebetiyle." *Belleten*, 15 (1951), 629–90.

"The Ottoman Economic Mind and Aspects of the Ottoman Economy." In M. A. Cook, ed., *Studies in the Economic History of the Middle East*, 207–18. Oxford, 1970.

"The Question of the Closing of the Black Sea under the Ottomans." In *Twelfth Spring Symposium of Byzantine Studies: 'The Byzantine Black Sea', 18–20 March, 1978*, 74–110. Athens, 1979.

Ishraqi, Ihsan. "Gilan dar hukumat-i Safaviyah." *Tarikh. Nashriyah-i tahqiqi-yi guruh-i amuzashi-yi tarikh* 2 (2536/1977), 63–81.

Islam, Riazul. A Calendar of Documents on Indo–Persian Relations (1500–1750). 2 vols. Tehran/Karachi, 1979.

Indo-Persian Relations: A Study of the Political and Diplomatic Relations Between the Mughul Empire and Iran. Tehran, 1970.

Israel, Jonathan I. *Dutch Primacy in World Trade 1585–1740.* Oxford, 1989.

European Jewry in the Age of Mercantilism 1550–1750. Oxford, 1985.

Issawi, Charles, ed. *The Economic History of Iran 1800–1914.* Chicago, 1971.

Iukht, A. I. "Armianskie remeslenniki v Astrakhane v pervoi polovinie XVIII v." *Teghekagir Hasarakakan Gitut'yunneri* (1958), 37–54.

"Indiiskaia koloniia v Astrakhani." *Voprosy Istorii* 3 (1957), 135–43.

Torgovlia s vostochnymi stranami i vnutrennii rynok Rossii (20–60–e gody XVIII veka). Moscow, 1994.

"Torgovye sviazi Astrakhani s vnutrennim rynkom (20–50–e gody XVIII v.)." *IZ*, 118 (1990), 139–201.

Ja'fariyan, Rasul. "Adabiyat-i zidd-i Masihi dar dawrah-i Safavi." in idem, *Maqalat-i tarikhi*, 211–57. Qum, 1375/1996.

Jodogne, Pierre. "La <<vita del Sofi>> di Giovanni Rota. Edizione critica." In M. Boni, ed., *Studi in onore di Raffale Spongano*, 215–34. Bologna, 1980.

Kellenbenz, Hermann. "Der russische Transithandel mit dem Orient im 17. Jahrhundert." *JGO*, new ser., 12 (1964), 481–500.

Keyvani, Mehdi. *Artisans and Guild Life in the Later Safavid Period: Contributions to the Social-Economic History of Persia.* Berlin, 1982.

Khachikyan, Shushanik. "Typology of the Trading Companies used by the Merchants of New Julfa." Paper presented at the 2nd Conference of Iranian Studies. Bethesda, MD, May 1998.

Khayadjian, Edmond. "La communeauté arménienne de Marseille." *Marseille: Revue Municipale*, 118 (1979), 31–9.

Khodarosvsky, Michael. *Where Two Worlds Met: The Russian State and the Kalmyk Nomads, 1600–1771.* Ithaca, 1992.

Kissling, Hans-Joachim. "Sāh Ismā'īl Ier, la nouvelle route des Indes et les Ottomans." *Turcica*, 6 (1975), 89–102.

Klein, Rüdiger. "Caravan Trade in Safavid Iran (First Half of the 17th Century)." In Jean Calmard, ed., *Etudes Safavides*. Paris and Tehran, 1993. 305–18.

"Trade in the Safavid Port City Bandar 'Abbas and the Persian Gulf Area (ca. 1600–1680): A Study of Selected Aspects." Ph.D. dissertation. London University, 1993/94.

Konovalev, S. "England and Russia: Three Embassies, 1662–5." *Oxford Slavonic Papers*, 10 (1962), 60–104.

Kortepeter, Karl Max. *Ottoman Imperialism during the Reformation: Europe and the Caucasus.* New York, 1971.

Kukanova, N. G. "Iz istorii russko-iranskikh torgovikh sviaziei v XVII veke." *Kratkie Soobshcheniia Instituta Vostokvedeniia*, 26 (1958), 41–53.

Ocherki po istorii russko-iranskiikh torgovykh otnoshenii v XVII–pervoi polovine XIX vv. Saransk, 1977.

"Rol' armianskogo kupechestva v razvitii russko-iranskoi torgovli v poslednoi treti XVII v." *KSINA*, 30 (1961), 20–34.

"Russko-iranskie torgovye otnosheniia v kontse XVII–nachale XVIII veka." *IZ*, 57 (1956), 232–54.

Kurkdjian, A. A. "La politique économique de la Russe en Orient et le commerce arménien au début du XVIIIe siècle." *REA*, new ser., 11 (1975–76), 245–53.

Kütükoğlu, Bekir. "Les relations entre l'empire ottoman et l'Iran dans la seconde moitié du XVIe siècle." *Turcica*, 6 (1975), 128–45.

Osmanlı–Iran siyasi münasebetleri, vol. 1, 1578–1590. Istanbul, 1962.

Lambton, Ann K. S. *Continuity and Change in Medieval Persia: Aspects of Administrative, Economic and Social History, 11th–14th Century*. London, 1988.

"The Internal Structure of the Seljuq Empire." *Cambridge History of Iran*, 5 (1968), 203–82.

Landlord and Peasant in Persia. London, 1962.

"The Tribal Resurgence and the Decline of the Bureaucracy in the Eighteenth Century." In Thomas Naff and Roger Owen, eds., *Studies in Eighteenth-Century Islamic History*, 108–29, 377–82. Carbondale, Ill., 1977.

Lane, F. C. "The Mediterranean Spice Trade: Further Evidence of its Revival in the Sixteenth Century." *American Historical Review*, 45 (1939–40), 581–90.

"Venetian Shipping during the Commercial Revolution." *American Historical Review*, 38 (1933), 219–37.

Laufer, Berthold. *Sino-Iranica: Chinese Contributions to the History of Civilization in Ancient Iran*. Chicago, 1919.

Le Strange, G. *The Lands of the Eastern Caliphate*. Cambridge, 1905.

Leue, H.-J. "Legal Expansion in the Age of the Companies: Aspects of the Administration of Justice in the English and Dutch Settlements of Maritime Asia, c. 1600–1750." In W. J. Mommsen and J. A. de Moor, eds., *European Expansion and Law: The Encounter of European and Indigenous Law in 19th- and 20th-Century Africa and Asia*, 129–58. Oxford, 1992.

Lieberman, Victor. "Abu Lughod's Egalitarian World Order: A Review Article." *Comparative Studies in Society and History*, 35 (1993), 544–50.

Lockhart, Laurence. "The Diplomatic Missions of Henry Bard, Viscount Bellomont, to Persia and India." *Iran*, 4 (1966), 97–104.

The Fall of the Safavi Dynasty and the Afghan Occupation of Persia. Cambridge, 1958.

Longrigg, Stephen Helmsley. *Four Centuries of Modern Iraq*. Oxford, 1925.

Lopez, Robert Sabatino. *Medieval Trade in the Mediterranean World*. New York, 1955.

"Silk Industry in the Byzantine Empire." *Speculum*, 20 (1945), 1–42.

Luft, Paul. "Iran unter Schāh 'Abbās II (1642–1666)." Phil. dissertation. Göttingen University, 1968.

Lystov, V. P. *Persidskii pokhod Petra I 1722–1723*. Moscow, 1951.

McChesney, Robert D. "Four Sources on Shah 'Abbas's Building of Isfahan." *Muqarnas*, 5 (1988), 103–34.

Macler, F., ed. *Quatre conférences sur l'Arménie faites en Hollande suivies d'une note sur la Hollande et les Arméniens*. Paris, 1932.

Magnusson, Lars, ed. *Mercantilist Economics*. Boston, 1993.

Mamedova, T. *Russkie konsuly ob Azerbaidzhane 20–60e gody XVIII veka*. Baku, 1989.

Mann, Michael. "The Autonomous Power of the State: Its Origins, Mechanisms and Results." *Archives Européennes de Sociologie*, 25 (1984), 185–213.

The Sources of Social Power. Vol. 1, *A History of Power from the Beginning to AD 1760.* Cambridge, 1986.

Mantran, Robert. "L'Empire ottoman et le commerce asiatique aux XVIe et XVIIe siècles." In D. S. Richards, ed., *Islam and the Trade of Asia*, 169–179. Oxford and Philadelphia, 1970.

Marcus, Abraham. *The Middle East on the Eve of Modernity: Aleppo in the Eighteenth Century.* New York, 1989.

Martineau, Alfred, ed. *Mémoires de François Martin fondateur de Pondicherry (1665–1696).* 3 vols. Paris, 1931–34.

Martirosian, A. U. *Armianskie poseleniia na territorii Irana v XI–XV vv.* Erevan, 1990.

Masson, Paul. *Histoire du commerce français dans le Levant au XVIIe siècle.* Paris, 1896.

Masters, Bruce. *The Origins of Western Economic Dominance in the Middle East: Mercantilism and the Islamic Economy in Aleppo, 1600–1750.* New York, 1988.

Matthee, Rudi (Rudolph). "Administrative Stability and Change in Late-17th-Century Iran: The Case of Shaykh 'Ali Khan Zanganah (1669–1689)." *International Journal of Middle East Studies*, 26 (1994), 77–98.

"Anti-Ottoman Politics and Transit Rights: The Seventeenth-Century Trade in Silk between Safavid Iran and Muscovy." *CMR(S)*, 35 (1994), 739–62.

"Between Venice and Surat: The Trade in Gold in Late Safavid Iran." *Modern Asian Studies*, 33:3 (1999), forthcoming.

"The Career of Mohammad Beg, Grand Vizier of Shah 'Abbas II (r. 1642–1666)." *IS*, 24 (1991), 17–36.

"The East India Company Trade in Kerman Wool, 1658–1730." In Jean Calmard, ed., *Etudes Safavides*, Paris and Tehran. 343–83.

"Iran's Ottoman Policy under Shāh Sulaymān, 1666/1076–1695/1105)." In Kambiz Eslami, ed., *Iran and Iranian Studies: Papers in Honor of Iraj Afshar.* 148–77. Princeton, 1998.

"Politics and Trade in late Safavid Iran: Commercial Crisis and Government Reaction under Shah Solayman (1666–1694)." Ph.D. dissertation. University of California, Los Angeles, 1991.

Mattiesen, Otto Heinz. *Die Kolonial- und Überseepolitik der kurländischen Herzöge im 17. und 18. Jahrhundert.* Stuttgart, 1940.

"Die Versuche zur Erschliessung eines Handelsweges Danzig–Kurland–Moskau–Asien besonders für Seide, 1640–1655." *JGO*, 3 (1938), 533–69.

Meilink-Roelofsz, M. A. P. "The Earliest Relations between Persia and the Netherlands." *Persica*, 6 (1977), 1–50.

"The Structures of Trade in the Sixteenth and Seventeenth Centuries: Niels Steensgaard's 'Carracks, Caravans and Companies', A Critical Appraisal." *Mare Luso-Indicum*, 4 (1980), 1–43.

"Een vergelijkend onderzoek van bestuur en handel der Nederlandse en Engelse handelscompagnieën op Azië in de eerste helft van de zeventiende eeuw." *Bijdragen en Mededelingen betreffende de Geschiedenis der Nederlanden*, 91 (1976), 196–217.

Melville, Charles, ed. *Persian and Islamic Studies In Honour of P. W. Avery.* Cambridge, 1990.

ed. *Safavid Persia: The History and Politics of an Islamic Society.* London, 1996.

Monahan, Martin J. "Trade and Diplomacy: Indo-Iranian Relations 1600–1635." Ph.D. dissertation. New York University, 1991.

Mu'izzi, Najaf-quli Husayn. *Tarikh-i ravabit-i siyasi-yi Iran ba dunya.* Tehran, 1326/ 1947.

Murphey, Rhoads. "Continuity and Discontinuity in Ottoman Administrative Theory and Practice During the Late 17th Century." *Poetics Today,* 14 (1993), 419–43.

The Outsiders: The Western Experience in India and China. Ann Arbor, 1977.

Nadel-Golobič, Eleonora. "Armenians and Jews in Medieval Lvov: Their Role in Oriental Trade 1400–1600." *CMRS,* 20 (1970), 345–88.

Nava'i, 'Abd al-Husayn, ed. *Ravabit-i siyasi-yi Iran va Urupa dar 'asr-i Safavi.* Tehran, 1372/1993.

Niewöhner-Eberhard, Elke. "Machtspolitische Aspekte des osmanisch-safawi-dischen Kampfes um Bagdad im 16/17. Jahrhundert." *Turcica,* 6 (1975), 103–27.

Olson, Robert W. *The Siege of Mosul and Ottoman–Persian Relations 1718–1743: A Study of Rebellion in the Capital and War in the Provinces of the Ottoman Empire.* Bloomington, 1975.

Pamuk, Sevket. "The Disintegration of the Ottoman Monetary System during the Seventeenth Century." *Princeton Papers in Near Eastern Studies,* 2 (1993), 67–81

"Money in the Ottoman Empire, 1326–1914." In Halil Inalcik and Donald Quataert, eds., *An Economic and Social History of the Ottoman Empire, 1300–1914,* 947–85. Cambridge, 1994.

Papazian, A. D. *Agrarnye otnosheniia v vostochnoi Armenii v XVI–XVII vekakh.* Erevan, 1972.

Pavlova, I. K. "Maloizvestniy istochnik po istorii Irana 30-kh godov XVII v." *Narody Azii i Afriki,* 6 (1986), 96–102.

Pearson, M. N. *Merchants and Rulers in Gujarat: The Response to the Portuguese in the Sixteenth Century.* Berkeley, 1976.

Perry, John R. "Deportations." *EIr.* 7. London, Boston and Henley, 1994, 309–10.

Petech, Luciano. "Les marchands italiens dans l'empire mongol." *JA,* 250 (1962), 549–74.

Petrushevskii, I. P. "Narodnoe vosstanie v Gilyane v 1629 godu." *Uchenye Zapiski Instituta Vostokvedeniia,* 3 (1951), 225–56.

Zemledelie i agrarnye otnosheniia v Irane XIII–XIV vekov. Moscow and Leningrad, 1960.

Pigulewskaja, N. *Byzanz auf den Wegen nach Indien: Aus der Geschichte des byzantinischen Handels mit dem Orient vom 4. bis 6. Jahrhundert.* Berlin, 1969.

Pigulevskaia, N. V. et al. *Istoriia Irana s drevneishikh vremen do kontsa 18 veka.* Leningrad, 1958.

Pope, A. Upham. *An Introduction to Persian Art since the Seventh Century AD.* London, 1930.

Prakash, Om. *The Dutch East India Company and the Economy of Bengal 1630–1720.* Princeton, 1985.

Rabino di Borgomale, H. L. "Les dynasties locales du Gîlân et du Daylam." *JA,* 237 (1949), 301–50.

Mazandaran and Astarabad, London, 1928.

Rahmani, A. A. *Azerbaidzhan v kontse XVI i XVII vekov.* Baku, 1981.

Raptschinsky, Boris. "Uit de geschiedenis van den Amsterdamschen handel op

Rusland in de XVIIe eeuw." *Jaarboek van het Genootschap Amstelodamum*, 34 (1937), 57–83.

Rapp, Richard, T. "The Unmaking of the Mediterranean Trade Hegemony: International Trade Rivalry and the Commercial Revolution." *JEH*, 35 (1975), 499–525.

Richard, Francis, ed. *Raphaël du Mans missionnaire en Perse au XVIIe s.* 2 vols. Paris, 1995.

Riedlmayer, Andras. "Ottoman–Safavid Relations and the Anatolian Trade Routes, 1603–1618." *Turkish Studies Association Bulletin*, 5 (1981), 7–10.

Römer, Claudia. "Die osmanische Belagerung Bagdads 1034–35/1625–26." *Der Islam*, 66 (1989), 119–36.

Röhrborn, Klaus Michael. *Provinzen und Zentralgewalt Persiens im 16. und 17. Jahrhundert*. Berlin, 1966.

Rossabi, Morris. "The 'Decline' of the Central Asian Caravan Trade." In James Tracy, ed., *The Rise of Merchant Empires: Long-Distance Trade in the Early Modern World 1350–1750*, 351–70. Cambridge, 1990.

Sanjian, Avedis K. *The Armenian Communities in Syria under Ottoman Domination*. Cambridge, Mass., 1965.

Sartor, Wolfgang. "Die Wolga als internationaler Handelsweg für persische Rohseide im 17. und 18. Jahrhundert." Phil. dissertation. Free University, Berlin, 1993.

Savory, Roger. *Iran under the Safavids*. Cambridge, 1980.

"The Sherley Myth." *Iran*, 5 (1967), 73–82.

"Tahlili az tarikh va tarikh-nigari-yi dawran-i Safavi." *Irannamah*, 13 (1995), 277–300.

Scheltema, Jacobus. *Rusland en de Nederlanden*. 4 vols. Amsterdam, 1818.

Schütz, Edmond. "An Armenian-Kipchak Document of 1640 from Lvov and its Background in Armenia and in the Diaspora." In G. Kara, ed., *Between the Danube and the Caucasus*, 247–330. Budapest, 1987.

Sella, D. *Commerci e industrie a Venezia nel secolo XVII*. Venice and Rome, 1961.

Sohrweide, Hanna. "Der Sieg der Safaviden in Persien und seine Rückwirkungen auf die Schiiten Anatoliens im 16. Jahrhundert." *Der Islam*, 41 (1965), 95–223.

Sotavov, N. A. *Severniy Kavkaz v russko-iranskikh i russkikh-turechkikh otnosheniiakh v XVIII v. Ot Konstantinopol'skogo dogovora do Kiuchuk–Kainardzhinskogo mira 1700–1774*. Moscow, 1991.

Steensgaard, Niels. *The Asian Trade Revolution of the Seventeenth Century: The East India Companies and the Decline of the Caravan Trade*. Chicago, 1974.

Steinmann, Linda Keehn. "Shah 'Abbas and the Royal Silk Trade 1599–1629." Ph.D. dissertation. New York University, 1986.

Stevens, Sir Roger. "European Visitors to the Safavid Court." *IS*, 7 (1974), 421–51.

"Robert Sherley: The Unanswered Questions." *Iran*, 17 (1979), 115–26.

Stewart, Devin J. "Taqiyyah as Performance: The Travels of Baha' al-Din al-'Amili in the Ottoman Empire (991–93/1583–85)." In Devin J. Stewart, Baber Johansen and Amy Singer, *Law and Society in Islam*, 1–70. Princeton, 1996.

Subrahmanyam, Sanjay, ed. *Merchants, Markets and the State in Early Modern India*. Delhi, 1990.

The Political Economy of Commerce in Southern India 1500–1650. Cambridge, 1990.

The Portuguese Empire in Asia 1500–1700: A Political and Economic History. London and New York, 1993.

Szuppe, Maria. "Un marchand du roi de Pologne en Perse, 1601–1602." *MOOI,* 3 (1986), 81–110.

Tadjirian, Elizabeth and Karapétian, Méroujan, "Les voies de transit du commerce arménien en Moscovie aux XVIIe et XVIIIe siècles." In H. Kévorkian, ed., *Arménie entre Orient et Occident. Trois mille ans de civilisation,* 157–161. Paris, 1996.

Tajbakhsh, Ahmad. *Iran dar zaman-i Safaviyah.* Tabriz, 1340/1961.

Tékéian, C.-D. "Marseille, la Provence, et les Arméniens." *Mémoires de l'Institut Historique de Provence* 6 (1929), 5–65.

Terpstra, H. *De opkomst' der Westerkwartieren van de Oost-Indische Compagnie (Suratte, Arabië, Perzië).* The Hague, 1918.

Tiepolo, Maria Francesca. *La Persia e la Repubblica di Venezia.* Tehran, 1973.

Tilly, Charles. *Coercion, Capital and European States, AD 990–1990.* Oxford, 1990.

Tivadze, T. G. "Svedeniia russkogo diplomata o votsarenii v Irane Shakha Sefi." *Izd. Akad. Nauk Gruzinskoi SSR. Seria ist., arkh., etnog. i ist. iskustva* (1989): 97–101.

Troebst, Stefan. *Handelskontrolle – "Derivation" – Eindämmung. Schwedische Moskaupolitik 1617–1661.* Wiesbaden, 1997.

"Isfahan–Moskau–Amsterdam. Zur Entstehungsgeschichte des moskauischen Transitprivilegs für die Armenische Handelskompanie in Persien (1666–1676)." *JGO,* 41 (1993), 180–209.

"Die Kaspi–Volga–Ostsee Route: Handelskontrollpolitik Karls XI. Die schwedischen Persien-Missionen unter Ludwig Fabritius 1679–1700." *FOG,* 54 (1998), 127–204.

"Narva und der Aussenhandel Persiens im 17. Jahrhundert. Zum merkantilen Hintergrund schwedischen Grossmachtpolitik." In Alexander Loit and Helmut Pürimäe eds., *Die schwedischen Ostprovinzen Estland und Livland im 16. und 18. Jahrhundert,* 161–78. Uppsala, 1993.

"Stockholm und Riga als Handelsconcurrentinnen Archangel'sk? Zum merkantilen Hintergrunde schwedischer Grossmachtpolitik 1650–1700." *FOG,* 48 (1993), 259–94.

Tucci, Ugo. "Le emissioni monetarie di Venezia e i movimenti internazionali dell'oro." In idem, *Mercanti, navi, monete nel Cinquecento veneziano,* 275–316. Bologna, 1981.

"Un ciclo di affari commerciali in Siria (1579–1581)." In idem, *Mercanti, navi, monete nel Cinquecento veneziano,* 95–143. Bologna, 1981.

Tumanovich, N. N. *Gerat v XVI–XVIII vekakh,* Moscow, 1989.

Udovitch, A.L. "Merchants and Amirs: Government and Trade in Eleventh-Century Egypt." *Asian and African Affairs,* 22 (1988), 53–72.

Uhlenbeck, C. C. *Verslag aangaande een onderzoek in de archieven van Rusland ten bate der Nederlandsche geschiedenis.* The Hague, 1891.

Ülker, Necmi. "The Rise of Izmir, 1688–1740." Ph.D. dissertation. University of Michigan, 1974.

Van Leur, J. C. *Indonesian Trade and Society: Essays in Asian Society and Economy.* Leiden. 1983.

Van Nierop, Leonie. "De zijdenijverheid van Amsterdam historisch geschetst." *Tijdschrift voor Geschiedenis*, 45 (1930), 18–40, 151–72.

Van Rooy, Silvio. "Armenian Merchant Habits as Mirrored in 17–18th-Century Amsterdam Documents." *REA*, new ser., 3 (1966), 347–57.

Van Santen, H. W. "De Verenigde Oost-Indische Compagnie in Gujarat en Hindustan, 1620–1660." Ph.D. dissertation. University of Leiden, 1982.

Vercellin, Giorgio. "Mercanti turchi a Venezia alla fine del Cinquecento." *Il Veltro,* 23 (1979), 243–76.

Vermeulen, U. "L'ambassade néerlandaise de Jan Smit en Perse 1628–1630)." *Persica*, 7 (1975–78), 155–63.

"L'ambassade persane de Musa Beg aux Provinces Unies (1625–1628)." *Persica,* 7 (1975–78), 145–53.

"La mission de Jan L. van Hasselt comme agent du Shah de Perse aux Provinces-Unies (1629–1631)." *Persica*, 8 (1979), 133–44.

Viner, Jacob. "Power versus Plenty as Objectives of Foreign Policy in the Seventeenth and Eighteenth Centuries." In D. C. Coleman, ed., *Revisions in Mercantilism*, 61–91. London, 1969.

Volovnikova, V. G. ed. *Poslannik Petra I na vostoke. Posol'stvo Florio Beneveni v Persiiu i Bukharu v 1718–1725 godakh*. Moscow, 1986.

Von Mende, Rana. *Muṣṭafā ʿĀlī's Furṣat-nāme. Edition und Bearbeitung einer Quelle zur Geschichte des persischen Feldzugs unter Sinān Pasa 1580–1581*. Berlin, 1989.

Von Nasackin, Nicolas. "Die kaukasische Seidencultur." *Oesterreichische Monatschrift für den Orient*, 3 (1877), 30–1.

Vorob'eva, A.G. "K voprosu o prebyvanii Stepana Razina v Azerbaidzhane i Persii." *Izvestiia Akademii Nauk Azerbaidzhanskoi SSR, seriia istorii, filosofii i prava* (1983), no. 3, 32–37.

Voskanian, V. K. "Les Arméniens à Moscou du XVe au XVIIe siècle." *REA*, new ser., 9 (1972), 425–44.

"Novo-torgoviy ustav i dogovor s armianskoi torgovoi kompanei v 1667." *Teghekagir*, 6 (1974), 29–43.

Wake, H. H. "The Changing Patterns of Europe's Pepper and Spice Imports, ca 1400–1700." *JEEH*, 8 (1979), 361–403.

Wallerstein, Immanuel. *The Modern World-System*. Vol. I, *Capitalist Agriculture and the Origins of the European World-Economy in the Sixteenth Century*. London, 1974.

Weber, Max. *Economy and Society: An Outline of Interpretive Sociology*. Ed. G. Roth and C. Wittich. 2 vols. Berkeley, 1978.

Wijnroks, E. H. "Jan van de Walle and the Dutch Silk-Trade with Russia 1578–1635," In J. Braat, A. H. Huussen, B. Naarden, and A. L. M. Willemsen, eds., *Russians and Dutchmen*, 41–58. Groningen, 1993.

Willan, T.S. *The Early History of the Russia Company 1553–1603*. Manchester, 1956; repr. 1968.

The Muscovite Merchants of 1555. Manchester, 1953.

Wills, John E. Jr. "European Consumption and Asian Production in the Seventeenth and Eighteenth Centuries." In John Brewer and Roy Porter, eds., *Consumption and the World of Goods*, 133–47. London, 1993.

Wilson, C. H. "Cloth Production and International Competition in the Seventeenth Century." *EHR*, 2nd ser., 13 (1960), 209–21.

Wirth, Eugen. "Alep et les courants commerciaux entre l'Europe et l'Asie du XIIe au XVIe siècles," *Revue du Monde Musulman et de la Méditerranée*, 55–6 (1990), 44–56.

Wolf, Eric. *Europe and the People Without History*. Berkeley, 1984.

Wolfe, Martin. "French Views on Wealth and Taxes from the Middle Ages to the Old Regime." In D. C. Coleman, ed., *Revisions in Mercantilism*, 190–209. London, 1969.

Woods, John E. *The Aqquyunlu. Clan, Confederacy, Empire. A Study in 15th/9th Century Turko-Iranian Politics*. Minneapolis and Chicago, 1976.

Zarinebaf-Shahr, Fariba. "Tabriz under Ottoman Rule (1725–1731)." Ph.D. dissertation. University of Chicago, 1991.

Zedginide, G. E. "Iz istorii pol'sko-russkikh diplomatichekikh otnoshenii s Iranom. Deiatel'nost Bogdana Gurdzhitskogo." Avtoreferat dissertatsii. Tiflis, 1971.

Zekiyan, L.B. "Xoǧa Safar ambasciatore di Shah 'Abbas a Venezia." *Oriente Moderno*, 58 (1978), 357–67.

"Le colonie armene del Medio Evo in Italia e le relazioni culturali Italo-armene." In G. Ieni and L. B. Zekiyan, eds., *Atti del primo simposio internazionale di arte armena*, 803–929. Venice, 1978.

Zevakin, E. S. "Konflikt Rossii s Persiei v serednie XVII stoletiia." *Azerbaidzhan v nachale XVIII veka*, 8/iv (Baku, 1929), 24–31.

"Persidskii vopros v russko-evropeiskikh otnosheniiakh XVII veke." *IZ*, 8 (1940), 129–62.

Zevenboom, K. M. C. "De gewichten die voor 1820 te Amsterdam werden gebruikt en de ijkwerken die daarop worden aangetroffen." *Jaarboek van het Genootschap Amstelodamum*, 45 (1953), 46–107.

Zulalian, M. K. *Armeniia v pervoi polovinie XVI veka*, Moscow, 1971.

Index